Analytical Grammar:

a systematic approach to language mastery

Teacher Book

Created by R. Robin Finley

Analytical Grammar: Teacher Book
©1996 R. Robin Finley
Published and distributed by Demme Learning

analyticalgrammar.com

1-888-854-6284 or +1 717-283-1448 | demmelearning.com
Lancaster, Pennsylvania USA

Revision Code 0196-B

Printed in the United States of America by The P.A. Hutchison Company
3 4 5 6 7 8 9 10

For information regarding CPSIA on this printed material call: 1-888-854-6284
and provide reference #0196-10192020

How Does the Three-Year Program Work?

The first year the parent would teach the first 10 units. This should take about 10 weeks. After that no more new grammar is taught that year. For the remainder of that year, one day every two weeks, a reinforcement exercise (from *Reinforcement and Review*) is done. This is independent "seatwork" the student can do on his own. He can even correct his own work, as the answers are contained in the book.

The second year begins with a week of review (in the *Reinforcement and Review* book), and then the parent would teach units #11 through 17 in the main book (about 8 weeks in all). This would complete the study of grammar, covering the four phrases and three clauses. That would be all the grammar taught that year. Every other week for the rest of the year, the student would do either a reinforcement exercise, also in *Reinforcement and Review*, or simply parse and diagram a sentence from a book he's reading.

The third year the parent would teach units #18 through 35 (about 17-18 weeks). These units cover all the rules of punctuation and usage. That would complete the formal study of grammar and language mechanics. After that the student needs to be held accountable for all mistakes in writing.

To facilitate the process of holding your student accountable, the Student Workbook turns into a reference book. The Table of Contents, all the notes, and the index are on perforated paper. At the end of each season, we suggest that the notes for that season be torn carefully out of the book, three-hole punched, and placed in a binder. That way, eventually, the student is left with a Table of Contents, all the notes from Unit #1 through 34, and an index. This binder will make for a very handy reference book in later years. I still get emails from former students in their 30s and 40s who tell me they still have their "Grammar Notebooks" on their desks at work!

So that's the Analytical Grammar program. I am a woman on a mission to convince parents that they don't need to be "doing" a grammar worksheet every day, all year long, for years and years! If grammar is taught sequentially and logically, there is no need for so much repetition.

YEAR ONE: - **Units 1 through 10**
                    - **One reinforcement (from *Reinforcement and Review*) one day every other week.**

YEAR TWO: - **Start with one week of review (from *Reinforcement and Review*)**
                    - **Units 11 through 17**
                    - **One reinforcement (from *Reinforcement and Review*) once a month.**

YEAR THREE: - **Units 18 through 35**

WHAT THEN? After repeated customer requests Analytical Grammar now has High School Reinforcement books. Any of the four books can be used at any time after completing the Analytical Grammar course and are written to help periodically reinforce grammar, punctuation, and usage concepts. The topics of the four books are American Authors, British Authors, World Authors, and Shakespeare's Plays. There are enough worksheets to do one every two weeks for a full school year.

If you have an older student and you want to get through more quickly, teach units 1 - 10 as above. Reinforce once a week until Christmas. After that, do units 11 through 17 (skip the review). Reinforce once a week until the end of the year. Year two would be units 18 - 35.

If you want to go through all in one year, you don't need to purchase *Reinforcement and Review*. Just go straight through using the shortcuts outlined on the last page of teacher notes in this front section.

FOR CHARTS THAT SHOW THESE SCHEDULES, LOOK IN OUR BROCHURE OR AT
WWW.ANALYTICALGRAMMAR.COM.

SCHEDULE FOR IMPLEMENTATION

Each unit of *Analytical Grammar* is set up in the same manner: a page of notes, 3 exercises, and a test (there is an optional writing assignment in each of the first 10 units). The following is a suggested schedule for delivery of this curriculum if you decide to do a unit a week.

Monday: Go over unit notes together with your student. Optional: You can use the DVD companion.

Have your student do Exercise #1. I suggest you do the first two sentences together and then assign the remainder for homework. This process should take you no longer than 20 minutes.

Tuesday: Go over the completed Exercise #1. This should take no more than 20 minutes. Note only the mistakes which pertain to the unit you are doing. In other words, if you are doing Unit #1 on Nouns, Articles, & Adjectives, just look at the words that are *supposed* to be marked. If your student has marked a verb as a noun, just ignore it. That is a mistake that will "correct itself" as he goes through the course.

Have your student do Exercise #2.

Wednesday: Do the same thing for Exercise #2 as you did for Exercise #1. Assign Ex. 3.

Thursday: Do the same thing for Exercise #3 as you did for Exercise #2. You can assign the writing assignment at this time, should you choose to do it.

Friday: Read the writing assignment and score it as you see fit.

Have your student do the test. I recommend that you make the test "open note"; in other words, allow your student to use his notes as he takes the test.

Monday: You and your student should grade the tests together, with you calling out the answers and him marking mistakes (see "Notes on Correcting Tests" on page 2). Using the little "scoring box" (which you will find on the test key) total up the correct answers and write the grade on the test.

After the test is graded, I introduce the next unit and start the process over again!

There are many ways you can "flex" the delivery of this curriculum. You can have your student "test out" of a unit by looking at the notes and, if he feels ready, taking the test. If the student scores at least 80% correct on the test, you can skip to the next unit. You can also give the student two exercises in one dayand have him do the "odds" or the "evens."

TEACHER NOTES

Since I've used these materials in my own classroom - with all sorts of students from "special ed" to gifted - I've learned a trick or two that I'd like to pass along to you! I'll talk about each unit, but first we need to talk about how to score tests. **Before I say anything else, however, I should tell you that I STRONGLY recommend that you make all test "open notes."** I want your students to use their Grammar Reference Books in the future, so they need to feel very comfortable with the notes.

Notes on Correcting Tests

When you and your student correct the tests for Units 1-5, it's important that you **check what's correct.** Don't try to mark the mistakes and then deduct that number from the "points possible" on each sentence. Since your student isn't yet marking all the words in the sentence, he might make the mistake of marking some word that is a part of speech he hasn't learned yet. That is a problem that will "solve itself" in time, so I just ignore these errors. I've learned that, if you **check what's correct and count up the checks**, it works out nicely.

It didn't take me very long to find out that trying to correct sentence diagrams is quite a trick. Here's what I recommend: when you see the test diagram keys, you'll see that each "point" is marked with a check mark. I go through the diagrams, check by check. If an item on the test I'm grading is in the right place, I make my own check mark beside it. If something is in the wrong place, I usually circle it so that the student can see where he made his mistake. When it comes to modifiers, as long as they are diagramed correctly and attached to the word they modify, they are correct - EVEN IF THE WORD THEY MODIFY IS IN THE WRONG PLACE. Get it? Let's try an example.

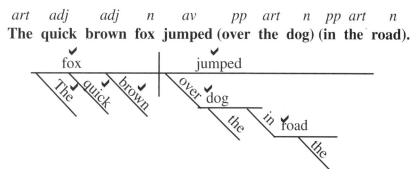

This diagram is worth 7 points. They are - the subject is *fox* (1); the verb is *jumped* (2); attached to *fox* are "capital" *The* (3), *quick* (4), and *brown* (5); attached to *jumped* is the prepositional phrase *over the dog* (6); attached to *dog* is the prepositional phrase *in the road* (7). Now, suppose that your student diagramed it like this:

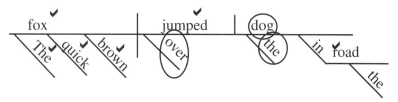

This diagram actually only loses 1 point because the prepositional phrase *over the dog* - since it was worth only 1 point - can lose only 1 point if it's diagramed incorrectly. The prepositional phrase *in the road* is still correct because it's attached to *dog*, even though *dog* is in the wrong place.

TABLE OF CONTENTS

Unit #1: Noun, Articles, and Adjectives

This is a relatively easy unit, but I think that's good because students build their confidence which tends to help them "ready themselves" for subsequent units. The one piece of advice that I'd like to give you is to have the students VERBALIZE what they are learning. For example, let's look at the sentence on the Notes about Elvis. My students have to "talk me through" the sentence. Here's how I insist my students do this sentence: First they must read it out loud. Then they must say, "The nouns are *teenagers* and *song*. Which teenagers? The teenagers. *The* is an article. Which song? Elvis Presley's famous song. *Elvis Presley's* is an adjective with wings. *Famous* is an adjective. Which 'Blue Suede Shoes'? It doesn't say."

This is a "multisensory" approach - involving the eyes, ears, and vocal chords of the students as well as their brains - which I believe pays off.

Unit #2: Pronouns

As it says in the Notes, pronouns need to be memorized - at least to the point where the students know one when they see one. When students are "verbalizing" the steps, they need to add to what they have said about nouns and say, "The pronouns are ---."

I also insist they use the word "antecedent" (instead of, for example, "stands for") on Exercise #1; otherwise, they don't remember what an antecedent is. This word becomes important not only in writing but in the Usage units at the end of this program. For example, "*he* is the pronoun and *John* is the antecedent."

Unit #3: Prepositional Phrases

This unit is also relatively easy. The verbalizing continues with, "_____ is a preposition and the prepositional phrase is _____." We begin in this unit to diagram - with "baby steps."

Unit #4: Subject & Verb

Again, be sure the students verbalize with, "_____ is a verb. Who or what _____? (Then answer the question). _____ is the subject and _____ is the verb." The students should immediately draw a baseline and write in the subject and verb. Make a big deal out of the fact that neither the subject nor the verb will be inside a prepositional phrase.

Unit #5: Adverbs

When verbalizing adverbs, it's good for the students to tell you that a certain adverb tells you *how* or *when* or *where* or *why* about the verb.

The point which must be emphasized over and over again is that **adverbs or prepositional phrases - when they modify verbs** - can almost always be moved to another position (or two) in the sentence without it sounding awkward or changing the meaning at all. If, on the other hand, a word cannot be moved because it must stay next to some other word, that means that the adverb modifies the word it must stay next to.

For example, in the sentence "Today we are learning about adverbs," the word *today* can be moved to a variety of places without changing the meaning of the sentence. That tells you that it modifies the verb *are learning*. In the sentence "We are working very hard," the adverb *very* cannot be moved away from the word *hard*; therefore, it modifies *hard*.

Remember the three "tests" talked about on the notes. Does your modifier (adverb or prepositional phrase) answer *how* or *when* or *where* or *why* about the verb? Can you move it around? If those test don't work, try the "read it together" test.

Also, don't miss the scoring note on the key for exercise #1.

Unit #6: Patterns 1 & 2

With the help of the partial Process Chart (a more complete explanation of the use of this chart is on the next page of these notes), it's very easy for the students to know when there is or is not a direct object.

The only problem which may occur is this: When the students ask, "(subject), (verb), what?" they will often try to find an answer even when there isn't one. It's important to make clear that the answer to this question tells you "what?" - not "when?" or "where?" or "how?" In other words, when the students ask "(subject), (verb), what?" - it's just as likely that there will be NO answer as it is that there will be one!

It is in this unit that I introduce the concept of "stripping down" a sentence - in other words, taking out ALL modifiers (articles, adjectives, adverbs, and prepositional phrases) and reading what's left over. What's left over is your baseline. If one noun and/or pronoun is left over, it's Pattern #1. If two nouns and/or pronouns are left over, then it's Pattern 2.

Unit #7: Pattern 3

This unit is a "piece of cake" if you tell students to parse the sentence and then "strip it down." If three nouns and/or pronouns are left over, then it's Pattern 3 - AND THE MIDDLE ONE IS ALWAYS THE INDIRECT OBJECT.

Unit #8: Linking Verbs & Patterns 4 & 5

This used to be the most difficult concept for students to master, until I came up with the Process Chart. This chart works like a charm, but you'd be surprised how many students resist using it! I make them actually put their fingers at Step 1 and then work through the sentence - following with their fingers. At some point in this process - - the light comes up in their eyes - and they GET IT!! It's always a high point for me!

Unit #9: Helping Verbs

As long as students memorize their helping verbs - so they don't mix helping verbs up with adverbs - this is an easy unit.

Unit #10: Conjunctions and Compound Situations

The first time students look at these notes, they shriek with terror! Looks so complicated! But really there's nothing new here except that when you have two (or more) of something, you need two (or more) lines in your diagram. I've included little extra instructions on the earlier exercises (See Notes A or B or whatever) and then they do fine.

If you and your student decide to take a break at this point, you can order my book called **Reinforcement and Review ($19.95).** *The reinforcement contains enough exercises for your student to do one every two weeks for the rest of the school year, so he won't forget his skills. There are review exercises to "gear up" before going on to Unit #11.*

INSTRUCTIONS FOR USING "THE PROCESS"
(Located on the back of the Unit #8 Notes)

I have found this little "flow chart" to be ENORMOUSLY successful with my students, and so I heartily recommend that you give it a try in your teaching. I know it looks a little intimidating at first, but I promise you that it will be well worth the effort to use it. In the following paragraphs, I will tell you how and when to use it.

Basically, this chart graphically illustrates the thought processes that your student must go through in order to analyze a subject-verb combination. Some verbs have direct objects and some don't. Some verbs are action verbs and some are linking verbs. Some linking verbs have predicate nominatives and some have predicate adjectives. It can be rather daunting to keep all of this straight, so I devised this chart. It consists mainly of questions the student must ask. Each question has two possible answers, represented by the arrows leading him to the next question, and so on.

FIRST USE:
Give this chart to your students after you have gone over the notes to **Unit #4: Subject and Verb.** At that point you need only go through Steps 1, 2, 3, 4, & 5. Your students must ask the question in Step 5 to determine whether the word that looks like a verb is a real verb (ie: it has a subject) or a verbal. If it is a verb, then your students can draw a baseline and fill in the subject and verb. If the verb doesn't have a subject, then it's a verbal. The student should just leave the word marked *v* and go on. Keep looking because there *will* be a verb.

SECOND USE:
This should occur when the students are about to do Exercise 3 of **Unit #6: Patterns 1 & 2.** At Step 6 on the chart, there is a question to ask. If there is no answer, then you have a Pattern 1 sentence; in other words, there is no direct object. If there is an answer, you have a Pattern 2 sentence.

THIRD USE:
This occurs when the students are doing **Unit #8: Patterns 4 & 5.** At this point you should be using the entire chart. I feel sure that, by this time, the logic of the entire chart will be apparant to you. Just ask the questions it says to ask and follow the arrows (depending on the answer) to the next step.

After a while the logic of this process will make so much sense to the students that they won't need to use the chart. But during the learning process, this chart helps the students to feel that they have something to lean on.

SUGGESTIONS FOR SHORTCUTS

Occasionally you might find the need to implement this program in less than the usual one-unit-per-week manner, especially if you are home schooling a 10th, 11th, or 12th grader. If you do, I have some ideas for you which will enable you to get through the program more quickly.

If you have a student who has a pretty good background in the basic parts of speech, he or she will probably find the first three or four units to be very easy. You can have this student "test through" these units by doing the following:

1.   Read through the notes with him.
2.   Have him do the first three sentences of each exercise, plus all the fill-in-the-blank items.
3.   Have him skip the Skills Support activity
4.   Give him the test. If he scores at a C+ level or better, he can keep moving on without further review.

At some point your student will feel the need to slow down. Or perhaps you have a student with very little grammar background, but you still want to move more quickly. In either case, you can cut one day off the delivery of each unit by doing the following:

1.   Read through the notes with her.
2.   Give her Exercise #1 as usual.
3.   After going over Ex. #1, give her Ex. #2 and Ex. #3 together, but tell her to do every other sentence.
4.   Skip the Skills Support.
5.   Give her the test as usual.

When I taught this course to my public-school 8th graders (and you can imagine how little grammar they had when they came to me!), I used the delivery method listed directly above. I was able to get through the entire book in about 20 weeks.

Season One

NOUNS, ARTICLES, & ADJECTIVES

THE NOUN is a word that <u>names a person, place, thing, or idea.</u>

A COMMON NOUN is a word that names a person, place, thing, or idea. These nouns are NEVER CAPITALIZED and always consist of ONE WORD ONLY. Examples:

PERSONS:	teacher, man, girl
PLACES:	school, yard, city
THINGS:	bridge, carrot, building, day
IDEAS:	anger, democracy, inspiration* (these are often called ABSTRACT nouns)

(*watch for the "ion" ending - that's a strong clue that the word is a noun)

A PROPER NOUN is the NAME of a person, place, etc. These words are CAPITALIZED and MAY CONSIST OF MORE THAN ONE WORD; however, no matter how many words are in a proper noun, it still equals only one noun. Examples:

PERSONS:	Mr. Jones, Mary, Thomas John Matthews
PLACES:	Cranford High School, Anchorage, Alaska, Russia
THINGS:	The Golden Gate Bridge, Thursday, The Empire State Building, April 1, 1492
IDEAS:	The Theory of Relativity, the Industrial Revolution

THE ARTICLE: There are only three articles; they are <u>A, AN, and THE.</u> They always come in front of the noun they modify. The article *A* is used in front of nouns which begin with consonants (a tree); the article *AN* is used in front of nouns which begin with vowels or vowel sounds (an apple).

THE ADJECTIVE: Adjectives describe or <u>MODIFY NOUNS and PRONOUNS.</u> They usually come in front of the noun they modify. Examples are TALL, SILLY, BEAUTIFUL, SEVERAL. For now, all the adjectives you will be studying will be <u>next to</u> the noun they modify. Watch out for PROPER ADJECTIVES, which are adjectives made out of proper nouns (England = English); they always begin with capital letters. Since a proper noun can consist of more than one word (Tim Smith), a proper adjective can also consist of more than one word (Tim Smith's house). If this is the case, then you would mark such an adjective "adj" and use "wings."(See Elvis Presley's" below)

We've just learned the NAMES of three words: noun, article, and adjective. Words also do certain JOBS: the job done by articles and adjectives is called MODIFIER. Nouns have five different jobs that they do; we'll learn about those jobs soon.

STEPS TO TAKE:

1. Find all the nouns in each sentence. Write N over the common nouns and PN over the proper nouns. If a proper noun consists of more than one word, write PN over the middle and draw lines ("wings") over all the words in the noun (see example).

   n   *n* ——— *pn* ———
   EXAMPLE: The teenagers loved Elvis Presley's famous song, "Blue Suede Shoes."

2. Go back to EACH noun you found and ask "Which?" Any word located next to that noun that answers this question is either an article or an adjective. Write ART over the articles and ADJ over the adjectives.

   Which teenagers? <u>the</u> teenagers. *the* is an article
   Which song? <u>Elvis Presley's famous</u> song. *Elvis Presley* is an adjective (with wings); *famous* is an adjective.
   Which "Blue Suede Shoes"? It doesn't say.

   art   *n*   —— *adj* —— *adj* *n*   —— *pn* ——
   EXAMPLE: The teenagers loved Elvis Presley's famous song, "Blue Suede Shoes.

NOUNS, ARTICLES, & ADJECTIVES:EXERCISE #1

NAME:_____DATE:_____

DIRECTIONS: *Write* **n** *over the common nouns,* **pn** *over the proper nouns (put "wings" [— pn—] over proper nouns that consist of more than one word),* **art** *over the articles, and* **adj** *over the adjectives.*

   adj   *n*   ————— *pn* —————   *adj adj* *n*
1. Every morning at Madison Middle School we salute our nation's flag.

   art   *n*   *adj n*   *adj n*   *adj n*
2. The students stand at their desks and put their hands over their hearts.

   adj   *n*   *art* ——— *pn* ———   *art* *n*
3. Some students do not choose to say the Pledge of Allegiance, but it is the custom
     adj   *n*   *n*   *art* *n*   *art* *n*
    for those students to stand quietly to show respect for the beliefs of the students

    who do.
     adj   *n*   *n* *adj n*   *n*   *art* ——— *pn* ———
4. In twelve years of school, each boy and girl will say the Pledge of Allegiance on
                   adj   *n*
    approximately 2,160 occasions.
   art *adj*   *n*   *art*   *n*   *n*   *art* *n*
5. The constant repetition of the pledge often means that students ignore the meaning of
  adj *adj* *n*
  this daily ritual.

DIRECTIONS: *Mark the nouns, articles, and adjectives as you were instructed above.*
  art *adj*   *n*   *art adj*   *n*   *art* *adj* ——— *adj* ——— *n*
1. The young boy was a recent immigrant from the war-torn Central American country
   —*pn* ———
  of El Salvador.
   adj adj n *adj adj* *n*   *pn*   *art* *n*   *adj*
2. On his first day at his new school in America, he noticed that the students stood every
   n   *art n*   *n*
   morning, faced the flag, and said words he didn't understand.
   art *adj*   *n*   *art adj adj*   *n*   *adj adj*
3. By the second week he was able to say the first few words by imitating his fellow
   n
  students.
  art adj   *n*   *art adj*   *n*   *art* *n*
4. The boy's family were happy to live in a prosperous country where the people could
     adj n   *adj n*   *n*   *n*
   work at their jobs and raise their children in peace and safety.
   art n *adj adj n*   *n* *pn*   *adj* *n*
5. By the end of his first month of school, Juan stood every morning and proudly
        n   *art n* *adj adj*   *n*
   pledged allegiance to the flag of his adopted country.

                                                                               (over)

WRITE THE DEFINITION OF A NOUN IN A COMPLETE SENTENCE.
(You will be tested on these definitions.)

A noun is the name of a person, place, thing, or idea.

WHICH TYPE OF NOUN BEGINS WITH A CAPITAL LETTER AND MAY CONSIST OF MORE THAN ONE WORD?

A proper noun.

NOUNS, ARTICLES, & ADJECTIVES: EXERCISE #2

NAME:_____   DATE:_____

DIRECTIONS: *Write **n** over the common nouns, **pn** over the proper nouns (with "wings" [——pn——] if necessary), **art** over the articles, and **adj** over the adjectives.*

    art   adj   n   art ——— pn ———   pn
1. The American flag was officially adopted by the Continental Congress in Philadelphia
     —— pn —
on June 14, 1777.

    art adj n   adj adj n   adj adj n   art
2. The first flag had seven red stripes and six white stripes to symbolize the
    adj   adj   n
original thirteen colonies.

     art adj adj   n   art n   art adj n   adj
3. In the upper left-hand corner, known as the canton, was a blue field with thirteen
    adj   n
white stars.

          pn   pn   art n   pn art n   adj n
4. After Vermont and Kentucky joined the union in 1795, the canton held fifteen stars
           adj   adj   n
and there were now fifteen red-and-white stripes.

     pn art   n   adj   adj   n   adj
5. In 1818 the decision was made to keep thirteen red-and-white stripes and add new
    n   art   n   art adj   n   n   art   n
stars to the canton to show the current number of states in the union.

    adj   n   adj adj   n   art adj   —pn ——
6. Many people believe that our American flag was made by the legendary Betsy Ross.

    adj n   art adj   n   adj adj   n
7. This story is probably not an accurate version of how our nation's symbol was made.

         art adj n art adj   n   —— pn —
8. According to the popular story, the young seamstress known as Betsy Ross sewed
         adj adj adj n   art   n   —— pn ———
and helped design our nation's first flag under the direction of George Washington.

    adj   n   —— pn — art adj   n   adj
9. Historical records show that Betsy Ross was a real flagmaker, but there is no
    n   art adj   —— pn ——
evidence that she made the first Stars and Stripes.

    adj adj   n   —— pn ——   n   art adj   n
10.This delightful legend about Betsy Ross gained popularity with the American public
    art n   art adj   n   pn
at the time of the national centennial in 1876.

WRITE THE DEFINITION OF THE ADJECTIVE IN A COMPLETE SENTENCE.

Adjectives modify or describe nouns.

NOUNS, ARTICLES, & ADJECTIVES: EXERCISE #3

NAME:_____DATE:_____

DIRECTIONS: *Write* ***n*** *over the common nouns,* ***pn*** *over the proper nouns (with "wings"* [——***pn***——] *if necessary),* ***art*** *over the articles, and* ***adj*** *over the adjectives.*

        art   n   art adj n   n   n
1. It is the tradition throughout the entire world to have rules and regulations about
  art adj   n   adj adj   n
  the proper method of displaying any country's flag.

        art adj   n   adj   n   adj   n
2. During the twentieth century flag etiquette received particular attention because
  n   art adj   n   n
  flags have become a prime focus of patriotism.

     art —— pn—— art   n   art adj   n   art —— pn—
3. In the United States the anniversary of the flag's adoption by the Continental
  ————   pn   —pn—
  Congress in 1777 has been celebrated as Flag Day.

    pn   art ———— pn————   art— pn—   adj   n
4. In 1942 the United States Congress adopted a Flag Code listing uniform rules
            art adj   n art adj   n
  for displaying the American flag in a respectful manner.

  adj adj   n   art adj   n   art n
5. Many legal battles have been waged over the so-called desecration of the flag.
  adj   n   art ———— adj ——   n   art pn
6. Political protesters, such as the anti-Vietnam War marchers of the 1960's, may
          adj adj   n   art n
  try to dramatize their particular causes by burning the flag.

  art adj   n   art n   art adj   n art
7. The highest courts in the land usually decide that, since the American flag is a
  adj   n   n   n
  powerful symbol of freedom, citizens should be free to treat it as they choose, even
  adj   n   n
  if this treatment causes outrage in others.

    adj   adj   n art n   art —— pn ——
8. In one American city , an artist was criticized for displaying the Stars and Stripes
  art adj   n   art n   adj   n   n
  in a disrespectful manner as a means of symbolizing his freedom of speech.

  adj   n   adj adj —— adj ————   n
9. Other citizens chose to exercise their own First Amendment rights by removing
  n   adj   n
  flags displayed in this manner.

   n   adj   n   art adj   n
10. Flags symbolize deep-felt emotion, and they have become an important means
    adj   n   adj   n
  of political communication on our planet.

LIST THE THREE ARTICLES IN OUR LANGUAGE.
   The articles are A, AN, and THE.

WHERE WILL THE ARTICLE BE LOCATED, IN RELATIONSHIP TO THE NOUN?
   Articles will always be located in front of the noun.

SKILLS SUPPORT

PARAPHRASING: On these Skills Support exercises, you will be asked to "paraphrase" something. Paraphrasing is a skill you will use in these tests, in writing book reports, and in writing essays and reports all through school. When you paraphrase, you take what someone else has written and you write it in your own words. Here's an example from a famous poem called "Casey at the Bat."

It looked extremely rocky for the Mudville nine that day;
The score stood two to four, with but one inning left to play.
So, when Cooney died at second and Burrows did the same,
A pallor wreathed the features of the patrons of the game.

My paraphrase:
Things didn't look good for the Mudville baseball team that day.
It was two to four in the bottom of the ninth.
So when Cooney was tagged out at second base and the same thing had happened to Burrows,
The fans' faces became deathly pale.

The next example is from Mark Twain's great classic* Tom Sawyer*:

"Hello, old chap, you got to work, hey?"
Tom wheeled suddenly and said:
"Why it's you, Ben, I warn't noticing."
"Say - I'm going in a'swimming, I am. Don't you wish you could? But of course you'd druther work - wouldn't you? Course you would!"
Tom contemplated the boy a bit, and said:
"What do you call work?"
"Why, ain't *that* work?"
Tom resumed his whitewashing, and answered carelessly: "Well, maybe it is, and maybe it ain't. All I know is, it suits Tom Sawyer."
"Oh, come now, you don't mean to let on that you like it?"
The brush continued to more.
"Like it? Well, I don't see why I oughtn't to like it. Does a boy get a chance to whitewash a fence every day?"
That put the thing in a new light. Ben stopped nibbling his apple. Tom swept his brush daintily back and forth - stepped back to note the effect - added a touch here and there - criticized the effected again - Ben watching every move and getting more and more interested, more and more absorbed. Presently he said:
"Say, Tom, let *me* whitewash a little."

My paraphrase:
"Hiya, pal, got chores to do, huh?"
Tom turned around quickly and said:
"Oh! It's you, Ben! Sorry, I wasn't paying attention."
"Hey, I'm goin' for a dip! Bet you wish you could go too. But I see you're really having a great time! SURE you are!"
Tom stared at Ben for a moment.
"Why shouldn't I be having a great time?"
"Are you trying to tell me that's fun?" Tom went back to his painting and remarked off-handedly:
"Maybe. Maybe not. All I can tell you is I enjoy it."
"Oh, please, Tom, don't tell me you're having fun!"
The paintbrush moved slowly back and forth.
"Why not? It's not every day a guy gets to whitewash a fence!"
This was a new slant on the situation. Ben stopped chewing his apple. Tom took a swipe with the brush - stood back to get the full effect - moved forward to dab again - moved back to look again - Ben watching like a hawk, becoming increasingly fascinated, increasingly hooked. After a few moments he said:
"Tom? Can I try it a little?"

DIRECTIONS: *Mark all the common and proper nouns, articles, and adjectives in the Pledge of Allegiance. Then, as neatly as you can, write a paraphrase of it. You will probably have to look some words up in the dictionary.*

n   *art* *n*
I pledge allegiance to the flag of

art _____ *pn* _____   *art*   *n*
the United States of America and to the republic

adj   *n*   *pn*
for which it stands, one nation under God, indivisible,

n   *n*
with liberty and justice for all.

NOUNS, ARTICLES, & ADJECTIVES: TEST

NAME:_____DATE:_____

(RAW SCORE:_____*/117*_____GRADE:_____)

DIRECTIONS: *Write* **n** *over the common nouns,* **pn** *over the proper nouns (with "wings" [—pn—] if necessary),* **art** *over the articles, and* **adj** *over the adjectives.*

          art   n   art adj   n   n   adj adj   n

__11__ 1. In the course of an average day, people rarely stop and think about their own country

          adj n

and its flag.

              adj adj   n   art   n   adj n   adj   adj

__11__ 2. As we lead our busy lives, the citizens of this country often overlook their hard-won

          adj   n

personal freedom.

             n adj   n   art   n   adj adj   n

__13__ 3. In school our teachers work to teach about the events of our early history, which

             art adj   n   art —— pn ————

help us understand the burning issues which led to the American Revolution.

           pn adj   n   art adj   n   n   art   adj

__12__ 4. Since 1775 many men and a growing number of women have made the ultimate

          n   art   n

sacrifice for the freedom which we enjoy now.

          art ————pn ———— art —pn—   adj adj   adj   n

__10__ 5. The Revolutionary War and the Civil War were fought on our own American soil to

               n   n

preserve freedom at home.

          adj n   art n   n   adj   n

_7_ 6. Other wars were fought to preserve the freedom of people in other countries.

          adj adj n   pn   n adj   n   n

__13__ 7. Every single day in America, lawyers, law officers, and judges struggle to protect

          art   n   adj adj   n

the freedom won in many desperate battles.

          adj   adj   n   adj adj adj   n   adj adj

__13__ 8. Our much-criticized politicians spend their entire working lives seeing that this huge,

           adj   n   adj   n

complicated country runs smoothly and that our freedom is preserved.

(over)

        adj   *n*   *adj*   *n*   *adj* *n*   *art* *n*

11 9. Many students have family members who have served their time in the military

                          adj   *adj*   *n*

protecting and preserving America's precious freedom.

                            art ——— *pn* ————   *adj* *n*   *art adj*

10 10. Perhaps when we say the Pledge of Allegiance, it is our way of thanking the many

        adj   *n*   *art* *n*

dedicated people who have struggled for the freedom we enjoy.

1 11. Define NOUN:

    A noun is the name of a person, place, thing, or idea.

1 12. Define ADJECTIVE:

    An adjective modifies a noun or a pronoun.

1 13. Which kind of noun always begins with a lower-case letter and can consist of only one word?

    A common noun.

3 14. List the ARTICLES in our language.

    The articles are A, AN, and THE.

===
117

Raw		Score	Grade	%
117	-	114 =	A++ =	98+
113	-	111 =	A+ =	95
110	-	105 =	A =	90
104	-	99 =	B+ =	85
98	-	93 =	B =	80
92	-	87 =	C+ =	75
86	-	81 =	C =	70
80	-	76 =	D+ =	65
75	-	70 =	D =	60

PRONOUNS

DEFINITION: A word that takes the place of one or more nouns. A pronoun can do anything a noun can do. Pronouns are even occasionally modified by adjectives! The only way to learn pronouns, unfortunately, is to MEMORIZE THEM. There are four main categories of pronouns in our language:

PERSONAL PRONOUNS: These pronouns occur in four "cases."

Subjective	Objective	Possessive	Reflexive
I	me	mine	myself
you	you	yours	yourself/yourselves
he	him	his*	himself
she	her*	hers	herself
it	it	its	itself
we	us	ours	ourselves
they	them	theirs	themselves

(Just memorize all these pronouns; you won't have to worry about which are objective and which are subjective for now.)

DEMONSTRATIVE PRONOUNS: this*, that*, these*, those*

INTERROGATIVE PRONOUNS: These also often come in "cases."

Subjective	Objective	Possessive	No Case
who	whom	whose	which, what
whoever	whomever	whosever	whichever, whatever

INDEFINITE PRONOUNS:

each*	anybody	many*
either*	anyone	more*
neither*	anything	much*
one*	everybody	most*
some*	everyone	both*
any*	everything	few*
other*	somebody	several*
another*	someone	all*
none	something	two*, three* etc.
	nobody	
	no one	
	nothing	

Pronouns do the same jobs that nouns do; we'll learn about those jobs later.

*NOTE: In the lists of pronouns on the first page, there were some that had asterisks next to them. Those pronouns with asterisks can also be used as adjectives sometimes. If the word in question is an adjective, you would already know it by now because it would have answered the question "Which?"   Look at the examples below:

>   *pn   adj   n*
>   Jack loaned me his book.   (Note that HIS is being used as an adjective in this sentence)

>   *pn   art   n   pro*
>   Jack said the book was his.(Note that HIS is a pronoun in this sentence)

Many words that you might think of as pronouns (such as MY, YOUR, OUR) can <u>only</u> be used as adjectives. That's why they are not listed with the personal pronouns on the first page. Some grammar books call these words "possessive pronouns." In this program, however, we call them adjectives if they are doing an adjective's job and pronouns if they are doing a pronoun's job.

ANTECEDENTS: An antecedent is the noun or nouns that the pronoun stands for. You usually concern yourself with antecedents when you are using the personal pronouns. Here's an example:

>   *pn   pro*
>   Jane said she was tired.   (The word <u>JANE</u> is the antecedent for <u>SHE</u>.)

PRONOUNS: EXERCISE #1

NAME: _____DATE:_____

DIRECTIONS: *The purpose of this exercise is to give you practice with personal pronouns. Write **n** over the nouns, **pn** over the proper nouns, **art** over the articles, **adj** over the adjectives, and **pro** over the pronouns. In the space below each sentence, write the pronoun and its antecedent for each personal pronoun that you find.*

```
                pn        art  adj   n    pro              pro
```
1. EXAMPLE: Ted fired at the distant target, but he just couldn't hit it.
           he = Ted   it = target

```
   pro       art   n    pro           art   n         pro          pro  pn
```
2. "I know the reason you missed the target, but do you know what it is, Ted?" asked
```
    pn
```
Jody.   ***I = Jody***   ***you & you = Ted***   ***it = reason***

```
    pn           pn    pro   adj  n     pro
```
3. Ted looked at Jody, but he had no idea what she meant.   ***he = Ted she = Jody***

```
   pn        pn    adj   n     pn                    adj   n        pro
```
4. Bill and Tom, both friends of Ted, were puzzled by her question themselves.
                    themselves = Bill and Tom
```
   pn          pro              pro  art   n          adj  adj  n
```
5. Ted muttered to himself, "Seems to me the problem must be this old rifle."
           himself & me = Ted
```
        pn       adj   n   pro           pro        pro
```
6. When Jody heard his response, she chuckled to herself about it.
           she & herself = Jody   ***it = response***
```
   pro        pn    pro   pro        art  n   pro          pro
```
7. She said to Ted, "If you think you can hit the target, you will hit it."
           She = Jody   you & you & you = Ted   it = target
```
   pro                     art  adj    n            art  adj  n
```
8. She knew that just thinking a positive thought could have a large impact on whether
```
   pro  art  n         pro
```
he hit the target or missed it.   ***She = Jody   he = Ted   it = target***

```
   pn        pro                pro            art   n   pro
```
9. Ted realized she was right and wished he had thought of the idea himself!
           she = Jody   he & himself = Ted
```
      art   n      art  adj     n     pn   adj  n
```
10. As if the situation were a self-fulfilling prophecy, Ted raised his rifle, thought about
```
   art   n            art  n   art  n    pro
```
the bullseye, and placed a shot in the center of it.
           it = bullseye

DEFINITIONS: A pronoun is a word which takes the place of a _____***noun***_____.

          The noun or nouns the pronoun takes the place of is called the _____***antecedent***_____.

Photocopying this product is strictly prohibited by copyright law.

PRONOUNS: EXERCISE #2

NAME: _____DATE:_____

DIRECTIONS: *This exercise is designed to give you extra practice in the demonstrative and interrogative pronouns, although it also contains personal pronouns. Write **n** over the nouns, **pn** over the proper nouns, **art** over the articles, **adj** over the adjectives, and **pro** over the pronouns. Since demonstrative and interrogative pronouns usually don't have antecedents, it won't be possible to write them down. As long as you know what an antecedent is, you're in fine shape!*

    ———*pn*——— *art n   adj   adj   n   pro   adj*
1. Once, Johnny Carson made a joke on his television show, but this caused some
        n   pro
    trouble for him.
    pro pro   pro   art n   adj   n   adj   n
2. What he claimed was that there was a shortage of paper towels in this country.
    pro   pro art   n   adj n   pro
3. He went on to describe what the consequences of this shortage might be, which
            adj   n   pro   pro
    alarmed many people who listened to him.
    art   n   adj n   pro   n   adj   n
4. The implication of this joke was that people had better stock up on paper towels
                art   n
    quickly or face the consequences.
        pro   art   adj   n   pro pro   art n   adj   n
5. This was a humorous skit to those who knew a shortage of paper towels did not exist.
            n   art adj   n   pro   pro
6. Within days, however, a real shortage developed which surprised everyone.

     pro   pro   art adj   n   pro
7. Those who did not realize there was not a real shortage went out and bought up all of
    art adj   n   pro
    the paper towels they could find.
     *pro   art adj   *   adj   n   pro   n*
8. This disrupted the normal paper towel distribution, which created shortages for
        pro   adj   n
    whoever really needed paper towels.
        pro   art n   pro   adj   n   art
9. Whoever believed the shortage to be true acted on it and, by his action, caused the
        n
    belief to become true.
        pro   adj   n   art   adj   n   pro
10. This is another example of a self-fulfilling prophecy which came about because of
    pro   n
    what people thought.

DEFINITIONS: A pronoun is a word which_____*takes the place*_____ of a noun.

        A noun is the name of _*a person, place, thing, or idea*___

        An adjective _____*modifies or describes a noun*_____

        An antecedent is _*the noun the pronoun takes the place of*___

* "paper" is not an adjective in this sentence because it doesn't modify the noun "distribution." It modifies the adjective "towel." We will learn in subsequent units what that word is. For now, no matter what a student writes above it, don't count it wrong. It would be a good idea to discuss it, however.

13

PRONOUNS: EXERCISE #3

NAME:_____DATE:_____

DIRECTIONS: *This exercise is designed to give you practice in the indefinite pronouns, but all the other types of pronouns are here too. Write **n** over the nouns, **pn** over the proper nouns, **art** over the articles, **adj** over the adjectives, and **pro** over the pronouns.*

    pro pro   pro pro   n   art adj   adj

1. Many who are successful at what they do in life have a positive mental

        n

   attitude.

    pro   pro n   adj n   adj   adj

2. Everyone knows that students in our school have positive and creative

        n

   attitudes.

  pro pro   adj n   art n   pro   pro art

3. All of us believe our school is the best and, because we think it is the

  n pro   n pro   pro art n

   best, we act in ways that make it the best.

    pro pro   adj n   art adj

4. Everyone who visits our school is impressed by the friendly and

  adj   n   n

   helpful students and faculty.

  pro pro   adj n   n   pro

5. All of us work to keep our halls and cafeteria clean so everyone can

      pro   pro   pro

   enjoy them as much as we do.

    pro   pro   pro   adj n pro

6. When we see someone who is careless about our school, we remain

           pro pro   art n

   positive and do whatever we can to correct the problem.

    pro   n   adj adj n   –pro–

7. Hundreds of people watch our sports teams, but no one has ever accused

 pro adj   n

   us of poor sportsmanship.

    pro pro art n   n   n   art

8. Anyone who has a question or problem can always get help from a

  n   art n   art n

   teacher, a counselor, or a principal.

(over)

   pro   *pro*   *adj*   *n*   *pro*   *adj*   *n*   *art*

9. We cannot manage everything at one time, so we manage one thing at a

    n

    time.

                    pro   *pro* *pro*   *pro*   *pro* *pro*   *pro*

10. Often if someone believes he or she can do something, he or she will do it!

DEFINITION: A pronoun _____ *takes the place of a noun* _____ .

                  The three articles are _____ *A, AN, and THE* _____

SKILLS SUPPORT

DIRECTIONS: *Mark all the nouns, proper nouns, articles, adjectives, and pronouns in the paragraph below. Then write a paraphrase of this paragraph. Remember: you must change as many words as you can, but try to leave the sentence structure as it was originally written. A good paraphrase should contain all the ideas that are in the original paragraph.*

        pn   *art*   *adj*   *n*   *pro*
Epictetus, an ancient philosopher, once said, "What concerns

        art   *n*   *n*   *art*   *n*   *n*
is not the way things are, but rather the way people think

   n   *pro*   *pro*   *art*   *n*   *n*
things are." He was aware that the world of thought overlaps

    art   *n*   *n*   *pro*   *pro*   *art*   *n*
the world of action. He knew that if a person believes

  pro   *pro*   *adj*
something to be true which may or may not be so, and acts on that

   n   *adj*   *n*   *art*   *n*
belief, often his actions can cause the belief to become true.

PRONOUNS: TEST

NAME: _____DATE:_____

(RAW SCORE: _____ */105* LETTER GRADE: _____)

DIRECTIONS: *Write* **n** *over the nouns,* **pn** *over the proper nouns,* **art** *over the articles,* **adj** *over the adjectives, and* **pro** *over the pronouns.*

    pn   *pro* *pn*   *pro*   *pro*   *pro*   *pro*
___ 1. Ted once said to me, "Bob, if you think something is true even if it isn't true, you can
 8   *pro*
    make it become true."

       art *n*   *pro pro* *art* *n*   *adj*   *n*   *pro*
___ 2. Once a teacher was told that she had a class of gifted children, but later it was found
 13 *pro pro*   *adj*   *n*
    that she had average students.

       pro   *adj*   *n*   *pro*   *adj* *n*
___ 3. Because she thought her students were gifted, she went out of her way to develop
 9   *n* *pro*   *pro*
    lessons that were challenging for them.

     art   *n* *pro*   *adj n* *pro pro*   *pro*   *art adj*   *n*
___ 4. The class itself had no idea that she thought it was a gifted class.
 11

    pro *art* *n*   *pro*   *pro* *pro pro*   *pro*
___ 5. This is an example of what can happen to many of us if we believe something to be
 8
    true.

    pro   *pro*   *pro art* *n*   *art*   *n*   *pro pro*
___ 6. Whatever you may think about it, the class responded to the challenge and few, if any,
 11   *art n*
    did poorly on the lessons.

    pro   *art adj*   *n*   *pro*   *art n* *pro*
___ 7. Everyone responded in a positive way, and they did quite well on the tests which were
 9   *pro*
    given to them.

 pro   *pro*   *pro*   *adj*   *n*   *pro*
___ 8. It was discovered that, because they were treated as gifted students, many had
 10   *adj*   *n*   *pro*   *pro*
    performed as gifted students and most were very pleased with themselves.

(over)

___
5
       pro   *pro*   *pro*   *pro*   *pro*

9. All of this happened because someone thought something was true even though it was

not true.

___
11
       pro   *pro*   *pro*   *pro art adj*   *adj*   *n*

10. Whatever one may think, few can deny that an unusual, difficult-to-explain event took

                          adj *n*

place in this classroom.   *PLACE is telling where in this sentence, it's an adverb. If you're student marked it a noun, don't worry about it! We'll get there later.*

===
95

DEFINITIONS: *Complete the sentences below.*

___
1
   1. A noun is ___***the name of a person, place, thing, or idea***___ .

___
1
   2. A proper noun always begins with ___***a capital letter***___

___
2
   3. A ___***common***___ noun can only consist of one word, but a

   ___***proper noun***___ can be more than one word.

___
3
   4. The articles are ___***A, AN, and THE***___

___
1
   5. An adjective ___***modifies nouns and pronouns***___

___
1
   6. A pronoun ___***takes the place of a noun***___

___
1
   7. An antecedent is ___***the noun the pronoun stands for***___ .

===
10

Raw		Score		Grade	%
105	-	102	=	A++	=98+
101	-	99	=	A+	= 95
98	-	94	=	A	= 90
93	-	89	=	B+	= 85
88	-	84	=	B	= 80
83	-	78	=	C+	= 75
77	-	73	=	C	= 70
72	-	68	=	D+	= 65
67	-	63	=	D	= 60

PREPOSITIONAL PHRASES

DEFINITION: A preposition is a word used to show the relationship between two nouns.

EXAMPLES: The package <u>under</u> the tree is mine. (<u>under</u> is the preposition)
The package <u>in</u> the tree is mine. (<u>in</u> is the preposition)
The package <u>near</u> the tree is mine. (<u>near</u> is the preposition)

NOTICE HOW THE RELATIONSHIP BETWEEN THE PACKAGE AND THE TREE CHANGES WHEN THE PREPOSITION CHANGES.

HOW TO FIND A PREPOSITION:

Almost all prepositions will fit into the following little sentence (it's very handy; memorize it!).

"THE MOUSE GOES _____ THE BOX (OR BOXES)."

Try it out with the prepositions underlined in the three sentences used for examples. They fit, don't they?

PREPOSITIONS ARE LABELED "PP."

There are, however, some prepositions that won't fit into the "mouse-box" sentence. There are nine very common ones, which may seem like a lot to remember. Here's a little memory aid: you may not be able to remember them, BUT AL DOES!

B = but (but me)	**A** = as (as a wink)	**D** = during (during recess)
U = until (until lunch)	**L** = like (like a dog)	**O** = of (of the homework)
T = than (than the others)		**E** = except (except Bob)
		S = since (since breakfast)

A word may fit into the "mouse-box" sentence and look like a preposition, but IT ISN'T A PREPOSITION UNLESS IT'S IN A PREPOSITIONAL PHRASE. To find a prepositional phrase, you say the preposition and ask, "What?" The answer you are looking for is a noun or pronoun that answers that question. That noun or pronoun is called the OBJECT OF THE PREPOSITION. Each prepositional phrase will -

> begin with a preposition, and
>> end with a noun or pronoun.
>>> If there are any words between the preposition and its object, they are modifiers for the object.

In the three sentences above, the prepositional phrases are "under the tree," "in the tree," and "near the tree" and "tree" is the object of the preposition in all three phrases.

PREPOSITIONAL PHRASES HAVE A JOB TO DO; THEY ARE ALWAYS **MODIFIERS**.

Look at the following three sentences:

I ate my lunch before recess.	(the prepositional phrase is "before recess")
I ate my lunch before.	("before" isn't a preposition because there's no object.)
I ate my lunch before I saw you.	("before" isn't a preposition because if you ask, "before what?", the answer would be "before I saw you." That's not a prepositional phrase because you won't have a verb in a prepositional phrase.)

DIAGRAMING: Sentence diagraming is a tool we use much like drawing pictures. We use diagrams to make it easier to understand concepts which might be hard to understand. Diagrams consist of three types of lines: horizontal (——), vertical (|), and diagonal (＼).
The basic diagram of a prepositional phrase looks like this:

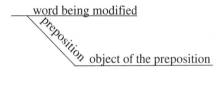

EXAMPLE: art   n   prep   adj   adj   n
                the class (after my lunch hour)

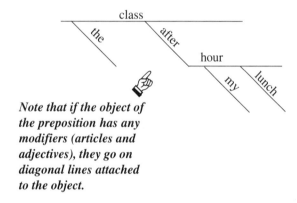

Note that if the object of the preposition has any modifiers (articles and adjectives), they go on diagonal lines attached to the object.

NOTE: A few prepositions consist of more than one word. They are *because of, on account of, in spite of, according to, instead of, contrary to* and *out of*. If you find one of these prepositions, label it "pp" with "wings" (as you do with proper nouns of more than one word).

PREPOSITIONAL PHRASES: EXERCISE #1

NAME:_____DATE:_____

DIRECTIONS: Mark all the nouns, proper nouns, articles, adjectives, pronouns, and prepositions in the sentences below. Put parentheses around the prepositional phrases. Then, on a separate sheet of paper (and as neatly as you can), diagram the prepositional phrases in each sentence. Sentence #1 has been done for you as an example. Notice that some of the words below are underlined. That will be explained to you on the other side of this page.

```
       pp  adj   n  pro  art adj     n    pp    n
1.  (In math class) we use a certain  method (of thinking).
```

(For now, we're not going to worry about what word goes on this line. Just diagram the prepositional phrases and leave that line blank.)

```
      art  n    pp  art n   pp  n     art    n     pp  adj    n
2.  A person (with a mind)( for math) has the advantage (over other people).
```

```
      adj     n       n    pp     adj      n
3.  Such people learn concepts (about mathematical principles) easily.
```

```
      pro          n    pp  n
4.  They solve problems( in math )quickly.
```

```
      adj     n   pp adj  n        n   pp  n
5.  Emotional blocks (in your mind) prevent success(in math).
```

```
      art  n   pp adj   n     pp art    n        pro art adj   n   pp    n
6.  A belief (in your ability)(as a mathematician) gives you a better chance (at success).
```

```
      art  n  pp     adj     n      pp adj  n
7.  The "gift" (of mathematical ability) exists (in all people).
```

(over)

    art n   pp   n   pp   adj   n   art n pp   n

8. A lack (of <u>success</u>)(with certain <u>problems</u>) seldom indicates a lack (of <u>ability</u>).

    pp   n   pro   pp art n pp   n   pp   n

9. (In <u>school</u>) we look (for the <u>key</u>)(to <u>success</u>)(in <u>mathematics</u>).

    — pp— adj   n   pp   n   pp n pro   adj adj n

10.(Instead of "special" <u>brains</u>)(with <u>ability</u>)(in <u>math</u>), we need more hard work!

All the underlined words in this exercise are doing the same job. Look at your notes and write what that job is.

    object of the preposition
    _____

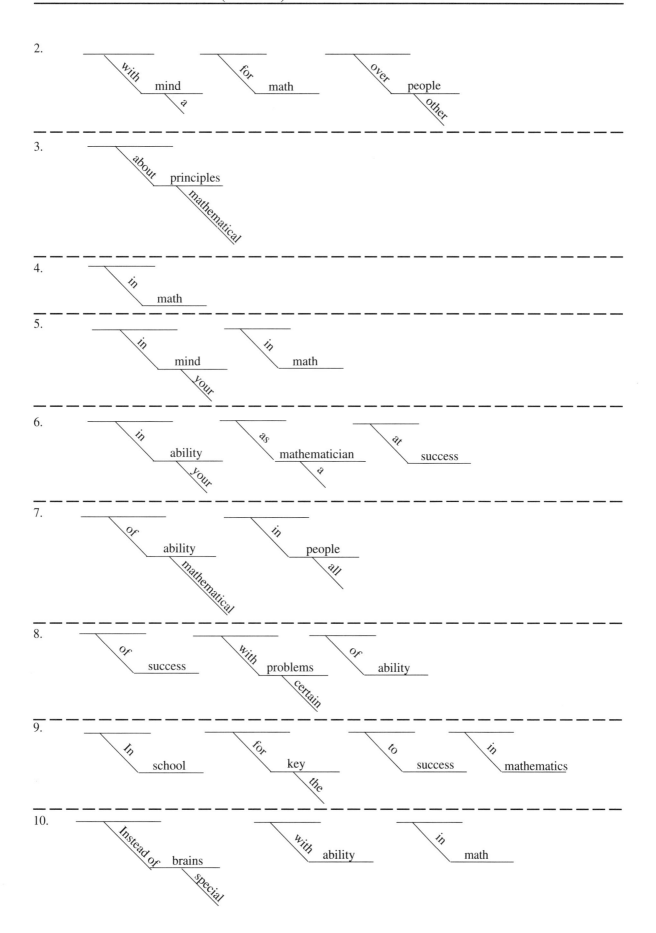

PREPOSITIONAL PHRASES: EXERCISE #2

NAME:_____DATE:_____

DIRECTIONS: *Mark all the nouns, proper nouns, articles, adjectives, pronouns, and prepositions in the sentences below. Put parentheses around the prepositional phrases. Then, on a separate sheet of paper, diagram the prepositional phrases in each sentence. Look on the back of this paper for additional work having to do with the underlined words below.*

      pn   *pp adj*   *n*   *pp adj*   *n*
1. Johnny counts (on his fingers)(in math <u>class</u>)!

      n   *pp adj*   *n*   *pro pp adj*   *adj*   *n*
2. Counting (on his fingers) helps him (with some <u>math</u> problems).

       pp ***   *adj*   *n*   *n*   *n* *pp*   *n*
3. Early (in many students' educations), teachers prohibit counting(on fingers).

> * Students want to call this word an adjective which modifies "educations," but in this sentence "many" modifies "students," doesn't it? This wouldn't count against them on the test (see teacher notes), but it's something they should just be aware of at this point.

      n   *pp adj*   *n* *pp*   *n*   *adj*   *n*
4. Counting (on their fingers)(in <u>public</u>) embarrasses some people.

       adj   *n*   *pp adj*   *n*
5. Do your math (in your head)!

     pp art   *n*   *pp*   *art n*
6. (In an emergency), finger-count (under the table)!

     pp adj   *n*   *adj*   *n*   *art*   *n*   *pp*   *n*
7. (In <u>many</u> cases), finger counting indicates an understanding (of arithmetic).

(over)

     pp   adj   pn   pro   art   adj   adj   n

8. (In ancient China), they used a sophisticated finger-counting machine called

     art   n

   an abacus.

     art   pn   art   n   pp adj adj   n

9. The Chinese still use the abacus (in their everyday <u>lives</u>).

     adj   adj   adj   n   pp adj   n

10. Clever, imaginative <u>finger-counting</u> schemes work effectively (for many people).

DIRECTIONS: *The underlined words in these sentences are doing one of two jobs. Choosing your answer from the jobs below, write what job each underlined word is doing.*

	MODIFIER	*OBJECT OF THE PREPOSITION*
<u>SENTENCE #</u>	<u>WORD</u>	<u>JOB</u>
1	class	*object of the preposition*
2	math	*modifier*
4	public	*object of the preposition*
7	many	*modifier*
9	lives	*object of the preposition*
10	finger-counting	*modifier*

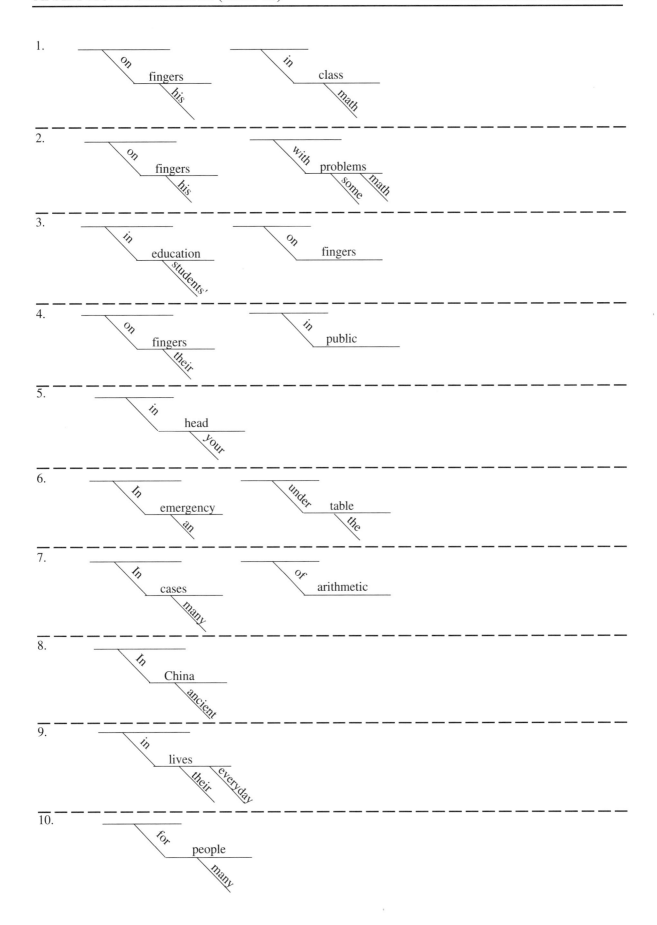

PREPOSITIONAL PHRASES: EXERCISE #3

NAME:_____DATE:_____

DIRECTIONS: *Mark all the nouns, proper nouns, articles, adjectives, pronouns, and prepositions in the sentences below. Put parentheses around the prepositional phrases. Then, on a separate sheet of paper, diagram the prepositional phrases in each sentence. The underlined words have to do with additional work on the other wide of this page.*

     — pp——   adj   n   pro   adj   n   pp adj   n
1. (Contrary to popular belief), you use your imagination (in math class).

        pp art   n   pp   n   art   n   pp   n   pp
2. Early (in the history)(of mathematics), the imagination (of <u>mathematicians</u>) led (to
    art   n   pp adj adj   adj   n
the discovery)(of each new mathematical theorem).

    art   n   pp   adj   n   art n   pp adj adj   n
3. The act (of mathematical creation) involves the use (of all <u>one's</u> abilities).

     pp adj   n   art n   pp   n   art n   pp art   adj   n
4. (In most cases), the gift (of logic) plays only a part (in the mathematical process).

     pp adj   n   pp   n   n   pp   n   art   adj   n   pp
5. (In your classes)(at school), success (in mathematics) requires an <u>intuitive</u> sense (of
   art   n   pp   n
the <u>rightness)</u>(of things).

     pro   art   n   pp art   n   art   adj   n
6. You often give the solution (to the problem) an "educated" guess.

          pro   art   n   pp   adj   n   pp art   adj
7. Sometimes you find the answer (without conscious awareness)(of the creative
    n
process).

    pp   adj   n   pro   art   n   pp art   n
8. (In your mind) you instinctively know the answer (to the problem).

(over)

      n   *pp adj* *n*   *pp n*
9. Creativity exists (in all aspects)(of math).

  art *adj*   *n pp adj* *n*   *art adj*   *adj*   *n pp n*
10. The <u>logical</u> part (of your mind) is not the only intellectual tool (in use).

DIRECTIONS: *Write what job the underlined words are doing. Choose your answer from among the following:*

      OBJECT OF THE PREPOSITION   *MODIFIER*

SENTENCE #	WORD	JOB
2	mathematicians	*object of the preposition*
3	one's	*modifier*
5	intuitive	*modifier*
5	rightness	*object of the preposition*
10	logical	*modifier*

1. contrary to / popular belief / in math class

2. in the history / of mathematics / of mathematicians / to the discovery / of each new mathematical theorem

3. of mathematical creation / of all one's abilities

4. In most cases / of logic / in the mathematical process

5. In your classes / at school / in mathematics / of the rightness / of things

6. to the problem

7. without conscious awareness / of the creative process

8. In your mind / to the problem

9. in all aspects / of math

10. of your mind / in use

SKILLS SUPPORT

DIRECTIONS: *Mark all the words in the passage below that you know. Put parentheses around the prepositional phrases. Diagram the prepositional phrases. Then paraphrase the entire paragraph.*

    n   *adj*   *n*   *pp* *art* *n*

Research has failed to show any difference (between the sexes)

  pp   *adj*   *n*   *art*   *n*   *pp* *n* *pp* *art* *adj*

(in mathematical ability). The perception (of math)(as a masculine

    n   *pp* *adj* *n*   *pp* *art* *n*   *n*

domain) stems (from other myths)(about the subject). Math is seen

 pp *art* *n*   *pp* *adj*   *adj*   *n*   *adj* *

(as the epitome)(of cool, impersonal logic) - nonintuitive and

   adj

abstract.

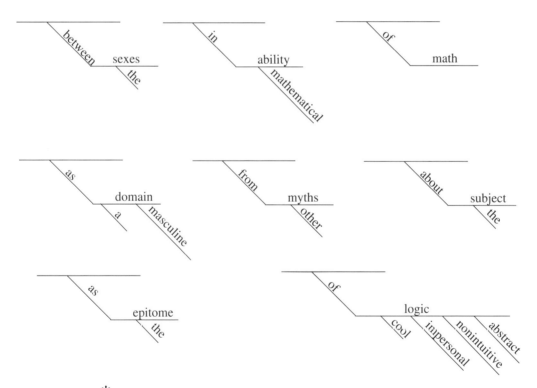

    ***** *These two adjectives modify the noun "logic" although they're*
not in their usual place. It's interesting to ask the student why
he thinks the writer chose to take these adjectives out of their
normal order. Ask the student which sentence is more dramatic
and why:
"We stared at the dark and deep ocean."
"We stared at the ocean - dark and deep."

PREPOSITIONAL PHRASES: TEST

NAME:_____DATE:_____

(RAW SCORE: _____ /279 GRADE:_____)

;

DIRECTIONS: *Mark all the nouns, proper nouns, articles, adjectives, pronouns, and prepositions in the sentences below and put parentheses around the prepositional phrases. Then, on a separate sheet of paper, diagram the prepositional phrases.*

___
10
> *n*   *adj   n   pp   n   pp   adj   n*
> 1. Men really have no advantage (over women)(in mathematical ability).

___
18
> *art   n   pp   n   pp art   adj   n   pp   adj   n   pp   art*
> 2. The perception (of math)(as a masculine domain) stems (from other myths)(about the
> *n*
> subject).

___
13
> *n   pp   n   pp art   n   pp adj   adj   n*
> 3. Ability (in math) is seen (as the triumph)(of cool, impersonal logic).

___
9
> *pro   pp   art   adj   n   pp   n*
> 4. This perhaps fits (with the stereotypical image)(of men).

From now on, each set of prepositional phrases will count as one point.

___
11
> *pp   adj   n   n   pp   n   pp   n*
> 5. (In many cases) men will not readily admit (to difficulty)(with math).

___
16
> *n   pp adj   n   pp   adj*
> 6. Women, early (in their schooling), will often admit too readily (to personal
> *n   pp art n   pp   n*
> inadequacy)(as a reason)(for failure).

___
12
> *adj   n   art adj   n   pp   n   pp adj   n*
> 7. Both sexes may be expressing the same fears (about math)(in different ways).

___
18
> *adj   n   pp   n   art adj   n   pp   n   pp   n*
> 8. Do female experts (in mathematics) have the same degree (of femininity)(as women)
> *pp   adj   n*
> (in other fields)?

(over)

  — *pp* — *n* *pp — pn* — *n* *pp* *adj* *n*

___ 9. (According to studies)(at U.C.L.A.), women (in math-related professions) actually

18 *adj* *adj* *n* *pp* *adj* *n*

  exhibit more <u>feminine</u> characteristics (than non-mathematics majors).

  pp *n* *pp* *adj* *n* *adj* *n*   *pro* *adj* *n* *pp* *adj*

___ 10.(In light)(of these studies), both sexes can give themselves high marks(in natural

17 *adj* *n*

  math <u>ability</u>).

===
142

DEFINITIONS:

1. The noun or pronoun at the end of the prepositional phrase is called the

       object of the preposition.

2. Pronouns are words that ___***take the place of one or more nouns.***___

3. A proper noun begins with a ___***capital letter.***___

4. A common noun ( ) can ☑ cannot consist of more than one word.

===
4

DIRECTIONS: *Write what job the underlined words are doing. Choose your answers from among the following:*

   OBJECT OF THE PREPOSITION   *MODIFIER*

SENTENCE #	WORD	JOB
1	ability	***object of the preposition***
2	subject	***object of the preposition***
3	cool	***modifier***
4	men	***object of the preposition***
5	many	***modifier***
6	inadequacy	***object of the preposition***
7	different	***modifier***
8	female	***modifier***
9	feminine	***modifier***
10	ability	***object of the preposition***

(5 points each)

===
50

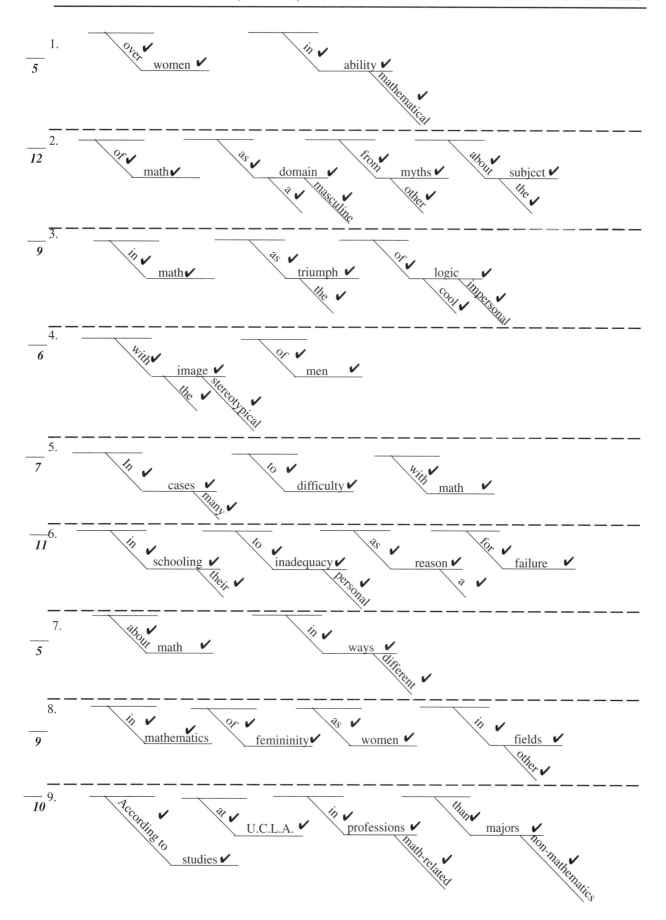

10.

$\dfrac{}{9}$

===
83

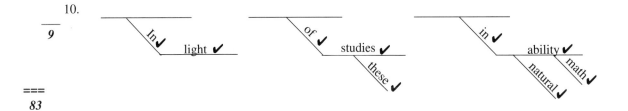

Raw		Score	Grade	%
279	-	273 =	A++	=98+
272	-	265 =	A+	= 95
264	-	251 =	A	= 90
250	-	237 =	B+	= 85
236	-	223 =	B	= 80
222	-	209 =	C+	= 75
208	-	195 =	C	= 70
194	-	181 =	D+	= 65
180	-	167 =	D	= 60

SUBJECT & VERB

The first thing we must discuss in this unit is the verb. In our language we have two kinds of verbs: action verbs and linking verb. This unit will be about action verbs; we will learn about linking verbs in Unit #8.

DEFINITION: An action verb is a word that expresses mental or physical action.

> EXAMPLES: (physical action) jump, search, carry, run, examine
> (mental action)   worry, think, believe, consider

A verb has a SUBJECT. The subject is the noun or pronoun that is DOING THE ACTION OF THE VERB.

> *art   n   pp art n   av   pp art adj   n*
> EXAMPLE: The horse (in the lead) raced (across the finish line).

> The verb is <u>raced</u>. Who or what "raced"? The horse, right? So <u>horse</u> is the subject of <u>raced</u>.
> **HANDY HINT: The subject will NEVER be inside a prepositional phrase.**

NOTE: If you find a word that looks like a verb but doesn't have a subject, you call it a "verbal." We'll learn all about verbals later on in Units #11, 12, and 13. For now, if you find a verbal just mark it "v." If it does have a subject, then it's a real verb, so for now mark it "av."

> *pn   av ▬ v▬ art pn pp adj   n*
> **EXAMPLE:**   Joe hopes to get an   A (on this test).

"To get" looks like a verb, but if you asked, "Who or what to get?" there is no stated answer in the sentence. A subject and verb always GO TOGETHER and sound right when spoken together. So "to get" in this sentence is a verbal. NOTE: Many verbals end in "ing" and any verb with "to" in front of it (to see, to throw) is always a verbal.

SIMPLE SUBJECT AND SIMPLE PREDICATE: These are terms that many language teachers and textbooks use, but they will not be used in this course. Just for your information, a "simple subject" is the noun or pronoun that is doing the action of the verb, without any of its modifiers. A "simple predicate" is just the verb by itself, without any modifiers. (We'll learn about those verb modifiers in the next unit.)

On the next page is the beginning of a "flow chart" which will be called THE PROCESS. It represents the mental steps you must take in order to figure out what the words in a sentence are doing, specifically the verbs.

I. *DIAGRAMING THE SUBJECT & VERB:*
A diagram shows the structure of a sentence by making a "picture" of it. Every diagram starts with a BASE LINE which contains the subject and the verb.

> EXAMPLE: *n   av*
> Lions roar.   Lions | roar

Notice that the base line is a horizontal line and that the subject and verb are separated by a vertical line which goes ALL THE WAY THROUGH the horizontal line. In a diagram, you capitalize the first word of the sentence, but you don't include punctuation.

II. *TO FIND THE SUBJECT AND VERB:* After marking n, art, adj, pp, and putting parentheses around the prepositional phrases, mark any word that looks like a verb "v." Then ask "Who or what (say the verb)?" The answer, a noun or a pronoun, will be the subject of that verb.

> EXAMPLE: *adj   n   av   adj   n   adj   n*
> My   uncle runs five miles every morning.

> 1. The verb is "runs."   uncle | runs
> 2. "Who or what runs?" Answer: uncle

35

III. *HOW TO DIAGRAM ARTICLES AND ADJECTIVES.*

   A.   Adjectives and articles are diagramed on diagonal lines attached to the noun or pronoun they
        modify. They should be diagramed in the order in which they come in the sentence.

        EXAMPLE: *adj   adj   n   av*
                   Our   special guest sang.

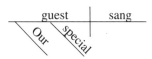

   B.   Two or more adjectives joined by a conjunction ("and," "but," or "or") are diagramed like this:

        EXAMPLE: *adj   adj   adj   n   av*
                   My   black and white dog barked.

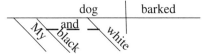

IV. *HOW TO DIAGRAM PREPOSITIONAL PHRASE:* From now on, if a prepositional phrase modifies the
subject, you must diagram it. Remember, if it modifies a noun, it will tell you "Which?" about that noun. In the
sentence on the other side of this page about the horse, the phrase "in the lead" tells you which horse. Look at the
diagram below.

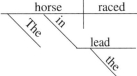

V. *HOW TO DIAGRAM A COMMAND:* It is a bit tricky to diagram a command or request, because it may
   appear that there is no subject.

        EXAMPLE: *av   adj   n*
                   Brush your   teeth.

   The verb is "brush," but if you ask "Who or what brush?" - it doesn't say. In the case of commands or
        requests, the subject is an understood "you."   The diagram will look like this:

   Notice that the "you" is in parentheses;
                                   this indicates that it is "understood."

VI. *HOW TO DIAGRAM AN "INVERTED" SENTENCE.* "Inverted" sentences are sentences which begin
    with "here" and "there." We use these sentences all the time in our language, but they may be a bit tricky to
    diagram. Once you find the verb and ask, "Who or what comes?" in the sentence below, you'll see that the
    subject is *principal.* It's tricky because you're used to seeing the subject in front of the verb - and these
    sentences are "inverted"!

        EXAMPLE: *av   art   n*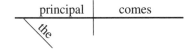
                          Here comes the principal.

The chart on the next page, which we call "The Process," represents the mental steps you must go through to analyze
a sentence grammatically. We will be adding steps to this chart, but at this point, as long as you understand what you
see now, you're in fine shape!

THE PROCESS

Step 1. Find and mark *n* all the nouns in the sentence. (*pn* over proper nouns)

Step 2. Find all the articles and adjectives (Ask, "Which (say the noun)?")

Step 3. Find all the pronouns.

Step 4. Find all the prepositions and put parentheses ( ) around the prepositional phrases.

Step 5. Find all words that look like verbs and mark them "v."

Step 6. Ask, "Who or what (say the verb)?"

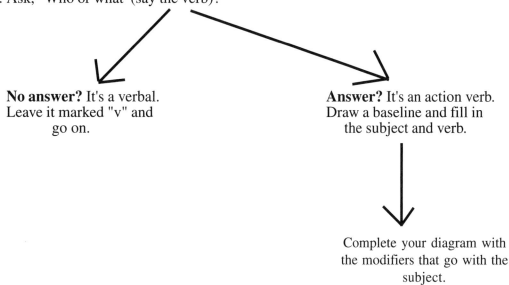

No answer? It's a verbal.
Leave it marked "v" and
go on.

Answer? It's an action verb.
Draw a baseline and fill in
the subject and verb.

Complete your diagram with
the modifiers that go with the
subject.

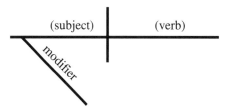

37

SUBJECT AND VERB: EXERCISE #1

NAME:_____DATE:_____

DIRECTIONS: Mark all the parts of speech that you know in the sentences below. Put parentheses around the prepositional phrases. In the space provided or on a separate piece of paper, diagram the subject and its modifiers (including prepositional phrases) and the verb. Since you don't know how to diagram anything else at this point, don't try.

    n   pp   pn   av   pp pn pp art   adj   adj   n
1. <u>People</u> (from <u>Mexico</u>) settled (in Texas) (in the seventeenth and eighteenth centuries). (See Notes III-B)

    adj   n   av   pp pn   pp   art   n   pp art pn
2. These people came (to Texas)(before the settlement)(of the Europeans).

    pro   av   n   n
3. They established farms and ranches there.

    adj   adj   n   av   art n
4. <u>These</u> early settlers plowed the land.

    adj   n   av pp art adj   adj   n
5. Their crops grew (in the harsh Texas climate).

    adj   pn   av   adj   n   pp adj   n
6. These Texans bestowed Spanish names (on their <u>towns</u>).

    pro   av pro pp adj   n   —— pn ——
7. They called one (of these towns) San Antonio.

    adj   n   av   pp pn   pp   art   adj   —— pn ——
8. Mexican culture spread (from Texas)(throughout the <u>southwestern</u> United States).

(over)

         Photocopying this product is strictly prohibited by copyright law.

av　adj　adj　adj　　n
9.　There went these early Texas pioneers.　(See Notes VI)

art　n　pp adj　n　　　av　　pp art　　n　　pp　adj　　　adj
10.　The names (of these states) <u>resulted</u>　(from the influence)(of these Spanish-speaking

n
settlers). (See Notes IV)

DEFINITIONS:

1.　A verb is not a "real" verb unless it has a _____*subject*_____.

2.　The articles in our language are _____*a*_____, _____*an*_____, and _____*the*_____.

DIRECTIONS: *Write what job the underlined words are doing. Choose your answers from among the following:*

　　SUBJECT　　　OBJECT OF THE PREPOSITION　　　VERB　　　MODIFIER

SENTENCE#	WORD	JOB
1	People	*subject*
1	Mexico	*object of the preposition*
4	These	*modifier*
6	towns	*object of the preposition*
8	southwestern	*modifier*
10	resulted	*verb*

1.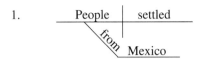

2.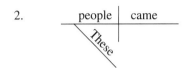

3.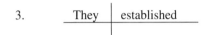

4.

5.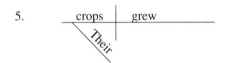

6.

7.

8.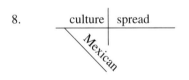

9.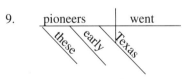

10.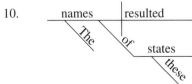

SUBJECT & VERB: EXERCISE #2

NAME: _____DATE: _____

DIRECTIONS: *Mark all the parts of speech that you know in the sentences below. Put parentheses around the prepositional phrases. Then, in the space provided or on a separate sheet of paper, diagram the subject and its modifiers and the verb. Do not try to diagram anything else at this point. HINT: Watch out for verbals!*

——— *pn* ———   *av art   n   pp   art adj   adj   n   pp   pn*
1. <u>Roberto Felix Salazar</u> wrote a poem (about the early Mexican settlers)(of Texas).

   adj   n   av   art   n   v   pp   pn
2. These people settled the land known (as Texas).

   adj   adj   n   av — v – art   n   pp art   n   pp adj
3. This Mexican-American <u>poet</u> wanted to tell the story (of the contributions)(of these
   adj   n
   Texas pioneers).

   adj adj   adj   n   av   adj   adj   n   n
4. This joyful and passionate poem <u>describes</u> these hard-working farmers and ranchers.
   (*See Notes III-B*)

   pro   av   adj   adj   adj   n   pp art adj adj n
5. They built their thick-walled <u>adobe</u> houses(from the dry Texas earth).

   adj   adj   n   av   — v —   adj   n
6. Devout Catholic people <u>struggled</u> mightily to build their churches.

   adj   adj   adj   adj   n   av   — v —   n   pp adj
7. Their strong but gentle Mexican wives willingly sacrificed to make homes (for their
   n
   <u>families</u>). (*See Notes III-B*)

(over)

av adj n pp adj adj n

8. <u>Read</u> this poem (at your first opportunity). *(See Notes V)*

adj adj adj n av art adj n

9. These brave Mexican settlers left a rich legacy.

art adj adj n pp adj n av pp adj n

10. The soft Spanish names (of their <u>towns</u>) survive (to this day). *(See Notes IV)*

DEFINITIONS:

1. If there are any words between a preposition and its object, they are _____*modifiers*_____.

2. Only a _____*proper noun*_____ can consist of more than one word.

3. If a word looks like a verb but doesn't have a subject, it's a _____*verbal*_____.

DIRECTIONS: *Write what job the underlined word is doing. Choose your answers from among the following:*

SUBJECT   OBJECT OF THE PREPOSITION   MODIFIER   VERB

SENTENCE #	WORD	JOB
1	Roberto Felix Salazar	*subject*
3	poet	*subject*
4	describes	*verb*
5	adobe	*modifier*
6	struggled	*verb*
7	families	*object of the preposition*
8	Rcad	*verb*
10	towns	*object of the preposition*

Photocopying this product is strictly prohibited by copyright law.

1.

| Roberto Felix Salazar | wrote |

6.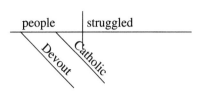

2.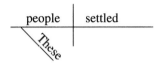

7.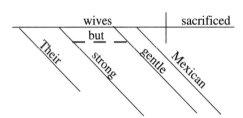

3.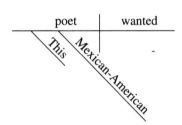

8.

| (you) | Read |

4.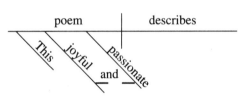

9.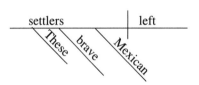

5.

| They | built |

10.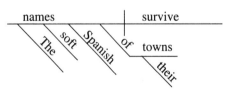

SUBJECT & VERB: EXERCISE #3

NAME: _____ DATE: _____

DIRECTIONS: *Mark all the parts of speech that you know in the sentences below. Put parentheses ( ) around the prepositional phrases. Then, in the space provided or on a separate sheet of paper, diagram the subject and its modifiers and the verb. Do not try to diagram anything else at this point.*

       pro av art   n   pp adj n pp   n   pp   adj

1. Today we study the contributions (of all <u>sorts</u>)(of people)(to American

    n

culture).

    ——— *pn* ———   *av*   *n* *pp* *adj* *n*

2. Roberto Felix Salazar obviously <u>took</u> pride (in his ancestors).

    ——— *pn* ——— *pp* ——— *pn* ———   *av*   *art*

3. "The Other Pioneers" (by Roberto Felix Salazar) celebrates the

         n   *pp* *adj* *adj*   *n*

accomplishments (of <u>these</u> Texas pioneers).

      pn   *pp* *art*   *adj* ——*pn*—— *av* *pp* *adj*   *adj*

4. Mexican-Americans (in the southwestern United States) identify (with these rugged

    n

<u>people</u>).

    adj   *adj*   *n*   *av* *adj* *n* *pp* *art* *adj*   *n*

5. <u>Mexican</u> and Anglo settlers left their mark (on the Texas landscape).

    adj   *n* *av* —*v*— *pp* *adj* *art* *adj*   *n*   *pp* *adj* *n*

6. American students try to learn (about all the different contributions)(to their culture).

    pp *art* *n*   *av* *art* *n* *pp* *adj* *adj*   *n*

7. Here (on the land) were the marks (of these early settlers). (See Notes VI)

   adj   *adj*   *n*   *av* *art* *n* *pp* *art* *adj*   *pn*

8. Anglo and Mexican culture really <u>shapes</u> the life (of the American Southwest).

      n   pp adj pro av pro——v——— pro pp adj   n

9. Poems (like this one) help us to understand more (about our country).

      adv av adj   n   n   pp adj   n

10. Please read these stories and poems (about your <u>antecedents</u>).

DEFINITIONS:

1. In a diagram, a _____*modifier*_____ goes on a diagonal lines attached to another word.

2. Pronouns are words that _____*take the place of nouns*_____.

3. Adjectives are words that _____*modify (or describe) nouns and pronouns*_____.

DIRECTIONS: *Write what job the underlined words is doing. Choose your answers from among the following:*

       SUBJECT   OBJECT OF THE PREPOSITION   VERB   MODIFIER

SENTENCE #	WORD	JOB
1	sorts	*object of the preposition*
2	took	*verb*
3	these	*modifier*
4	people	*object of the preposition*
5	Mexican	*modifier*
8	shapes	*verb*
10	antecedents	*object of the preposition*

1. we | study

6. students | try
   American

2. Roberto Felix Salazar | took

7. marks | were
   the / of / settlers / these / early

3. "The Other Pioneers" | celebrates
   by Roberto Felix Salazar

8. culture | shapes
   Anglo / Mexican / and

4. Mexican-Americans | identify
   in United States / the / southwestern

9. Poems | help
   like / one / this

5. settlers | left
   Mexican / Anglo / and

10. (you) | read

SKILLS SUPPORT

DIRECTIONS: *Below is a stanza from "The Other Pioneers" by Roberto Felix Salazar. Mark all the parts of speech that you know. Paraphrase this stanza.*

   pro av art adj n av   *pp   adj   n*
They saw the Texas sun rise golden-red (with promised wealth)

      av art adj   n   av   *pp   n*
And saw the Texas sun sink golden yet, (with wealth) unspent.

        pro   av   *– v –*   *–v –*
"Here," they said. "Here to live and here to love."

      av art n pp adj n   *art n pp adj n*
"Here is the land (for our sons and the sons)(of our sons)."

      pro av art   n   pp adj   pn
And they sang the songs(of ancient Spain)

      pro av   adj   n   – v– adj   n
And they made new songs to fit new needs.

 pro   av   art   n   *av   art   n*
They cleared the brush and planted the corn

      av   adj   n   av   *pp   n pp n*
And saw green stalks turn black (from lack)(of rain).

 pro   av   art   n   *pp   art   n*
They roamed the plains (behind the herds).

      av   art   adj   adj   n
And stood the Indian's cruel attacks.

      av   n   *av   n*
There was dust and there was sweat.

        av   n   art   n   av
And there were tears and the women prayed.

SUBJECT & VERB: TEST

NAME:_____DATE:_____

(RAW SCORE: _____ /206   GRADE: _____)

DIRECTIONS: *Mark all the nouns, proper nouns, pronouns, articles, adjectives, prepositions, and action verbs in the sentences below. Put parentheses around the prepositional phrases. Then, on a separate sheet of paper, diagram the subject and verb of each sentence. Add to your diagram the modifiers for the subject, including articles, adjectives, and prepositional phrases.*

     av adj adj   n pp adj adj   n

9 1. <u>Study</u> this beautiful poem (about Texas' early settlers).

     n pp adj   n   av art   n   pp adj adj n

—— 2. Students (of <u>American</u> culture) read the literature (of all our poets).

13

     pro av   n   pp   adj   adj   n

—— 3. They want information (about America's early <u>settlers)</u>.

8

     n pp adj n   av   n   pp adj n pp   n

—— 4. <u>Students</u> (in this school) read examples(of this type)(of literature).

14

     pro av adj   n   pp adj   n

—— 5. They want <u>more</u> information(about their roots).

8

     art   n   pp adj n av pro —— v ——   pro

—— 6. An <u>understanding</u> (of our roots) helps us to understand ourselves.

10

     adj adj   pn   av art adj   n   pp adj   adj

—— 7. All patriotic Americans appreciate the many contributions (of America's different

13

     adj   n

   cultural <u>groups</u>).

     art adj n pp pn   av art adj   n pp n pp adj n

—— 8. The best writers (in America) created a great body(of <u>work)</u>(on this subject).

17

(over)

          adj   *n*   *pp*   *adj* *adj*   *n*   *av* *pro* *n*   *pp*   *pro*

—— 9.   Great literature (about our early ancestors)<u>gives</u> us pride (in ourselves).
13

                   av   *adj*   *adj*   *n*   *pp*   *adj*   *n*

—— 10. Here comes that positive <u>self-esteem</u> (about our ancestors)!
8

===
113   ***DEFINITIONS:***

—— 1.   A verb is a "real" verb when it has a _____ *subject* _____.
1

—— 2.   The articles in our language are __*a*__, __*an*__, and __*the*__.
3

—— 3.   Which kind of noun begins with a capital letter? ____ *a proper noun* ____.
1

—— 4.   Which kind of noun consists of only one word? ____ *a common noun* ____.
1

—— 5.   A pronoun is a word that __ *takes the place of one or more a nouns* __.
1

—— 6.   Adjectives are words that _____ *modify nouns and pronouns* _____.
1

—— 7.   If a word looks like a verb but doesn't have a subject, it's a ____ *verbal* ____.
1
===
9

DIRECTIONS: *Write what job the underlined words are doing. Choose your answers from among the following:*

SUBJECT   *MODIFIER*   *VERB*   *OBJECT OF THE PREPOSITION*

SENTENCE #	WORD	JOB
1	Study	*verb*
2	American	*modifier*
3	settlers	*object of the preposition*
4	Students	*subject*
5	more	*modifier*
6	understanding	*subject*
7	groups	*object of the preposition*
8	work	*object of the preposition*
9	gives	*verb*
10	self-esteem	*subject*

5 points each

Raw		Score	Grade	%
206	-	201	= A++	=98+
200	-	195	= A+	= 95
194	-	185	= A	= 90
184	-	175	= B+	= 85
174	-	164	= B	= 80
163	-	154	= C+	= 75
153	-	144	= C	= 70
143	-	133	= D+	= 65
133	-	123	= D	= 60

===
50

I suggest you score the diagrams separately from the parsing. Refer to your instructions on how to grade diagrams. Each check mark represents a point. Remember, the first word of a sentence must be capitalized in the diagram.

FROM NOW ON, COUNT PREPOSITIONAL PHRASES - CORRECTLY DIAGRAMED AND ATTACHED TO THE RIGHT WORD - AS ONE POINT.

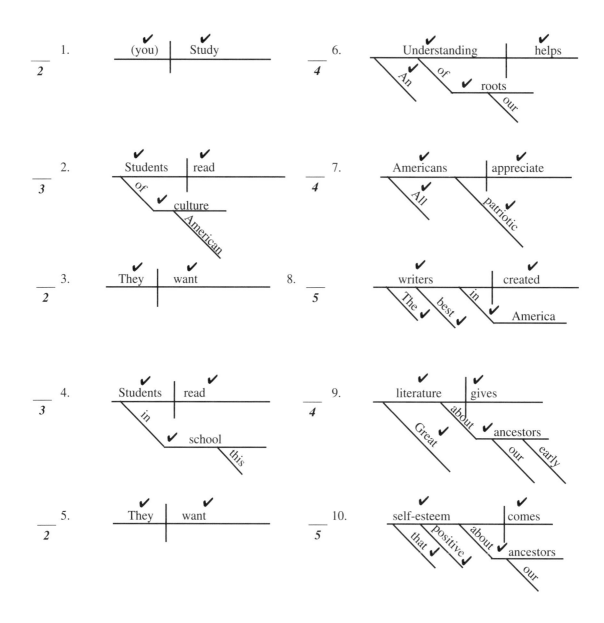

```
  2   1.    (you) | Study

  3   2.    Students | read
                of / culture
                  American

  2   3.    They | want

  3   4.    Students | read
                in / school
                  this

  2   5.    They | want

  4   6.    Understanding | helps
             An   of / roots
                    our

  4   7.    Americans | appreciate
             All        patriotic

  5   8.    writers | created
             The  best   in / America

  4   9.    literature | gives
             Great   about / ancestors
                       our   early

  5   10.   self-esteem | comes
             that positive  about / ancestors
                                    our
```

===
34

ADVERBS

DEFINITION: An adverb is an "all-purpose" **MODIFIER.** It can modify a **verb,** an **adjective**, or another **adverb**.

As is stated above, adverbs modify three different things. We will discuss these things in order.

1. When an adverb modifies a VERB, it tells you IN ONE WORD "How?" "When?" "Where?" or "Why?" about that verb.

art   n   av   adv   adv

EXAMPLE: The students arrived promptly today.

What does "promptly" tell you? Yes, it tells you HOW the students ARRIVED. It's an adverb, so it's marked "adv."

What does "today" tell you? Right, it tells you WHEN the students ARRIVED. It's also an adverb. Here's how you diagram this sentence:

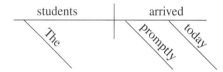

ADVERBS THAT MODIFY VERBS ARE MOVEABLE.

This is extremely important and that's why it's in such big type! This concept will be tremendously helpful to you when it comes to figuring out what an adverb modifies. Words in our language usually have to be in a certain place in a sentence (articles must come before nouns, helping verbs must come before verbs, subjects usually precede verbs, etc.), but that's not true of ADVERBS WHICH MODIFY VERBS. You can usually move such adverbs to two or three different places in the sentence without it sounding odd or changing the meaning in any way. Let's try it out with the sentence above. Can "promptly" be moved around? How about "today"?

Today the students arrived promptly.
The students promptly arrived today.
The students arrived today promptly.

All three of these variations make complete sense, don't they? So if you see a word in a sentence that can be moved without changing the sentence's meaning, that tells you two things: 1.) it's an adverb, and 2.) it modifies the verb! If it's an adverb and it <u>cannot</u> be moved, then <u>it modifies the word that it must stay next to.</u>

2. Adverbs that modify adjectives tell you "How?" or "To what extent?" about adjectives.

art   adv   adj   n   av pp art   adj   n

EXAMPLE: The extremely nervous patient sat (in the dentist's chair).

What does "extremely" tell you? Yes, it tells you HOW NERVOUS. It's an adverb. Notice also that "extremely" is NOT moveable. It must stay next to the word "nervous," because it modifies an adjective, not a verb. Here's how you diagram it.

*We call this nifty little construction
a "dog's hind leg"!*

51

3.   Adverbs that modify other adverbs also tell you "How?" or "To what extent?" about adverbs.

adj   n   av   adv   adv

EXAMPLE: Our guest left quite abruptly.

What does *quite* tell you? Yes, it tells you HOW ABRUPTLY. It's an adverb. Notice, also, that it cannot be moved away from the word *abruptly*. Here's how to diagram it:

You use a "dog's hind leg" every time you have a modifier that modifies another modifier.

4.   Prepositional phrases can modify verbs and other modifiers too. When they do, they answer the same "How?" "When?" , etc. questions as adverbs do Here are a few examples of how to diagram them.

pro   av   n   pp art   n

EXAMPLE: We ate lunch (in the park).   (*in the park* tells you WHERE we ATE)

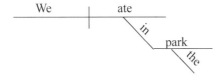

pro av pro adv pp art n

EXAMPLE: I saw him later (in the day).   (*in the day* tells you LATER TO WHAT EXTENT)

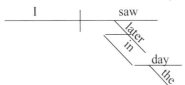

If you're having a little trouble understanding that *in the day* modifies *later*, remember that, if it modified the verb, it would be <u>moveable</u>. Since it can't be moved away from *later*, it must modify it.

In the sentence above this one, you can move *in the park* to the front of the sentence without changing its meaning. That tells you that it modifies the verb.

SOME HANDY LITTLE NOTES:

Many adverbs end in "ly." In our language you can change many adjectives (such as beautiful) into adverbs by adding the suffix "ly" (beautifully). Not all adverbs end in "ly," and not all words that end in "ly" are adverbs. Only adjectives with the "ly" suffix are adverbs.

The words *how, when, where,* and *why* are frequently adverbs. For now, mark them that way.

The words *not, never, really,* and *very* are very commonly used adverbs.

If you just can't figure out what a word is, it's probably an adverb!

<u>When your having a hard time figuring out where a modifier (adverb or prepositional phrase) goes,</u> try saying the modifier together with the word you think it modifies. For instance, in the last sentence above "saw in the day" doesn't sound right, but "later in the day" does! That tells you that "in the day" goes with "later"! This, along with the "moveability" trick and using the questions (how, when, where or why), will almost always show you what an adverb or prepositional phrase modifies.

ADVERBS: EXERCISE #1

NAME: _____DATE: _____

DIRECTIONS: *Mark all the nouns, articles, adjectives, prepositions, action verbs, and adverbs in the sentences below. Then diagram the subject and the verb and their modifiers. Don't attempt to diagram anything else.*

       pro   av   ———— pn ———— pp art adv adj adj   pn

1.   We recognize Dr. Martin Luther King, Jr. (as a truly great black <u>American</u>).

       — *pn*—   *adv av art adj   adj   n*

2.   Dr. King <u>certainly</u> had a brilliant, well-disciplined mind.

       pp art adv adj n   pn adv   av   n

3.   (At a very young <u>age</u>), Martin sadly experienced prejudice.

       art adj   adj   n   adv   av   adv

4.   The black and white children <u>always</u> played separately.

       pro   av   pn   adv

5.   <u>This</u> bothered Martin deeply.

       pro adv   av   pp art adj   n   pp adj n

6.   He always wondered (about the unequal <u>treatment</u>)(of his people).

       pp   n   pn   adv   av   pp ———— pn ———— pp pn

7.   (At fifteen) Martin proudly <u>enrolled</u> (at Morehouse College)(in Atlanta).

        pn   av   adv   pp adj n pp n

8.   Martin worked diligently (for his future)(in life).

       pro adv   av   art   n   pp adj   n

9.   He <u>finally</u> chose the ministry (as his profession).

       adj — pn — adv   av   adj   n   pp adj adj   n   pp

10.   Young Dr. King always inspired his congregation (with his <u>fiery</u> sermons)(against

        n

    injustice).

(over)

DEFINITIONS:

1.   A pronoun is a word that _____ *takes the place of a noun or another pronoun* _____

2.   An antecedent is _____ *the noun that the pronouns stands for* _____

3.   Adverbs are words that modify _____ *verbs, adjectives, and other adverbs* _____

4.   An adverb which can be moved modifies _____ *the verb* _____

5.   If an adverb cannot be moved, it modifies _____ *the word it must stay next to* _____

DIRECTIONS: *Write what jobs the words below are doing Choose your answer from among the following:*

> *SUBJECT   VERB   MODIFIER   OBJECT OF THE PREPOSITION*

SENTENCE #	WORD	JOB
1	American	*object of the preposition*
2	certainly	*modifier*
3	age	*object of the preposition*
4	always	*modifier*
5	This	*subject*
6	treatment	*object of the preposition*
7	enrolled	*verb*
9	finally	*modifier*
10	fiery	*modifier*

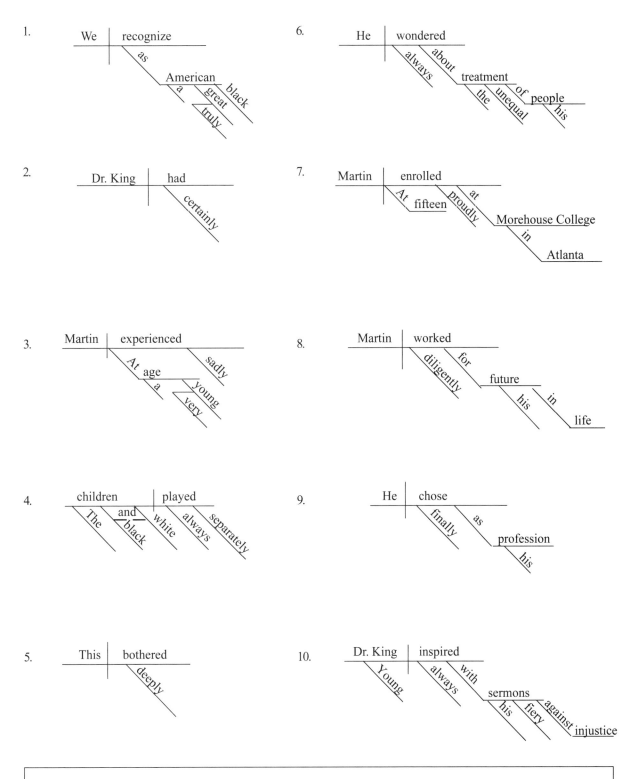

ADVERBS: EXERCISE #2

NAME: _____DATE: _____

DIRECTIONS: *Mark all the nouns, articles, adjectives, prepositions, action verbs, and adverbs in the sentences below. Put parentheses around the prepositional phrases. Then diagram the subject and the verb and their modifiers. There may be words you can't yet diagram; if so, just leave them alone for now.*

——————— *pn* ———— *adv*   *av*   *pp*—————— *pn* ————

1. <u>Martin Luther King, Jr.</u> ultimately graduated (from Morehouse College).

     pro adv   av   art   n   pp —————— *pn* —————
2. He then <u>received</u> a scholarship (to Crozer Theological Seminary).

     art   n   pp ——— *pn* ——— *adv   av   pn*
3. The teachings (of Mahatma Gandhi) <u>totally</u> fascinated Martin.

     pp   adj   n   pn   adv   av   adj   n   pp   adj
4. (With non-violent <u>methods)</u>, Gandhi successfully freed his people (from British

     n
   domination).

     pn   adv   av   pp art   n   pp adj   n
5. Martin sincerely believed (in the <u>success</u>) (of this method).

     pro   av   adv pp adj   adj   n   pp ——— *pn* ———
6. <u>He</u> studied hard(for his doctoral degree)(at Boston University).

     pp   adj   n   ——pn—— av adj adj   n pp art adv   adj   n
7. (Upon his graduation,) Dr. King started his adult life (as the very young <u>pastor)</u>

     pp art   n   pp   pn
   (of a church)(in Alabama).

     pp adj   n   pp adj   n   art   n   av   art   n   pp art   n
8. (At that time)(in our <u>history</u>),the law mandated the separation (of the races).

     pp adj   adj   n   ——pn—— adv   av   adj   adj   n
9. (In his Sunday sermons), Dr. King <u>bravely</u> denounced these unjust laws.

     * —— *pp* —— *adj   n   art adj   n   pp art   n   adv   av   art*
10. *(Because of Martin's words), the <u>black</u> leaders (in the community) also favored the

      n   pp adj   n   *(See Notes: Unit #3, pg. 6)
   use (of Gandhi's methods).

(over)

DEFINITIONS:

1.   Which kind of noun begins with a lower case letter and consists of one word only?

_____ *a common noun* _____

2.   If a word looks like a verb, but it doesn't have a subject, it's called a

_____ *verbal* _____

3.   If you find a verb and ask ,"Who or what - (and say the verb)?" - what are you looking for?

_____ *the subject* _____

DIRECTIONS: *Write what jobs the words below are doing. Choose your answers from among the following:*

SUBJECT   MODIFIER   VERB   OBJECT OF THE PREPOSITION

SENTENCE #	WORD	JOB
1	Martin Luther King, Jr.	*subject*
2	received	*verb*
3	totally	*modifier*
4	methods	*object of the preposition*
5	success	*object of the preposition*
6	He	*subject*
7	pastor	*object of the preposition*
8	history	*object of the preposition*
9	bravely	*modifier*
10	black	*modifier*

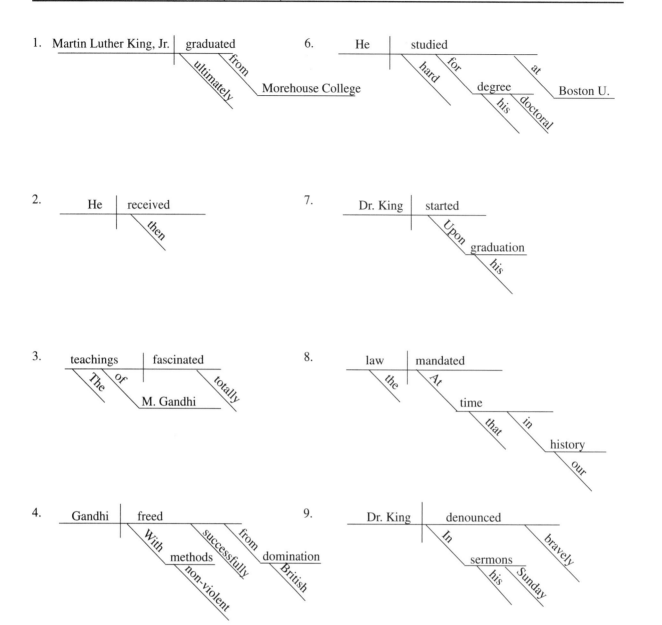

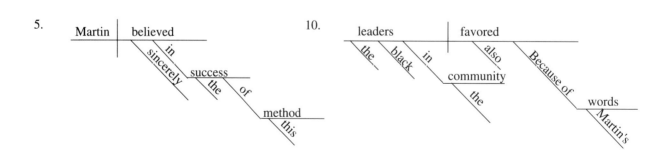

ADVERBS: EXERCISE #3

NAME: _____DATE: _____

DIRECTIONS: *Parse(mark all the parts of speech)in the sentences below. Then diagram the subject and its modifiers and the verb and its modifiers.*

1.
     — adj—   *n*   *pp*   *adj*   *n*   *pp* *adj* *n*   *adv*
    Dr. King's <u>message</u> (about non-violent resistence) (to segregation laws) certainly
    av art n   pp art n   pp adj   pn
    struck a chord (in the hearts)(of many Americans).

2
     —— *pn* ——   *pp art adj n pp   n*   *av*   *art*   *n*   *pp art*
    <u>Mrs. Rosa Parks</u>, (with a simple act)(of bravery), provided an opportunity (for the
                n   *pp— adj— n pp n*
    implementation)(of Dr. King's plan)(of action).

3.
     pp   *art n*   *pp adj n* —— *pn*—   *adv av pp art* — *adj* ——
    (Against the laws)(of her city), Mrs. Parks simply sat (in a "Whites Only"
       n   *pp art adj n*
    <u>section</u>)(of a city bus).

4.
     art adj   n   adv   av   pro pp adj n
    The city police <u>quickly</u> arrested her (for her "crime.")

5.
     —— *pn* —   *adv*   *av   art   pn pp adj n pp art adj n*
    Dr. King promptly <u>organized</u> the Blacks (of that city)(in a bus boycott).

6.
     art ———— *pn* ——— *adv   av art adj n pp   n*
    The Selma Bus Company soon <u>suffered</u> the daily loss(of money).

7.
     adv —pn— av   adj   *n*   *pp n*   *pp adj adv*
    Now Dr. King <u>led</u> non-violent marches (in protest)(against these completely
    adj   n
    unjust laws).

8.
     adv pp ——— *pn* ——— *art* ————— *pn* ———— *av art*
    Finally, (on <u>November 12, 1956</u>), the United States Supreme Court issued a
       n   pp   n   pp adj adv adj   n
    decision (in support)(of these civil rights crusaders).

(over)

59

9.
   pp ——— *pn* —— *pp* *pn* — *pn* — *av* *art* *adv* *adj* *adv*
(In Washington, D. C.), (in 1963), Dr. King delivered a very beautiful and <u>now</u>
    adj *n* *pp* *adj* *n* *pp* *adj* *n* *pp* *pn*
famous speech (about his dream)(of racial equality)(for America).

10.
     adv *pp* *pn* *art* *adj* *n* *av* *art* *n* *pp* *adj* *adv* *adj*
Tragically (in 1968), a white <u>ex-convict</u> ended the career (of this truly great
    adj *n*
American hero).

DEFINITIONS:

1.   The three articles are   _____ *A, AN, and THE* _____

2.   A proper noun begins with a _____ *capital letter* _____

     and may consist of   _____ *more than one word* _____

3.   An action verb expresses _____ *mental or physical action* _____

     and must have a   _____ *subject* _____

4.   If a word looks like a verb but doesn't have a subject, it's a _____ *verbal* _____

DIRECTIONS: What jobs are the words below are doing? Choose your answers from among the following:

SUBJECT   MODIFIER   VERB   OBJECT OF THE PREPOSITION

SENTENCE #	WORD	JOB
1	message	*subject*
2	Mrs. Rosa Parks	*subject*
3	section	*object of the preposition*
4	quickly	*modifier*
5	organized	*verb*
6	suffered	*verb*
7	led	*verb*
8	November 12, 1956	*object of the preposition*
9	now	*modifier*
10	ex-convict	*subject*

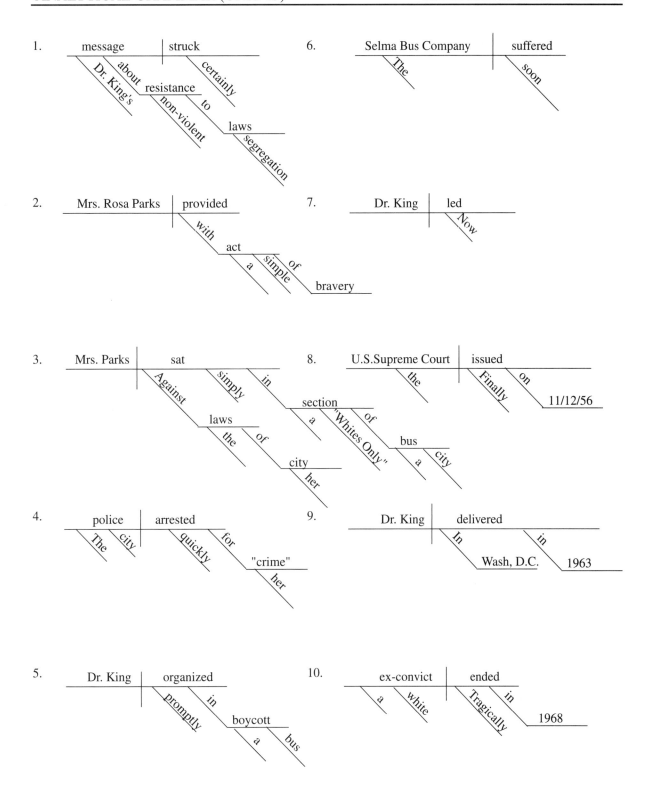

SKILLS SUPPORT

DIRECTIONS: The following is an exerpt from Dr. Martin Luther King, Jr.'s historic "I Have a Dream" speech, given on the steps of the Lincoln Memorial in 1963. Parse the words that you can in the passage below. Then paraphrase it.

*pro av — v — art n pp n * adv * art n*
"We refuse to believe the bank (of justice) is bankrupt...Now is the time

— v — n art n pp pro pp adj n
to make justice a reality (for all) (of God's children)...

pro avart n adv
I have a dream today."

*These are linking verbs, so we're just going to ignore them for now.

ADVERBS: TEST

NAME: _____ DATE: _____

(RAW SCORE _____ */251* GRADE: _____)

DIRECTIONS: *Mark all the nouns, articles, adjectives, pronouns, prepositions, action verbs, and adverbs in the sentences below and put parenthese around the prepositional phrases. Then, on a separate sheet of paper, neatly diagram the subject and verb and their modifiers.*

      art   n   pp art ——— pn ——— adv   av   ——— pn ———

___1.   The crowds (at the Lincoln Memorial) joyfully received Martin Luther King, Jr.

9

      adj   pn   av   adj   n pp adj adv adj   n

___2.   All Americans take tremendous pride (in this often repeated speech).

11

      adj   pn   pp adj   n   adv   av pro pp art n

___3.   Many Americans (in that generation) instantly hailed him (as a hero).

13

      adv adj   n   av   pn   pp adj n

___4.   Today his courage inspires Americans (of all colors).

9

      —— pn ——   av   n   pp art adv   adj   n   pp art   n

___5.   Dr. King emphasized discipline (as a very important aspect)(of the struggle)

16   *pp   n*

      (against injustice).

      —— pn ——   av   pn   pp art   n   pp   n   pp adj n   pp adj

___6.   Dr. King reminded Americans (of the guarantee)(of equality)(for all people)(in our

18   *pn*

      Constitution).

      adv   art ——— pn ——   av adj   n   pp art n   pp adj

  7.   Constitutionally, the Founding Fathers formed this country (as a home)(for all

15   *adj   n*

      God's children).

      n   pp adj   n   pp art n   av pp adj adj   n pp n

___8.   People (from all corners)(of the world) come (to this sweet land)(of liberty.)

18

      adv   ——— pn — av   pn   pp art n pp adj adv adj   n

___9.   Tragically, James Earl Ray robbed America (of the life)(of this truly great man).

14

      adv   pn   pp adj n   av   art   n   pp adj n pp n

___10. Today Americans (of all colors) remember the courage (of this man)(of peace).

16

                                                (over)

DEFINITIONS:

___1.   A noun is the name of _____*a person, place, thing, or idea.*_____
1

___2.   A _____*common*_____ noun begins with a lower-case letter.
1

___3.   A _____*proper*_____noun begins with a capital letter.
1

___4.   A _____*common*_____noun can consist of only one word.
1

___5.   An adjective is a word that _____*modifies a noun or a pronoun*_____
1

___6.   The articles in our language are ___*a*___, ___*an*___, and ___*the*___.
3

___7.   A pronoun is a word that _____*takes the place of a noun*_____.
1

___8.   An antecedent is _____*the noun the pronoun stands for*_____.
1

___9.   A word may look like a preposition, but it's not unless it has a(n) _____*object*_____.
1

___10.   Adverbs modify _____*verbs*_____, _____*adjectives*_____, and
3

        _____*adverbs*_____.

===
14

DIRECTIONS: *Write what jobs the words below are doing. Choose your answers from among the following:*

SUBJECT   VERB   MODIFIER   OBJECT OF THE PREPOSITION

SENTENCE #	WORD	JOB
1	crowds	*subject*
2	speech	*object of the preposition*
3	hailed	*verb*
4	Today	*modifier*
5	aspect	*object of the preposition*
6	Dr. King	*subject*
7	home	*object of the preposition*
8	People	*subject*
9	robbed	*verb*
10	colors	*object of the preposition*

(5

points

each)

===
50

Raw		Score		Grade		%
251	-	245	=	A++	=	98+
244	-	238	=	A+	=	95
237	-	225	=	A	=	90
224	-	213	=	B+	=	85
212	-	200	=	B	=	80
199	-	188	=	C+	=	75
187	-	175	=	C	=	70
174	-	163	=	D+	=	65
162	-	150	=	D	=	60

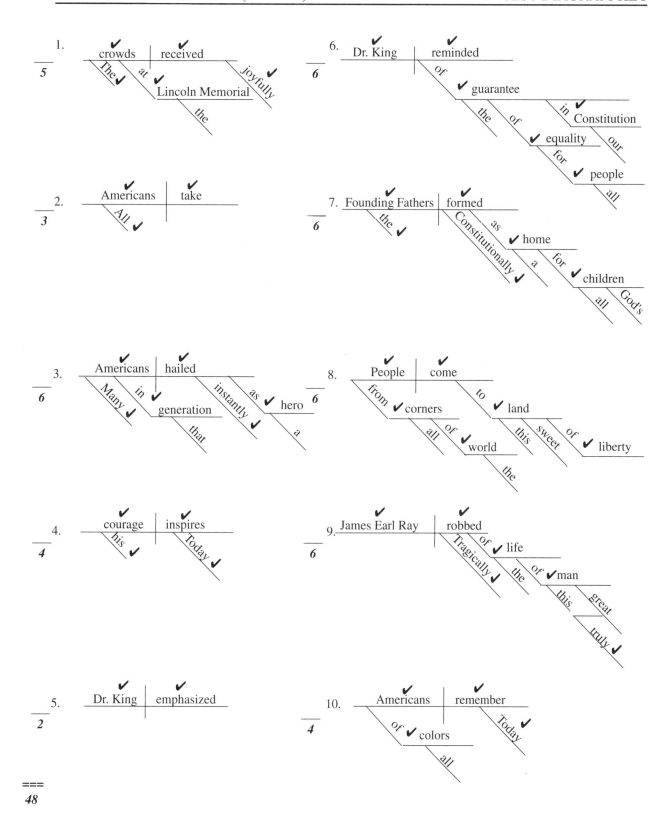

PATTERNS 1 & 2

Now that you know the basics of diagraming, it is necessary for you to know the FIVE SENTENCE PATTERNS. No matter how different sentences may look, they all fall into one of five basic patterns. This unit deals with PATTERNS 1 & 2. These two patterns contain ACTION VERBS ONLY.

PATTERN 1: N - V

The N-V pattern contains only two items on the baseline: a subject (N) and an action verb (V). The subject and verb may have modifiers, and there may be prepositional phrases in the sentence, but THERE WILL BE NO OTHER NOUNS OR VERBS.

> EXAMPLE: *art   n   av   prep art   adj   n*
> The boy stood (on the boat's deck).

As you already know, this sentence should be diagramed like this:

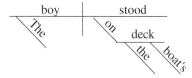

(EXERCISE #1 features the N-V pattern; but to complete it keep reading)

PATTERN 2: N - V - N

To learn about Pattern 2, you must become familiar with a new "job" called the DIRECT OBJECT. The N-V-N pattern contains three main parts: a subject (N), an action verb (V), and a DIRECT OBJECT (N). All three parts may have modifiers, and there may be prepositional phrases in the sentence, but THERE ARE NO OTHER NOUNS OR VERBS.

To find the DIRECT OBJECT, you first find the subject and the verb. Then you simply SAY THE SUBJECT, SAY THE VERB, AND ASK "WHAT?" The answer will be a noun or a pronoun and is called the DIRECT OBJECT.

> EXAMPLE: *adj adj   n   av   art adj   n*
> My best friend had   a birthday party.

The subject is FRIEND; the verb is HAD. Now say, "friend had WHAT?" The answer is PARTY - which is your DIRECT OBJECT. The diagram for this Pattern 2 sentence is like this:

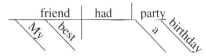

(Exercise #2 features these N-V-N patterns; Exercise #3 contains
sentences which are both Pattern 1 and Pattern 2; do them now)

THE PROCESS:

On the back of this page is an expanded version to the flow chart that was introduced in Unit #4. We will be adding new mental steps, but for now - as long as you understand what you see - you're doing fine!

THE PROCESS

Step 1. Find and mark *n* all the nouns in the sentence. (*pn* over proper nouns)

Step 2. Find and mark all the articles and adjectives (Ask, "Which [say the noun]?")

Step 3. Find and mark all the pronouns.

Step 4. Find all the prepositions and put parentheses around the prepositional phrases.

Step 5. Find any word that looks like a verb and mark it "v."

Step 6. Ask, "Who or what (say the verb)?"

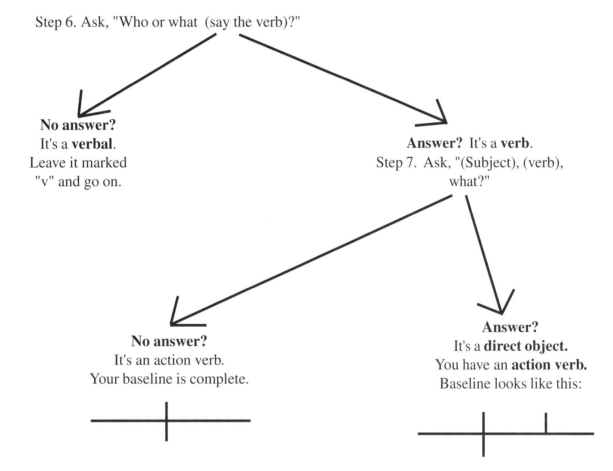

No answer?
It's a **verbal**.
Leave it marked
"v" and go on.

Answer? It's a **verb**.
Step 7. Ask, "(Subject), (verb),
what?"

No answer?
It's an action verb.
Your baseline is complete.

Answer?
It's a **direct object.**
You have an **action verb.**
Baseline looks like this:

PATTERNS 1 & 2: EXERCISE #1

NAME:_____DATE:_____

DIRECTIONS: *All the sentences below are Pattern 1. Parse them and put parentheses around the prepositional phrases. Diagram the subject and verb and their modifiers, including the prepositional phrases.*

    adv   *adj*   *n*   *av pp adj   n*

1. Many Americans' <u>grandparents</u> live (in other states).

      pro pp pro av pp adv   adj   n   adv adv

2. Many (of us) <u>go</u> (to our grandparents' houses) very rarely.

     n   *pp adj*   *n*   *adv   av pp adj   n   pp art   n   pp*

3. People (in former generations)seldom moved (to other <u>places)</u>(with the frequency)(of
   adj   *n*
today's families).

     adj   *adj*   *n*   *av pp art adj   n   pp adj   n*

4. Most American children <u>lived</u> (in the same town)(as their grandparents).

     pro   *av*   *adv pp adv*   *adj*   *n*

5. They visited often (in <u>their</u> grandparents' homes).

     pp   *adj adj*   *adj*   *n pro*   *av*   *pp art n pp art*

6. (During these long and frequent visits) they learned (about the lives) (of the
      n
<u>grandparents.</u>)

     n   *pp*   *pn*   *adv av pp adj*   *n*   *pp   adj   n*

7. Children (in America) today <u>visit</u> (with their grandparents)(during short vacations).

     n   *pp adj adj*   *n*   *av   adv*   *pp   n pp n*

8. Families (from all economic <u>levels</u>) move frequently (from place)(to place).

(over)

    art adj pro av   pp adj   n   pp art adj   n
9. A lucky <u>few</u> visit (with their grandparents)(for a long time).

     pp   art n pp adv   adj   n   av pp pro pp adj   n   pp
10. (Before the <u>end</u>)(of your grandparents' lives), speak (to them)(of your gratitude)(for
  adj adj n
    all their love). (See Notes, Unit #4, p. 8, IV)

DEFINITIONS:

1. Pronouns are words that _____ *take the place of nouns* _____.

2. To look for the direct object you say the _____ *subject* _____, say the _____ *verb* _____,

    and ask _____ *what?* _____.

3, A verb must have a _____ *subject* _____ to be a "real" verb.

DIRECTIONS: *Write what job the underlined words are doing. Choose your answers from among the following:*

    SUBJECT   *OBJECT OF THE PREPOSITION*   *VERB*   *MODIFIER*

<u>SENTENCE #</u>	<u>WORD</u>	<u>JOB</u>
1	grandparents	*subject*
2	go	*verb*
3	places	*object of the preposition*
4	lived	*verb*
5	their	*modifier*
6	grandparents	*object of the preposition*
7	visit	*verb*
8	levels	*object of the preposition*
9	few	*subject*
10	end	*object of the preposition*

    69

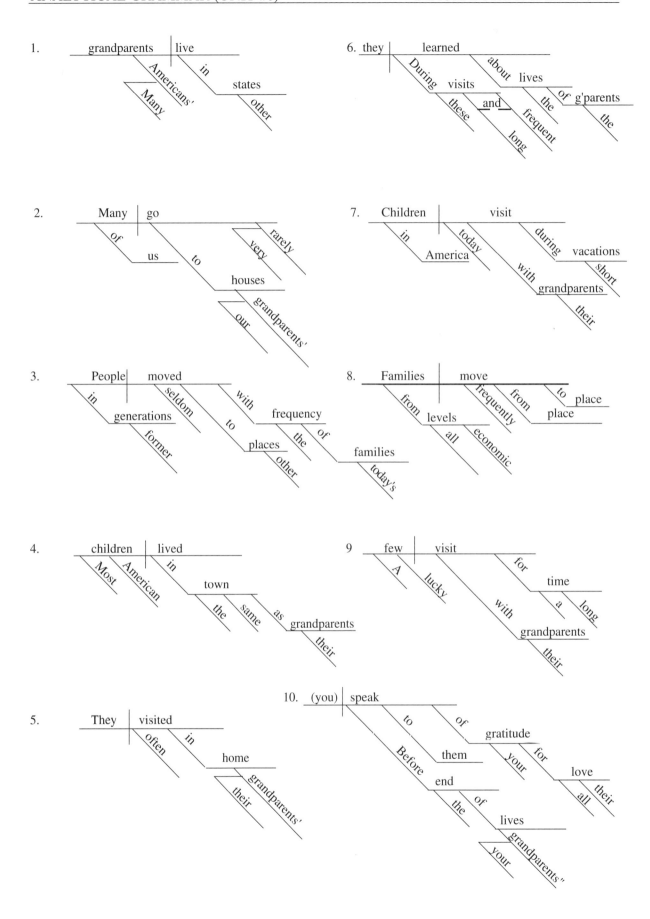

PATTERNS 1 & 2: EXERCISE #2

NAME:_____DATE:_____

DIRECTIONS: *All the sentences below are Pattern 2. Parse them and put parentheses around the prepositional phrases. Diagram the entire sentence. Remember to use your Process chart.*

```
    pp   adj        adj      n  pro  adv    av      art   n   pp  adj  n
1.  (In today's youth-oriented society) we seldom appreciate the wisdom (of our elders).
```

```
    art  n   av   adj   adj    n   pp  adj  adj   n
2.  The past gives many valuable lessons (for our modern lives).
```

```
    adj    n    adv  adv  av  adj    n       pp art   n    pp art
3.  Young people today rarely show their appreciation (for the lessons)(of the
      n
    past).
```

```
    adj    n    adv   av    n    pp   adj    n
4.  Older people sometimes lack  patience (with younger people).
```

```
    adj    n      adv     av      n         pp   adj       adj
5.  These conflicts occasionally cause misunderstandings(between younger and older
      n
    people).
```

```
    art  adj   n   pp art adj    n     av    n   pp  art  n   pp pro
6.  An enjoyable hour (with an older person) opens doors (from the past)(for you).
```

```
    adj   n   pp  art  n  av   n  pp  n   pp adj  adv   adj
7.  These doors (from the past) shed light (on things)(in our often confusing
      n
    world).
```

(over)

    adj   adj   n   pp adj   n   adv av   n   pp   adj   n

8. Some older people (in <u>nursing</u> homes) never get visits(from younger people).

    art n   pp pro   av   pro pp pro

9. A visit (like this) benefits <u>both</u> (of you)!

    av   n   —pp— adj   adj   n pp art n   pp art adj   n

10. <u>Take</u> time (out of your busy life)(for a visit)(with an older person). (See Notes: Unit #3, pg. 6)

DIRECTIONS: *Write what job the underlined words are doing. Choose your answers from among the following:*

SUBJECT   DIRECT OBJECT   OBJECT OF THE PREPOSITION   VERB   MODIFIER

SENTENCE #	WORD	JOB
1	wisdom	*direct object*
2	past	*subject*
3	appreciation	*direct object*
4	Older	*modifier*
5	misunderstandimgs	*direct object*
6	person	*object of the preposition*
7	light	*direct object*
8	nursing	*modifier*
9	both	*direct object*
10	Take	*verb*

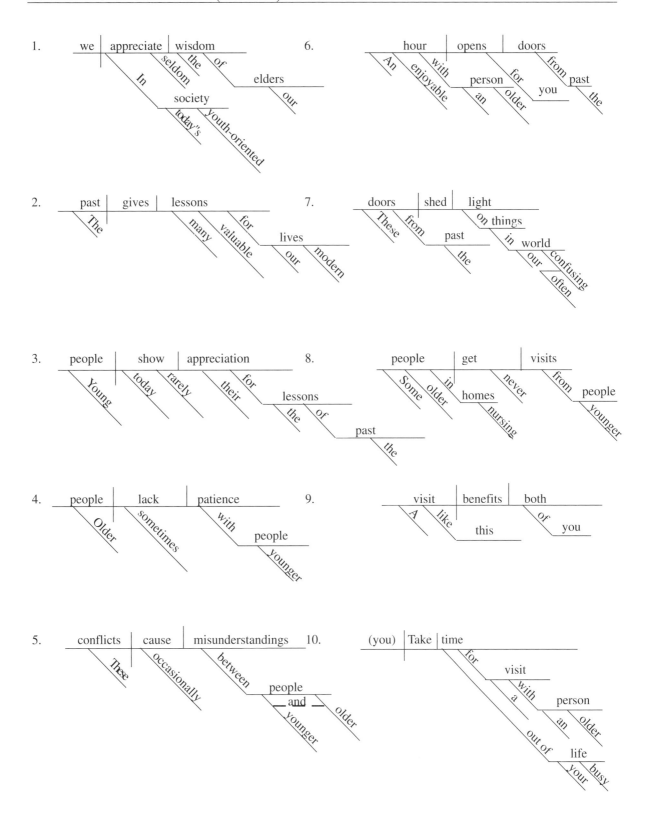

PATTERNS 1 & 2: EXERCISE #3

NAME:_____DATE:_____

DIRECTIONS: *The sentences below are either Pattern 1 or Pattern 2. Parse them and put parentheses around the prepositional phrases. Diagram the entire sentence. Remember to use your process chart.*

          pn   *av* *art* *n*   *pp*   *adj*   *n*
1. Rudolfo A. Anaya wrote a <u>story</u> (about his grandfather).

   adj *adj* *n*   *av* *pp* *art* *n*   *pp* *art*___ *pn* ____ *pp* __ *pn* ____
2. This old <u>farmer</u> <u>lived</u> (in a valley)(on the Pecos River)(in New Mexico).

      adj   *n*   *av*   *n*   *pp*   *n*
3. Rudolfo's culture teaches respect (for <u>elders</u>).

  pro *av* *pp* *adv*   *adj*   *n*   *pp*   *art*   *n*
4. He lived (on his <u>grandfather's</u> farm)(during the summer).

   adj   *n*   *adv* *av*   *pp* *adj*   *n*   *pp* *art* *adj*   *n*
5. His uncles <u>also</u> lived (in that valley)(beside the grandfather's farm).

    adj   *n*   *av* *adj* *n*   *pp*   *n*
6. Rudolfo's grandfather used few words (for advice).

     av *pp* *n*
7. "<u>Pray</u> (for rain)."

   pp *adj*   *n*   *pp* *art* *n*   *pn*   *av* *pp* *n*
8. (Beside his grandfather)(in the wagon), Rudolfo <u>drove</u> (into town)
   pp   *n*
(for supplies).

(over)

      Photocopying this product is strictly prohibited by copyright law.

     art   adj   n   pp adj   n   av pp art adj   adj   n

9. The beloved <u>grandfather</u> (of his childhood) died(after a long and <u>useful</u> life).

     pn   av art adj   n   pp   n   pp adj adj   n   pp adj

10. Rudolfo gained a great <u>deal</u> (of wisdom)(from his close association)(with his

     n

grandfather).

DIRECTIONS: *Write what job the underlined words are doing. Choose your answers from among the following:*

SUBJECT   DIRECT OBJECT   OBJECT OF THE PREPOSITION   VERB   MODIFIER

<u>SENTENCE #</u>	<u>WORD</u>	<u>JOB</u>
1	story	*direct object*
2	farmer	*subject*
2	lived	*verb*
3	elders	*object of the preposition*
4	grandfather's	*modifier*
7	Pray	*verb*
8	drove	*verb*
9	grandfather	*subject*
9	useful	*modifier*
10	deal	*direct object*

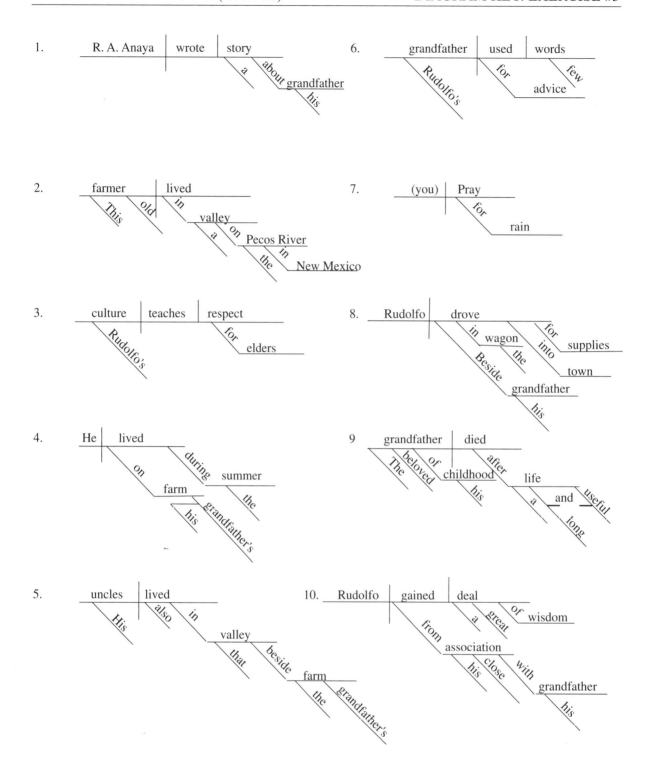

SKILLS SUPPORT

The following is an exerpt from a poem. Mark the nouns, articles, adjectives, pronouns, prepositions, adverbs, and verbs in the lines below and put parentheses around the prepositional phrases. Then paraphrase these two stanzas.

LEGACY II

Leroy V. Quintana

  ADV PRO AV   ADV
NOW I LOOK BACK
  ADV ADJ   N   V
ONLY TWO GENERATIONS REMOVED
  AV   PRO   PRO   *PP ART ADJ N
REALIZE I AM NOTHING (BUT A POOR FOOL)
  PRO AV   PP   N
WHO WENT (TO COLLEGE)

    V   — V— ADJ N   ADV
TRYING TO FIND MY WAY BACK
  PP ART   N   PP ART   N
(TO THE CENTER)(OF THE WORLD)
   ADV   N   AV
WHERE GRANDFATHER STOOD
  ADJ N
THAT DAY

(SEE NOTES UNIT #3 - "BUT AL DOES.")

PATTERNS 1 & 2: TEST

NAME:_____DATE:_____

(RAW SCORE:_____*/254*__GRADE:_____)

DIRECTIONS: *Parse the sentences below and put parentheses around the prepositional phrases. Then, on a separate sheet of paper, diagram the entire sentence.*

       art adj n av   adv   pp art n   pp art n
___ 1. An old man sat quietly (on a <u>bench</u>)(in the park).
13

       adj   n   pp   art   n   av art n pp   n   pp art adj   adj
___ 2. <u>Some</u> boys (from the neighborhood) <u>played</u> a game (of baseball) (in a nearby vacant
18   ***n***
       lot).

       pn av art   n   pp art   n   pp   art adv adj   n
___ 3. Paul hit the <u>ball</u> (over the fence)(onto the old man's bench).
14

       art   n   pp adj   n   av pp adj   n
___ 4. "The baseball (from our game) fell (on your bench)."
11

       adj   adj   n   adv av pro pp art   n
___ 5. "Your stupid ball nearly hit <u>me</u> (on the head)!
10

       adv   av pro adv   adv
 5 6. Please take <u>it</u> away immediately!"

       pn   av   art adj n pp art   n   pp art n
___ 7. Paul studied the old man (on the bench) (for a moment).
13

(over)

           Photocopying this product is strictly prohibited by copyright law.

         pp art adj   n   pro   av   pp art adj n
___ 8. (In a polite tone), he <u>apologized</u> (to the old man).
12

        art adj n pp art   n   av   pp pn pp   n
___ 9. The old man (on the bench) smiled (at Paul)(in <u>surprise</u>).
14

        pro   adv   av adv adj   n
——10. "You certainly have very nice manners!"
6

        art adj   n   pp art pro av pp adj adj   n   pp art n
—— 11. A real <u>friendship</u> (between the two)grew (from this chance <u>encounter</u>)(in the park).
17

===
133

DIRECTIONS: *Write what job the underlined words are doing. Choose your answers from among the following:*

SUBJECT   DIRECT OBJECT   OBJECT OF THE PREPOSITION   VERB   MODIFIER

SENTENCE #	WORD	JOB			
1	bench	*object of the preposition*			
2	Some	*modifier*			
2	played	*verb*			
3	ball	*direct object*			
5	me	*direct object*			
6	it	*direct object*			
8	apologized	*verb*			
9	surprise	*object of the preposition*			
11	friendship	*subject*			
11	encounter	*object of the preposition*			

5

points

each

Raw		Score	Grade	%
254	-	248 =	A++	=98+
247	-	241 =	A+	= 95
240	-	228 =	A	= 90
227	-	215 =	B+	= 85
214	-	203 =	B	= 80
202	-	190 =	C+	= 75
189	-	177 =	C	= 70
176	-	165 =	D+	= 65
164	-	152 =	D	= 60

===
50

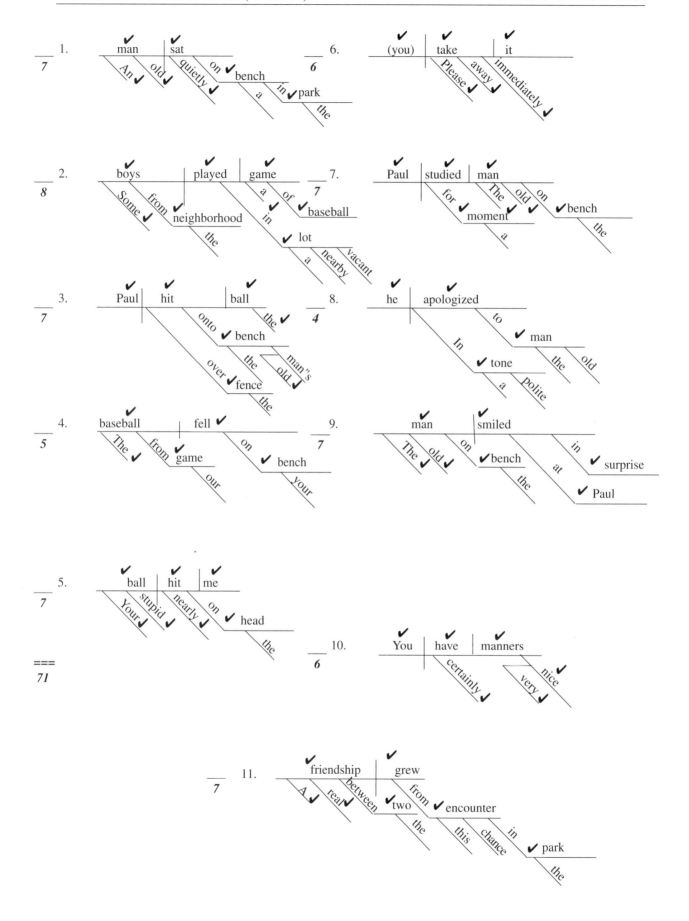

PATTERN #3

To learn about Pattern 3, you must learn a new concept called the <u>INDIRECT OBJECT</u>.

PATTERN 3:   N-V-N-N

It consists of four main parts IN THIS ORDER: the subject (N), an action verb (V), an indirect object (N), and a direct object (N). All four parts may have modifiers, and there may be prepositional phrases in the sentence, but THERE WILL BE NO OTHER NOUNS OR VERBS.

IMPORTANT: <u>A SENTENCE CANNOT HAVE AN INDIRECT OBJECT UNLESS IT</u> HAS A DIRECT <u>OBJECT.</u>

      EXAMPLE: *pn   av   pro art   n   pp   n*
                Mom gave   me   a dollar (for candy).

If you "strip down" this sentence (take out all the modifiers and prepositional phrases), what would be left?

           Mom   gave   me   dollar

When you "strip down" a sentence as you did above, count the number of nouns (or pronouns) left over. If you have one noun left over, you have a Pattern 1 (N-V) sentence. If you have two nouns left over, you have a Pattern 2 (N-V-N) sentence. If you have three nouns left over, you have Pattern 3 (N-V-N-N); the first noun will be the subject, the second will be indirect object, and the third will be the direct object.

   The diagram of the complete sentence would look like this:

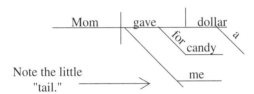

Note the little
"tail."

VERY IMPORTANT: The INDIRECT OBJECT will always be located <u>between</u> the VERB and the DIRECT OBJECT in the sentence. The words will ALWAYS come in this order:

     SUBJECT - VERB - INDIRECT OBJECT - DIRECT OBJECT.

     These sentences will only contain ACTION VERBS.

The easiest way to determine which sentence pattern you have is to "strip the sentence down." That means to take out all the modifiers. Then look to see how many NOUNS are left over. If there are three nouns (or pronouns), then the MIDDLE NOUN IS THE INDIRECT OBJECT.

PATTERN 3: EXERCISE #1

NAME:_____DATE:_____

DIRECTIONS: All the sentences below are Pattern 3. Parse them and put prepositional phrases in parentheses.
Then, in the space provided or on a separate sheet of paper, diagram the entire sentence

       pn   *av*   *pn*   *adj* *adj*   *pn*
1. African-Americans gave <u>America</u> many great Congressmen.

     ———— *pn* ———— *av*   *pn* *adj adj* *n* *pp* *pn*   *pp pn*
2. <u>Blanche Kelso Bruce</u> gave Missouri its first school(for Blacks)(in 1864).

   pp *pn* *art*   *adj*   *n*   *av* —*pn*— *adv* *adj* *adj* *adj*   *pn*
3. (In 1874) the Mississippi legislature made Mr. Bruce that state's first black Senator.

   pp *pn* ———— *pn* ————   *av* — *pn*—— *adj adj* *adj*   *pn*
4. (In 1888) Henry Plummer Cheatham gave North Carolina its first black <u>Congressman</u>.

    pp *adj* *n* *pp* *pn*   *pn*   *av* — *pn*———— *art*   *n*   *pp*
5. (After his defeat)(in 1892), Cheatham gave North Carolina an orphanage (for
   adv *adj*   *n*
   two hundred students).

    ———— *pn* ———— *pp* ———— *pn*——————— *av* ———— *pn*——————— *adj*
6. Wood High School (in Charleston, South Carolina), gave <u>Robert Carlos DeLarge</u> his
   adj   *n*
   early education.

   pp *pn* *art* —*adj*————   *n*   *av* *pro* *adj*   *n*   *pp* *n*
7. (In 1870) the South Carolina legislature appointed <u>him</u> land <u>commissioner</u> (in charge)

   pp *adv* *adj*   *adj*   *n*
   (of that state's public lands).

                                                      (over)

    art adj adj   n   av pro art   n   pp   n   pp art

8. The same state legislature gave him the nomination (for representative)(of the

   ——————— *pn* ———————

Second Congressional District).

   pp pn   pn   av art ——pn——adj adj adj   pn   pp art adj

9. (In 1966) Massachusetts gave the United States its first <u>black</u> Senator (from a popular

   n

election).

   ——————————— *pn* ——————————   *av art n   pp   pn   adj   n*

10. Senator Edward William Brooke III gave the people (of Massachusetts) twelve years

   pp   adj   n   pp art pn

(of dedicated <u>service</u>)(in the Senate).

DIRECTIONS: *Write what job the underlined words are doing. Choose your answers from among the following:*

       SUBJECT   DIRECT OBJECT   INDIRECT OBJECT

       OBJECT OF THE PREPOSITION   MODIFIER   VERB

SENTENCE #	WORD	JOB
1	America	*indirect object*
2	Blanche Kelso Bruce	*subject*
4	Congressman	*direct object*
6	Robert Carlos DeLarge	*indirect object*
7	him	*indirect object*
7	commissioner	*direct object*
9	black	*modifier*
10	service	*object of the preposition*

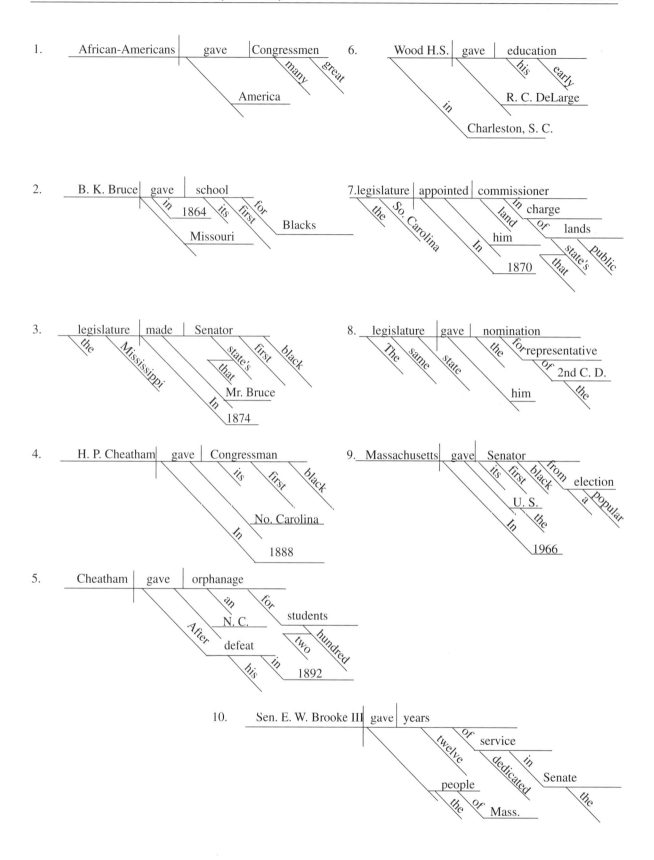

PATTERN 3: EXERCISE #2

NAME:_____DATE:_____

DIRECTIONS: *The sentences below are either Pattern 2 (N-V-N) or Pattern 3 (N-V-N-N). Parse the sentences and then, in the space provided or on a separate sheet of paper, diagram the entire sentence.*

      adj   pn   av   pn pp adj n pp adj n
1. Black Americans represent <u>America</u> (in all aspects)(of our culture).

     —— *pn* ——   *av art   adj   —— pn — pro pp adj adj*
2. Mary McLeod Bethune gave the southeastern <u>United States</u> one (of its finest
        adj   n
   teacher-training institutions).

   art —— *pn* ——   *av — pn* ——   —— *pn* —— *pp adj*
3. The Brooklyn Dodgers named Roy Campanella "Most Valuable Player" (in three
     adj   n
  different years).

    —— *pn* —— *av adv adj   adj   n   pp   adj   n*
4. Wilt Chamberlain broke almost every scoring record (in professional basketball).

   pp pn —— *pn* —— *av art adj   n   pp art   n   pp art adj n*
5. (In 1839) <u>Joseph Cinque</u> led a successful revolt (against the captain)(of a slave ship).

    —— *pn* —— *av adj   n   adj   n   pp   art adj*
6. Harriet Tubman <u>gave</u> many slaves their freedom (through the famous
   ——   *pn* ——
  <u>Underground Railroad</u>).

    pp adj adj   n   pp   n   pp pn —— *pn* ——   *av   n*
7. (After his own escape)(to freedom)(in 1835), Frederick Douglas denounced <u>slavery</u>

   pp adj adj   n
  (in his fiery speeches).

                                            (over)

   —— *pn* ——   *av*   *art* ————————————— *pn* —————————

8. W. E. B. Dubois founded the National Association for the Advancement of Colored

People.

   ——*pn* ——   *av*   *art*   *n*   *adj*   *adj*   *n*   *pp* ——— *pn* —

9. James Baldwin gave the world such <u>magnificent</u> essays (as "The Fire Next

Time.")

   ———— *pn* ———   *av*   *art* ——————————— *pn* ——————— *pp adj*

10. Lorraine Hansberry won the New York Drama Critics Circle Award(for her
   ——— *pn* ———
A Raisin in the Sun).

DIRECTIONS: *Write what job the underlined words are doing. Choose your answers from among the following:*

    SUBJECT   *DIRECT OBJECT*   *INDIRECT OBJECT*

             OBJECT OF THE PREPOSITION   *MODIFIER*   *VERB*

SENTENCE #	WORD	JOB
1	America	*direct object*
2	United States	*indirect object*
3	"Most Valuable Player"	*direct object*
4	every	*modifier*
5	Joseph Cinque	*subject*
6	gave	*verb*
6	Underground Railroad	*object of the preposition*
7	slavery	*direct object*
9	magnificent	*modifier*

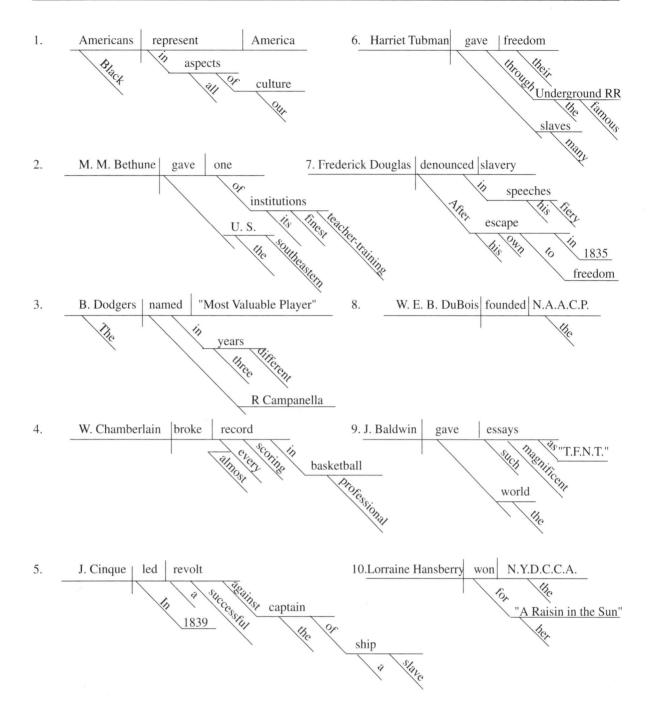

PATTERN 3: EXERCISE #3

NAME:_____DATE:_____

DIRECTIONS: *The sentences below are either Pattern 1(N-V), Pattern 2 (N-V-N), or Pattern 3 (N-V-N-N). Parse the sentences and then, in the space provided or on a separate sheet of paper, diagram the entire sentence.*

```
      ──── pn ────      av    n   pp adj  adj      n    pp art adj
```
1. Langston Hughes achieved <u>fame</u> (from his magnificent poems)(about the black
```
        n     pp    pn
```
    experience)(in America).

```
      ────── pn ───    av adj   n     pp art  n    pp ──── pn ─────   pp
```
2. Langston Hughes <u>made</u> his entrance (into the world) (in Joplin, Missouri), (on
```
      ─────  pn ────
```
    February 1, 1902).

```
    adj   n    av  art   n   pp    pn   pp art n pp   n    pp       n
```
3. His father left the family (for Mexico)(in a fit)(of <u>rage</u>)(over discrimination).

```
    adj    n     av adj n  art adj   n      pp adj   n
```
4. His mother gave her <u>son</u> the best home (within her power).

```
    adj      n    pp  adj    n     av  pro adj   n
```
5. His classmates (in grammar school) elected him class <u>poet</u>.

```
    pp adj adj   n   pn    av    adj    n   pp  n  pp pro
```
6. (On that same day) <u>Langston</u> wrote sixteen verses(in praise)(of them).

```
    pp adv adj    n       pn      av  pp  pn  pp adj adj   n   pp adj
```
7. (At his father's request) Langston moved (to Mexico)(in his junior year)(in high
```
      n
```
    school).

(over)

    pro   av   adj adj   n   pp   adj adj   n

8. He published his first <u>poem</u> (during his senior year).

    pn   av   pro   pp   —— pn——   pp   pn

9. Langston put himself (through Lincoln College)(in Pennsylvania).

    pp   adj adj   n   ——————pn—— av   pn   art   adj   n   pp

10. (Throughout his long career) Langston Hughes gave <u>America</u> the priceless <u>legacy</u> (of

    adj   n

    his <u>poetry</u>).

DIRECTIONS: *Write what job the underlined words are doing. Choose your answers from among the following:*

SUBJECT	DIRECT OBJECT	INDIRECT OBJECT	OBJECT OF THE PREPOSITION
	VERB	MODIFIER	

SENTENCE #	WORD	JOB
1	fame	*direct object*
2	made	*verb*
3	rage	*object of the preposition*
4	son	*indirect object*
5	poet	*direct object*
6	Langston	*subject*
8	poem	*direct object*
10	America	*indirect object*
10	legacy	*direct object*
10	poetry	*object of the preposition*

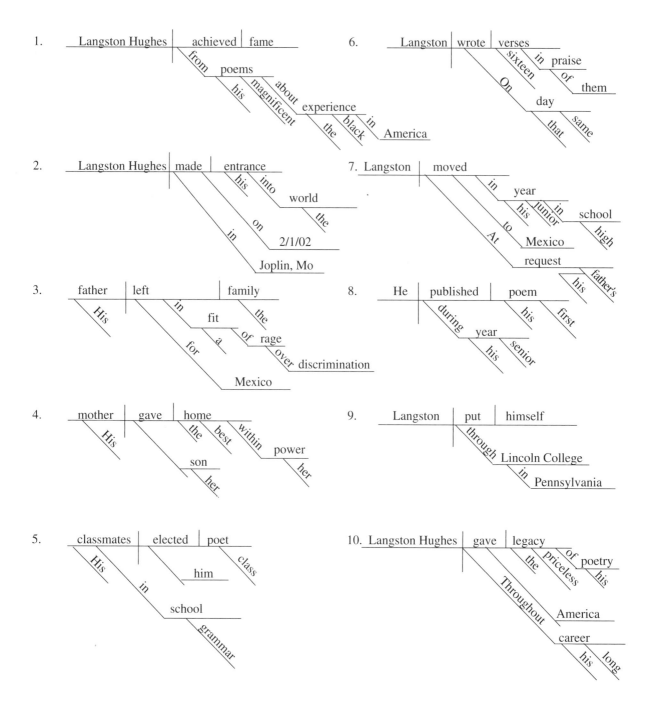

SKILLS SUPPORT

Parse and diagram the first line of this poem. Then paraphrase the poem.

I, TOO, SING AMERICA

by Langston Hughes

pro adv av   pn
I,   too, sing America.

I am the darker brother.

They send me to eat in the kitchen

When company comes,

But I laugh,

And eat well,

And grow strong.

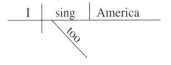

Tomorrow,

I'll be at the table

When company comes.

Nobody'll dare

Say to me,

"Eat in the kitchen,"

Then.

Besides,

They'll see how beautiful I am

And be ashamed —

I,   too, sing America.

PATTERN #3: TEST

NAME: _____ DATE:_____

(RAW SCORE: _____ /255 GRADE: _____)

DIRECTIONS: *Parse the sentences below and put prepositional phrases in parentheses. Then, on a separate sheet of paper, diagram the entire sentence.*

             pn   av art —— pn—— adj n pp adj n   pp adj

1. African-Americans give the <u>United States</u> their gifts (in all areas) (of American

             n

$\overline{14}$ culture).

           adj   n   av adj n   pp adj   n

2. Black <u>writers</u> touch our hearts (with their <u>stories)</u>.

$\overline{9}$

           adj   n   av pp adj   n pp n pp n

3. Black soldiers come (to <u>America's</u> aid)(in time)(of war).

$\overline{13}$

           adj   n   pp adj n   av   pp art n   pp   adj

4. Show business (in this country) benefits (from the talents)(of African-American

             n

$\overline{15}$ entertainers).

           adj   n   av pro n   pp adj   n

5. Black poets write <u>us</u> <u>poems</u> (of great beauty).

$\overline{9}$

        art   n   pp adj adj   n   av art adj   n   pp   pn

6. The <u>talents</u> (of great black athletes) enrich the sports scene(in America).

$\overline{14}$

           adj   n   av art n pp adj adj   n

7. <u>American</u> history <u>contains </u>the names(of many black patriots).

$\overline{10}$

(over)

```
        art   n   pp    adj     pn   av  pro  adj     adj     n
```
—— 8. The ranks (of America's Blacks) give <u>us</u> countless dedicated <u>educators</u>.
11

```
         n    pp   n      av    adv  pp adj  n   pp   adj    n
```
—— 9. Citizens (of color) contribute <u>greatly</u> (to all walks)(of American life).
14

```
        pn       av    pp   art     n      pp adj adj  adj    n
```
—— 10. America <u>prospers</u> (from the contributions)(of all her cultural <u>groups)</u>.
12

DIRECTIONS: Write what job the underlined words are doing. Choose your answers from among the following:
===
121
      SUBJECT   DIRECT OBJECT   INDIRECT OBJECT

      OBJECT OF THE PREPOSITION   VERB   MODIFIER

SENTENCE #	WORD	JOB
1	United States	*indirect object*
2	writers	*subject*
2	stories	*object of the preposition*
3	America's	*modifier*
5	us	*indirect object*
5	poems	*direct object*
6	talents	*subject*
7	American	*modifier*
7	contains	*verb*
8	us	*indirect object*
8	educators	*direct object*
9	greatly	*modifier*
10	prospers	*verb*
10	groups	*object of the preposition*

5

points

each

Raw		Score		Grade		%
255	-	249	=	A++	=	98+
248	-	242	=	A+	=	95
241	-	229	=	A	=	90
228	-	216	=	B+	=	85
215	-	204	=	B	=	80
203	-	191	=	C+	=	75
190	-	178	=	C	=	70
177	-	165	=	D+	=	65
164	-	153	=	D	=	60

===
70

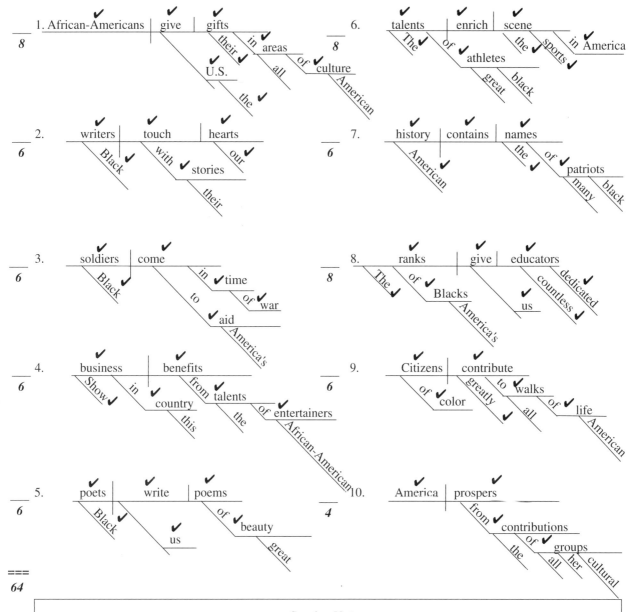

LINKING VERBS AND PATTERNS 4 & 5

DEFINITION: A linking verb is a word that links its subject with a noun (or pronoun) or an adjective in the predicate. (The predicate is everything except the subject and its modifiers)

THE SUBJECT OF AN ACTION VERB IS <u>DOING</u> SOMETHING.

THE SUBJECT OF A LINKING VERB IS <u>BEING</u> SOMETHING.

There are only a small group of verbs that can be linking verbs. For the most part, they are -

BE (is, are, am, was, were, being, been)	SMELL	STAY
SEEM	TASTE	APPEAR
BECOME	LOOK	REMAIN
	FEEL	GROW

Some of these verbs are always linking verbs (such as *seem* and *become*), but most of them can be action verbs too. In order to be sure it's a linking verb, you have to determine if it's in a LINKING VERB SENTENCE PATTERN.

PATTERN 4 - N-LV-N: This is the first linking verb sentence pattern. We call it "noun - linking verb - noun." The first noun (or pronoun) is the SUBJECT, next comes the LINKING VERB, and then comes the second noun which is called the PREDICATE NOMINATIVE. The most important thing to remember is that the **subject and the predicate nominative are always the same person or thing.**

EXAMPLE:

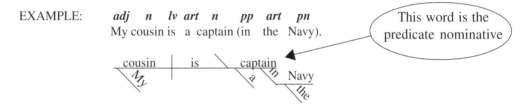

Notice how *cousin* and *captain* are the same person in this sentence? If the sentence said, "My cousin married a captain in the Navy," that wouldn't be the case, would it? Notice how the base line differs from a Pattern 2 sentence: the line which separates the action verb from its direct object is **vertical**, whereas the line which separates a linking verb from its predicate nominative is **diagonal** and slants upward to the left. The **predicate nominative** is the noun or pronoun that completes the linking verb pattern.

PATTERN 5 - N-LV-ADJ: This is the second linking verb pattern. We call it "noun - linking verb - adjective." The noun is the SUBJECT, then comes the LINKING VERB, and then comes an adjective called the PREDICATE ADJECTIVE. **The predicate adjective always describes the subject.**

EXAMPLE:

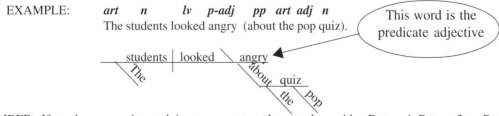

REMEMBER: If you have an action verb in your sentence, then you have either Pattern 1, Pattern 2, or Pattern 3. If, however, you have a linking verb, then you have either Pattern 4 or Pattern 5. In a Pattern 4 sentence the linking verb LINKS the subject with another noun or pronoun in the predicate. In a Pattern 5 sentence the linking verb LINKS the subject to an adjective in the predicate. On the back of this page is the completed Process chart. Use it as you do these exercises. If you understand the Process chart, it will be your "best friend" in mastering this material.

THE PROCESS

Step 1. Find & mark "n" all the nouns in the sentence.

Step 2. Find & mark all the articles and adjectives (Ask, "Which [say the noun]?")

Step 3. Find & mark all the pronouns.

Step 4. Find & mark all the prepositions and put parentheses around the prepositional phrases.

Step 5. Find all words that look like verbs and mark them "v."

Step 6. Ask, "Who or what (say the verb)?"

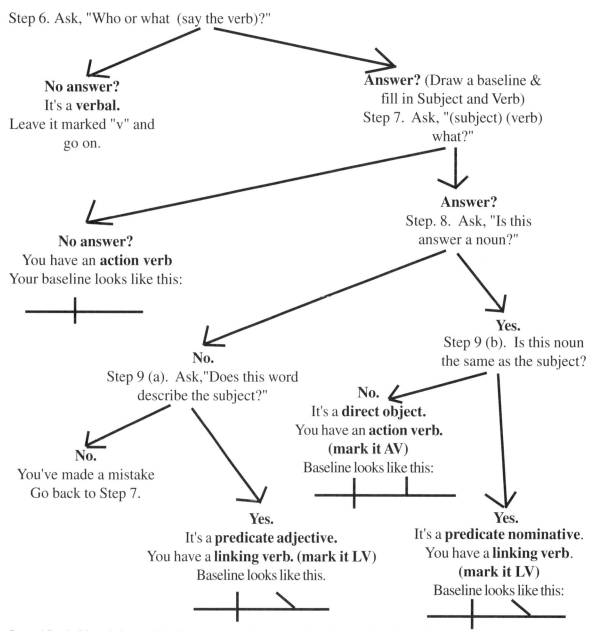

No answer?
It's a **verbal.**
Leave it marked "v" and
go on.

Answer? (Draw a baseline &
fill in Subject and Verb)
Step 7. Ask, "(subject) (verb)
what?"

No answer?
You have an **action verb**
Your baseline looks like this:

Answer?
Step. 8. Ask, "Is this
answer a noun?"

No.
Step 9 (a). Ask,"Does this word
describe the subject?"

Yes.
Step 9 (b). Is this noun
the same as the subject?

No.
You've made a mistake
Go back to Step 7.

No.
It's a **direct object.**
You have an **action verb.**
(mark it AV)
Baseline looks like this:

Yes.
It's a **predicate adjective.**
You have a **linking verb. (mark it LV)**
Baseline looks like this.

Yes.
It's a **predicate nominative**.
You have a **linking verb**.
(mark it LV)
Baseline looks like this:

Step 10. Add articles, adjectives, prep. phrases, adverbs, and conjunctions to the diagram.

Step 11. Pat yourself on the back! You've successfully "parsed" and diagramed the sentence!

PATTERNS 4 & 5: EXERCISE #1

NAME:_____DATE:_____

DIRECTIONS: *All the sentences below are either the N-LV-N or N-LV-ADJ pattern. Parse and diagram the sentences.*

      pn   *lv*   *adj*   *n*   *pp*   *adj*   *n*
1. Jewish-Americans are important <u>contributors</u> (to American culture).

      —— *pn* — *lv* *pro* *pp* *adj*   *adv* *adj*   *n*
2. George Burns was one (of America's most beloved <u>comedians)</u>.

    art   *adv*   *adj* —— *pn* —— *lv* *art* *adj*   *adj*   *n*
3. The <u>extremely</u> talented Barbra Streisand is a great popular singer.

    —— *pn* —— *lv*   *adj*   *adj* —— *pn* ——   *pp* *art* *adj*
4. Henry Kissinger <u>was</u> America's powerful Secretary of State (during the Nixon
          n
    administration).

    adj   *adj*   *adj*   *n*   *lv* — *pn* ——
5. One influential Jewish-American publisher was <u>Joseph Pulitzer</u>.

   ——*adj* ——   *adj*   *n*   *lv* *adv*   *p-adj*
6. Dr. Jonas Salk's polio <u>vaccine</u> was terribly important.

   ——*adj* ——   *n*   *lv* *adv* *p-adj*   *pp* *adj* *pro*
7. Albert Einstein's mind was more <u>brilliant</u> (than any other).

(over)

```
          adj           pn      lv    adv    p-adj
```
8. Baseball Hall of Fame's Sandy Koufax was greatly respected.


```
    adj              n    lv    adv      p-adj
```
9. George Gershwin's music was incredibly beautiful.


```
  art   n   pp pn   pp   pn   lv   adv   p-adj
```
10. The history (of Jews)(in America) is indeed great.

DIRECTIONS: Write what job the underlined words are doing. Choose your answers from among the following:

SUBJECT   PREDICATE NOMINATIVE   PREDICATE ADJECTIVE

OBJECT OF THE PREPOSITION   MODIFIER   VERB

SENTENCE #	WORD	JOB
1	contributors	*predicate nominative*
2	comedians	*object of the preposition*
3	extremely	*modifier*
4	was	*verb*
5	Joseph Pulitzer	*predicate nominative*
6	vaccine	*subject*
7	brilliant	*predicate adjective*
10	Jews	*object of the preposition*

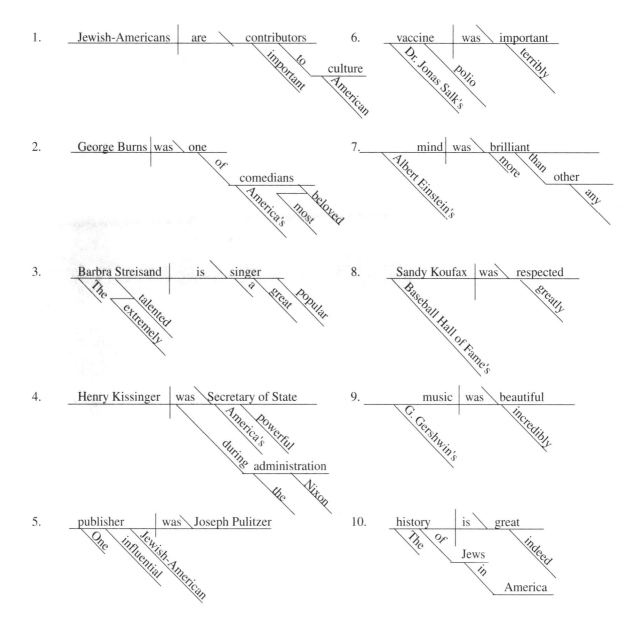

PATTERN 4 & 5: EXERCISE #2

NAME: _____ DATE:_____

DIRECTIONS: *All of the sentences below are either N-LV-N or N-LV-ADJ. Parse and diagram the entire sentence.*

    art adj n lv p-adj pp art n pp art adj adj   n
1. The young girl was terrified (by the <u>guns</u>)(of the Nazi prison guards).

    art   n   pp adj n   lv   n   pp art   adj   adj   n
2. The <u>members</u> (of her family) were <u>prisoners</u> (of the anti-Jewish German government)
    pp art adj pn
    (in the early 1940's).

    pro lv art adj   n pp   pn   pp pn
3. She was a helpless inmate (of Camp Mittelsteine)(in Germany).

    art   adj   adj   n   pp adj n lv   n*
4. The prisoner identification number (on her arm) was 55082.

    pn   lv p-adj   pp   n
5. Riva <u>grew </u>weaker (from hunger).

    adj adj   n lv   adv   p-adj pp adj   n
6. This young girl felt desperately lonely (for her <u>parents</u>).

    pro lv   n   pp art adj   n   pp art adj   n
7. They were prisoners (of a death camp)(in a <u>different</u> place).

    art   n   pp adj   n   lv   adv   adv   p-adj
8. The guards (at Riva's camp) were almost unbelievably <u>cruel</u>.

* Students were told that numbers are pronouns; however, this is such a specific number that I would call it a noun. In the "grand scheme of things," however, it doesn't much matter because they function in the same way!

                                                            (over)

            Photocopying this product is strictly prohibited by copyright law.

    art   adj   n   pp   n   lv   p-adj
9. The mere idea (of escape) looked hopeless.

    pn   lv adv   p-adj   pp art adj   n   pp adj   n
10. Riva felt less <u>miserable</u> (in the secret world)(of her poetry).

DIRECTIONS: *Write what job the following words are doing. Choose your answers from among the following:*

    SUBJECT   PREDICATE NOMINATIVE   OBJECT OF THE PREPOSITION

        MODIFIER   PREDICATE ADJECTIVE   VERB

SENTENCE #	WORD	JOB
1	guns	*object of the preposition*
2	members	*subject*
2	prisoners	*predicate nominative*
5	grew	*verb*
6	parents	*object of the preposition*
7	different	*modifier*
8	cruel	*predicate adjective*
10	miserable	*predicate adjective*

1.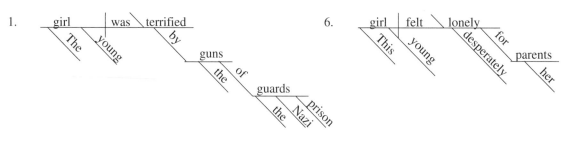

2.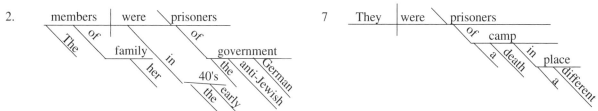

3.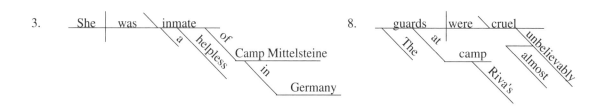

4.

5.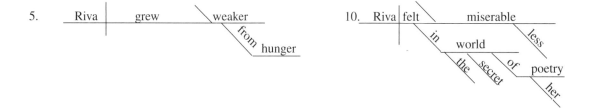

6. girl | felt \ lonely — desperately — for — parents / This / young / her

7. They | were \ prisoners — of — camp — a / death / in — place / different / a

8. guards | were \ cruel — at — camp — unbelievably / almost / The / Riva's

9. idea | looked \ hopeless — The / mere / of — escape

10. Riva | felt \ miserable — less — in — world — of — poetry / the / secret / her

PATTERNS 4 & 5: EXERCISE #3

NAME:_____DATE:_____

DIRECTIONS: *The sentences below represent all five sentence patterns: N-V, N-V-N, N-V-N-N, N-LV-N, and N-LV-ADJ. Parse and diagram the entire sentence.*

    art adj n pp pn pp pn   av   pp   pn   pp — pn ——— pp
1. The first group (of Jews)(in America) <u>came</u> (from Brazil)(to New Amsterdam)(in
   pn
   1654).

    art adj   adj   n   pp art adj   n   lv art n pp   pn
2. The second Jewish <u>settlement</u>(in the American colonies) was the <u>village</u> (of Newport)
  pp — pn —— pp pn
  (in Rhode Island)(in 1658).

    pn lv art adj n   —— pp — adj adj   n
3. Jews were "an alien nation" (according to some <u>ignorant</u> settlers).

    art adj pn pp   pn   av   pp art pn   pp art — pn —
4. The <u>first</u> Jews(in Pennsylvania) traded (with the Indians)(along the Delaware
   ____   *pp pn*
   River)(in 1655).

    art adj pn pp   pn   av pro art adv adj   n   pp
5. The devout Jews (of Philadelphia) built<u> themselves</u> a very beautiful <u>synagogue</u>(in
   pn
   1770).

    pp art n pp art ____ pn _____   adv   adj pn av pp art
6. (At the time)(of the American Revolution), approximately 2,500 Jews lived (in the
   adj   n
   American colonies).

(over)

103

     adj adj   adj   n   lv   adv   p-adj   pp   art n   pp

7. This tiny Jewish <u>minority</u> became historically important (during the days)(of

     adj   n   pp   n   pp —— pn ——

    our fight)(for freedom)(from Great Britain).

     pn   av   art   adj   n pp art   adj   n pp art   n

8. Jews played an <u>important</u> part (in the revolutionary struggle)(from the start).

     pn   pp   pn   adv av   pp art   n   pp   n

9. Jews (from Europe) also joined (into the fight)(for freedom).

     lv p-adj pp adj   adj   adj   n

10. Be <u>proud</u> (of these early Jewish patriots)!

DIRECTIONS: Write what job the underlined words are doing. Choose your answers from among the following:

   SUBJECT   DIRECT OBJECT   INDIRECT OBJECT   PREDICATE NOMINATIVE

   OBJECT OF THE PREPOSITION   MODIFIER   PREDICATE ADJECTIVE   VERB

SENTENCE #	WORD	JOB
1	came	*verb*
2	settlement	*subject*
2	village	*predicate nominative*
3	ignorant	*modifier*
4	first	*modifier*
5	themselves	*indirect object*
5	synagogue	*direct object*
7	minority	*subject*
8	important	*modifier*
10	proud	*predicate adjective*

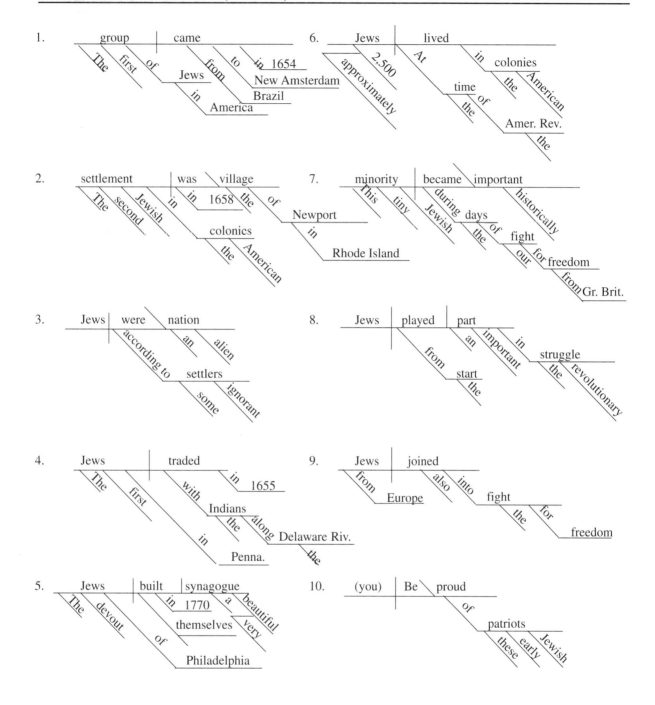

SKILLS SUPPORT

DIRECTIONS: *Below is a poem written by a young girl in a German concentration camp during World War II. Parse and diagram lines 1 and 13.   Then paraphrase the entire poem.*

WHY?

Written by Riva Minska, Number 55082
Camp Mittelsteine, Germany
January 14, 1945

Translated from the Yiddish
by Ruth Minsky Sender, Free Person
New York City, U.S.A.
1980

<pre>
adv adv pro av   pp art   n
All alone, I stare (at the window)
</pre>

Feeling my soul in me cry,

Hearing the painful screams of my heart

Calling silently: Why?

Why are your dreams scattered, destroyed?

Why are you put in this cage?

Why is the world silently watching?

Why can't they hear your rage?

Why is the barbed wire holding me prisoner,

Blocking to freedom my way?

Why do I still keep waiting and dreaming

Hoping...maybe...someday...

<pre>
pro av   pp pro art   adj   n
I   see (above me) the snow-covered mountains,
</pre>

Majestic, proud, and high.

If like a free bird I could reach their peaks

Maybe (from there) the world will hear my cry...

Why?

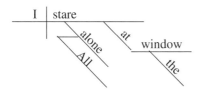

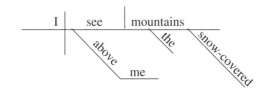

PATTERNS 4 & 5: TEST

NAME: _____ DATE: _____

(RAW SCORE: _____ */248*____ GRADE: _____)

DIRECTIONS: *The sentences below represent all five sentence patterns. Parse and diagram the entire sentence.*

           pro av art   n   pp art pn   pp art pn

___1.   We find the <u>history</u> (of the Jews)(in the Bible).
12

                      n or

    art pro pp art adj   n   lv   pn   pp art n pp   pn

___2.   The first (of the Jewish <u>patriarchs</u>) was Abraham (from the land)(of Canaan).
16

        _____ *pp*____ *art   n pp art pn   pn   av   pn   adj n pp adj   n*

___3   (According to the story)(in the Bible), God <u>gave</u> Abraham this <u>land</u> (for all time).
17

            adj   n   lv art n pp art adj   n

___4.   Abraham's great-grandson became a <u>slave</u>(to the Egyptian pharaoh).
10

            adv adj   n   lv   p-adj   pp   pn   pp   n

___5.   Later this pharaoh became <u>dependent</u> (upon Joseph) (for advice).
11

            pp   n   adj   adj   n   av adj art   pn

___6.   (In time) another Egyptian pharaoh enslaved all the <u>Israelites</u>.
10

(over)

       adj   n   av   adj   adj   adj   n   pp   pro
___ 7. This pharaoh murdered all <u>Jewish</u> male babies(except one).
10

       adj adj   adj   n   lv   pn
___ 8. That one lucky <u>baby</u> was <u>Moses</u>.
6

       pn   av   art _____   pn ____   adj   n   adv adv
___ 9. Moses gave the <u>Children of Israel</u> their freedom once again.
8

       pn   adv   av   art   n   adj   _____pn _____
10. Moses also gave the world God's <u>Ten Commandments</u>.
7

=== **DIRECTIONS:** *Write what job the underlined words are doing. Choose your answers from among the following:*
107

  SUBJECT   PREDICATE NOMINATIVE   OBJECT OF THE PREPOSITION   VERB

     DIRECT OBJECT   INDIRECT OBJECT   MODIFIER   PREDICATE ADJECTIVE

SENTENCE #	WORD	JOB
1	history	*direct object*
2	patriarchs	*object of the preposition*
3	gave	*verb*
3	land	*direct object*
4	slave	*predicate nominative*
5	dependent	*predicate adjective*
6	Israelites	*direct object*
7	Jewish	*modifier*
8	baby	*subject*
8	Moses	*predicate nominative*
9	Children of Israel	*indirect object*
10	Ten Commandment	*direct object*

(5

points

each)

Raw		Score	Grade	%
248	-	243 =	A++	=98+
242	-	235 =	A+	= 95
234	-	223 =	A	= 90 -
222	-	210 =	B+	= 85
209	-	198 =	B	= 80
197	-	186 =	C+	= 75
185	-	173 =	C	= 70
172	-	161 =	D+	= 65
160	-	148 =	D	= 60

===
60

109

* Whether or not the second line of the base line is VERTICAL or DIAGONAL will count one point from now on.

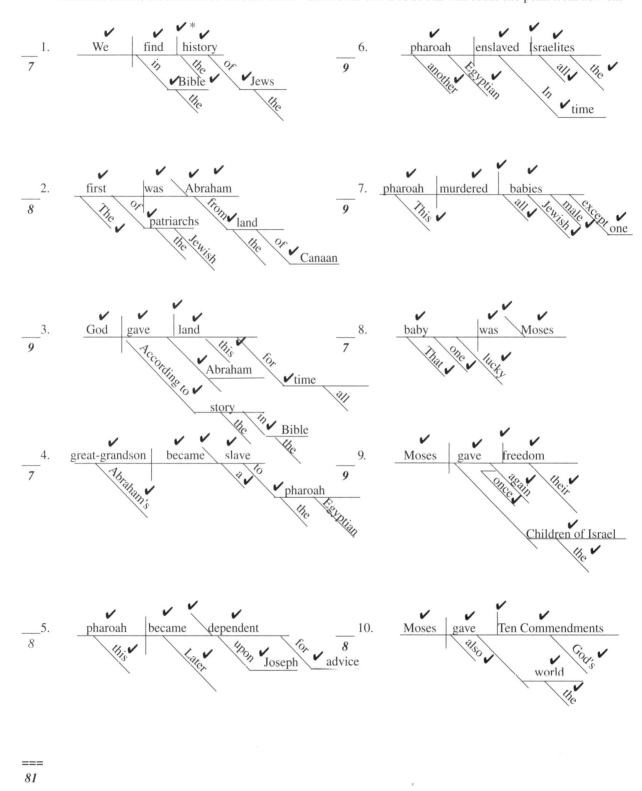

===
81

HELPING VERBS

DEFINITION: A word (or words) which comes before an action or linking verb and helps form different tenses. The helping verb and the main verb make up the VERB PHRASE. (Helping verbs are sometimes called "auxiliary verbs.")

EXAMPLES:

(main verb)	CRAWL	
(verb phrase)	will crawl	(*will* is the helping verb)

(main verb)	LISTEN	
(verb phrase)	has been listening	(*has* and *been* are helping verbs)

(main verb)	FIND	
(verb phrase)	would have been found	(*would, have,* and *been* are helping verbs)

THE BEST WAY TO LEARN HELPING VERBS IS TO MEMORIZE THEM. THEY ARE LISTED BE-LOW:

is	has	will	may
am	have	would	might
are	had	shall	must
was	do	should	
were	does	can	
be	did	could	
being			
been			

You may have noticed that some of the helping verbs listed above were taught to you as ACTION VERBS (such as DO and HAVE). If one of these verbs is the LAST word in the verb phrase, then it is an action verb. If, however, it is NOT the last word in the verb phrase, it is a helping verb.

<pre>
               pro hv av adj   n
</pre>
EXAMPLE: I will do my homework.   (*will do* is the verb phrase and *do* is an action verb.
<pre>
               pro hv adv av   adj   n
</pre>
I do not want any lunch.   (*do want* is the verb phrase and *do* is a helping verb)

You may also have noticed helping verbs in the list above which were taught to you as LINKING VERBS (is, am, are, etc.). If one of these words is the LAST word in the verb phrase, it is a linking verb; otherwise, they are helping verbs.

<pre>
              pn   hv lv art   n
</pre>
EXAMPLE: John will be a senior.   (*will be* is the verb phrase and *be* is a linking verb)
<pre>
              pn   hv hv av   pp   n
</pre>
John will be going (to college).   (*will be going* is the verb phrase & *be* is a helping verb)

NOTE: A favorite spot for adverbs to "live" is between a helping verb and the main verb (I should *really* do my homework.) That's why you need to know those helping verbs by heart; otherwise, you might mistake an adverb for a helping verb.

HOW TO DIAGRAM HELPING VERBS: Helping verbs are just part of the verb, so they are diagramed like this:

<pre>
            pn   hv lv adj adj   n pp adj   n
</pre>
Josephine will be my study partner (in algebra class).

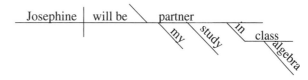

HOW TO DIAGRAM QUESTIONS: Most of the questions in our language are formed by moving the words in a statement around and putting them in a different order. Look at the following examples:

EXAMPLES: (statement)   I should do my homework.
             (question)   Should I do my homework?

Notice that, in order to form a question, the helping verb is simply moved in front of the subject.

             (statement)   He walked to school.
             (question)   Did he walk to school?

In this case, because the original statement did not have a helping verb, a helping verb is added to the sentence - again in front of the subject.

To diagram a question, the helping verb still goes in the verb slot, but it is capitalized to show that it came first in the sentence. Look at the diagram below:

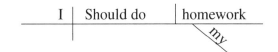

Photocopying this product is strictly prohibited by copyright law.

HELPING VERBS: EXERCISE #1

NAME: _____ DATE:_____

DIRECTIONS: *Parse and diagram the sentences below.*

1.
       ——— *pn* ——— *hv av pp pn pp pn*
       Santha Rama Rau was born (in India)(in 1923).

2.
       pro hv hv   av   n   pp art adj   n
       She has been writing novels (for a long time).

3.
       ———————— *pn* ——— *hv adv lv   p-adj pp adj adj   n*
       Santha Rama Rau has long been famous (for her superb essays).

4.
       pro hv adv hv   lv   p-adj pp adj   n   adv
       She could easily have been popular (for her novels) also.

5.
       pp ———————— *pn* ——— *pro hv   av   art   adj   n   pp*
       (In "By Any Other Name") she has portrayed the cultural conflict (in

       pn ——— *pp*— *art adj   n*
       India)(because of the English colonization).

6.
       hv pro av   pro   pp   adj   n
       Do you know anything (about cultural conflicts)?

7.
       adj   n   hv   av pro pp art   n   pp adj   n
       This essay might help you (to an understanding)(of such conflicts).

8.
       adj   adj   n   hv   av pp art n   pp   adj   n
       Two Indian sisters were sent (to a school)(for English children).

(over)

      adj   *adj*   *n* *hv* *hv* *av* *pp* *adj*   *n*   *pp* *n*

9.   This Anglo-Indian school had been taught (by British teachers)(for years).

      adj   *adj*   *n* *hv* *hv* *av* *adj* *adj*   *n*   *pp* *adj* *adj*

10.   This British-run school must have caused many cultural problems (for its Indian

      n

students).

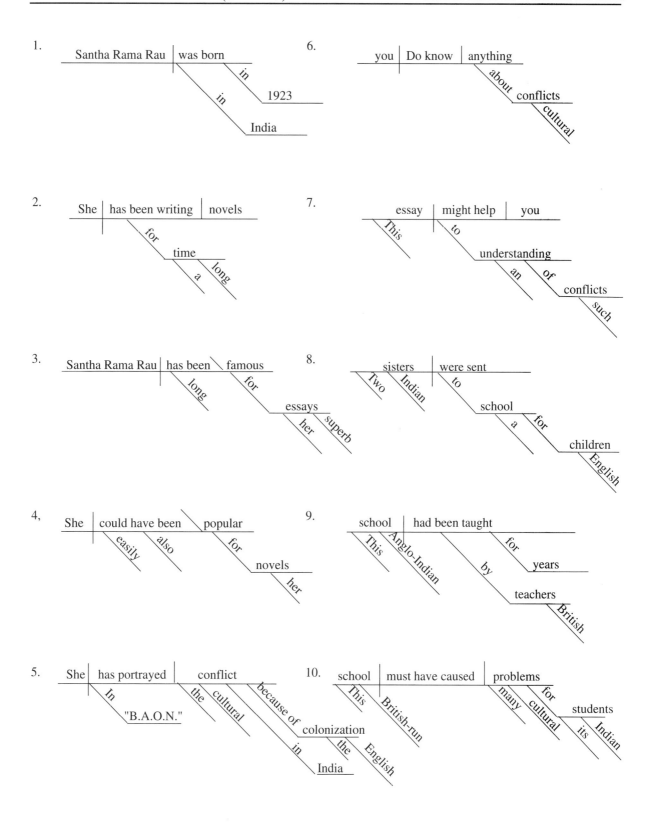

HELPING VERBS: EXERCISE #2

NAME:_____DATE:_____

DIRECTIONS: *Parse and diagram the sentences below*

    art adj   n   hv   hv   av   adj   adj   adj   n   pp adj   n
1. The two sisters had been given two beautiful Indian names (by their parents).

    pp art adj n pp n   art   n   hv   av   adj   n   pp   adj
2. (On the first day)(of school), the teacher had indicated her helplessness (with Indian

    n

    names).

    adj   adj   n   hv   lv   pn
3. Santha's new name would become Cynthia.

    pn   hv hv av pp pn
4. Premila would be known (as Pamela).

    art n   hv adv   av   art   n   pp adj adj   n
5. The girls could not understand the reason (for these new names.)

    pro hv   adv   av   art   n   pp adv adj   n   pp adj adj
6. They would soon understand the reasons(for their mother's anxiety)(about this new
    adj   n
    English school).

    adj adj   adj   n   hv hv   av   pp art adj   n pp art adj n
7. Four other Indian children had been assigned (to the same class)(with the two sisters).

    pro pp art adj   adj n   hv   av art adj   n   —— pp — adj adj
8. One (of the other Indian girls) was wearing a cotton dress (instead of her native
    adj   n
    Indian clothes).

(over)

   art n   hv av adj   n   pp art   n   pp   adj   n   pp

9. The girls <u>would ask</u> their mother (about the possibility)(of English-style dresses)(for

    pro

   themselves).

   hv pro av art adj   n   pp adj   n   pp   adj   n

10. Did <u>they</u> have a good reason (for their desire)(for different clothes)?

DIRECTIONS: *Write what JOB each of the underlined words on the front of this exercise is doing. Choose your answers from among the following:*

SUBJECT   DIRECT OBJECT   VERB   OBJECT O THE PREPOSITION   INDIRECT OBJECT

PREDICATE NOMINATIVE   MODIFIER   PREDICATE ADJECTIVE

SENTENCE #	WORD	JOB
1	Indian	*modifier*
2	teacher	*subject*
3	Cynthia	*predicate nominative*
4	Pamela	*object of the preposition*
5	new	*modifier*
6	reasons	*direct object*
7	Four	*modifier*
8	clothes	*object of the preposition*
9	would ask	*verb*
10	they	*subject*

DEFINITIONS:

1. Helping verbs are verbs that come _____*before*_____ main verbs

   and help form different ____*tenses*____.

2. Adjectives are words that _____*modify nouns and pronouns*_____

3. A pronoun is a word that _____*takes the place of a noun*_____

4. The helping verb and the main verb together make up the

   _____*verb phrase*_____

    117

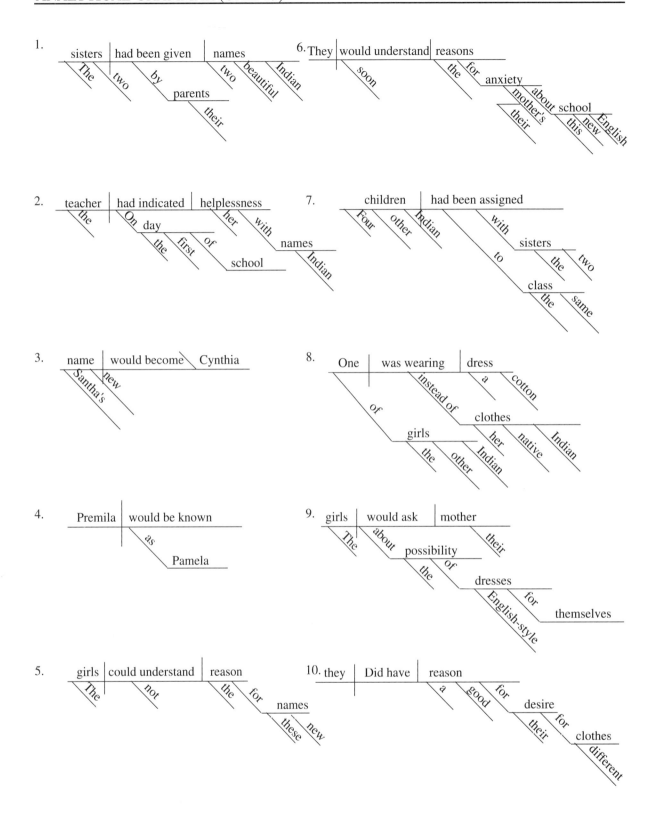

HELPING VERBS: EXERCISE #3

NAME:_____DATE:_____

DIRECTIONS: *Parse and diagram the sentences below*

    adj adj n pp   n   pp art adj   n   hv lv   adv p-adj
1. That first <u>day</u> (of school) (for the two sisters) had been very difficult.

    pn   hv   hv   av   pp art   n   pp adj adj   n
2. Santha <u>had been asked </u>(by the teacher) (for her new name).

    pro hv   adv   av   pro
3. She could not remember <u>it</u>!

    art   n   pp art   n   hv   av   pp pro
4. The rest (of the <u>class</u>) had laughed (at her).

    pro hv   lv art adv   adj   n
5. She had been a very embarrassed <u>girl</u>!

    pp   n   art adj adj   n   hv   av   n   — pp —   adj
6. (At <u>lunchtime</u>) the other Indian students were eating sandwiches (instead of normal
    adj   n
Indian food).

    pp   n   pro hv adv   av   art   adj   n
7. (At recess) she could not understand the competitive <u>games</u>.

    pp   n   art n hv   hv   av   n   pp   adj   n   pp adj   n
8. (At home) the <u>girls</u> had been taught kindness (to younger children)(in their <u>games</u>).

    adj   adj   n   hv adv   av art adj   n
9. These English children did not return the <u>same</u> courtesy!

(over)

119

art adj   n   hv   lv p-adj pp art n   pp   n   pp adj adj   n
10. The two sisters would feel <u>glad</u> (at the close)(of school)(on that first day)

DIRECTIONS: Write what JOB each underlined word is doing. Choose your answers from among the following:

SUBJECT   PREDICATE NOMINATIVE   MODIFIER   PREDICATE ADJECTIVE

VERB   DIRECT OBJECT   INDIRECT OBJECT   OBJECT OF THE PREPOSITION

SENTENCE #	WORD	JOB
1	day	*subject*
2	had been asked	*verb*
3	it	*direct object*
4	class	*object of the preposition*
5	girl	*predicate nominative*
6	lunchtime	*object of the preposition*
7	games	*direct object*
8	girls	*subject*
9	same	*modifier*
10	glad	*predicate adjective*

DEFINITIONS:

1. An antecedent _____ ***is the noun the pronoun stands for*** _____

2. In a noun - linking verb - noun pattern the second noun is called the

    predicate nominative

3. In a noun - linking verb - adjective pattern the adjective is called the

    predicate adjective

4. A noun is _____ ***the name of a person, place, thing, or idea.*** _____

5. What are the modifiers in this sentence?

    the   this   in this sentence

6. The verb phrase is made up of the _____ ***helping verbs and main verb*** _____ .

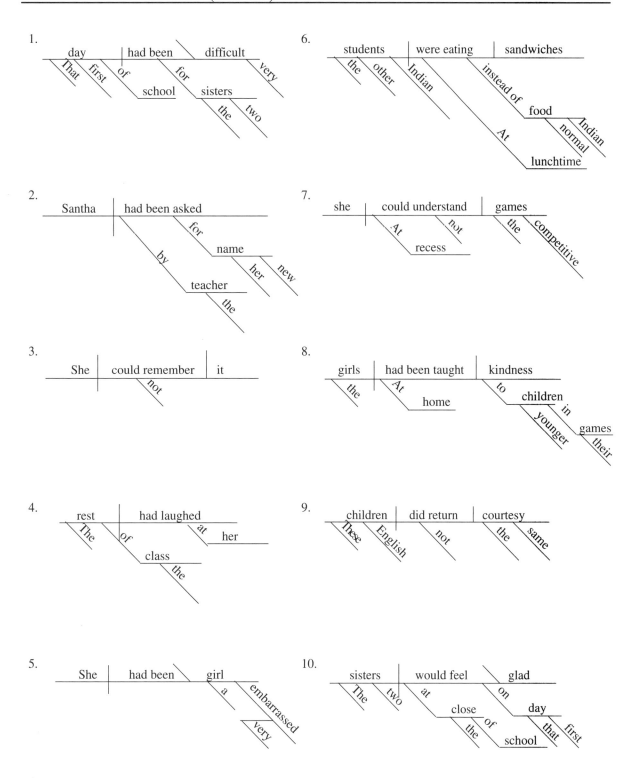

SKILLS SUPPORT

DIRECTIONS: *Below is an exerpt from Santha Rama Rau's essay "By Any Other Name." Mark all the parts of speech that you know in the passage. Diagram "He still remains insular." Then paraphrase the entire passage.*

    pn   hv   av —v—   pn   pp n   pp art   adj   n   pp adj

...Mother had refused to send Premila (to school)(in the British-run establishment)(of that

   n   pro hv av pro hv av art adj n pp adj   n   pro adv

time), because, she would say, "You can bury a dog's tail (for seven years) and it still

   av   adv adv   pro hv av art   pn   adv pp adj n   pp art   n

comes out curly, and you can take a Britisher away (from his home)(for a lifetime), and

pro adv   lv   p-adj

he still remains insular."

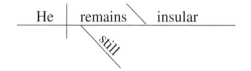

HELPING VERBS: TEST

NAME:_____DATE:_____

(RAW SCORE:_____/253_GRADE:_____)

DIRECTIONS: Parse and diagram all the sentences below.

     pp art n pp adj adj n art adj n hv   av   pp art adj n

___ 1. (On the day)(of Premila's first test), the girls' <u>lives</u> would change (in a big way).
19

     pn hv av   adv   pp art n pp adj   n

___2. Premila had marched suddenly (through the <u>door</u>) (of Santha's classroom).
12

     pro hv av adj n   adv

___3. "We <u>are leaving</u> this place now!"
6

     pn hv lv   adv   p-adj   pp adj   n

___4. Santha had been completely <u>dumbfounded</u> (by Premila's behavior).
9

     pro hv adv   av   adj n   adv

___5. She could not disobey her <u>sister</u>, however.
7

     pro hv adv   av adj n   adv

___6. "I can never attend <u>that</u> school again,"
7

     pp art n pp adj n   pn hv   av   pp art n   pp adj adj

___7.(On the way)(to their home), Santha was wondering(about the reason)(for their sudden
20   *n*

<u>departure</u>).

     pp n   pn   hv   av pp art n

___8. (At home), <u>Mother</u> would ask (for a reason).
10

(over)

> art   adj   n   hv   av   adj art adj   n   pp   n or v   pp   n

___9. The British teacher <u>had accused</u> all the Indian students (of cheating)(on tests)!
15

> pp adj   adj   pn   adv   adj adj   n   hv   av   pp art n pp art

___10. (To happy little Santha), however, this bad thing had happened (to a girl)(by the
22

> n   pp   pn

===   name)(of <u>Cynthia</u>)!
127

DIRECTIONS: *Write what JOB the underlined words are doing. Choose your answers from among the following:*

SUBJECT   PREDICATE NOMINATIVE   MODIFIER   PREDICATE ADJECTIVE

VERB   OBJECT OF THE PREPOSITION   DIRECT OBJECT   INDIRECT OBJECT

SENTENCE #	WORD	JOB
1	lives	*subject*
2	door	*object of the preposition*
3	are leaving	*verb*
4	dumbfounded	*predicate adjective*
5	sister	*direct object*
6	that	*modifier*
7	departure	*object of the preposition*
8	Mother	*subject*
9	had accused	*verb*
10	Cynthia	*object of the preposition*

(5 points each)

Raw		Score		Grade	%
253	-	247	=	A++	=98+
246	-	240	=	A+	= 95
239	-	227	=	A	= 90
226	-	215	=	B+	= 85
214	-	202	=	B	= 80
201	-	189	=	C+	= 75
188	-	177	=	C	= 70
176	-	164	=	D+	= 65
163	-	151	=	D	= 60

===
50

DEFINITIONS:

1. A helping verb helps the main verb form different _____ *tenses* _____.

2. A verb is not a verb unless it has a _____ *subject* _____.

3. Which word in this sentence is the predicate nominative? _____ *nominative* _____.

4. An adjective is a word that _____ *describes or modifies a noun or pronoun* _____.

5. A pronoun is a word that _____ *takes the place of a noun* _____.

6. What is an antecedent? _____ *the noun the pronoun stands for* _____.

7. Which kind of noun can consist of more than one word? _____ *a proper noun* _____.

8. The helping verb and the main verb make up the _____ *verb phrase* _____.

===
8

Photocopying this product is strictly prohibited by copyright law.

REMEMBER: *Whether the line which separates the verb and its complement (direct object, predicate nominative, or predicate adjective) is vertical or diagonal is worth a point.*

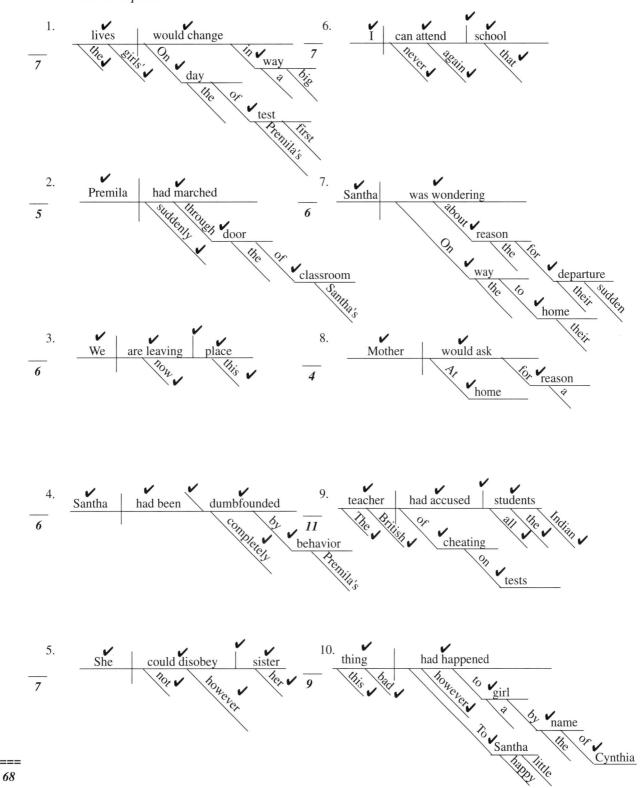

CONJUNCTIONS & COMPOUND SITUATIONS

A conjunction is a word (or words) that joins grammatical equals (noun to noun, verb to verb, etc.)

THERE ARE THREE KINDS OF CONJUNCTIONS:

        Coordinating conjunctions
            Correlative conjunctions
                Subordinating conjunctions (these will be covered later in Unit #16)

COORDINATING CONJUNCTIONS

and	or	for (when it means *because*)
but	nor	yet (when it means *but*)

EXAMPLES:

                conj
Anne cleaned the kitchen and the bedroom. (*and* joins 2 nouns: *kitchen* and *bedroom*)
                conj
We will go to the store and then to the cleaners. (*and* joins 2 prepositional phrases: *to the store* and *to the cleaners*)

CORRELATIVE CONJUNCTIONS

These conjunctions are always found in pairs with other words in between. They are....

either....or	both....and
neither....nor	not only....but (also)

EXAMPLES: Take special note of the way correlative conjunctions are marked.

You can take either the pie or the cake. (*either...or* joins 2 nouns: *pie* and *cake*)
                conj

The girl was both beautiful and kind. (*both...and* joins 2 predicate adjectives: *beautiful* and *kind*)
                conj

COMPOUND SITUATIONS:

A "compound situation" is when there are two (or more) of something joined by a conjunction in a sentence. Two (or more) subjects is called a "compound subject" and two or more verbs is called a "compound verb" and so forth. When you have a compound situation in a sentence diagram, you go to the place where that word (if it were only one word) would be diagramed - and then you "branch off." You make as many branches as you need to illustrate the compound situation in the sentence; so if you have a sentence with a **quadruple** subject (Kim, Tracy, Jean, and Mary all wore the same dress to the Prom), you would need four separate lines in the subject place in the diagram!

On the following pages of notes, you will find a sample diagram for all the possible compound situations you might encounter.

A.   <u>COMPOUND SUBJECT:</u>   *pn   conj   pn   av   adv*
                                    John and Jim walked home.

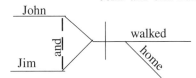

B.   <u>COMPOUND VERB</u>:   EXAMPLE #1:   *pn   hv   av   conj   av   art   n*
                                    John was washing and waxing the car.

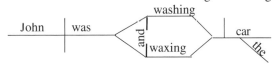

            EXAMPLE #2:   *pn   av   art   n conj   av   art   n*
                                    John washed the car and mowed the lawn.

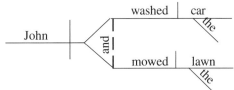

NOTE: In the first diagram above, we had to "rejoin" the base line after the compound verb **because** both verbs shared a direct object. In the second diagram each verb has its own direct object.

C.   <u>COMPOUND DIRECT OBJECT:</u>   *pn   av   art   n   conj art adj   n*
                                    Mom cleaned the kitchen and the living room.

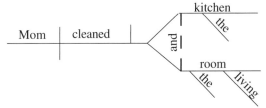

D.   <u>COMPOUND INDIRECT OBJECT:</u>   *pn   av   adj   n   conj pro art n*
                                    Sally sent my brother and me a present.

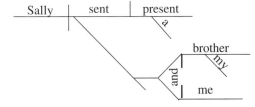

E.   <u>COMPOUND PREDICATE NOMINATIVE OR PREDICATE ADJECTIVE:</u>
                    pro   lv   p-adj conj p-adj
                    She felt hungry and tired.

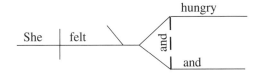

F.   COMPOUND PREPOSITIONAL PHRASES:

pro av pp art   n conj   pp   art   n
We rode (over the river) and (through the woods).

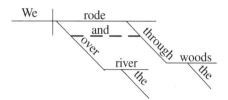

G.   <u>PREPOSITIONAL PHRASE WITH COMPOUND OBJECT:</u> *pro   av   pp art adj   n conj   n*
She dusted (under the new table and chairs).

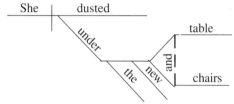

Notice that *the* and *new* are diagramed on the line that is shared by *table* and *chairs*. That's because these two modifiers modify both nouns.

H.   <u>COMPOUND SENTENCE:</u> *pn   av   art   n conj pn   av pro*
John washed the car and Jim waxed it.

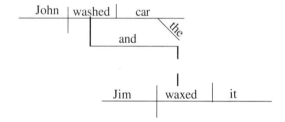

I.   <u>MULTIPLE COMPOUND SITUATIONS:</u>   *pn conj pn   av conj av   art n*
John and Jim washed and waxed the car.

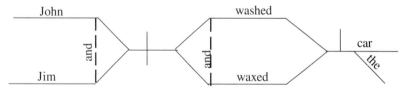

J.   <u>DIAGRAMING CORRELATIVE CONJUNCTIONS:</u>   *pn   pn av adj   n   adv*
<u>Both</u> Sean <u>and</u> Jason left their bikes outside.
conj

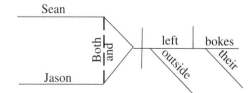

Photocopying this product is strictly prohibited by copyright law.

K.   <u>COMPOUND MODIFIERS</u>:

You learned how to diagram compound modifiers in Unit #4: Subject and Verb.

L.   <u>THREE OR MORE OF SOMETHING</u>:   *pn   pn   conj   pn   av   n*
                                          John, Joe, and Jim ate lunch.

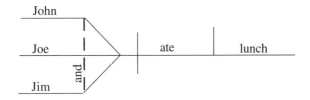

COMPOUND SITUATIONS: EXERCISE #1

NAME:_____DATE:_____

DIRECTIONS: *Parse and diagram the sentence below.*

    adj   n conj adj   n   av   adj   adj   n

1. Fairy tales and nursery rhymes entertain most American children. (See Notes A)

    adj   n   av   av pro adj adj   n

2. Our parents <u>either</u> read <u>or</u> tell us these favorite stories. (See Notes B-1 & J)
                     conj

    adj adj   n   av art   n conj av art adj   n   pp pro

3. Our first teachers tell the stories and sing the nursery rhymes (with us).
    (See Notes B-2)

    pro av adj   n   conj adj   n

4. I loved nursery rhymes and fairy tales. (See Notes C)

    adj   n   hv   av adj   n   conj pro   n   pp   n

5. My mother would read my brothers and me stories (before bedtime). (See Notes D)

    pro lv   adv p-adj conj p-adj

6. We were always quiet and spellbound. (See Notes E)

    pro   hv   av pro   pp art adj   n   pp adj   n

7. She would read them <u>either</u> (in the living room) <u>or</u> (in our bedrooms).
    (See Notes F & J)   *conj*

(over)

           Photocopying this product is strictly prohibited by copyright law.

　　　　pro　av　adj　　n　pp art　　n　conj　　n　　pp art　　n
8.　She had special voices (for the animals and characters)(in the stories). (See Notes G)

　　　　pro　av　————　pn　————　conj adj　n　　av　　pn
9.　I loved "Little Red Riding Hood" and my brothers loved "Pinnochio." (See Notes H)

　　　pn　　pn　conj pro lv　adv　adj　　n　　pp　　adj　n
10. Billy, George, and I were always perfect children (during story time)! (See Notes L)

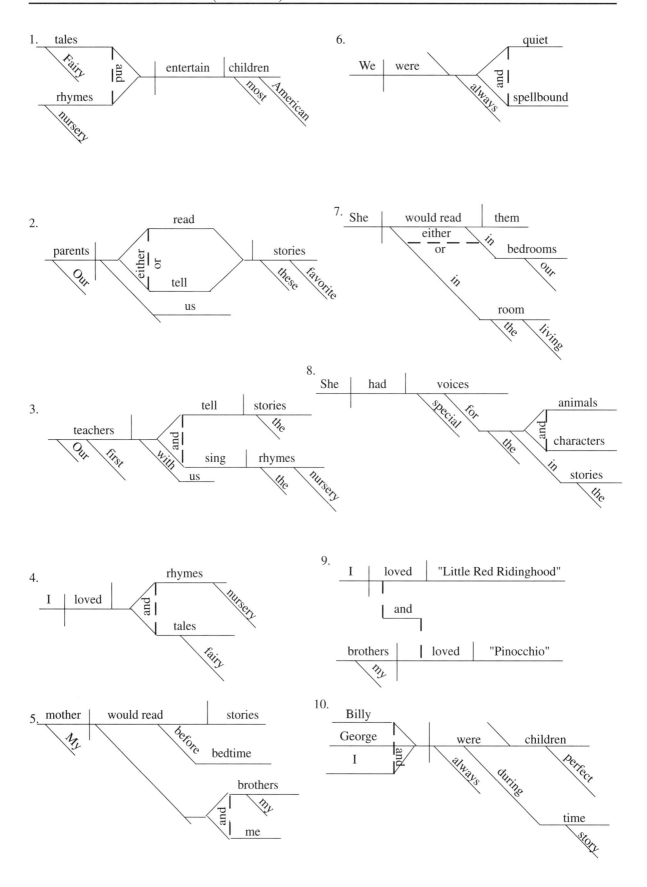

COMPOUND SITUATIONS: EXERCISE #2

NAME:_____DATE:_____

DIRECTIONS: *Parse and diagram the sentences below.*

    ———— *pn* ———— *conj adj   n   av   adj   n   pp   n   pp adj*
1. Little Red Ridinghood and her mother packed her <u>basket</u> (with cookies)(for her
    n
    grandma.)

    art   n   pp   adj   n   av   pp   art   n conj pp art n
2. The <u>path</u> (to grandma's house) went (through the forest) and (up the hill).

    ———— *pn* ———— *av conj   av   pp art adj   n*
3. Little Red Ridinghood ran and <u>skipped</u> (down the forest path).

    art adj adj   n   av   pp art n conj ———— *pn* ———— *av   adv*
4. The big bad wolf waited (behind a tree), and Little Red Ridinghood skipped <u>past</u>.

    art adj adj   n   av   pp art   n   conj pp n pp ———— *pn* ————
5. The big bad wolf jumped (from the <u>bushes</u>) and (in front)(of Little Red **Ridinghood**).

    art n   av ————*pn* ———— *art n conj   n   pp adj   n*
6. The <u>wolf</u> asked Little Red Ridinghood the purpose and destination (of her **journey**).

    pro hv   av   pp adj   n   conj pro lv   adv p-adj pp pro
7. "I am going (to my <u>grandma's</u>), and I am not <u>afraid</u> (of you)!"

(over)

————— *pn* ————— *av adj n conj av adj n*
8. Little Red Ridinghood grabbed her basket and continued her journey.

adj   n   lv   p-adj   p-adj pp pro
9. Her grandma looked both big and strange (to her).
                         conj

art adj adj   n   av   pp ————— *pn* ————— *conj   av pro adv*
10. The big bad wolf jumped (on Little Red Ridinghood) and gobbled her up!

DEFINITIONS:

1. Two or more subjects in a sentence is called a _____ *compound subject* _____.

2. When the noun in front of the verb is the same thing as the noun after the verb, what kind of verb do you have?
    _____ *a linking verb* _____

3. An adverb modifies _____ *a verb* _____, _____ *an adjective* _____, and _____ *another adverb* _____.

DIRECTIONS: *Write what job the underlined words are doing. Choose your answer from among the following:*

SUBJECT   DIRECT OBJECT   INDIRECT OBJECT   OBJECT OF THE PREPOSITION

PREDICATE NOMINATIVE   PREDICATE ADJECTIVE   MODIFIER   VERB

SENTENCE #	WORD	JOB
1	basket	*direct object*
2	path	*subject*
3	skipped	*verb*
4	past	*modifier*
5	bushes	*object of the preposition*
6	wolf	*subject*
7	grandma's	*object of the preposition*
7	afraid	*predicate adjective*
8	journey	*direct object*
9	big	*predicate adjective*
10	wolf	*subject*

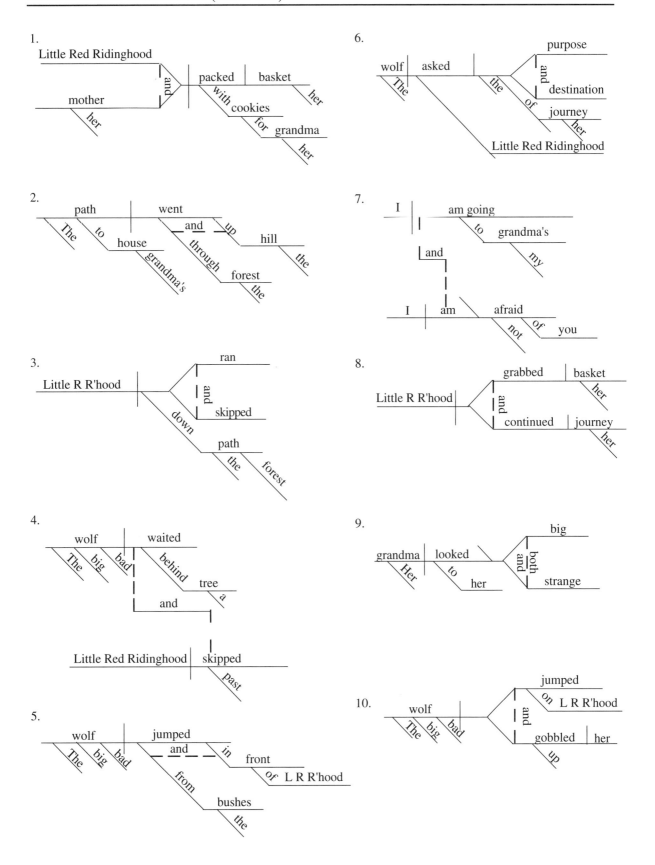

COMPOUND SITUATIONS: EXERCISE #3

NAME:_____DATE:_____

DIRECTIONS: *Parse and diagram the sentences below.*

            adj   n   adj   n   av   n   n conj n   pp

1. Not only fairy tales but also nursery rhymes teach children values and lessons (in

      n   conj
    life).

     pro pp adj adv adj   n   hv   av   pp ——— pn ——————— conj art

2. Many (of our most beloved tales) were written (by Hans Christian Anderson and the

    ——— *pn ———*
    Brothers Grimm).

    ——————— *pn*———————   *av ——— pn ——— conj ——— pn ———*

3. Hans Christian Anderson wrote "The Ugly Duckling" and "The Little Mermaid."

    art ——— pn ———   av pro ——— pn ——— conj ——— pn ———

4. The Brothers Grimm gave us "Little Red Ridinghood" and "Hansel and Gretel."

    ——————— *pn ———   hv av pp pn conj art ——— pn ——— hv*

5. Hans Christian Anderson was born (in Denmark), and the Brothers Grimm were

    av pp pn
    born (in Germany).

     adj adj n conj adj   n   lv   n   pp art adj   adj

6. These fairy tales and nursery rhymes are examples (of the strong European

       n   pp adj adj   n
    influence)(in our country's culture).

     pro pp adj adj   n   av pp   pn conj adj   n hv hv av

7. Most(of our fairy tales) come (from Europe), but children's stories have been told

    pp adj   n   conj pp adj n
    (in all countries) and (in all cultures).

                                                     (over)

       Photocopying this product is strictly prohibited by copyright law.

> *adj   n   av   pp   pn   pn   conj art — pn —*

8. <u>Popular</u> stories come (from China, India, and the Middle East).

> *adv   pro pp pro   av art adj   n conj   n   pp   n*

9. <u>Interestingly</u>, all (of them) teach the same values and lessons (to children).

DEFINITIONS:

1. A noun is a word that _____ *names a person, place, thing, or idea.* _____.

2. The articles in our language are _____ *a* _____, _____ *an* _____, and _____ *the* _____.

3. An antecedent is _____ *the word the pronoun takes the place of* _____.

4. In a noun - linking verb - adjective pattern, the adjective is called _____ *the predicate adjective* _____

5. List 3 jobs that a noun can do: _____

> *subject, predicate nominative, direct object, indirect object, object of the preposition* (any 3 of these)

DIRECTIONS: *Write what job the underlined words are doing. Choose your answer from among the following:*

SUBJECT	*DIRECT OBJECT*	*INDIRECT OBJECT*	*OBJECT OF THE PREPOSITION*
PREDICATE NOMINATIVE	*PREDICATE ADJECTIVE*	*MODIFIER*	*VERB*

SENTENCE #	WORD	JOB
1	children	*indirect object*
2	Many	*subject*
3	wrote	*verb*
4	"Hansel and Gretel	*direct object*
5	Denmark	*object of the preposition*
6	examples	*predicate nominative*
7	Europe	*object of the preposition*
8	Popular	*modifier*
9	Interestingly	*modifier*

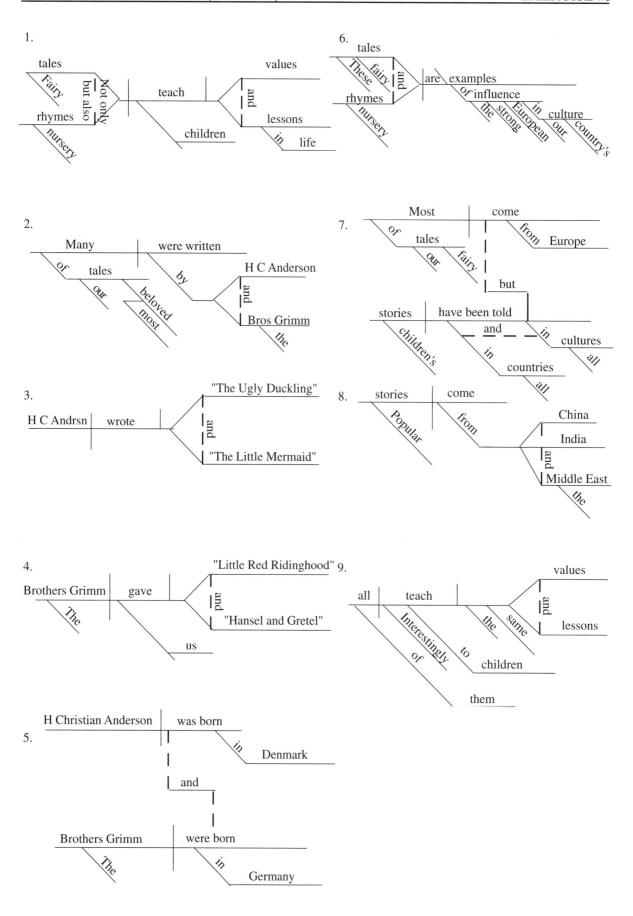

SKILLS SUPPORT

DIRECTIONS: _Parse all the words in the poem below and diagram the second sentence. Then write your own version of this nursery rhyme - only this time the names are Dick and Jane. The more rhymes you change, the higher your score - so try to come up with NEW RHYMES instead of all the old ones! (NOTE: For now, treat "TUMBLING" as a noun.)_

PN   CONJ   PN
Jack and Jill

AV   PP ART N
Went (up the hill)

---V---   ART N   PP   N
to fetch a pail (of water).

PN   AV   ADV
Jack fell down

CONJ   AV   ADJ   N
And broke his crown,

CONJ PN   AV   N   ADJ
and Jill came tumbling after!

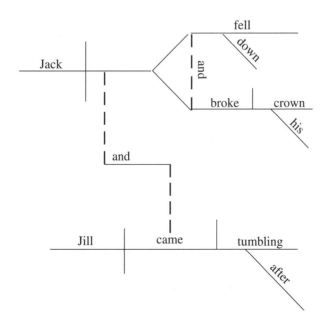

COMPOUND SITUATIONS: TEST

NAME:_____DATE:_____

(RAW SCORE: _____ */329* GRADE:_____)

DIRECTIONS: *Parse and diagram the sentences below.*

       n   hv   av adj n conj adj   n   pp adj   n

___ 1. <u>Parents</u> should read fairy tales and nursery rhymes (to their <u>children</u>).

12

          hv   n   av adj   n   pro av   adj   adj   n   adv

___ 2. <u>Not only</u> do children love these <u>stories, but</u> they learn many valuable lessons too.

12   —— *conj*——

       ——— *pn* ———   *hv av   n   n   conj   n pp adj*

___ 3. "The Ugly Duckling" can teach <u>children</u> kindness and tolerance (of others'

11   *n*

    differences).

       pn   lv   adv p-adj conj p-adj conj pro hv   av   pp art n

‾‾4. Cinderella was always <u>good</u> and patient, and she was rewarded (in the end).

14

       adj adj n   av adj   n   pp   n conj n conj art adj n av adj   n

___ 5. Two little pigs <u>built</u> their houses (of straw and wood), but the third pig built his house

21   *pp   n*

    (of brick).

       adj   n conj adj n   av adj adj adv adj   n

___ 6. Good planning and hard work saved all three little <u>pigs'</u> lives.

11

(over)

          Photocopying this product is strictly prohibited by copyright law.

       — pn —   av   art   n   conj   av   art   adv   adj   n   pp   art   adj   n

___7. Snow White helped the dwarfs and escaped the evil queen's plot (at the same <u>time</u>).
15

       adj   n conj   n   av pro adv pp adj   n   conj   av   adj   n

___8. Pinocchio's lies and stories led him <u>away</u> (from his father) and lengthened his nose!
15

      ——————— pn ——————— lv art n   pp   art   n   pp   n   conj adj

9. "The Emperor's New Clothes" is a story (about the dangers)(of dishonesty and false
       n
14 pride).

       pro   av   adj   adj   adj   n   pp adj   adj   n   conj   n

10. <u>We</u> learn many valuable life lessons (in our childhood stories and rhymes).

___
13

===
138

PART II: DIRECTIONS: *Write what job the underlined words are doing. Choose your answers from among the following:*

SUBJECT   DIRECT OBJECT   INDIRECT OBJECT   OBJECT OF THE PREPOSITION

    PREDICATE NOMINATIVE   PREDICATE ADJECTIVE   VERB   MODIFIER

SENTENCE #	WORD	JOB
1	Parents	*subject*
1	children	*object of the preposition*
2	stories	*direct object*
3	children	*indirect object*
4	good	*predicate adjective*
5	built	*verb*
6	pigs'	*modifier*
7	time	*object of the preposition*
8	away	*modifier*
10	We	*subject*

5 points each

===
50

Raw		Score	Grade	%
329	-	322 =	A++	=2098+
321	-	312 =	A+	= 95
311	-	296 =	A	= 90
295	-	279 =	B+	= 85
278	-	263 =	B	= 80
262	-	246 =	C+	= 75
245	-	230 =	C	= 70
229	-	213 =	D+	= 65
212	-	197 =	D	= 60

DEFINITIONS:

___1.   A noun is a word that _____ *names a person, place, thing, or idea.* _____
 1

___2.   The articles in our language are _____ *a, an, and the* _____
 3

___3.   An adjective is a word that _____ *modifies a noun or a pronoun* _____
 1

___4.   A pronoun is a word that _____ *takes the place of a noun* _____
 1

___5.   An antecedent is _____ *the noun the pronoun stands for* _____
 1

___6.   A verb isn't a real verb unless it has a _____ *subject* _____
 1

___7.   True or False: A direct object occurs with a linking verb _____ *false* _____
 1

___8.   In a N-LV-N sentence, the 2nd noun is called the _____ *predicate nominative* _____
 1

___9.   An adverb is a word that _____ *modifies a verb, adjective, or adverb* _____
 1

___10.   Prepositional phrases do the job of _____ *modifier* _____
 1

___11.   A word can't be a preposition unless it's in a _____ *prepositional phrase* _____
 1

___12.   Two or more subjects in a sentence is called a _____ *compound subject* _____
 1

___13.   The helping verb(s) and the main verb make up the _____ *verb phrase* _____
 1

___14.   Write an example of a correlative conjunction *either...or   neither...nor not. only.....but (also) both....and*
 1

___15.   The adjective following a linking verb is called _____ *predicate adjective* _____
 1

===
17

NOTE: Prepositional phrases with compound objects are counted as follows:
Otherwise, prepositional phrases are still counted as one point.

1.

2.

3.

4.

5.

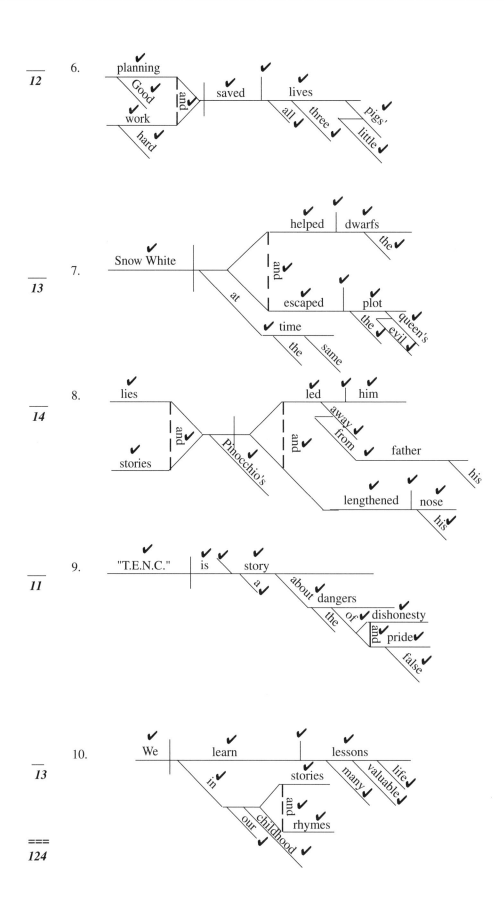

Season Two

NOTES FOR TEACHERS

GENERAL NOTES: I believe there are a couple of ways to go about mastering the information in Book #2 of *Analytical Grammar*. If your student has just finished Book 1 - and he or she is ready to go forward - then you can skip the review and go right into Unit 11. You should use the same weekly schedule as you did for Units 1 through 10; however, if you and your student have found shortcuts that work for you, then by all means, use them!

Should you decide to take a break between Books 1 & 2 of *Analytical Grammar*, then a little review might be in order. I have included three worksheets for each unit of Sentence Parts and Their Functions, should you need them.

You and your student could review the notes of the first unit of review and do one worksheet. If, in your opinions, no more work is needed, go on to the next review unit.

I don't have teacher notes for each separate unit in this book, so I'll just share with you the little things I have gleaned over the years.

UNITS 11 - 13: THE VERBALS

Students often have a hard time keeping the three verbals straight in their minds. To that end, I have my students make a chart, which I have demonstrated below. I do not recommend that you copy my chart. I really believe that students internalize and retain the information in the chart if I draw a blank for them and "talk them through it" as they copy. Each portion of the chart needs to make sense to your student as he or she writes it down.

I don't introduce the chart until Unit 12 , and then I have students add to it in Unit 13.

<table>
<tr><td colspan="5" align="center">THE VERBALS</td></tr>
<tr>
<th>Type of Verbal</th>
<th>What Does It Look Like?</th>
<th>What Job Does It Do?</th>
<th>How Is It Diagramed?</th>
<th>Removeability?</th>
</tr>
<tr>
<td>Participial</td>
<td>Verb + "ing"
or
Fits into "I have__"</td>
<td>Modifier</td>
<td></td>
<td>Removeable</td>
</tr>
<tr>
<td>Gerund</td>
<td>Verb + "ing"</td>
<td>Noun</td>
<td></td>
<td>Not Removeable</td>
</tr>
<tr>
<td rowspan="2">Infinitive</td>
<td rowspan="2">to + verb</td>
<td>Modifier</td>
<td></td>
<td>Removeable</td>
</tr>
<tr>
<td>Noun</td>
<td></td>
<td>Not Removeable</td>
</tr>
</table>

As soon as you introduce Unit 12: Gerunds, the question will probably immediately arise, "If all gerunds end in 'ing' and some participals end in 'ing,' how are you supposed to be able to tell them apart?" Well, that's where this issue of "removeability" comes in. Modifiers can always be removed from a sentence, and there will still be a meaningful sentence there. The sentence without the modifiers may sound like the Lone Ranger's faithful companion Tonto talking, but it is a sentence!

This is not true of nouns, however. If you pull just the noun out of the sentence, you'll be left with a sentence without a subject or a direct object, or perhaps a preposition with no object. Nouns are really essential.

So, tell the student that if he finds a verbal phrase that could be either a participial phrase or a gerund phrase, he should try to remove the phrase from the sentence. If he can remove it, it's a participial phrase; if he can't, it's a gerund phrase.

If an infinitive phrase is acting as a noun, it won't be removable; if it's acting as a modifier, it will be.

I have little names for the diagraming constructions for each verbal; this just makes it easier to talk about them. The construction on which you diagram a participal I call a **"dogleg."** The gerund is diagramed on a **"stilt and a stairstep."** When an infinitive is a modifier, it's on a **"broken dogleg,"** and when it's a noun it's on a **"stilt and a broken dogleg."**

SCORING TESTS

When you and your student are correcting diagrams, remember the technique used in Units 1 - 10. **Check what's correct and count the checks.** If you try to deduct the errors from the points possible on each diagram, you'll both go stark raving mad!

UNIT 14

I don't have any nifty little tricks with this unit. I find that students have very little trouble with appositives. When you do the sentence-combining exercises, your student may combine two sentences using an adjective clause rather than an appositive; it's not a bad idea to caution him.

For example, suppose your student were to combine these two sentences:

Jake is my best friend.

He is going to math camp this summer.

The answer, "Jake, who is my best friend, is going to math camp this summer," would be incorrect because "who is my best friend" is an adjective clause. The correct way to combine these two sentences would be, "Jake, my best friend, is going to math camp this summer."

UNIT 15 - 17

CONGRATULATIONS!! Once you get through these units, your student will "know it all." This is all the grammar there is to know. Some grammarians would argue that there are some very arcane topics (such as subjective complements and objective complements) which we haven't covered, but that's because

a.)   We have covered them; we've just called them by other names.

b.)   There is no practical application for this knowledge. In other words, there are no <u>punctuation rules</u> that depend upon an understanding of these concepts.

That's why I don't spend any time on them.

PARTICIPIAL PHRASES

For the next three units we'll be learning about those verbals we talked about back in Unit #4. There are three verbals in our language: participles, gerunds, and infinitives. This unit is about the participle.

DEFINITION: A participial phrase is a group of words beginning with a participle which acts as an ADJECTIVE.

A participle is a verb form that acts like an adjective. There are two kinds of participles:
1.)   PRESENT PARTICIPLES are verbs that end in "ing." (giving, taking, being, etc.)
2.)   PAST PARTICIPLES are verbs that will fit into the phrase "I have ____" (walked, given, done, been, etc.)

If you found a participle all by itself in a sentence, you would call it an adjective because that is how it acts. You would also diagram it as a regular adjective.

EXAMPLE: art adj   n   av   pro
                  A smiling policeman helped us.

If, however, your participle comes in a PHRASE, it must be diagramed in a special way. You know you have a PARTICIPIAL PHRASE when your verb form acts like a verb as well as an adjective. For example, it may have a direct object, etc.

Since a participial phrase acts like an adjective, it is attached in the diagram to the noun or pronoun it modifies. The pattern looks like this (it's called a "dogleg"):

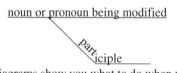

The following example diagrams show you what to do when you have a—

A.   PARTICIPLE WITH DIRECT OBJECT:

EXAMPLE: art n   v   art adj   n hv   av
                 A box containing a birthday gift was delivered.

(notice that the participle is marked "v" - not "av" - because it's a verbal.)

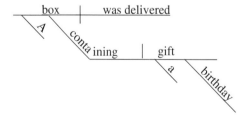

(over)

B. PARTICIPLE WITH MODIFIERS:

    EXAMPLE: pro av art   n   v   pp   pn
                     I   read   a   book <u>written (by   Dickens).</u>

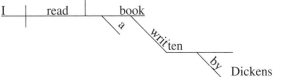

C. PARTICIPIAL PHRASE WITH PREDICATE NOMINATIVE OR ADJECTIVE:

    EXAMPLE: v   p-adj   art   n   hv   av   pp   pn
                 <u>Smelling delicious</u>, the turkey   was   carved (by   Dad).

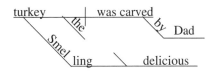

IMPORTANT: A participial phrase is an adjective. It can modify any noun or pronoun in the sentence. By the way, when a participial phrase is INTRODUCTORY (in other words, it comes at the beginning of the sentence), it is set off from the rest of the sentence by a comma.

PARTICIPIAL PHRASES: EXERCISE #1

NAME:_____ DATE:_____

PART I: DIRECTIONS: *Look at each verb below. If it looks like a PRESENT PARTICIPLE, mark "pres" in the space at the left. If it looks like a PAST PARTICIPLE, mark "past." If the verb could not possibly be a participle, write "verb."*

___*pres*___1. spinning   ___*verb*___6. win

___*verb*___2. was   ___*verb*___7. behave

___*past*___3. heard   ___*past*___8. placed

___*verb*___4. has gone   ___*verb*___9. look

___*pres*___5. having   ___*verb*___10. could

PART II: DIRECTIONS: *Parse the sentences below and put prepositional phrases in parentheses. Underline the participial phrases. Diagram the sentences. CHECK THE BACK FOR ADDITIONAL WORK.*

       v   art n   art n adv av
1.   Outrunning the hounds, the fox easily escaped.

      pro av pro v   adv   pp art n
2.   I saw him fishing contentedly (by the river).

        v pp art adj   n   art   n   av   art n
3.   Tackled(on the one-yard line), the quarterback fumbled the ball.

       adv   v   pp art n pro   av   adj   n
4.   Wildly cheering (for the team), we celebrated their victory.

      art n   av   art n   art n   v   pp adj   n   conj v   pp adj n
5.   The clerk handed the customer a box wrapped (in white paper) and tied (with red ribbon).

      v   art n   pp adj n   art n   av   adv   pp art n
6.   Balancing a book (on her head), the girl walked slowly (across the room).

      art   n   av art n   v   adj   n   pp art n
7.   The professor wrote a note expressing her approval (of the plan).

      art   n   av art   n   v pp art   n
8.   The children found an arrowhead buried (on the riverbank).

PART III: DIRECTIONS:

    1.) Make up a participial phrase to modify the SUBJECT of the following sentence. Diagram your completed sentence.   **Answers will vary; here are some examples:**

        THE COACH, *GESTURING WILDLY,* SIGNALLED A TIME-OUT.

    2.) Make up a participial phrase to modify the DIRECT OBJECT of the following sentence. Diagram your completed sentence.

        I HAVE THREE FRIENDS *TAKING THE HONORS CLASS.*

(over)

Write what job the following words are doing in the sentences in PART II. Choose your answers from among the following:

SUBJECT   PREDICATE NOMINATIVE   OBJECT OF THE PREPOSITION   DIRECT OBJECT   VERB

INDIRECT OBJECT   PREDICATE ADJECTIVE   MODIFIER

SENTENCE #	WORD	JOB
1	fox	*subject*
2	contentedly	*modifier*
3	line	*object of the preposition*
4	Wildly	*modifier*
5	customer	*indirect object*
5	box	*direct object*
6	girl	*subject*
7	wrote	*verb*

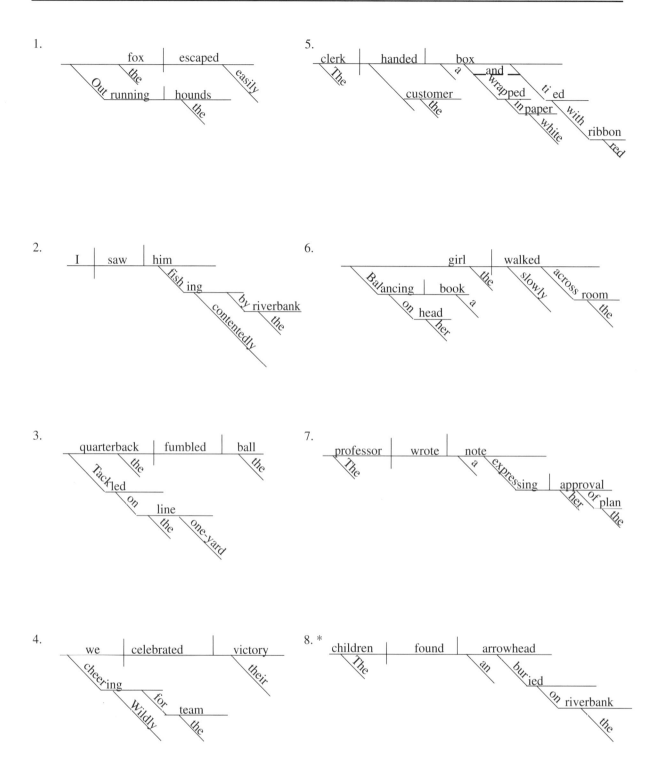

* This sentence is an excellent one for demonstrating what a "dangling participle" is. Try putting the phrase "buried on the riverbank" next to "children" - as in "Buried on the riverbank, the children found an arrowhead." We get a pretty funny mental picture here (I see little heads sticking out of the sand!) because the participial phrase is "dangling" out there next to the wrong noun. It must be next to the noun it modifies, or it will appear to modify the noun it's near.

PARTICIPIAL PHRASES: EXERCISE #2

NAME:_____DATE:_____

PART I: DIRECTIONS: *Parse the sentences below and put prepositional phrases in parentheses. Underline the participial phrases. Diagram the entire sentence.*

```
            v      adv  pp art    n     art    n      av    art    n
```
1.   Smiling happily(at the audience), the actress accepted the flowers.


```
        hv  pro av  pn    v     adj    n      adv
```
2.   Did you see Fred riding his bicycle today?


```
        art  n    v      pp art  adj   n    conj    adv        v       lv  art   n   pp art   n
```
3.   The cake, baked (by a master chef) and beautifully decorated, was the hit (of the party).


```
        v  art  adj    n   pro   adv  av  adj    n     pp   adj     n
```
4.   Being a devout coward, I naturally avoid any contact (with violent people).


```
        adv    av  adj    n     v    pp   adj     n        pp   adj n  *
```
5.   Please read three books written (by American authors) (during this year).


```
        v      pp art  n   pp adj  n     pn   av  art   n   pp  adj    n
```
6.   Screeching (at the top)(of her lungs), Tillie hit the man (with her bag).


```
        av  art  n    v      pp adj   n      adj    n   pp   n
```
7.   Give the lady seated (by my mother) this glass (of lemonade).


```
        v   art  adj    n   pp   n     pp  art   n   pn    av    adv conj   av    adj   n
```
8.   Choosing a huge piece (of chocolate)(from the box), Mimi yawned lazily and continued her reading.

   ✱ *This sentence lends itself nicely to a discussion about ambiguity. Ask the kids to paraphrase
      what it means. Can it be taken two ways? How could you fix it so that there's no confusion - if
      you mean the books are to be read "during this year"? What about if the books were to have
      been written "during this year"? How important is all this? What if you were taking a college
      class and your entire grade rested on following these directions to the letter?*

PART II: DIRECTIONS: *Make up a participial phrase to modify the INDIRECT OBJECT of the following
sentence.*

   I TOLD THE STUDENTS ***SEATED IN FRONT OF ME*** A STORY.

(over)

153

DIRECTIONS: *Write what job the following words are doing in the sentences in PART I. Choose your answers from among the following:*

SUBJECT	PREDICATE NOMINATIVE	OBJECT OF THE PREPOSITION

DIRECT OBJECT	INDIRECT OBJECT	MODIFIER	PREDICATE ADJECTIVE	VERB

SENTENCE #	WORD	JOB
1	flowers	*direct object*
2	bicycle	*direct object*
3	hit	*predicate nominative*
4	coward	*predicate nominative*
4	contact	*direct object*
5	books	*direct object*
6	lungs	*object of the preposition*
7	lady	*indirect object*
7	glass	*direct object*
8	lazily	*modifier*

Photocopying this product is strictly prohibited by copyright law.

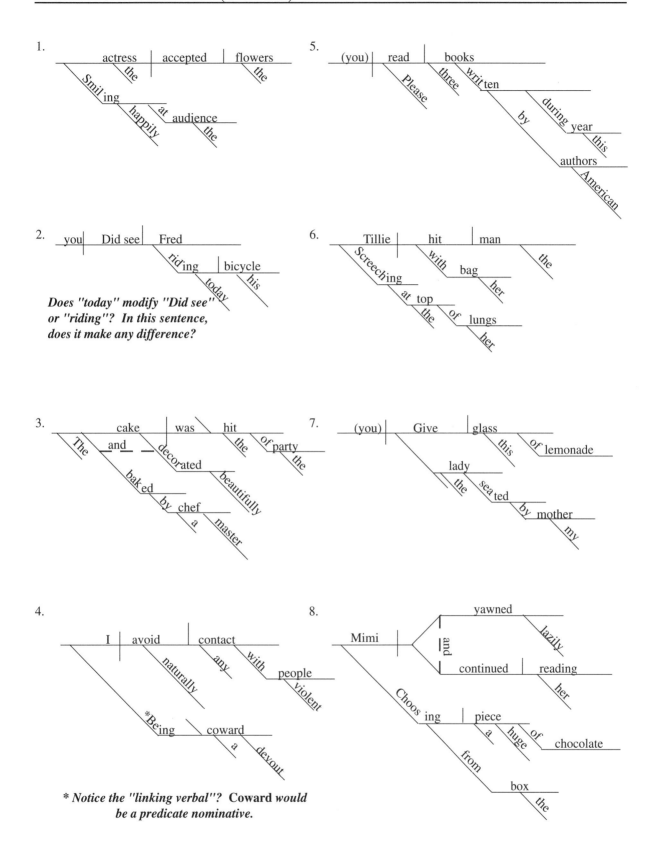

2. *Does "today" modify "Did see" or "riding"? In this sentence, does it make any difference?*

4. ** Notice the "linking verbal"? Coward would be a predicate nominative.*

PARTICIPIAL PHRASES: EXERCISE #3

NAME:_____DATE:_____

PART I: DIRECTIONS: *Parse the sentences below and put prepositional phrases in parentheses. Underline the participial phrases. Diagram the entire sentence.*

       v   art adj   n   art   n   av   pp   art n

1.   <u>Carrying a large package</u>, the messenger stumbled (across the room).

       art   n   v   pp art n pp   n   av adv pp art n

2.   The dog, <u>attracted (by the smell)(of meat)</u>, trotted over (to the stranger.)

       art   n   v   n   pp art adj   n   av pro

3.   The men <u>playing golf (at the country club)</u> helped us.

       pro av art adj   n   v   adv pp art n

4.   We noticed an old cowboy <u>tanned deeply by the sun)</u>.   .

       art   n   hv av   pp   n   adv   v   conj   v   pp   n

5.   The store was packed (with customers) <u>Christmas shopping</u> and <u>looking (for bargains)</u>.

       v   adv   p-adj pp adj   n   art   n   av art n

6.   <u>Feeling suddenly bored (by her guests)</u>, the hostess stifled a yawn.

       pro pp adj   n   v   n   lv adj   n

7.   Which (of those men) <u>wearing suits</u> is your boss?

       av pro art n   v   pp adj   n conj   adj   n

8.   Bring me   a sundae <u>smothered (in hot fudge and whipped cream)</u>.

       hv art n   v   art   n   adv av pp adj   n

9.   Did a lady <u>carrying a baby</u> just run (by this house)?

       adv   v   pp adj   n   pn   av   pp   n   pp adj   n

10.   <u>Easily tired (since her operation)</u>, Emily rested (after lunch)(in her room).

PART II: DIRECTIONS:

      1.) Make up a participial phrase to modify the PREDICATE NOMINATIVE of the following sentence. Diagram your completed sentence.

        HE WAS AN OLD MAN ***SITTING PEACEFULLY IN THE SUNSHINE***

      2.) Make up a participial phrase to modify the OBJECT OF THE PREPOSITION in the following sentence. Diagram your completed sentence.

        I SENT A LETTER TO MY AUNT ***LIVING IN GERMANY.***

(over)

DIRECTIONS: Write what job the following words are doing in the sentences in PART I. Choose your answers from among the following:

SUBJECT   OBJECT OF THE PREPOSITION   PREDICATE NOMINATIVE

DIRECT OBJECT   INDIRECT OBJECT   MODIFIER   PREDICATE ADJECTIVE   VERB

SENTENCE #	WORD	JOB
1	package	*direct object*
2	meat	*object of the preposition*
2	stranger	*object of the preposition*
3	men	*subject*
3	us	*direct object*
4	deeply	*modifier*
5	was packed	*verb*
6	bored	*predicate adjective*
7	suits	*direct object*
8	hot	*modifier*
9	house	*object of the preposition*
10	Emily	*subject*

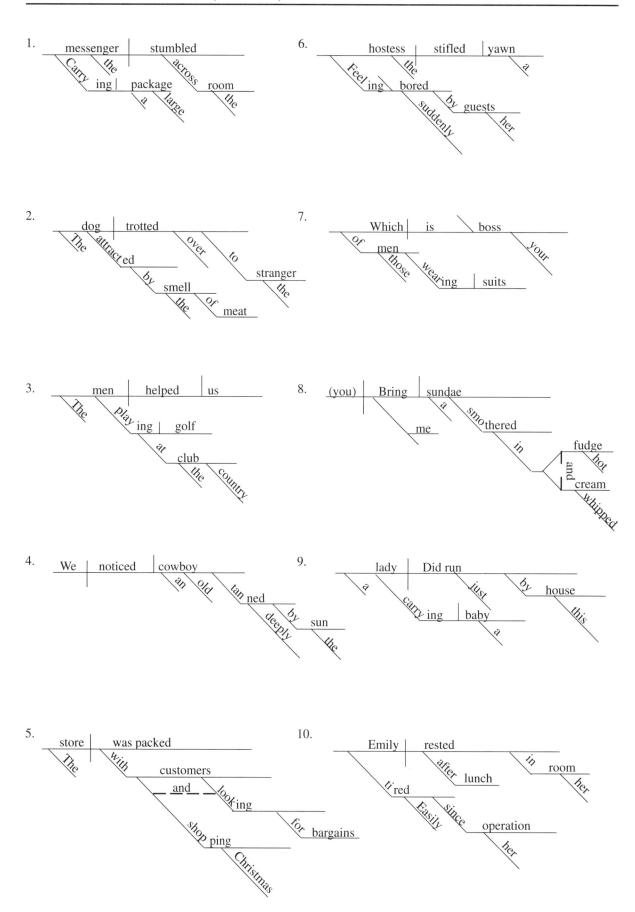

PARTICIPIAL PHRASES: TEST

NAME:_____PERIOD:_____DATE:_____

(Raw Score:_____/309 Grade:_____)

PART I: DIRECTIONS: *Parse the sentences below and put parentheses around the prepositional phrases. Under-*
line the participial phrases. Diagram the sentences. CHECK THE BACK FOR MORE WORK.

<pre>
              adv   av pro pp adj   n   v   art adj   n
___ 1.   Please introduce me (to that man) wearing the blue sweater.
12
</pre>

<pre>
              art   n   lv   adj   n   v   art   n   adj n pp art n
___ 2.   The thief was either that man carrying the briefcase or that boy (with the bike).
16   ‾conj‾
</pre>

<pre>
          v   pp n   art   n   lv adv p-adj
___ 3.   Painted (in oils), the picture was very beautiful.
10
</pre>

<pre>
              adv pro av   n   v   pp art adj   adj   n
___ 4.   Yesterday we heard speeches given (by the major political candidates).
12
</pre>

<pre>
          pro av adj   n   v   pp pn   art adj   n
___ 5.   I sent my cousin living (in Germany) a graduation announcement.
12
</pre>

<pre>
           v   art   n conj v   art n adv art adj n   av   pp n
___ 6.   Winding the clock and putting the cat out, the old man prepared (for bed).
17
</pre>

<pre>
          pro lv art   n   v   pp   n
___ 7.   It was a marriage made (in heaven).
9
</pre>

<pre>
           v   p-adj   pp art n   art n   av   pp   pro pp art n
___ 8.   Becoming conscious (of the smoke), the boy looked (around him)(for a fire).
17
</pre>

<pre>
          lv art   n   v   adj adj n   adj n
___ 9.   Is the woman wearing that fur coat your aunt?
10
</pre>

<pre>
              art   n   v   pp art adj n   av   adv   pp art n
___ 10.   The boy, munching (on a large roll), ambled slowly (down the street),
15
</pre>

===
130

(over)

159

DIRECTIONS: **PART II:** *Write what job each word is doing. Choose your answers from among the following:*

SUBJECT   DIRECT OBJECT   PREDICATE NOMINATIVE   INDIRECT OBJECT

OBJECT OF THE PREPOSITION   MODIFIER   PREDICATE ADJECTIVE   VERB

SENTENCE #	WORD	JOB
1	introduce	*verb*
1	sweater	*direct object*
2	man	*predicate nominative*
3	beautiful	*predicate adjective*
4	we	*subject*
4	speeches	*direct object*
5	cousin	*indirect object*
5	announcement	*direct object*
6	clock	*direct object*
7	It	*subject*
7	marriage	*predicate nominative*
8	conscious	*predicate adjective*
9	fur	*modifier*
9	aunt	*predicate nominative*
10	boy	*subject*
10	roll	*object of the preposition*

(5

points

each)

===
80

RAW SCORE		GRADE		%
309 - 302	=	A++	=	98+
301 - 293	=	A+	=	95
292 - 278	=	A	=	90
277 - 262	=	B+	=	85
261 - 247	=	B	=	80
246 - 231	=	C+	=	75
230 - 216	=	C	=	70
215 - 200	=	D+	=	65
199 - 185	=	D	=	60

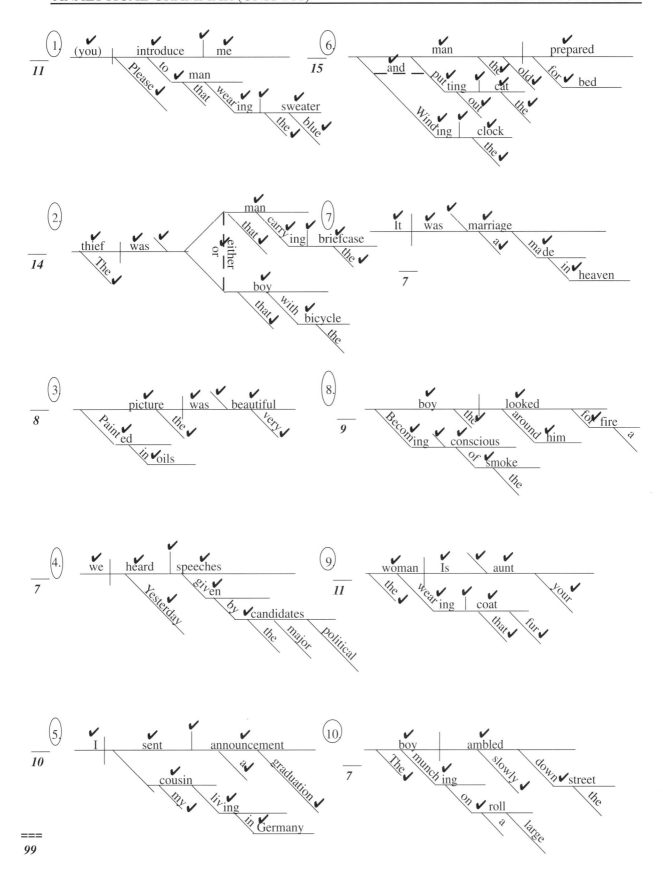

GERUND PHRASES

DEFINITION: A **GERUND** is a verb ending in "ing" which is used as a noun.

EXAMPLE: **v or n   lv   adj   n**
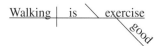

"Walking," which is usually thought of as a verb, is the subject of the above N-LV-N sentence.

A gerund can do any job a noun can do: subject, direct object, predicate nominative, indirect object, or object of the preposition.

But sometimes gerunds behave like verbs, too. They can, for example, take a direct object, etc. When they behave like verbs - as well as nouns - they are called **GERUND PHRASES** and must be diagramed in a special way.

The gerund phrase goes on a little "stilt" up above the place in the sentence for the noun the gerund phrase is substituting. For example, if the gerund phrase is a subject, the stilt goes in the subject space; if it is a direct object, the stilt goes in the direct object space; etc. Here are some examples of various types of gerund phrases doing various types of jobs:

A. <u>GERUND PHRASE AS A SUBJECT</u>

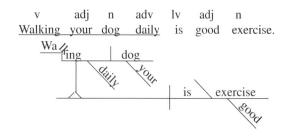

B. <u>GERUND PHRASE AS DIRECT OBJECT</u>

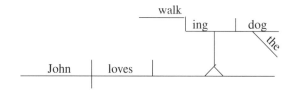

(over)

C. GERUND PHRASE AS PREDICATE NOMINATIVE

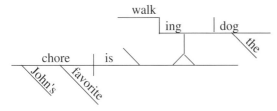

    adj   adj   n   lv   v   art   n
    John's favorite chore is walking the   dog.

D. GERUND PHRASE AS OBJECT OF THE PREPOSITION

    pn   lv   p-adj   pp   v   art   n
    John   is   crazy (about walking the dog.)

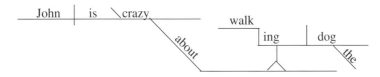

E. GERUND PHRASE AS INDIRECT OBJECT

    pn   av   v   art   n   adj   adj   n
    John calls walking the dog his favorite chore.

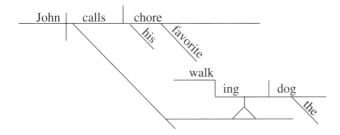

GERUND PHRASES: EXERCISE #1

NAME:_____DATE:_____

DIRECTIONS: *Parse the sentences below and put prepositional phrases in parentheses. Underline the gerund phrases. Diagram the sentences.*

       v   n   lv art adj n pp adj n
1.   Writing essays is a   major part (of our course).

       v   art   n   pp n   hv   av   pro
2.   Playing the radio (at night) may disturb others.

       pro hv adv   av   v   n
3.   I have always enjoyed playing chess.

       art   n av adv pp   v   art n art n
4.   The thief got in (by telling the guard a lie).

       adj   n   hv adv lv v   n   adv   pp adj   n
5.   His hobby has always been arguing politics heatedly (with his friends).

       art n   av pro n   pp v   pn
6.   The class gave me practice (in speaking Spanish).

       pn   av   v   art n art adj n
7.   Mortimer gives playing the guitar a bad name.

       *adj   v   art n   pp art n   av   art n
8.   Molly's rattling the dishes (in the kitchen) awakened the baby.

*Since a gerund is a verb that acts like a noun, the word _Molly's_ could be parsed as either an adjective or an adverb.

       adj adj   n   lv v   pro   adj   n
9.   Her favorite pastime is telling everyone her troubles.

       pro av   v   art adj n
10.   I dislike teasing the little boy.

(over)

        Photocopying this product is strictly prohibited by copyright law.

DIRECTIONS: *Write what jobs the following words are doing. Choose your answers from among the following:*

SUBJECT	*PREDICATE NOMINATIVE*	*DIRECT OBJECT*	*INDIRECT OBJECT*
OBJECT OF THE PREPOSITION	*PREDICATE ADJECTIVE*	*MODIFIER*	*VERB*

Sentence #	Word	Job
1	essays	*direct object*
1	part	*predicate nominative*
2	others	*direct object*
3	I	*subject*
4	guard	*indirect object*
5	heatedly	*modifier*
6	me	*indirect object*
7	guitar	*direct object*
8	Molly's rattling the dishes in the kitchen	*subject*
9	pastime	*subject*
9	everyone	*indirect object*
10	boy	*direct object*

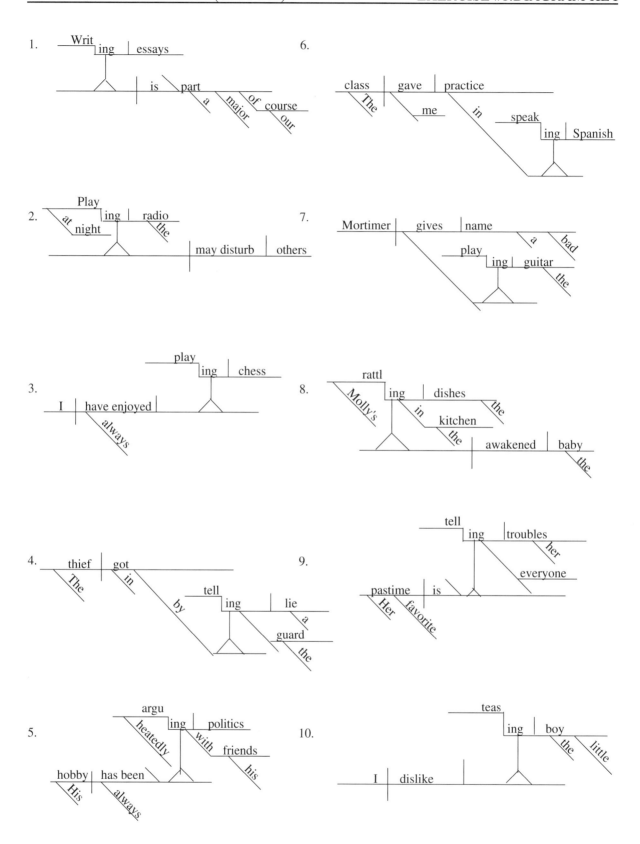

GERUND PHRASES: EXERCISE #2

NAME:_____DATE:_____

DIRECTIONS: *Parse the sentences below and put prepositional phrases in parentheses. Underline the participial phrases ONCE and the gerund phrases TWICE. Diagram the sentences.*

       v art n   pp art adj n   pn av   v   n

1. Being a man (with a big heart), Jim likes helping people.

       v art n pp art n   v   pp art n   lv art adv   adj n pp   n   pp art n

2. Giving a dollar (to the man) begging (in the street) was the wealthy woman's act (of charity) (for the day).

       adj   n   adv   v   pp   n   av   v   adj   n   pp art n art adj

3. My counselor, carefully trained (in psychology), considers sharing your troubles (with a friend) a good

       n

   idea.

       v art adj   n   pro av   v   pp art   n

4. Being an incurable romantic, I love walking (in the moonlight).

       v pp art n   adv   av   n   v pp art n

5. Crying (in the movies) usually embarrasses people caught (in the act).

       art adj n pp adj n   v pp art n   lv   v   art n pp   art n

6. The last act (of their day) spent (in the desert) was watching the sunset (from the mesa).

(over)

DIRECTIONS: *Write what jobs the following words are doing. Choose your answers from among the following:*

SUBJECT   PREDICATE NOMINATIVE   DIRECT OBJECT   INDIRECT OBJECT

OBJECT OF THE PREPOSITION   PREDICATE ADJECTIVE   MODIFIER   VERB

SENTENCE #	WORD	JOB
1	man	*predicate nominative*
1	people	*direct object*
2	man	*object of the preposition*
2	woman's	*modifier*
2	charity	*object of the preposition*
3	idea	*direct object*
4	incurable	*modifier*
4	romantic	*predicate nominative*
5	usually	*modifier*
5	act	*object of the preposition*
6	desert	*object of the preposition*

1.

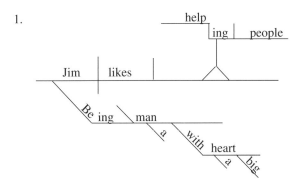

2.

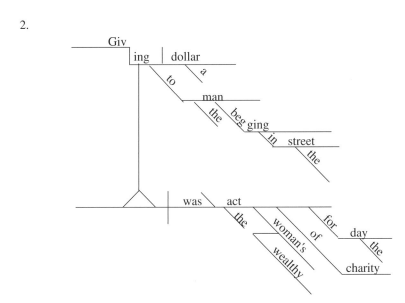

3.

(over)

169

4.

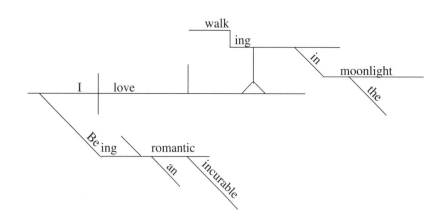

5.

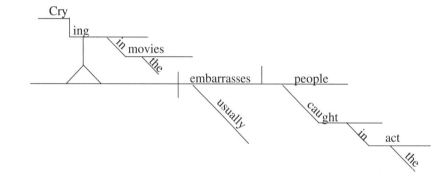

6.

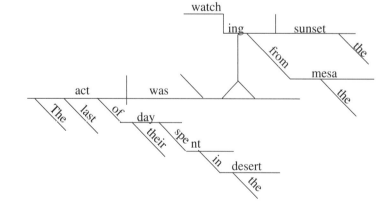

GERUND PHRASES: EXERCISE #3

NAME:_____DATE:_____

DIRECTIONS: *Parse the sentences below and put parentheses around the prepositional phrases.*
Underline the participial phrases ONCE and the gerund phrases TWICE. Diagram the sentences.

1.
        n   v   adv   pp art   n   hv   av   pp   v   art   n
    Flowers picked especially (for the occasion) were used (for decorating the ballroom).

2.
        adj   n   v   pp   adj   n   lv   v   n   pp n
    My hobby, developed (over many years), is embroidering samplers (on linen).

3.
       — pn —   av   v   n   v   pp art adj   n
    Mr. Gardner enjoys reading books written (in the 18th century).

4.
       adv   v   art adj   n   av   pro   v   pp art adj   n art adj   n
    Fluently speaking a foreign language gives anyone interested (in a diplomatic career) a distinct advantage.

5.
       adj   n   v   n   pp art pn   av   v   n art adj   n
    Many students attending college (in the Thirties) made swallowing goldfish a huge fad.

6.
       pro av — pn ——   pp   v   adj adj n   v   adv pp art   n
    I helped Mrs. Willows (by visiting her little boy) cooped up (in the hospital).

(over)

DIRECTIONS: *Write what jobs the following words are doing. Choose your answers from among the following:*

SUBJECT   PREDICATE NOMINATIVE   DIRECT OBJECT   INDIRECT OBJECT

OBJECT OF THE PREPOSITION   PREDICATE ADJECTIVE   MODIFIER   VERB

SENTENCE #	WORD	JOB
1	occasion	*object of the preposition*
1	ballroom	*direct object*
2	hobby	*subject*
2	many	*modifier*
3	books	*direct object*
4	language	*direct object*
4	advantage	*direct object*
5	made	*verb*
5	fad	*direct object*
6	boy	*direct object*
6	hospital	*object of the preposition*

1.

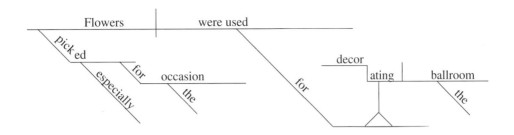

2.

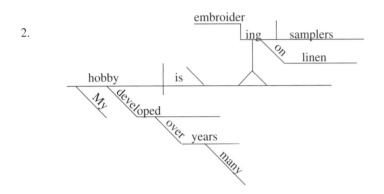

3.

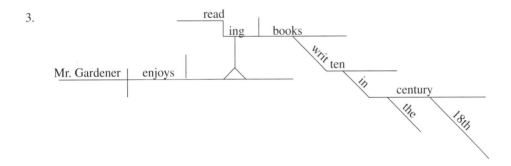

(over)

4.

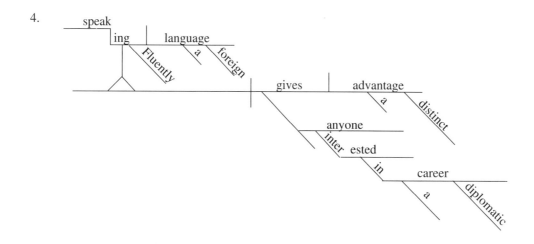

5.

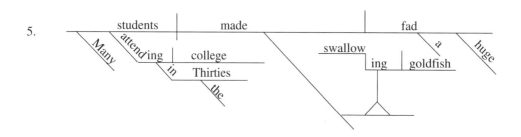

6.

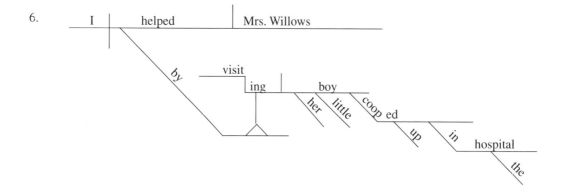

GERUND PHRASES: TEST

NAME:_____DATE:_____

(Raw Score:_____ */398* Grade:_____) */20*

DIRECTIONS: *Parse the sentences below and put parentheses around the prepositional phrases. Underline the participial phrases once and the gerund phrases twice. Diagram the sentences.*

              v   adj   n   pp pn lv art   n   pp adj   n   v   art adj   n

___ 1.   Photographing big game (in Africa) is the profession (of that man) wearing the brown jacket.
19

           art   n   v   pp art   n   av   v   art   n pp   n

___ 2.   The students seated (in the auditorium) hated hearing the bell (for class).
16

             v   art adj   n   lv art adj   n   v   pp art   n

___ 3.   Ringing the church bells is the danger signal chosen (by the villagers).
15

            adj   n   pp   v   art   n   lv   p-adj   pp art   n   v   art   n

___ 4.   His excuse (for breaking the law) sounded ridiculous (to the officer) writing the ticket.
18

        pro lv p-adj pp   v   n   conj pro av art adj   n   pp art n   v   pp— pn—

___ 5.   I was sick (of studying algebra), but I expected a good grade (on the test) given (by Mr. Wolf).
23

        adj   n   v   pp   adj   n   av   v   n   pp   n   adj adj   n

___ 6.   My cousin going (to boarding school) makes playing tricks (on people) his major pastime.
18

        art   n   v   pp art adj   n   adv   av   v   art   n

___ 7.   The car, speeding (down a narrow road), just missed hitting a child.
15

         pp   v   adj   n   pn   av   adj   n   v   art adj   n

___ 8.   (By ironing her dress), Jan helped her friend catching the early plane.
15

        adj   n   adv   v   pp art   n   av   v   art adj   n   pp pro

___ 9.   My horse, recently broken (to the saddle), enjoys exploring the bridle paths (with me).
18

          pn   v   pp adj   n   pp   n   av   v   n

___10.   Mother, accustomed (to large groups) (of people), adores planning parties.
14

===
171

(over)

     175

PART II: DIRECTIONS: *Write what jobs the following words are doing. Choose your answers from among the following:*

SUBJECT   PREDICATE NOMINATIVE   DIRECT OBJECT   INDIRECT OBJECT

OBJECT OF THE PREPOSITION   PREDICATE ADJECTIVE   MODIFIER   VERB

SENTENCE #	WORD	JOB
1	game	*direct object*
1	Africa	*object of the preposition*
1	profession	*predicate nominative*
1	brown	*modifier*
2	hated	*verb*
3	signal	*predicate nominative*
4	excuse	*subject*
4	law	*direct object*
4	ridiculous	*predicate adjective*
5	sick	*predicate adjective*
5	expected	*verb*
5	grade	*direct object*
6	boarding	*modifier*
6	people	*object of the preposition*
7	missed	*verb*
7	child	*direct object*
8	Jan	*subject*
9	horse	*subject*
10	people	*object of the preposition*

(5 points each)

RAW SCORE		GRADE		%
398 - 390	=	A++	=	98+
389 - 378	=	A+	=	95
377 - 358	=	A	=	90
357 - 338	=	B+	=	85
337 - 318	=	B	=	80
317 - 298	=	C+	=	75
297 - 278	=	C	=	70
277 - 258	=	D+	=	65
257 - 238	=	D	=	60

===
95

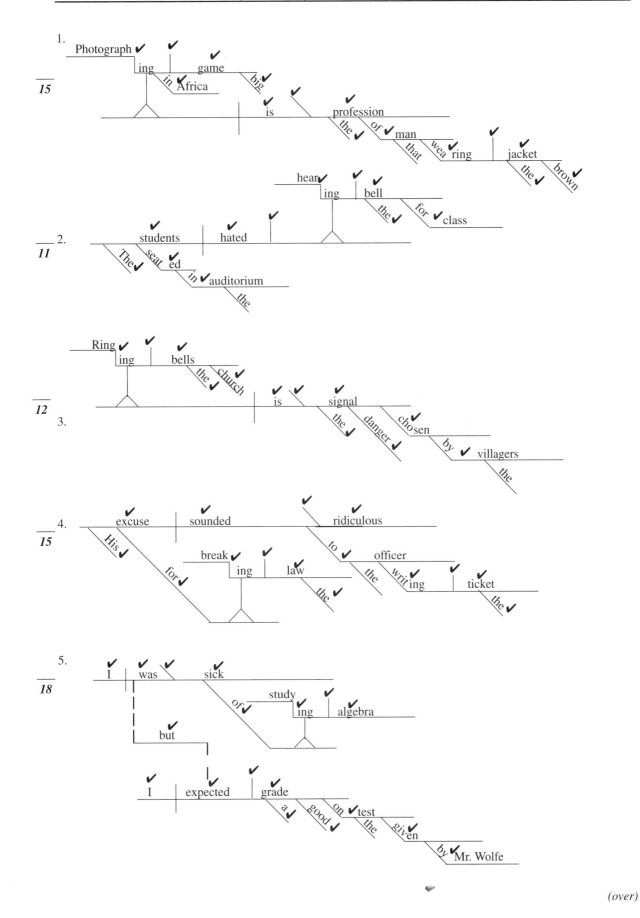

(over)

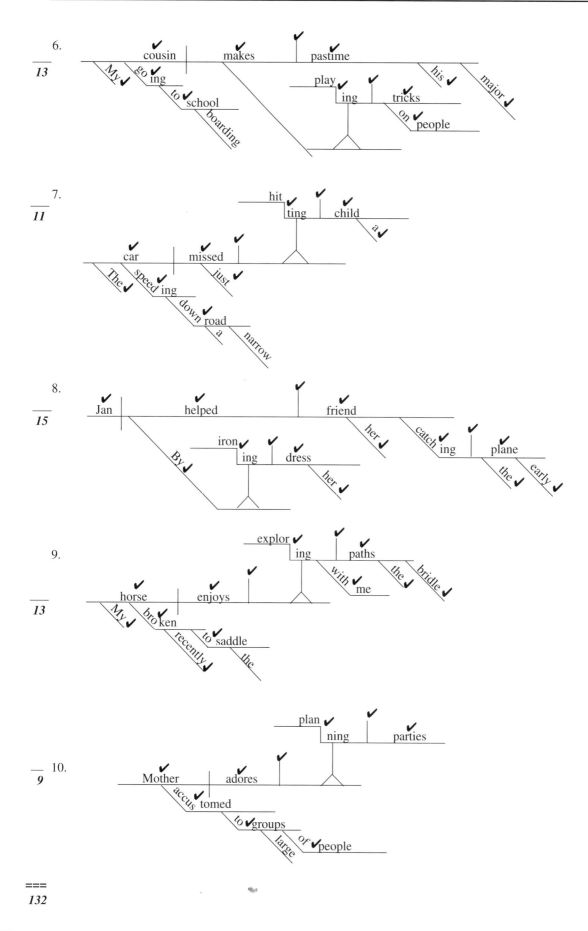

INFINITIVE PHRASES

DEFINITION: An infinitive is a verb form, almost always preceded by "to," which is used as a noun, adjective, or adverb.

EXAMPLES: Lydia refused to help. ("to help" is the direct object, a noun's job)

That was a day to remember. ("to remember" modifies "day," an adjective's job)

The senator rose to speak. ("to speak" modifies the verb "rose," an adverb's job)

Sometimes an infinitive behaves like a verb, too. It may take, for example, a direct object or be modified by an adverb. When this occurs, we call it an INFINITIVE PHRASE. Infinitives and infinitive phrases must be diagramed in a special way, depending on the job they are doing.

A.   WHEN AN INFINITIVE IS A NOUN:

EXAMPLE: -v-   pp   art   pn   lv   adj   n
            To enlist (in   the   Navy) is   his   plan.

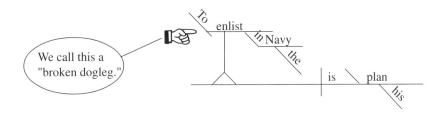

When an infinitive is a noun, your "stilt" and "broken dogleg" go above the space where that noun would go ordinarily. It can be a subject, a direct object, or a predicate nominative.   The other parts of the infinitive phrase are diagramed as if the infinitive were the verb of a sentence (for example, the infinitive's direct object is diagramed as a direct object, etc.)

B.   WHEN AN INFINITIVE IS A MODIFIER:

EXAMPLE: pro hv av   -v- art   n
            We are going to see the parade.

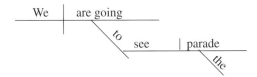

When an infinitive is a modifier, your "broken dogleg" goes underneath the word that the infinitive modifies.

(over)

C.   <u>INFINITIVE WITHOUT THE "TO":</u>

Sometimes the "to" is "understood" in an infinitive.

EXAMPLE: pn   av   v   art   n
            Dad helped <u>bake the cake</u>.

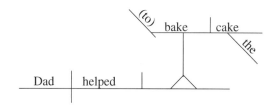

D.   <u>WHEN AN INFINITIVE HAS A SUBJECT</u>:

The infinitive is the only one of the VERBALS which may have a subject. When it does,
it is called an INFINITIVE CLAUSE. (We'll discuss clauses further in Units 19-21.) See below how to
diagram it.

EXAMPLE: pro av   pro -v- pro   pp   adj   n
            I wanted <u>him to help me (with   my   algebra.)</u>

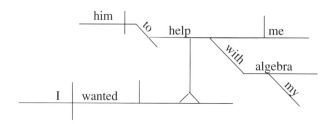

HINT: Whenever you spot a noun or a pronoun in front of your infinitive, always ask yourself, "Is that noun or
pronoun DOING THE ACTION of the infinitive?" If the answer is yes, then you have a subject for your infinitive;
in other words, you have an infinitive clause.

INFINITIVE PHRASES: EXERCISE #1

NAME:_____DATE:_____

DIRECTIONS: *Parse the sentences below and put parentheses around the prepositional phrases. Underline the infinitives and infinitives phrases. Diagram the sentences. CHECK THE BACK FOR MORE WORK.*

          — v — n   lv art adj   n
1.   To give advice is a simple matter.

          pro hv   av   - v—   art   n
2.   We were hoping to solve the puzzle.

          pn   av — v —
3.   James plans to go.

       pro av pp art   n   — v— pp pro
4.   I went (to the library) to look (for him).

         art   adj   n - v– art   n   lv— v— pro
5.   The best way to keep a secret is to forget it.

          pro   av — v — art   n   pp art   n
6.   They started to discuss the plans (for the dance).

       pro hv   av art   n   — v —
7.   I could feel the impulse to scream.

       —v— art adj   n lv art adj   n
8.   To be a good friend is an important thing.

          pn conj pn   av   v   art n
9.   Phil and Claude helped move the couch.

       art   n   lv p-adj —v —
10.   The door is difficult to open.

(over)

181

DIRECTIONS: *Write what job the following words are doing. Choose your answers from among the following:*

SUBJECT   PREDICATE NOMINATIVE   DIRECT OBJECT   INDIRECT OBJECT

OBJECT OF THE PREPOSITION   PREDICATE ADJECTIVE   MODIFIER   VERB

SENTENCE #	WORD	JOB
1	To give advice	*subject*
1	matter	*predicate nominative*
2	were hoping	*verb*
3	to go	*direct object*
4	him	*object of the preposition*
5	to keep a secret	*modifier*
6	plans	*direct object*
7	impulse	*direct object*
8	important	*modifier*
9	move the couch	*direct object*
10	difficult	*predicate adjective*

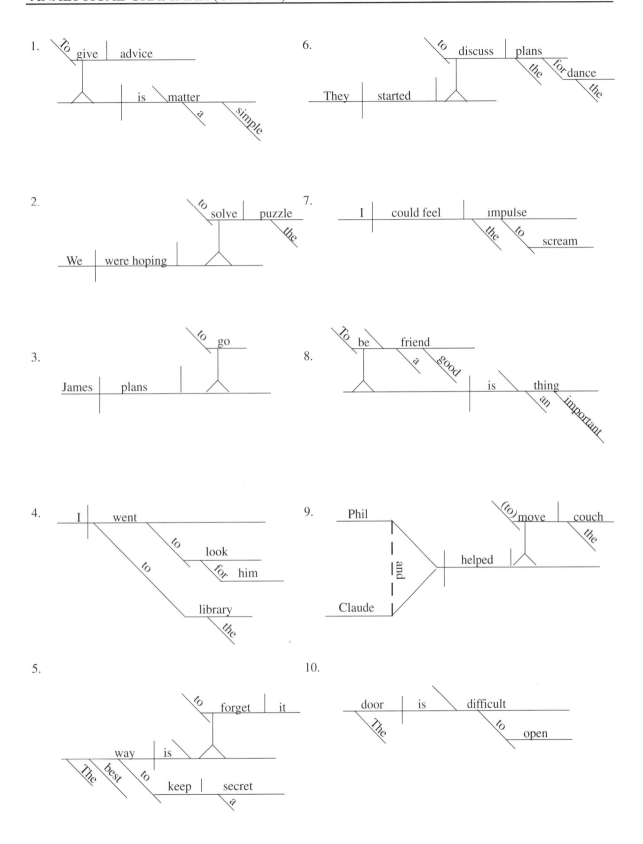

INFINITIVE PHRASES: EXERCISE #2

NAME:_____DATE:_____

DIRECTIONS: Parse the sentences below and put parentheses around the prepositional phrases. Underline the infinitives and infinitive phrases. Diagram the sentences. CHECK THE BACK FOR MORE WORK.

```
        pro  av  − v—      adv      pp    n
1.      We hope to leave immediately (after school).
```

```
     pn   hv  adv  av   v  pro art adj  n
2.      Cathy did not dare tell us the bad news.
```

```
     pro  hv  av  —v— art   n    v    pp  — pn —
3.      We are going to see the parade coming (down Main Street).
```

```
      v    adj    n     pn  av  —v—pro
4.      Hearing our footsteps, Fido ran to greet us.
```

```
     — v — art  adj   n    av  art adj   n
5.      To reach the fifth floor, take the other stairs.
```

```
       pp    v   adj   n  pro  av  — v—  art  n
6.      (After hearing her speech), I decided to become a doctor.
```

```
      hv  pro  av   pro      pp    v   art   n
7.      Have we done everything (except wash the dishes)?
```

```
     art   n    v    pp art   n    av   v  adj   n
8.      The man digging (in the quarry) helped find our baseball.
```

```
     art   n    v   pp adj    n       av  —v—art  adj   n
9.      The girls living (in my neighborhood) want to start a softball team.
```

```
     pro lv   adv    p-adj    —v—   n
10.     It is sometimes embarrassing to ask directions.
```

(over)

DIRECTIONS: *Write what job the following words are doing. Choose your answers from among the following:*

SUBJECT   PREDICATE NOMINATIVE   DIRECT OBJECT   INDIRECT OBJECT

OBJECT OF THE PREPOSITION   PREDICATE ADJECTIVE   MODIFIER   VERB

SENTENCE #	WORD	JOB
1	immediately	*modifier*
2	tell us the bad news	*direct object*
3	parade	*direct object*
4	Hearing our footsteps	*modifier*
5	stairs	*direct object*
6	hearing her speech	*object of the preposition*
7	everything	*direct object*
8	baseball	*direct object*
9	to start a softball team	*direct object*
10	embarrassing	*predicate adjective*

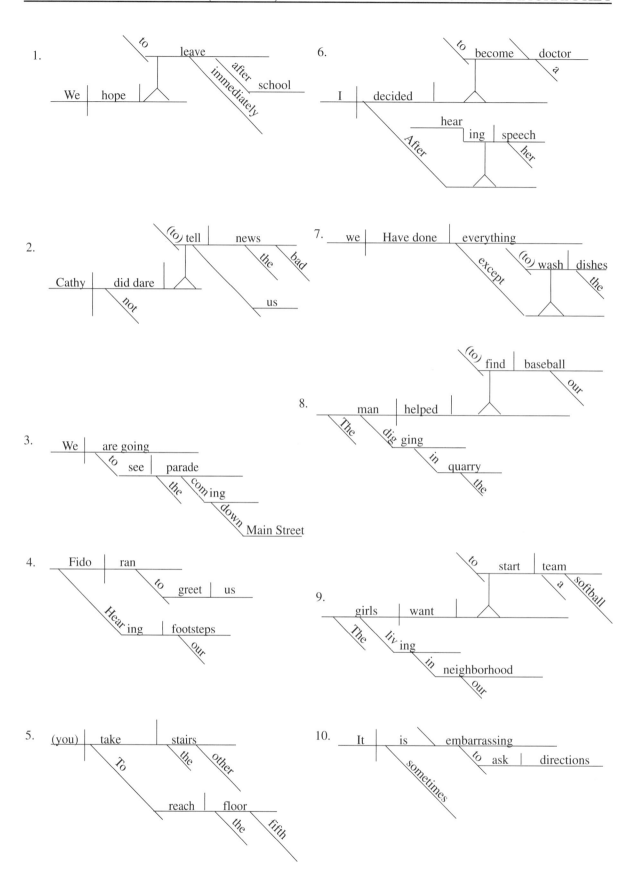

INFINITIVE PHRASES: EXERCISE #3

NAME:_____DATE:_____

DIRECTIONS: *Parse the sentences below and put parentheses around the prepositional phrases. Underline the infinitives, infinitive phrases, and infinitive clauses.. Diagram the sentences. CHECK THE BACK FOR MORE WORK.*

                n   v   pp adj   n   hv adv av — v —   art   n
1.   Persons untrained (in scuba diving) are not allowed <u>to demonstrate the equipment.</u>

               — v —   n   av art adj   n
2.   <u>To write poetry</u> requires a good vocabulary.

               pro hv av   pn —v— adj   n
3.   We are helping <u>Bob to paint his house.</u>

               pro hv av   — v —   n   v   n
4.   We are learning <u>to diagram sentences </u>containing phrases.

               ——v — art   n   v   pp pro lv p-adj
5.   <u>To interrupt a person</u> speaking (to you) is impolite.

               pro   av   art n —v — adj   n pp n
6.   We needed <u>the vet to see Prince's leg</u> (at once).

               pro lv art   n   —v — pp art n   v   pp art n
7.   She is the person <u>to see</u> (about the job) advertised (in the paper).

               hv pro av art   n   v adj n
8.   Did you see <u>the center foul our man</u>?

               pro lv p-adj —v— adj   n   v   pp art n
9.   They were glad <u>to hear his voice</u> coming (over the phone).

               pn hv adv av pro v   adv   pp   n
10.   Mom will not let <u>us swim</u> immediately (after lunch)

NOTE: Sentences 3, 6, 8, & 10 contain INFINITIVE CLAUSES. Give the students a hint about this when you hand out this homework. They should look at their notes carefully before doing this exercise.

(over)

DIRECTIONS: *Write what job the following words are doing. Choose your answers from among the following:*

SUBJECT   PREDICATE NOMINATIVE   DIRECT OBJECT   INDIRECT OBJECT

OBJECT OF THE PREPOSITION   PREDICATE ADJECTIVE   MODIFIER   VERB

SENTENCE #	WORD	JOB
1	untrained in scuba diving	*modifier*
2	To write poetry	*subject*
3	Bob	*subject*
4	phrases	*direct object*
5	speaking to you	*modifier*
6	the vet to see Prince's leg at once	*direct object*
7	advertised in the paper	*modifier*
8	man	*direct object*
9	glad	*predicate adjective*
10	lunch	*object of the preposition*

Photocopying this product is strictly prohibited by copyright law.

1.

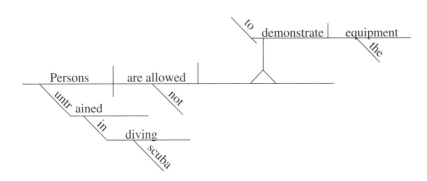

2.

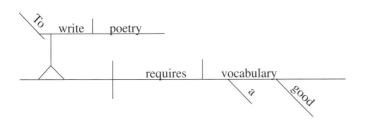

3.

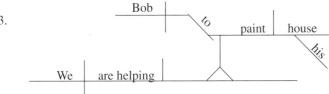

4.

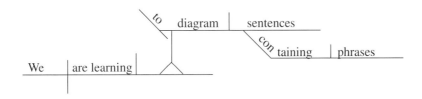

5.

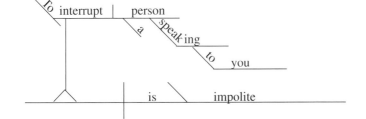

(over)

6.

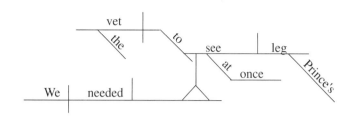

7.

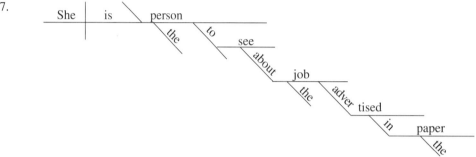

8.

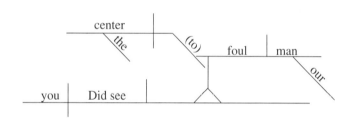

9.

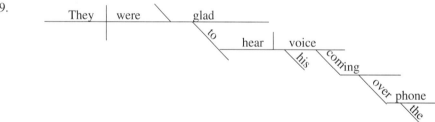

10.

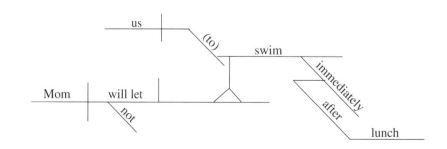

INFINITIVE PHRASES: TEST

NAME:_____DATE:_____

(Raw Score:_____/308_ Grade:_____)

PART I: DIRECTIONS: *Parse the sentences below and put prepositional phrases in parentheses. Underline the INFINITIVE PHRASES and INFINITIVE CLAUSES. Diagram the sentences. CHECK THE BACK FOR MORE WORK.*

```
           adj    n    av   pro— v — art   n
___ 1.     My father helped me to wash the car.
 8
```

```
           pn   hv  adv  av — v — adv  pp   n
___ 2.     Dad does not want to go out (after dinner).
 10
```

```
           hv  pro  av   pn    v   adj  adj    n    *adv
___ 3.     Did you hear Rochelle sing your favorite song yesterday?
 10
```

```
           pro hv   av   — v — art  adj      n     v    adv *adv
___ 4.     I am expecting **to meet the six-o'clock train arriving here today.
 11
```

```
           — v — adj   n    lv  adj adj   n    pp   v    pp    pn
___ 5.     To see movie stars was our main motive (for going) (to Hollywood).
 14
```

```
           pro lv  adv   p-adj  pp art adj    n   — v — adv   adv
___ 6.     It is often necessary (in a crowded bus) to step very carefully.
 13
```

```
           art  adj   n   v    art  adj  n  hv  av  — v —  p-adj    pp art  n
___ 7.     The young lady wearing the plaid coat is trying to look interested (in the game).
 16
```

```
           hv  pro  av art  n    v   adj    adj       n
___ 8.     Did you see the team play their championship game?
 10
```

```
           pn   av  pro — v — pp art  adj    n    pp    n
___ 9.     Jack dared us to walk (by the haunted house) (at midnight).
 13
```

```
           pn    av      — v —pro art adj  n     adv      v    pp   v    n
___ 10.    Jim wanted **to tell us  a ghost story especially designed (for scaring people).
 14
```

*These adverbs modify either the verbal or the main verb; either answer is correct - in the underlining and in the diagram.

===   ** The underlining point should count if they underlined what's shown plus the modifiers
119   "arriving here today" and "especially designed for scaring people."

(over)

PART II: DIRECTIONS: *Write what job each of the following words is doing. Choose your answers from among the following:*

SUBJECT   PREDICATE NOMINATIVE   DIRECT OBJECT   INDIRECT OBJECT

OBJECT OF THE PREPOSITION   PREDICATE ADJECTIVE   MODIFIER   VERB

SENTENCE #	WORD	JOB
1	me	*subject*
2	not	*modifier*
2	dinner	*object of the preposition*
3	yesterday	*modifier*
4	am expecting	*verb*
4	arriving here today	*modifier*
5	To see movie stars	*subject*
5	going to Hollywood	*object of the preposition*
6	It	*subject*
6	necessary	*predicate adjective*
6	very	*modifier*
7	wearing a plaid coat	*modifier*
8	you	*subject*
8	game	*direct object*
9	house	*object of the preposition*
10	us	*indirect object*
10	scaring people	*object of the preposition*

(5 points each)

RAW SCORE		GRADE		%
308	301	=	A++ =	98+
300 -	292	=	A+ =	95
291 -	277	=	A =	90
276 -	261	=	B+ =	85
260 -	246	=	B =	80
245 -	231	=	C+ =	75
230 -	215	=	C =	70
214 -	200	=	D+ =	65
199 -	184	=	D =	60

===
85

1.

<u>9</u>

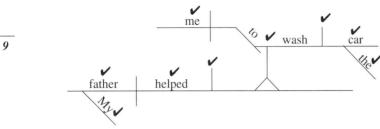

2.

<u>7</u>

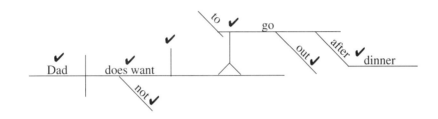

3.

<u>10</u>

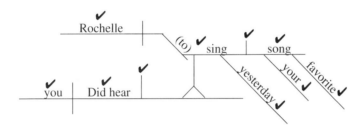

4.

<u>11</u>

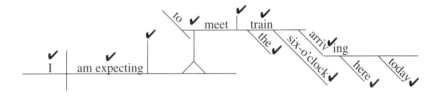

5.

<u>12</u>

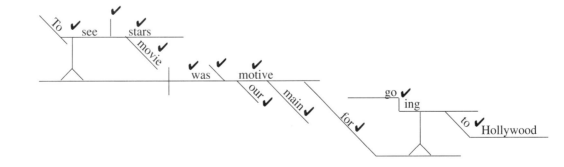

(over)

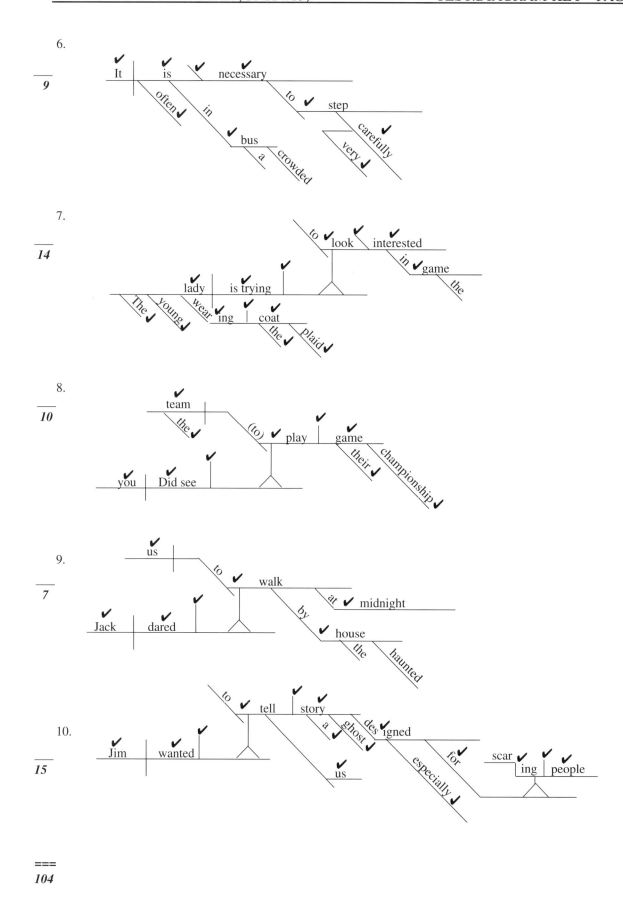

6.

___
9

7.

___
14

8.

___
10

9.

___
7

10.

___
15

===
104

APPOSITIVE PHRASES

DEFINITION: An **APPOSITIVE** is a noun or a pronoun which usually follows another noun or pronoun and **RESTATES** it to help identify or explain it. When the appositive has modifiers, it is called an **APPOSITIVE PHRASE.**

>   EXAMPLE: Jimmy, <u>a star athlete</u>, will surely get a scholarship to college.

>   "a star athlete" restates who Jimmy is. It is an appositive phrase.

>   Occasionally, the appositive or appositive phrase comes in front of the noun being restated.

>   EXAMPLE: <u>A man of integrity</u>, Mr. Aldritch never cheats anyone.

THE PATTERN FOR DIAGRAMING AN APPOSITIVE PHRASE IS BELOW:

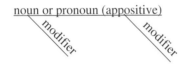

>   EXAMPLE: adj   adj   n   art   n   pp   art   n   lv   art   n   pp
>   Our honored guest, <u>the author (of   the book)</u>, is   a   friend (of

>   —n—   adj   n
>   Mr. Williams, <u>our mayor)</u>.

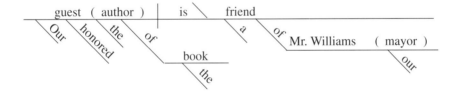

APPOSITIVE PHRASES: EXERCISE #1

NAME:_____DATE:_____

DIRECTIONS: *Parse the sentences below and put prepositional phrases in parentheses. Underline the appositives and appositive phrases. Diagram the sentences. CHECK THE BACK FOR MORE WORK.*

```
      adj   n   av art  adj   n   art  — pn ———
```
1.   Our school has a dramatic club, the Thespian Society.

```
      —  pn —  art   adj    n   lv art adj   n
```
2.   Mrs. Hinckley, an English teacher, is the club sponsor.

```
      n    pp art n   adj      n        av  art   n   pp art adj    n
```
3.   Officers (of the club), mostly upperclassmen, planned a program (for the next assembly).

```
      art   n   hv  av   pp   pn   art n  pp adj  adj    n
```
4.   The program was presented (on Tuesday), the day (of our weekly meeting).

```
      — pn —  art adj    n       av    — pn ——    n   pp art adj   adj     n
```
5.   Jim Carson, the program chairman, introduced David Haynes, director (of the city's repertory company).

```
      pp    — pn ——     n   pp art  — pn ——    — pn —   av  adj  n   pp n
```
6.   (From Nina Mason,) president (of the Thespian Society), Mr. Haynes received our award (of merit,)
```
      art n    v    pp adj   n
```
      a plaque designed (by club members).

(over)

DIRECTIONS: *Write what job each of the words below is doing. Choose your answers from among the following:*

SUBJECT   PREDICATE NOMINATIVE   DIRECT OBJECT   INDIRECT OBJECT

OBJECT OF THE PREPOSITION   PREDICATE ADJECTIVE   MODIFIER   VERB

SENTENCE #	WORD	JOB
1	school	*subject*
2	English	*modifier*
2	sponsor	*predicate nominative*
3	program	*direct object*
4	Tuesday	*object of the preposition*
5	introduced	*verb*
6	Nina Mason	*object of the preposition*

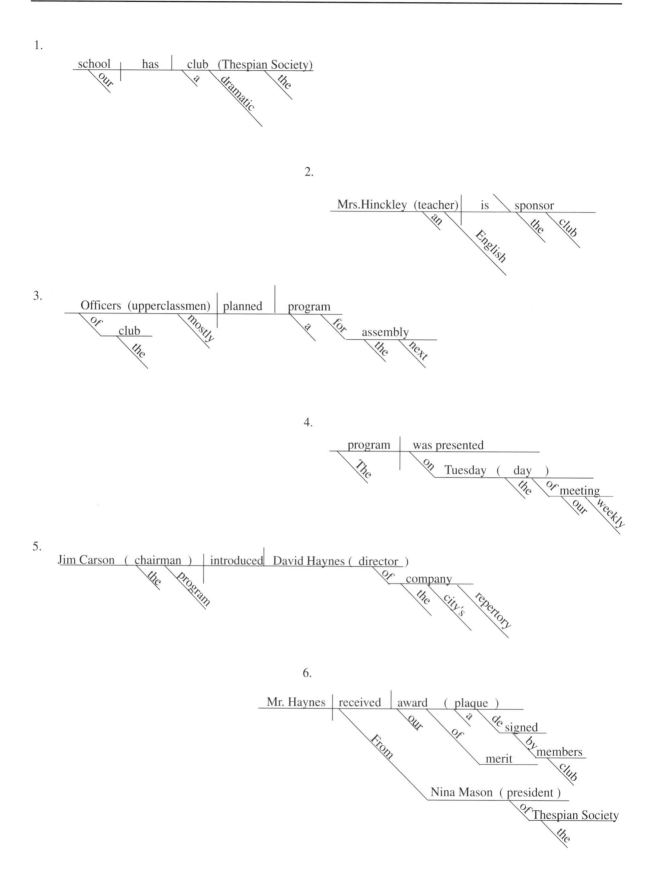

APPOSITIVE PHRASES: EXERCISE #2

NAME:_____DATE:_____

DIRECTIONS: *Parse the sentences below and put prepositional phrases in parentheses. Underline the appositives and appositive phrases. Diagram the sentences. CHECK THE BACK FOR MORE WORK.*

    pn adj adj n adv av v adj n

1. Jason, <u>my little nephew</u>, still enjoys hearing nursery rhymes.

   adj n − pn — hv av pro pp v pp pn

2. My friend <u>Mary Jo</u> will visit us (before leaving)(for Europe).

   ‾‾ pn ‾ art n pp art ‾ adj‾ n lv art adj n pp adj n v

3. Carolyn Keene, <u>the author (of the Nancy Drew stories)</u>, is a popular writer (with young people) interested

   pp n

   (in mysteries).

    hv pro av — pn —— adj adj n

4. Have you met Marie Ritterman, <u>my best friend</u>?

    n adj adj n v adv adv lv adv p-adj pp adj n

5. Science, <u>my favorite class taken this year</u>, gets more fascinating (with each month).

    art adj n n pp art adj n av − v — pp n adv

6. The Randolph twins, <u>members (of the track team)</u>, have to report (for practice) soon.

     pn art adj n   adv av pro pp adj n pp art n

7. Archimedes, <u>a Greek physicist</u>, supposedly made one (of his discoveries) (in the bathtub).

(over)

DIRECTIONS: *Write what job each of the following words is doing. Choose your answers from among the following:*

SUBJECT   DIRECT OBJECT   INDIRECT OBJECT   PREDICATE NOMINATIVE

OBJECT OF THE PREPOSITION   PREDICATE ADJECTIVE   MODIFIER   VERB

SENTENCE #	WORD	JOB
1	hearing nursery rhymes	*direct object*
2	will visit	*verb*
3	writer	*predicate nominative*
3	mysteries	*object of the preposition*
4	best	*modifier*
5	Science	*subject*
5	fascinating	*predicate adjective*
6	soon	*modifier*
7	supposedly	*modifier*

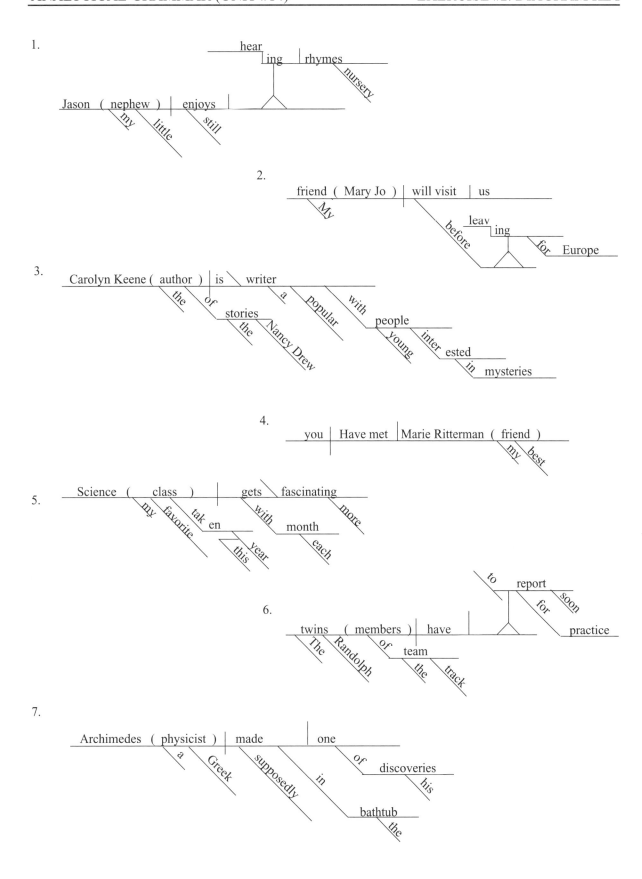

APPOSITIVE PHRASES: EXERCISE #3

NAME:_____DATE:_____

DIRECTIONS: *Parse the sentences below and put parentheses around the prepositional phrases. Underline the appositives and appositive phrases. Diagram the sentences. CHECK THE BACK FOR MORE WORK.*

    art n v adv adv av — v— pp adj n art   adj   adj   n

1.   The boy living next door loved to work (on his car,) <u>a dilapidated old wreck.</u>

    adj pro pp art   n   art n conj art n   hv av   pp art n   v   pp   n

2.   Only two (of the animals), <u>a horse and a cow</u>, were saved (from the fire) started (by lightning).

    art adj   adj   n   n pp art n   av art n   – v— pp art   n

3.   A black funnel-shaped cloud, <u>sign (of a tornado)</u>, forced the family to hide (in the cellar).

    —— pn —— art adj   n pp adj   n   lv art n pp adj   n   v   adv

4.   *Little Women*, <u>a favorite book (for young people)</u>, was a part (of my education) considered absolutely

    p-adj

    necessary.

    — pn — adj   adj   n   adv av   n   v   adv pp art n   pp art — pn ——

5.   Mr. Chang, <u>my geography teacher</u>, once visited natives living deep (in the jungles)(of the Amazon Valley).

    v   art   n   lv art n pp adj n   — pn —   pp —— pn ———

6.   Catching a sailfish is the goal (of my uncle), <u>Ray Belson (of Richmond, Virginia).</u>

(over)

          Photocopying this product is strictly prohibited by copyright law.

DIRECTIONS: *Write what job each of the following words is doing. Choose your answers from among the following:*

SUBJECT   PREDICATE NOMINATIVE   DIRECT OBJECT   INDIRECT OBJECT

OBJECT OF THE PREPOSITION   PREDICATE ADJECTIVE   MODIFIER   VERB

SENTENCE #	WORD	JOB
1	living next door	*modifier*
2	two	*subject*
2	lightning	*object of the preposition*
3	family	*subject*
4	part	*predicate nominative*
4	considered absolutely necessary	*modifier*
5	natives	*direct object*
6	Catching a sailfish	*subject*
6	uncle	*object of the preposition*

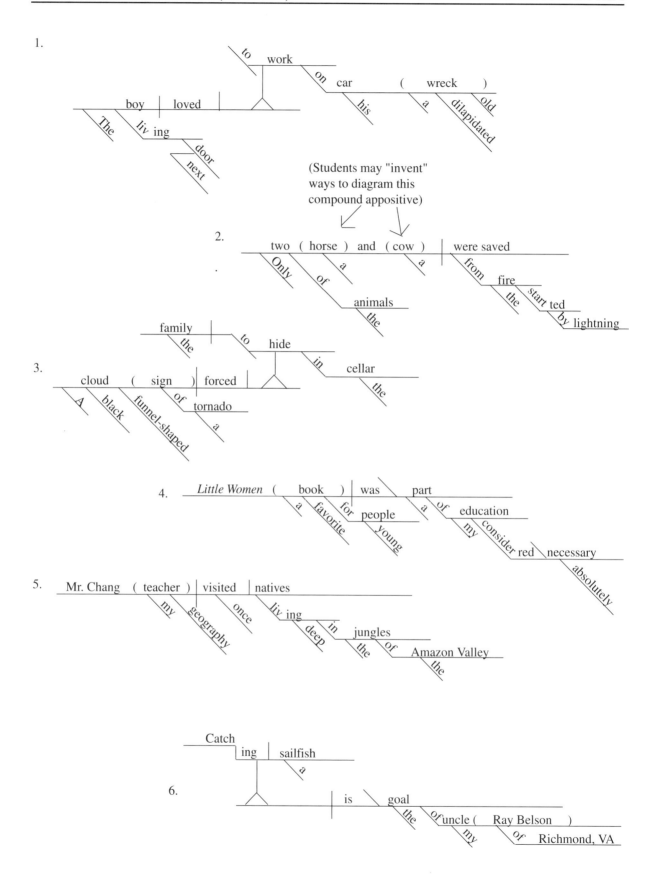

1.

(Students may "invent"
ways to diagram this
compound appositive)

2.

3.

4.

5.

6.

APPOSITIVE PHRASES: TEST

NAME:_____DATE: _____

(RAW SCORE:_____ _/37*4*_ GRADE:_____)

DIRECTIONS: *Parse the sentences below and put prepositional phrases in parentheses. Underline appositives and appositive phrases. Diagram the sentences. CHECK THE BACK FOR MORE WORK.*

        pp   v —— pn ——   adj adv adj n pro adv av — v — art n
___ 1.   (After seeing *Gone With the Wind*), <u>my very favorite movie</u>, I usually want to re-read the book.
15

      art adj   adj   n   —— pn —— lv art adj   adj   adj   n   v pp art n
___ 2.   The story's main character, <u>Scarlett O'Hara</u>, is a beautiful, spoiled southern belle living (on a plantation)
19   *v   pn*
     named Tara.

        — v — — pn ——   n pp art adj   n   lv adj adj n
___ 3.   To marry Ashley Wilkes, <u>heir (to a neighboring plantation)</u>, is her one desire.
13

      pn hv   av   — v —— pn   art adj adj   n   v   pp pro
___ 4.   Ashley is engaged to marry Melanie,<u> a sweet young woman beloved (by everyone).</u>
14

      — pn — art n   av conj av pp n   pp   pn
___ 5.   Rhett Butler, <u>a gambler,</u> meets and falls (in love)(with Scarlett).
13

      art — pn — adj adj   n   — v — art   n   av adv conj av adj adj   n
___ 6.   The Civil War, <u>that tragic struggle to free the slaves</u>, comes along and destroys their privileged way
19   *pp n*
     (of life).

      pn hv   av conj pn   n pp art pn   hv   av —v — adj   n
___ 7.   Tara is destroyed and Scarlett, <u>head (of the O'Haras),</u> must struggle to feed her family.
16

      pn   av   — pn — art adj n   v   pp   n
___ 8.   Scarlett marries Rhett Butler,<u> a rich man yearning (for respectability).</u>
11

> I have found it helpful over the years to explain a little about the story of *Gone With the Wind* before
> students take this test. They need to have it explained, for example, that <u>Tara</u> is a plantation and that <u>Ashley</u>
> <u>Wilkes</u> is a <u>man</u>! They might also need to be told what a "southern belle" is. Then they do just fine!

(over)

              adj   n   art   adj   pro   av   pp art   n   pp adj adj   n   art   n

__19__ 9.   Their marriage, <u>an unhappy one</u>, ends (at the death)(of their only child,) <u>a daughter</u>.

              pn art adj   n   pp   n   adv   av   conj pn   adv   v   adj   n

__21__ 10.   Rhett, <u>a good man (at heart,)</u> finally leaves, and Scarlett, now realizing her mistakes,

              av — v —   pp pn

===   decides to return (to Tara).

__160__

PART II: *Write what job the following words are doing. Choose your answers from among the following:*
          SUBJECT   PREDICATE NOMINATIVE   DIRECT OBJECT   MODIFIER

OBJECT OF THE PREPOSITION   VERB   INDIRECT OBJECT   PREDICATE ADJECTIVE

SENTENCE #	WORD	JOB
1	to re-read the book	*direct object*
2	main	*modifier*
2	belle	*predicate nominative*
2	named Tara	*modifier*
3	To marry Ashley Wilkes	*subject*
3	neighboring	*modifier*
4	Melanie	*direct object*
5	Rhett Butler	*subject*
5	Scarlett	*object of the preposition*
6	slaves	*direct object*
6	privileged	*modifier*
7	must struggle	*verb*
8	Rhett Butler	*direct object*
8	respectability	*object of the preposition*
9	unhappy	*modifier*
9	child	*object of the preposition*
10	to return to Tara	*direct object*

(5

points

each)

RAW			
SCORE		GRADE	%
374 - 366	=	A++	= 98+
365 - 355	=	A+	= 95
354 - 336	=	A	= 90
335 - 317	=	B+	= 85
316 - 299	=	B	= 80
298 - 280	=	C+	= 75
279 - 261	=	C	= 70
260 - 243	=	D+	= 65
242 - 224	=	D	= 60

===

__85__

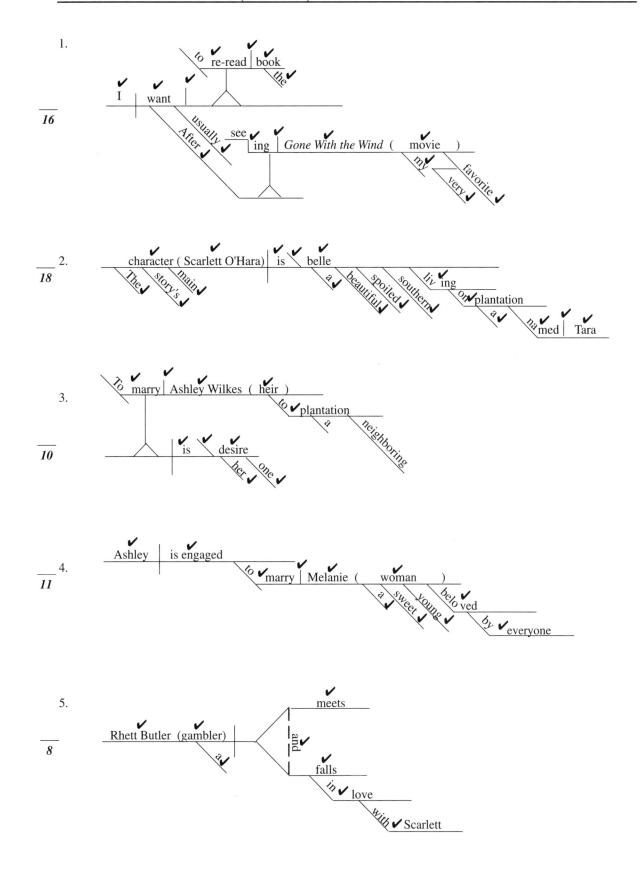

1.

16

2.

18

3.

10

4.

11

5.

8

(over)

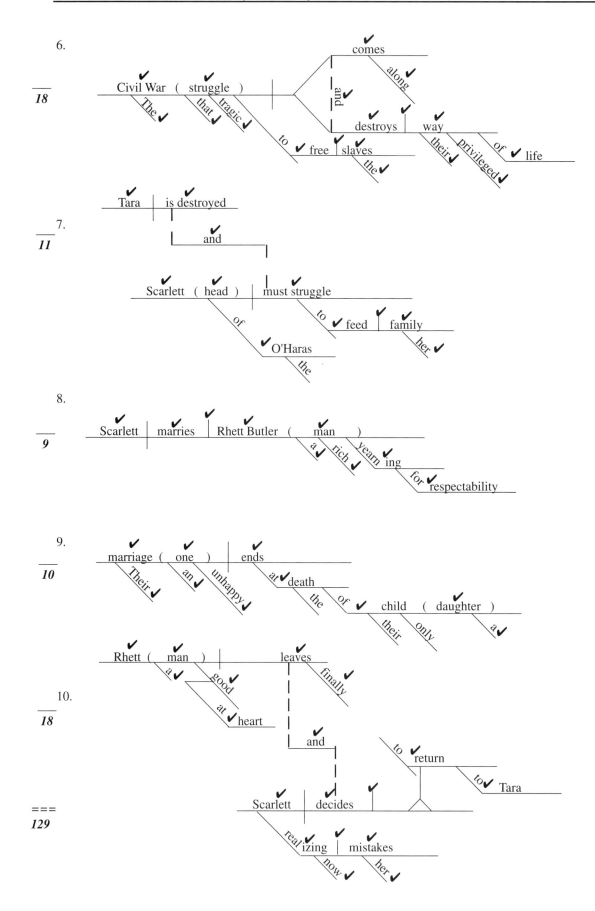

ADJECTIVE CLAUSES

Before discussing ADJECTIVE CLAUSES in particular, it is necessary to discuss CLAUSES in general. A CLAUSE is a group of words that contains a verb <u>and its subject</u> and is used as part of a sentence. If a clause expresses a <u>complete thought</u>, then we call it a SENTENCE (if it's all by itself) or an INDEPENDENT CLAUSE (if it's attached to another clause). If a clause does NOT <u>express a complete thought</u>, then we call it a DEPENDENT or SUBORDINATE CLAUSE.

DEPENDENT or SUBORDINATE clauses need INDEPENDENT clauses to complete their meaning.

     EXAMPLE: <u>After it stopped raining</u>, we played softball.

     The subordinate clause "After it stopped raining" is not a complete thought by itself. Put together with the independent clause "we played softball," it has meaning.

     (EXERCISE #1 IS BASED ON THE ABOVE INFORMATION ABOUT CLAUSES IN GENERAL.)

We will now discuss ADJECTIVE CLAUSES. Obviously, an adjective clause is a clause that does the work of an adjective. In other words, it modifies a noun or pronoun. The easiest way to spot an adjective clause is to look at the FIRST WORD OF THE CLAUSE. Adjective clauses are introduced by RELATIVE PRONOUNS. You must memorize them. They are WHO, WHOM, WHOSE, WHICH, and THAT. Use WHICH or THAT when referring to things and WHO, WHOM, and WHOSE when referring to people.

The relative pronoun does two things at once. First, it "stands for" or relates to the word in the independent clause that the adjective clause is modifying. Second, it serves as part of the clause. For example, the relative pronoun might be the subject of the clause or its direct object. The following sample diagram will show you how these adjective clauses work:

     EXAMPLE: pn   pro   av   pp   pn   adv   av   pn
            Yvette, <u>who lived (in France)</u>, quickly learned English.

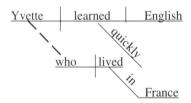

     The relative pronoun "who" (1) acts as the subject of the subordinate clause, and (2) shows that "who" stands for "Yvette."

Study the following sample diagrams:

     EXAMPLE: art   n   pro   pro av   adv   av   art   n
            The man <u>whom you met yesterday</u> bought a house.

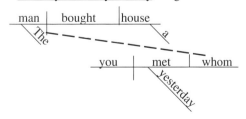

     The relative pronoun "whom" (1) acts as the direct object of the subordinate clause and (2) shows you that "whom" stands for "man" in the independent clause.

                                                                       (over)

EXAMPLE: adj n pp   pro   pro av art n av   pro art   n
               My aunt, (to whom) I sent a gift, wrote me a   letter.

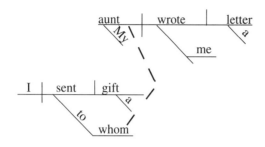

The relative pronoun "whom" (1) acts as the object of the preposition "to" and (2) shows you that "whom" stands for "aunt" in the independent clause.

EXAMPLE: pro   av   art n *pro/adj n   pro hv   av
               We thanked the man whose shovel we had borrowed.

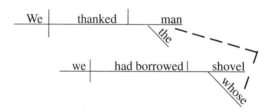

The relative pronoun "whose" (1) acts as a modifier for "shovel" and (2) shows you that "whose" stands for "man" in the independent clause.

*"Whose" is the relative pronoun, but it is acting like an adjective so it's also correct to call it an adjective. Either answer is correct here.

ADJECTIVE CLAUSES: EXERCISE #1

NAME:_____DATE:_____

DIRECTIONS: *In each sentence below, underline the subordinate clause. Look at each clause and see if you can tell whether the clause is acting like an adjective (answering the question "Which?" about a noun) or acting like an adverb (answering the questions "How?" "When?" "Why?" "Where?" about a verb, an adjective, or an adverb).*

1.   When my family went to New York last summer, we visited the Theodore Roosevelt museum.
                    *(Adverb Clause; tells **when** we "visited")*

2.   The museum has been established in the house in which Roosevelt was born.
                    *(Adjective Clause: tells **which** "house")*

3.   It is located on the basement floor of Roosevelt's birthplace, which is on East Twentieth Street.
                    *(Adjective Clause; tells **which** "birthplace")*

4.   The museum contains books, letters, and documents that pertain to Roosevelt's public life.
                    *(Adjective Clause; tells **which** "books, letters, and documents")*

5.   There are mounted heads of animals, a stuffed lion, and zebra skins from big-game hunts that Roosevelt

        went on in Africa.
                    *(Adjective Clause; tells **which** "hunts")*

6.   Because Roosevelt was once a cowboy, there are also branding irons.
                    *(Adverb Clause; tells **why** there "are" branding irons)*

7.   Before Theodore Roosevelt became President, he fought in the Spanish-American War.
                    *(Adverb Clause; tells **when** he "fought")*

8.   During the war he led the Rough Riders, who made the charge up San Juan Hill.
                    *(Adjective Clause; tells **which** "Rough Riders")*

ADJECTIVE CLAUSES: EXERCISE #2

NAME:_____DATE:_____

DIRECTIONS: *Parse the sentences below. Underline the subordinate clause and circle the relative pronoun.*
Diagram the entire sentence. CHECK THE BACK FOR MORE WORK.

         —— pn ——   av   art   n pro pro hv av
1.   Mrs. Dalton recommended the movie that I am seeing.

          adv av art   n   pro pro av   pp pro
2.   Here is the letter that I wrote (to you).

          n   pro av — v — n   hv   av   adv   adv
3.   People who want to learn languages must study every day.

          n   pro av art adj n   adv   av adv
4.   Students who read a great deal usually write well.

          pro   pp art   n   pro hv av pp   n   av pp adj   n
5.   Some (of the paintings) that were done (by students)sold (for   big money).

          pn   pro   lv art   n   pp art n   av   adj   n
6.   Mercury, who was the messenger (of the gods), wore winged sandals.

          art n   pro art   n   av   lv —pn — art adj   n
7.   The man whom the policeman wants is Jake the Snake, a petty thief.

          hv art   n adj or pro n   lv p-adj adv   av pp art   n
8.   Will the person whose lights are on please report (to the desk)?

(The word "whose" in this sentence
could be parsed as either an adjective
or a pronoun, since it is a relative
pronoun acting like an adjective)

          art n pro   av   pro   pp art n   hv adv av art   n
9.   A person who knows nothing (about a topic) should not express an opinion.

          pro lv art n   pp   pro pro av art n
10.   He is the man (from whom) I bought the car.

(over)

Photocopying this product is strictly prohibited by copyright law.

DIRECTIONS: *Write what job the following words are doing. Choose your answers from among the following:*

SUBJECT   PREDICATE NOMINATIVE   DIRECT OBJECT   INDIRECT OBJECT

OBJECT OF THE PREPOSITION   PREDICATE ADJECTIVE   MODIFIER   VERB

SENTENCE #	WORD	JOB
1	that	*direct object*
2	Here	*modifier*
3	languages	*direct object*
4	Students	*subject*
5	that	*subject*
5	money	*object of the preposition*
6	messenger	*predicate nominative*
7	whom	*direct object*
8	please	*modifier*
9	nothing	*direct object*
9	not	*modifier*
10	whom	*object of the preposition*

1.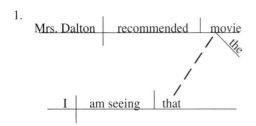

2.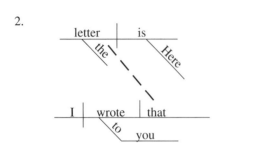

3.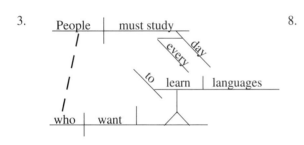

4.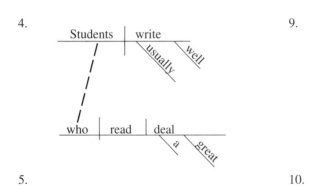

5.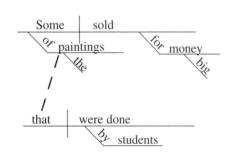

6.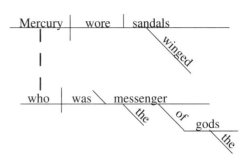

7.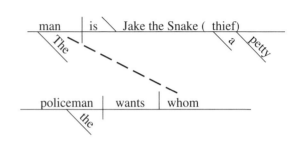

8.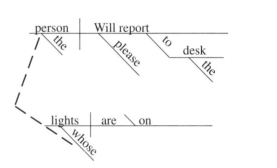

9.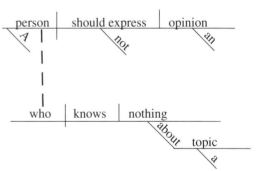

10.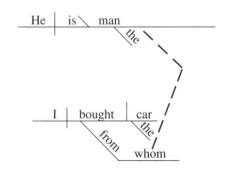

ADJECTIVE CLAUSES: EXERCISE #3

NAME:_____DATE:_____

DIRECTIONS: *Parse the sentences below. Underline the adjective clauses, circle the relative pronouns, and diagram the sentences. CHECK THE BACK FOR MORE WORK.*

　　　　pro av adv pp art n   pro —pn —   av   adv
1.　　I   did well (on the test) (that) Mrs. Freeman gave yesterday.

　　　　adj   n pro   av   adj   n   av   n   pp adj   n
2.　　My cousin, (who) enjoys practical jokes, put pepper (into my popcorn).

　　　　pn   av   pp art n pp pro pro av adj adj   n
3.　　Dad disappeared (into the shed) (in which) he kept his gardening tools.

　　　　adj   n   pro   adj   n   lv p-adj   av adj adj n
4.　　My sister, (whose) horsebackriding skills are amazing, won seven blue ribbons.

　　　　adj   n   pro lv adv p-adj pp pro hv av pn
5.　　This dress, (which is) too long (for you) may fit Mary.

DIRECTIONS: *The following pairs of sentences are short and choppy. Re-write them and combine the* <u>two</u> *sentences into* <u>one</u> *sentence using ADJECTIVE CLAUSES. You may change words, add words, delete words — your sentence must (1) contain ALL the ideas that were in the original two and (2) contain an adjective clause.*

1.　　Morris drove the white convertible. The convertible led the parade.

　　　　Morris drove the white convertible which led the parade.
　　　　The white convertible, which Morris drove, led the parade.

2.　　Einstein did not do well in school. He was a genius.

　　　　Einstein, who was a genius, did not do well in school.
　　　　Einstein, who did not do well in school, was a genius.

3.　　I ordered this hamburger. It is cold!

　　　　This hamburger that I ordered is cold.

4.　　That man is my uncle.   I have admired him for a long time.

　　　　I have admired that man, who is my uncle, for a long time.
　　　　That man, whom I have admired for a long time, is my uncle.

5.　　The policeman's badge is lost. He is retiring in 2008.

　　　　The policeman, who lost his badge, is retiring in 2008.
　　　　The policeman, who is retiring in 2008, lost his badge.

(THESE ANSWERS WILL VARY. YOU HAVE TO USE YOUR JUDGEMENT. THE PRONOUNS "WHICH" AND "THAT" ARE INTERCHANGE-ABLE.)

DIRECTIONS: *Write what job the following words are doing. Choose your answers from among the following:*

SUBJECT   DIRECT OBJECT   INDIRECT OBJECT   PREDICATE NOMINATIVE

OBJECT OF THE PREPOSITION   PREDICATE ADJECTIVE   MODIFIER   VERB

SENTENCE #	WORD	JOB
1	well	*modifier*
1	that	*direct object*
2	who	*subject*
3	which	*object of the preposition*
4	ribbons	*direct object*
5	long	*predicate adjective*

Photocopying this product is strictly prohibited by copyright law.

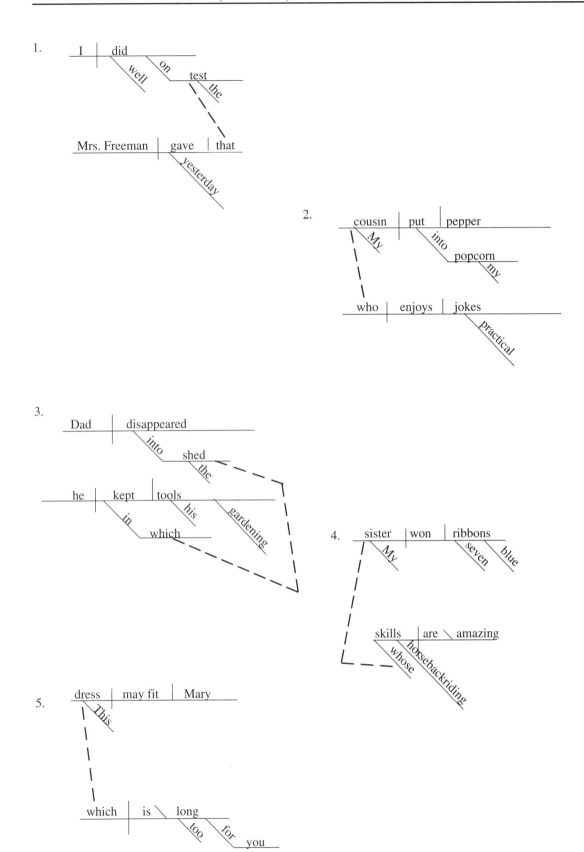

ADJECTIVE CLAUSES: TEST

NAME:_____ DATE:_____

(RAW SCORE:_____ */381* GRADE:_____)

PART I: DIRECTIONS: *Parse the sentences below. Underline the adjective clauses, circle the relative pronouns, and diagram the sentences. CHECK THE BACK FOR MORE WORK.*

                 n   lv   n   ~~pro~~ av adj   n
____1. Antonyms are words (which) have opposite meanings.
9

         adj   n   lv art n ~~pro~~ hv adv   lv   adv p-adj
____2. Scuba diving is a sport (that) is now becoming very popular.
13

       pn ~~pro~~ lv art adj   n   pp   pn   av adj n   ̄ v ̄   adv   pp   art n
____3. Pluto, (which) is the farthest planet (from Earth), takes 248 years to revolve once (around the sun).
20

      art   n   hv   av pp art pro ~~adj~~ adj n   lv p-adj
____4. A scholarship was awarded (to the one) (whose) short story was best.
15

      pro av   pro ~~pro~~ pro av pp art n
____5. We invited everyone (whom) we knew (to the party).
12

       n   pp adj   n   pro   av   pp   n   lv adv p-adj pp   n   ̄ v ̄
____6. Words (in our language) (which) begin (with "th") are often hard (for foreigners to pronounce).
19

     ̄ pn ̄   pro pp adj   n   lv adj   adj   adj   n   av pp pn
____7. Robert Frost, (who) (for many years) was our unofficial national poet, died (in 1963).
17

     pp adj n pn av art n   pp   pro   ~~pro~~ pro av conj av
____8. (In her diary) Jane kept a record (of everything) (that) she did and thought.
18

      pn   lv art adj   n   pro hv hv   av   adv pp art n
____9. Achilles was the Greek warrior (who) could be wounded only (in the heel).
16

    adv av art n   pp art n   pp pro art   n   hv   av
____10. Here is a picture (of the man) (for whom) the police are searching.
17

===
156

(over)

PART II: *Write what job the following words are doing. Choose your answers from among the following:* SUBJECT, PREDICATE NOMINATIVE, DIRECT OBJECT, INDIRECT OBJECT, OBJECT OF THE PREPOSITION, PREDICATE ADJECTIVE, MODIFIER, VERB.

SENTENCE #	WORD	JOB
1	words	*predicate nominative*
2	popular	*predicate adjective*
3	248	*modifier*
3	sun	*object of the preposition*
4	whose	*modifier*
5	whom	*direct object*
6	Words	*subject*
6	hard	*predicate adjective*
6	foreigners to pronounce	*object of the preposition*
7	years	*object of the preposition*
7	poet	*predicate nominative*
8	record	*direct object*
9	warrior	*predicate nominative*
9	could be wounded	*verb*
10	Here	*modifier*
10	picture	*subject*
10	whom	*object of the preposition*

(5 points each)

===
85

PART III: *DIRECTIONS: The following pairs of sentences are short and choppy. Re-write them and combine the* <u>*two*</u> *sentences into* <u>*one*</u> *sentence using ADJECTIVE CLAUSES. You may change words, add words, delete words — your sentence must (1) contain ALL the ideas that were in the original two and (2) contain an adjective clause. Remember: you use* which *or* that *when referring to things and* who/whom *when referring to people.*

1. My cousin loves old movies. He stayed home this afternoon to watch TV.

    My cousin, who loves old movies, stayed home this afternoon to watch TV.
    My cousin, who stayed home this afternoon to watch TV, loves old movies.

2. Dad built a "worm fence." It has zigzagging rails.

    Dad built a worm fence which (or that) has zigzagging rails.
    The worm fence that Dad built has zigzagging rails.

3. The dress once belonged to my aunt. It has a poodle on the skirt.

    That dress, which once belonged to my aunt, has a poodle on the skirt.
    That dress, which has a poodle on the skirt, once belonged to my aunt.

4. Johnny is too old to play with you. He wants to play with Jimmy.

    Johnny, who is too old to play with you, wants to play with Jimmy.
    Johnny, who wants to play with Jimmy, is too old to play with you.

(2

points

each)

5. Mary wrote a book. It was on the best-seller list.

    Mary wrote a book which (or that) was on the best-seller list.
    The book which Mary wrote was on the best-seller list.

6. I fell madly in love with the artist. He lives next door.

    I fell madly in love with the artist who lives next door.

7. I stumbled over the scooter. It was lying on the sidewalk.

    I stumbled over the scooter which (or that) was lying on the sidewalk.
    The scooter which I stumbled over was lying on the sidewalk.

8. My father paid $100 for that chair. It once belonged to the mayor.

    My father paid $100 for that chair which (or that) once belonged to the mayor.
    That chair, which my father paid $100 for, once belonged to the mayor.

9. The little boy had lost his temper. He was screaming at his sister.

    The little boy, who had lost his temper, was screaming at his sister.
    The little boy who was screaming at his sister had lost his temper.

10. That tall man coaches our football team. You met him yesterday.

    Yesterday you met that tall man who coaches our football team.
    That tall man, whom you met yesterday, coaches our football team.

===
20

(THESE ANSWERS WILL VARY. AS LONG AS THEIR SENTENCE MEANS THE SAME AS THE ORIGINAL TWO SENTENCES AND CONTAINS AN ADJECTIVE CLAUSE, I GIVE FULL CREDIT. IF THEY USE "THAT" OR "WHICH" FOR PEOPLE, INSTEAD OF "WHO," I GIVE ONLY 1 POINT.)

220

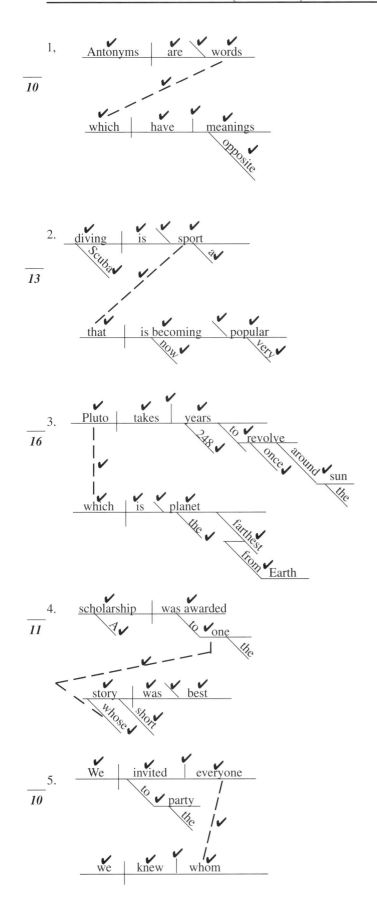

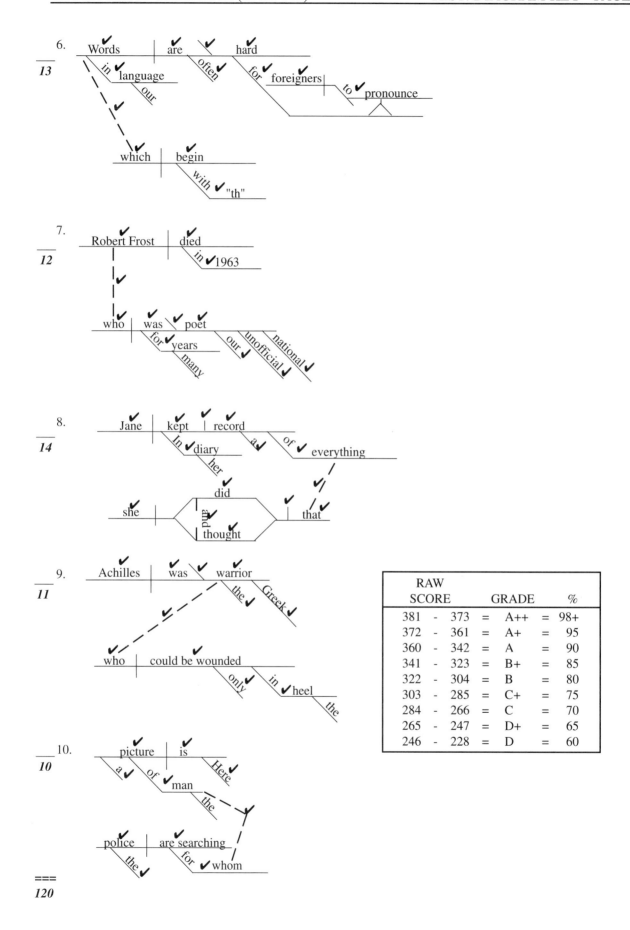

RAW SCORE			GRADE		%
381	-	373	= A++	=	98+
372	-	361	= A+	=	95
360	-	342	= A	=	90
341	-	323	= B+	=	85
322	-	304	= B	=	80
303	-	285	= C+	=	75
284	-	266	= C	=	70
265	-	247	= D+	=	65
246	-	228	= D	=	60

ADVERB CLAUSES

DEFINITION: An **ADVERB CLAUSE** is a group of words with a subject and a verb that modifies a verb, an adjective, or an adverb. It answers the questions "How?" "When?" "Where?" or "Why?" about one of those words located in the independent clause.

      EXAMPLE: <u>Before the game started</u>, we ate lunch.

              The subordinate clause "Before the game started" tells you WHEN we ate. It is an adverb clause modifying the verb "ate."

      EXAMPLE: I am glad <u>that you are coming</u>.

              The subordinate clause "that you are coming" tells WHY I am glad. It is an adverb clause modifying the predicate adjective "glad."

Adverb clauses are introduced by <u>SUBORDINATING CONJUNCTIONS</u>. You should become very familiar with these words:

after	before	unless
although	if	until
as	in order that	when
as if	since	whenever
as long as	so that	where
as soon as	than	wherever
because	though	while

(WHEN YOU PARSE A SUBORDINATING CONJUNCTION, MARK IT "<u>S C</u>.")

HERE'S A TRICK: If you think a group of words is an adverb clause, but you're not sure, try this: cover up the subordinating conjunction with one thumb. Cover up the independent clause with the other thumb. What's left over? The little sentence left over in the first example is "the game started." In the second example it's "you are coming." If what is left over is a little sentence, you have an adverb clause. Try it with the example sentences above. This is called the <u>Mrs. Finley's Never-Fail Thumb Test</u>.

HOW TO DIAGRAM A SENTENCE WITH AN ADVERB CLAUSE:

      EXAMPLE: s c   art   n   av art   n   pro av   adj n
                Before the guests left the ballroom, they thanked their hosts.

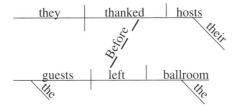

The subordinating conjunction is on a dotted line which goes from the verb of the subordinate clause to whatever word in the independent clause it modifies.

(over)

ADVERB CLAUSES: EXERCISE #1

NAME:_____DATE:_____

DIRECTIONS: Parse the sentences below and put parentheses around the prepositional phrases. Remember to parse subordinating conjunctions as "s c." Underline the adverb clause. Diagram the sentences.

    sc art n av pp adj n   pn av pro adv
1. Because the present came (from her aunt,) Diane opened it immediately.

    pro hv av art n sc pro av pp n
2. I will attend the party if it starts (by seven).

    adj n   av adv sc pro av
3. My brother slept later than I did.

     sc pro lv adv art __pn __ pro av v   adj   n
4. Although I am not a Sherlock Holmes, I enjoy solving difficult puzzles.

    pro av art n pp art n sc pro hv av art n
5. He saw the author (of the play) when he was leaving the theatre.

    sc pro av art n pp art n   av pp adj n
6. After you add the eggs (to the mixture), beat (for ten minutes).

     pn av – sc –pro hv av art n
7. John looked as if he had seen a ghost.

    art   n   hv adv av sc art n   av adv adj n pp pro
8. The driveway will not set if the concrete has too much water (in it).

    hv pro av art n – sc –pro hv lv art adj   n
9. Can you plan the party so that it will be a complete surprise?

    sc adj n   av adj n pro hv adv av pp art n
10. Unless my dad changes his mind, I can not go (to the dance).

      Photocopying this product is strictly prohibited by copyright law.

1.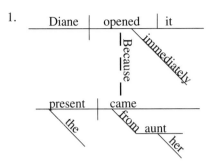

2.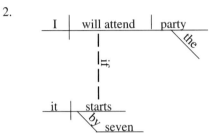

3.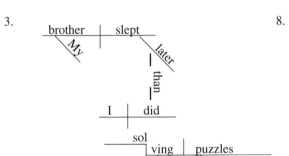

4.

5.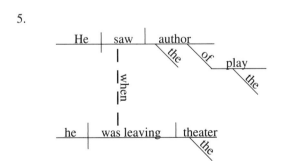

6.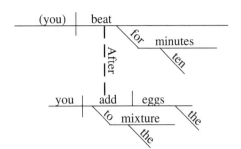

7.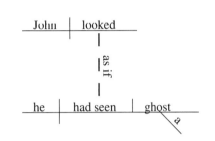

8.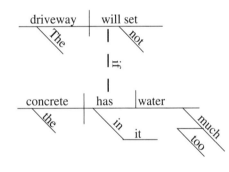

9.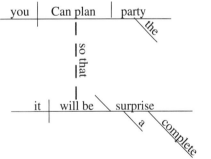

10.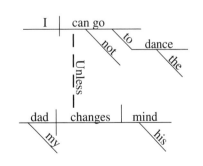

ADVERB CLAUSES: EXERCISE #2

NAME:_____DATE:_____

DIRECTIONS: *Parse the sentences below and put parentheses around the prepositional phrases. Underline the adverb clauses. Diagram the sentences.*

sc pro av _v _ art   n   av   adj   n   pn
1.   If you wish to ruin a friendship, watch my friend Morris.

sc   art adj   n   hv   av   pn   av   pro
2.   When the other person is speaking, Morris interrupts him.

— sc ——   pro   av   v   art n pro av art adj   n   adv
3.   As soon as someone starts telling a joke, he gives the punch line away.

adv pro av _sc _art   n   lv   adv p-adj
4.   Then he acts as if the joke was not funny.

pro   av   art   n   _sc _pro hv   av   pp   pro
5.   He changes the subject so that he can brag (about himself.)

sc   pro hv av   pp   adj adj   n   conj adj   n   pro adv   av pp   adj conj
6.   While he is talking (about his heroic deeds and great intelligence), he always goes (into lengthy and
adj   n
uninteresting detail).

sc   pro av   v   art adj   n   pro   av   art adj adj   n   pro pro
7.   Before he describes saving a child's life, he mentions the other heroic things that he
hv   av pp adj n
has done (in his life).

sc   pro av art   n   pro   av   adj adj   n
8.   Whenever he gets a chance, he criticizes his other friends.

sc   pro   av   adj   n   pro lv p-adj conj av
9.   Unless he monopolizes every conversation, he gets angry and sulks.

av   —v—   pp   pn   sc pro adv av ——v—— adj n
10. Remember to act (like Morris) if you never want to have any friends!

1.

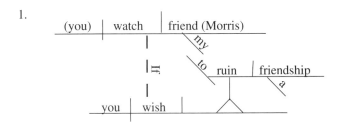

2.

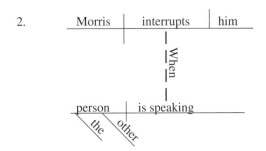

3.

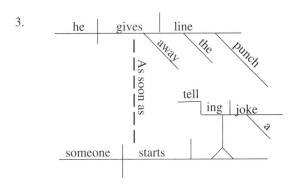

4.

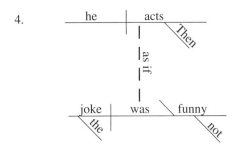

5.

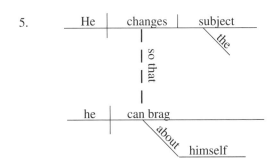

6.

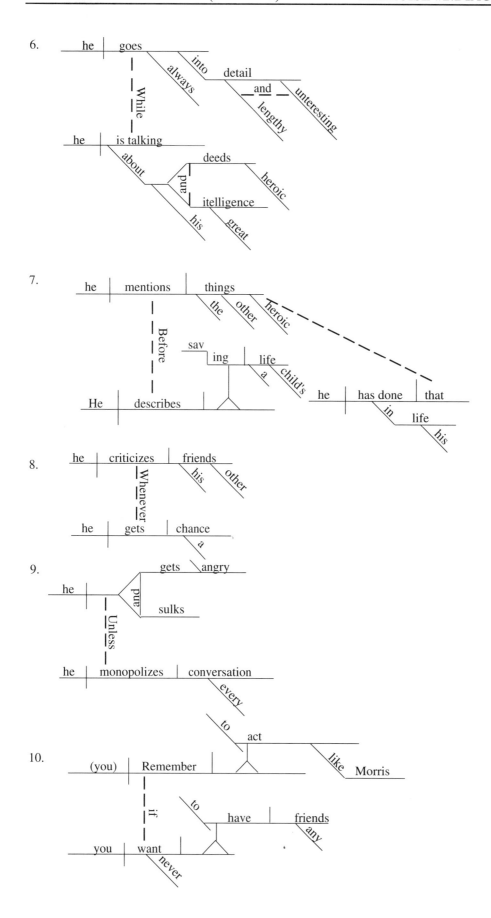

7.

8.

9.

10.

ADVERB CLAUSES: EXERCISE #3

NAME:_____DATE:_____

DIRECTIONS: *Underline the adjective & adverb clauses in the sentences below.   Circle the relative pronouns and the subordinating conjunctions. Above the clause write whether it's an adverb or adjective clause and what word in the main clause it modifies.   This is what you will have to do on the test, so be sure you know what you're doing!*

1. *adverb - borrowed*   *adjective - Mary*
    Since I did not have my math book, I borrowed one from Mary, who is always prepared for class.

2. *adjective - class*   *adverb - seem*
    This class, which is considered to be the hardest in the school, will not seem so hard after it is finished.

3. *adjective - teacher*   *adjective - teacher*
    My science teacher, who loves to build strange machines, and my math teacher, who gets his kicks from

    adverb - be
    solving difficult puzzles, will be the recipients of the state Teacher of the Year award because they are

    such excellent teachers.

4. *adjective - girl*   *adverb - acted*
    The girl who was sitting in the back row acted as if she had not heard the teacher's instructions.

5. *adverb - become*   *adjective - idea*
    When I finally graduate from high school, the idea of going to college, which seems like a dream, will

    actually become a reality.

6. *adverb - asked*   *adjective - man*
    Before I left the auditorium, I asked the man who had given the speech for an autograph.

7. *adjective - souvenir*   *adverb - get*
    I always get a souvenir which my little brother will like whenever I am on a trip.

8. *adjective - students*   *adverb - do*
    Students who read directions carefully usually do well when they are tested.

9. *adverb - like*   *adjective - something*
    Whenever I go on vacation, I like to buy something that reminds me of the place.

10. *adverb - decided*   *adjective - book*
    Since I had no homework, I decided to read a book which I had been wanting to read.

SUBORDINATE CLAUSES: TEST

NAME:_____DATE:_____

(RAW SCORE:_____ */100*   GRADE:_____)

DIRECTIONS: *There are twenty subordinate clauses in the story below. On a separate sheet of paper, do the following things: 1.) copy the entire subordinate clause, 2.) on the line below it, write either ADJECTIVE CLAUSE or ADVERB CLAUSE, whichever it is, 3.) circle the relative pronoun or the subordinating conjunction, and 4.) write the word in the main clause that the subordinate clause modifies. Try to number your clauses <u>in the order in which they come in the story.</u>*

EXAMPLE: The old boxer who had retired from the ring was teaching the young fighter.

1.   (who) had retired from the ring

          adjective clause   boxer

Robert Browning, who was a poet of the Victorian period, wrote a poem about Childe Roland, a daring knight who set out on a dangerous quest for the Dark Tower. Many brave knights had been killed because they had searched for the Tower, but Roland was determined not to rest until he found it.

After Roland had searched for years, he came upon an old man who pointed the way to the Tower. Following the old man's directions, Roland found himself in a land which was horrible beyond belief. As he passed across the eerie wasteland, he saw all around him the signs of savage struggles that had taken place here in the past. Although Roland now felt doomed, he rode on. He saw sights that would have convinced the bravest of men to turn back. But Roland would not give up while he had strength to continue.

Finally, when he had become discouraged, a large black bird swooped down over his head. As he watched it fly away, he saw in the distance the place which the old man had described to him. A dark tower loomed up before him as if a huge stone had arisen out of the valley. He felt like a sailor looking at a rocky shelf at the very moment that his ship crashes into it. While Roland paused to look, he heard ringing in his ears the names of all those who had died in the quest for the Tower. Then, on the hillsides, he saw in a sheet of flame the figures of the knights who had perished. But, in spite of the horror, Roland raised his horn to his lips and blew: "Child Roland to the Dark Tower came!"

EXTRA CREDIT: *In this story there is one appositive phrase, four infinitive phrases, and three participial phrases. Find as many as you can and copy them out on your test paper. Be sure to tell what each item is before you write it down. What is the appositive restating? What jobs is each infinitive doing? What is each participial phrase modifying.? The example below shows you how to do this exercise.*

EXAMPLE: Bowser, my three-legged dog, falls over in a stiff wind..

          my three-legged dog - appositive phrase - restates Bowser.

PART I: 4 points each. Total points = 80.

1.   (Who) was a poet of the Victorian period.

              adjective clause   *Robert Browning*

2.   (who) set out on a dangerous quest for the Dark Tower.

              adjective clause   *knight*

3.   (because) they had searched for the Tower

              adverb clause   *killed (answer may include helping verbs)*

4.   (until) he found it

              adverb clause   *(to) rest*

5.   (after) Roland had searched for years

              adverb clause   *came*

6.   (who) pointed the way to the Tower

              adjective clause   *man*

7.   (which) was horrible beyond belief

              adjective clause   *land*

RAW					
SCORE		GRADE		%	
100	- 98	=	A++	=	98+
97	- 95	=	A+	=	95
94	- 90	=	A	=	90
89	- 85	=	B+	=	85
84	- 80	=	B	=	80
79	- 75	=	C+	=	75
74	- 70	=	C	=	70
69	- 65	=	D+	=	65
64	- 60	=	D	=	60

8.   (as) he passed across the eerie wasteland

              adverb clause   *saw*

9.   (that) had taken place here in the past

              adjective clause   *struggles*

10.   (although) Roland now felt doomed

              adverb clause   *rode*

11.   (that) would have convinced the bravest of men to turn back

              adjective clause   *sights*

12.   (While) he had strength to continue

              adverb clause   *(would) give*

13.   (When) he had become discouraged

              adverb clause   *swooped*

14. (as) he watched it fly away

   adverb clause   saw

15. (which) the old man had described to him

   adjective clause   place

16. (as if) a huge stone had arisen out of the valley

   adverb clause   loomed

17. (that) his ship crashes into it

   adjective clause   moment

18. (while) Roland paused to look

   adverb clause   heard

19. (who) had died in their quest for the Tower

   adjective clause   those

20. (who) had perished

   adjective clause   knights

===
80

PART II: There are 24 correct responses below - one point for saying what kind of phrase it is, one for copying out the phrase correctly, and one point for what it restates, modifies, or what job it does. If they have partial answers, I give credit for what's there. (In all, there's a whopping possible 24 extra credit points!!)

appositive phrase - a daring knight - restates Child Roland

Infinitive phrase - (not) to rest - modifier

Infinitive phrase - to turn back - modifier

infinitive phrase - to continue - modifier

Infinitive phrase - to look - modifier

participial phrase - following the old man's directions - modifies Roland

participial phrase - looking at a rocky shelf - modifies sailor

participial phrase - ringing in his ears - modifies names

PART II: DIRECTIONS: *The sentences below are choppy and sound childish. Using ADJECTIVE and ADVERB CLAUSES, combine the pairs of sentences into one sentence. To get credit here, your sentence must 1.) contain an adjective or adverb clause, and 2.) contain all the ideas of the original two sentences. You may have to change words, delete words, and/or add words.*

1. Henry Borsini is getting bald. He is also overweight and out of shape.
   Henry Borsini, who is getting bald, is also overweight and out of shape.

2. I didn't have a warm coat. I borrowed one from a friend.
   Since I didn't have a warm coat, I borrowed one from a friend.

3. I was almost asleep. I heard a sound that jerked me awake.
   I was almost asleep when I heard a sound that jerked me awake.

(2 points each)

4. Amy has never been outside the United States. She speaks German beautifully.
   Amy, who has never been outside the United States, speaks German beautifully.

Answers will vary

5. The Lawsons are our neighbors. They have gone to Hawaii for two weeks.
   The Lawsons, who are our neighbors, have gone to Hawaii for two weeks.

6. That glass has become chipped. It is dangerous.
   That glass, which has become chipped, is dangerous.

7. Ray searched for many days. He found the perfect gift.
   After Ray searched for many days, he found the perfect gift.

8. Jane wanted to talk to that man. He was eating lunch in the same restaurant.
   Jane wanted to talk to that man who was eating lunch in the same restaurant.

9. The twins had never seen a waterfall. Their uncle took them to Niagara Falls.
   The twins had never seen a waterfall before their uncle took them to Niagara Falls.

=== 20

10. The women couldn't walk very easily. They changed into flat-heeled shoes.
    The women, who couldn't walk very easily, changed into flat-heeled shoes.

These items are worth 2 points each. I usually give the full two points as long as the sentences contain adjective or adverb clauses and mean the same thing as the original two sentences. When a sentence is correct but the student uses "that" or "which" for people, instead of "who" or "whom," I give him 1 out of 2 for that item.

NOUN CLAUSES

DEFINITION: A NOUN CLAUSE is a subordinate clause which is used as a noun in the sentence. It may be a subject, a complement (direct object, indirect object, predicate nominative), or the object of a preposition.

EXAMPLES: 1.)   pro pro av   av   pro
                         <u>What he said</u> surprised me.

(The noun clause "What he said" acts as the subject of the verb "surprised.")

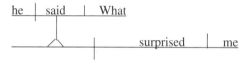

2.)   art   n   hv lv   pro   av
                The champion will be <u>whoever wins.</u>

(The noun clause "whoever wins" acts as the predicate nominative of "will be.")

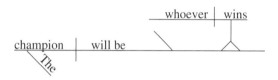

3.)   pn   av   pro adj   n   lv
                Jane knows <u>what your secret is.</u>

(The noun clause "what your secret is" is the direct object of "knows.")

4.)   pro hv av   pro   av art   n
                I   will give <u>whoever comes</u> a ticket.

(The noun clause "whoever comes" is the indirect object of "give.")

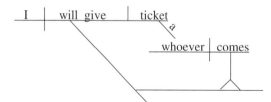

(over)

5.)   pro av   n pp   pro   lv p- adj
She brings food (to <u>whoever is ill</u>.)

(The noun clause "whoever is ill" is the object of the preposition "to.")

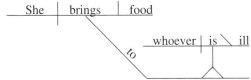

Noun clauses are usually introduced by the following pronouns:

that	what	who	whom
	whatever	whoever	whomever

And sometimes by the following adverbs:

where	when	why	how
wherever	whenever	whyever	however

THESE INTRODUCTORY WORDS HAVE NO SPECIAL NAME OF THEIR OWN; JUST PARSE THEM EITHER "PRO" OR "ADV."

IMPORTANT NOTE: Most of the time the introductory word has some job to do in the clause (see the above diagrams); however, sometimes (with the word "that") it has no function in the clause at all. Its only function is to connect the subordinate clause to the main clause.

EXAMPLE: pro   av   pro pro lv p-adj
She thought <u>that I was sick</u>.

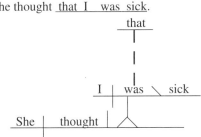

NOUN CLAUSES: EXERCISE #1

NAME:_____DATE:_____

DIRECTIONS: *Parse the sentences below. Underline the noun clause. Diagram the sentence and, to the side of your diagram, indicate what job each clause is doing.*

        pro art   n   av   lv art adj   n
1.   What the club wanted was a spook house.

       adj   n   lv pro pro hv   adv av adv pp   n
2.   His message was that he would not be home (for dinner).

       art n   av   pp adv art   n   av
3.   A guide pointed (to where the picture was.)

       art   n   av   pro   hv av art   n art adj n
4.   The teacher gave whoever had read the story a short quiz.

      pn   adv av art adj   n   pp   pro   pro av
5.   Tammy always had a cheery hello (for whomever she knew).

      pro   av   art adj   n   pp   n   hv av art n
6.   Whoever guesses the correct number (of jellybeans) will win a prize.

      art   n   pp art adj   n   lv pro adv   av
7.   The outcome (of the whole thing) is what really matters.

      art   n   av   pp pro adv   n   hv av
8.   A beekeeper explained (to us) how honey is made.

      pro pro hv adv   av   lv   adv p-adj
9.   That she was not coming was quite obvious.

      pro lv p-adj   pp pro   av   adv   adv
10.   We were astonished (by what happened here yesterday).

1.

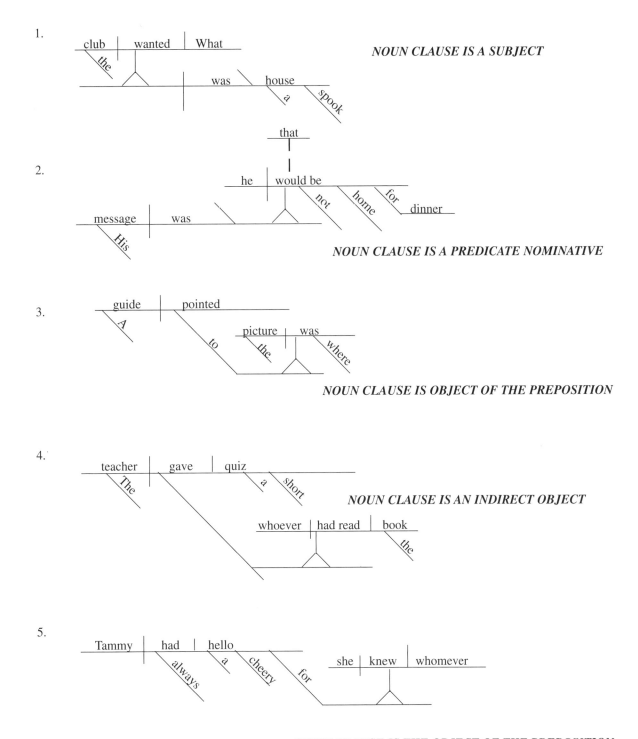

NOUN CLAUSE IS A SUBJECT

2.

NOUN CLAUSE IS A PREDICATE NOMINATIVE

3.

NOUN CLAUSE IS OBJECT OF THE PREPOSITION

4.

NOUN CLAUSE IS AN INDIRECT OBJECT

5.

NOUN CLAUSE IS THE OBJECT OF THE PREPOSITION

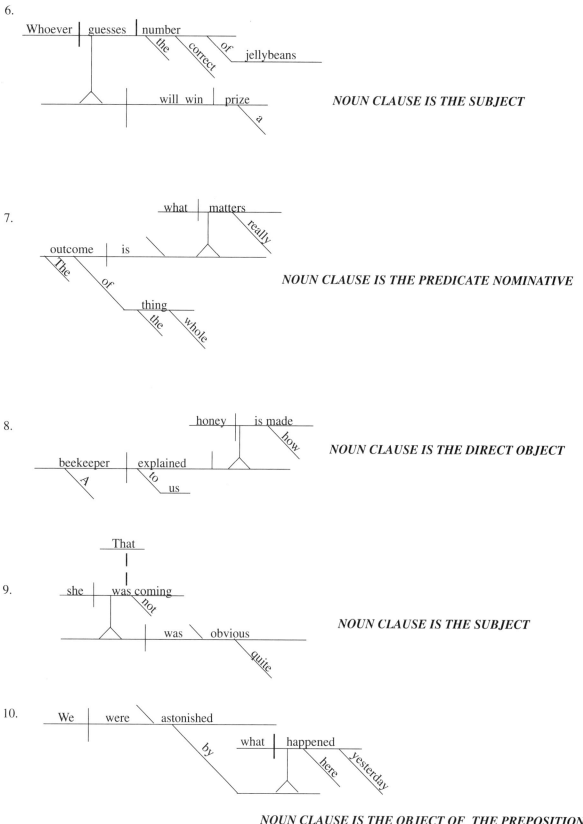

6.

NOUN CLAUSE IS THE SUBJECT

7.

NOUN CLAUSE IS THE PREDICATE NOMINATIVE

8.

NOUN CLAUSE IS THE DIRECT OBJECT

9.

NOUN CLAUSE IS THE SUBJECT

10.

NOUN CLAUSE IS THE OBJECT OF THE PREPOSITION

NOUN CLAUSES: EXERCISE #2

NAME:_____DATE:_____

DIRECTIONS: *Below each sentence, underline and identify every phrase (participial, gerund, infinitive, or appositive) and every clause (adjective, adverb, or noun). If it's doing a job, write what job it's doing; if it's modifying something, write what it's modifying.*

EXAMPLE: When he heard Maria's speech, Mark felt that he should try harder.
            (Adverb clause - modifies "felt")   *(Noun clause - direct object)*

1.   What he does best is playing the piano.
    (Noun clause - subject)   *(Gerund phrase - predicate nominative)*

2.   Mr. Allen is the man who taught us origami.
                        (Adjective clause - modifies "man")

3.   Screaming with fear, Jenny sat up suddenly when the tent collapsed.
    (Participial phrase - modifies "Jenny")   *(Adverb clause - modifies "sat")*

4.   My brother's family, our favorite relatives, surprise us whenever they arrive on time.
                (Appositive phrase - restates "family") *(Adverb clause - modifies "surprise")*

5.   I could not understand what the directions said to do before entering the restricted area.
            (Noun clause - direct object") *(Infinitive - direct object)**(Gerund phrase - obj. of the preposition)*

6.   Where we sat was the row of seats located near the exit.
    (Noun clause - subject)   *(Participial phrase - modifies "row")*

7.   Wolfman Jack, who was a disc jockey, loved to play old songs on "The Midnight Special."
        (Adjective clause - modifies "Wolfman Jack") *(Infinitive phrase - direct object)*

8.   The oranges that we picked when we were in Florida were very juicy.
    (Adjective clause - modifies "oranges")(Adverb clause - modifies "picked")

9.   Gene, a thoughtful person, brought sandwiches for whoever was hungry.
        (Appositive phrase - restates "Gene")   *(Noun clause - object of the preposition)*

10.   Horses, considered stupid by many people, have strong feelings about where they go.
            (Participial phrase - modifies "Horses")   *(Noun clause - obj. of the preposition)*

NOUN CLAUSES: EXERCISE #3

NAME:_____ DATE:_____

DIRECTIONS: *Below each sentence, underline and identify every phrase (participial, gerund, infinitive, or appositive) and every clause (adjective, adverb, or noun). If it's doing a job, write what job it's doing; if it's modifying something, write what it's modifying. It would probably be best to use a separate sheet of paper and copy the phrases and clauses out, since this is what will be required on the test.*

1.   Joe, who was Mary's partner in the dance contest, refused to leave the dance floor
             (Adjective clause - modifies "Joe")   *(Infinitive phrase - direct object)*

        when the judge tapped him on the shoulder.
        (Adverb clause - modifies "to leave")

2.   Professor Watkins, lecturing about the Amazon, absentmindedly left the room after the break
             (Participial phrase - modifies "Prof. Watkins")
        because he thought the class was over.
         (Adverb clause - modifies "left")

3.   The argument was all about what Teresa had said when Jill told her a joke.
             (Noun clause - obj. of the preposition) *(Adverb clause - modifies "had said")*

4.   Although they were already exhausted, the first string players stayed in the game
        (Adverb clause - modifies "stayed")

        because the score was tied.
        (Adverb clause - modifies "stayed")

5.   Jason, who is taller than Kyle, thinks that it would be funny
        (Adjective clause - modifies "Jason")(Noun clause - direct object)

        if he played the part of Scarlett O'Hara in the *Gone With the Wind* parody.
             (Adverb clause - modifies "funny")

6.   Saving the environment has become an obsession with Tracy, whom I was telling you about.
        (Gerund phrase - subject)   *(Adjective clause - modifies "Tracy")*

7.   Karen, burdened with a huge pile of books, was staggering down the hall and Kevin,
             (Participial phrase - modifies "Karen")

        who is very thoughtful, offered to help her out.
        (Adjective clause - modifies "Kevin")(Infinitive phrase - direct object)

8.   I turned around and only had a moment to see a shadow, which I felt was that of a man,
                   (Infinitive phrase - modifies "moment") *(Adjective clause - modifies "shadow")*

        flitting past the open doorway.
        (Participial phrase - modifies "shadow")

NOUN CLAUSES: TEST

NAME:_____ DATE:_____

(RAW SCORE:_____ /80 GRADE:_____)

DIRECTIONS: PART I: *On a separate sheet of paper, write out the entire subordinate clause in each sentence below. Write what kind of a clause it is. If it is a noun clause, write what job it is doing. If it is an adjective or adverb clause, write what word it modifies.*

1.   Len claims that he knows judo.

2.   Amy blushed when she read the letter.

3.   The bait that worked best was shrimp.

4.   Everyone who travels needs a map.

5.   No one saw Diane after she left practice.

6.   The wolf attacked because it was trapped.

7.   The robot will do whatever you ask.

8.   The test, which was quite hard, lasted one hour.

9.   We went to the circus when it came to town.

10.   What I like best is talking on the phone with friends.

11.   The champion beat whomever he fought.

12.   A person who designs buildings is an architect.

13.   Kenny Loggins is the one who plays guitar.

14.   Whoever returns the stolen jewels will get a reward.

15.   The dog followed Jeff wherever he went.

16.   Although she prefers hockey, Grace plays center on the basketball team.

17.   Many people watch television because they are bored.

18.   We could see the lake from where we stood.

19.   Slavery was what divided the country.

20.   Radar, which locates distant objects, is used to track spacecraft.

(Answers on next page)

1.	that he knows judo	noun clause	direct object
2.	when she read the letter	adverb clause	modifies "blushed"
3.	that worked best	adjective clause	modifies "bait"
4.	who travels	adjective clause	modifies "Everyone"
5.	after she left practice	adverb clause	modifies "saw"
6.	because it was trapped	adverb clause	modifies "attacked"
7.	whatever you ask	noun clause	direct object
8.	which was quite hard	adjective clause	modifies "test"
9.	when it came to town	adverb clause	modifies "went"
10.	What I like best	noun clause	subject
11.	whomever he fought	noun clause	direct object
12.	who designs buildings	adjective clause	modifies "person"
13.	who plays guitar	adjective clause	modifies "one"
14.	Whoever returns the stolen jewels	noun clause	subject
15.	wherever he went	adverb clause	modifies "followed"
16.	Although she prefers hockey	adverb clause	modifies "plays"
17.	because they are bored	adverb clause	modifies "watch"
18.	where we stood	noun clause	object of the preposition
19.	what divided the country	noun clause	predicate nominative
20.	which locates distant objects	adjective clause	modifies "radar"

(3

points

each)

===
60

PART II: DIRECTIONS: *On this test paper, copy out the clauses (adjective, adverb, or noun) and phrases (participial, gerund, infinitive, or appositive) that you find in the sentences below. Identify what kind of clause or phrase it is. (These sentences were taken from "The Hound of the Baskervilles" by Sir Arthur Conan Doyle) BE SURE TO COPY OUT THE ENTIRE PHRASE OR CLAUSE. (If the phrase or clause is too long to fit on the line provided below, write the first word of it, then an ellipsis [...], and the last word.)*

EXAMPLE: On the night of Sir Charles's death, Barrymore the butler, who made the discovery, sent Perkins the groom on horseback to me. (3 items in this sentence)

1.	"the butler"	Appositive phrase
2.	"who....discovery"	Adjective clause
3.	"the groom"	Appositive phrase

1. I whisked round and had just time to catch a glimpse of something which I took to be a large black calf passing at the head of the drive. (4 items in this sentence)

2. A hound it was, an enormous coal-black hound, but not such a hound as mortal eyes have ever seen. (2 items in this sentence)

3. With long bounds the huge black creature was leaping down the track, following hard upon the footsteps of our friend. (1 item in this sentence)

4. Never have I seen a man run as Holmes ran that night. (1 item in this sentence)

5. The gleam of the match which he struck shone upon his clotted fingers and upon the ghastly pool which widened from the crushed skull of the victim. (2 items in this sentence)

(Up to 5 points extra credit for correctly diagraming sentence #5 in Part II)

TEACHER NOTE: Use your own discretion as to where phrases & clauses begin and end. I would accept, for example, "to be a large black calf passing at the head of the drive."

SENTENCE #	WORD GROUP	IDENTIFICATION
1	*to catch a glimpse of something*	*infinitive phrase*
1	*which I took to be a large black calf*	*adjective clause*
1	*to be a large black calf*	*infinitive phrase*
1	*passing at the head of the drive*	*participial phrase*
2	*an enormous coal-black hound*	*appositive phrase*
2	*as mortal eyes have ever seen*	*adverb clause*
3	*following hard upon the footsteps of our friend*	*participial phrase*
4	*as Holmes ran that night*	*adverb clause*
5	*which he struck*	*adjective clause*
5	*which widened from the crushed skull of his victim*	*adjective clause*

(2 points each)

===
20

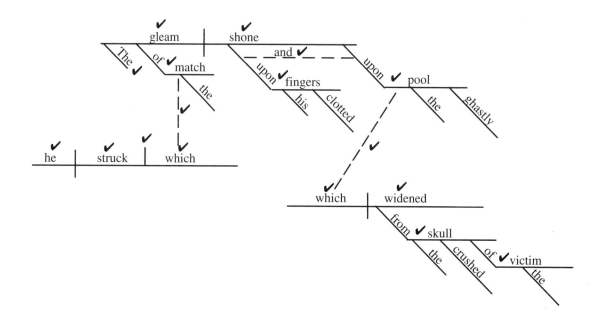

WHEN GRADING THESE EXTRA CREDIT DIAGRAMS, START OUT WITH 5 POINTS. DEDUCT A POINT FOR EACH MISTAKE MADE. IF MORE THAN 5 MISTAKES ARE FOUND, YOU CAN DISCONTINUE GRADING THE DIAGRAM, AS THE STUDENT WILL NOT EARN ANY POINTS. THERE ARE 17 POSSIBLE CORRECT RESPONSES IN THIS DIAGRAM (corresponding with the check marks). ADD THE EXTRA CREDIT POINTS TO THE RAW SCORE.

RAW SCORE			GRADE		%
80 - 78	=	A++	=	98+
77 - 76	=	A+	=	95
75 - 72	=	A	=	90
71 - 68	=	B+	=	85
67 - 64	=	B	=	80
63 - 60	=	C+	=	75
59 - 56	=	C	=	70
55 - 52	=	D+	=	65
51 - 48	=	D	=	60

Season Three

NOTES FOR TEACHERS

GENERAL NOTES: Many teachers today despair of ever teaching their students the rules of punctuation. They attempt short cuts, such as, "Whenever there's a pause, put in a comma!" This may sound simple but, based on my over 30 years in the classroom, I can tell you that it doesn't work! People pause in all sorts of places for dramatic effect, but that doesn't mean a comma would be correct in that place. How is a student supposed to know?

I therefore determined that students must understand the grammar of the English language before they can be expected to internalize rules of punctuation.

This is a comprehensive study of the rules of punctuation. It is designed to be used after the student has completed Analytical Grammar, Units 1 - 17.

I designed all the tests in Analytical Grammar so that the student can correct his own paper. This is, in my opinion, a good learning opportunity for him to either see how well he's doing or the mistakes he's making.

In the tests for Units 19 through 22 - the comma rules - I tell students that "bad punctuation cancels out good punctuation." In other words, if a sentence is supposed to have one comma in it, it's worth one point. But, if the sentence on the student's test paper has two commas in it (and one of them is right and one of them is wrong), then that sentence earns zero points. If a sentence shouldn't have any commas inserted, it's worth one point. Tell your student that, from now on, he should never put a comma in a sentence unless he knows why he's doing it. He should actually know the "buzzword" for the comma rule he's using. If he puts commas in because, "I don't know; it just look right," he risks losing points!

When you get to Units 23 - 28, it can get a bit challenging for your student to correct these tests. I would recommend, however, that you keep with it. In time you will become more efficient in conveying to the student what he needs to do.

I think it's very important for students to learn to write dialogue correctly, and so a few tests contain little "sketches" which have dialogue in them. These have to be re-written complete with correct paragraphing, punctuation, and capitalization.

Before you start correcting these, tell the student what each paragraph is worth and have him write that in the left-hand margin. As you go through that paragraph, verbalize everything that needs to be done in it: "Paragraph - open quote - Capital 'The' - and so on." Tell the student to make a mark whenever he sees a mistake (and that includes stuff that is missing AS WELL AS stuff that's there and shouldn't be). At the end of that paragraph, tell him to count the mistakes and deduct that number from the number of points the paragraph is worth. It works out, so stick with it! Just pride yourself on teaching your student more than he's ever known about punctuation.

REINFORCEMENT: Once you have finished this course, your student should be held accountable in everything he writes for every mistake made in punctuation and capitalization. And remind him to go back to his Grammar Notebook (the collection of all the Notes of every unit that he started way back when he was learning the Parts of Speech) if he gets a bit "rusty" on something. That's what it's there for!

245

COMMA ERRORS

There are two kinds of comma errors: comma SPLICES and comma SPLITS.

A comma SPLICE is a comma which incorrectly joins two sentences. Sometimes you write two sentences next to each other that just *feel* like they ought to go together, so you just *put* them together with a comma. Such as --

We could prove we'd spent the whole day at the beach, we had the sunburn to prove it!

But what you've got there is a comma splice, which is a "no-no." In the case of the above sentences, you could fix the "no-no" in one of three ways:

1. Just write two separate sentences.
2. Join the two sentences with a subordinating conjunction, such as "because."
3. Join the two sentence with a semicolon (See Unit #26)

A comma SPLIT is when you put a comma where it doesn't belong. *The following is a list of places where a comma should <u>not</u> be:*

1. There should never be ONE comma separating the SUBJECT AND VERB.

   EXAMPLE: The butler carrying a tray, walked into the room.

2. There should never be ONE comma separating the VERB AND ITS DIRECT OBJECT.

   EXAMPLE: We discovered after searching carefully, many things.

3. There should never be ONE comma separating a LINKING VERB AND ITS COMPLEMENT.

   EXAMPLE: James felt, absolutely wonderful.

4. There should never be ONE comma separating a MODIFIER AND ITS NOUN.

   EXAMPLE: The soft, cuddly, sweater was gorgeous.

5. There should never be ONE comma separating a VERB AND ITS INDIRECT OBJECT.

   EXAMPLE: I wrote, my aunt in Florida a letter.

6. There should never be ONE comma separating an INDIRECT OBJECT AND ITS DIRECT OBJECT.

   EXAMPLE: I wrote my aunt in Florida, a letter.

SO REMEMBER THE SIX DEADLY SPLITS!

1.	*Subject and verb*	*4.*	*Modifier and its noun*
2.	*Verb and direct object*	*5.*	*Verb and indirect object*
3.	*Linking verb and complement*	*6.*	*Indirect object and direct object*

Photocopying this product is strictly prohibited by copyright law.

COMMA RULES 1, 2, & 3

COMMA RULE 1:   **The "buzzword" for this rule is** *ITEMS IN A SERIES*: use commas to separate items in a series of grammatical equals. This may be a series of nouns, verbs, prepositional phrases, adjective clauses, etc.

NOTE THAT THERE IS A COMMA SEPARATING THE LAST TWO ITEMS.

EXAMPLE: John, Uncle Hank, Aunt Jean, and Anne went to church. (nouns)

The happy, carefree, and enthusiastic kids enjoyed the picnic. (adjectives)

We searched under the desks, behind the shelves, and in the trashcan for the missing keys. (prepositional phrases)

NOTE: If all the items are separated by "and" or "or," do not use commas to separate them.

EXAMPLE: I bought jeans and a shirt and a sweater.

NOTE: When writing a sentence containing a series of items, make sure the sentence is PARALLEL.

EXAMPLE: A good bedtime routine is a hot shower, flossing and brushing your teeth, and to get your clothes ready for the next morning.

(The above sentence makes sense, but it is not PARALLEL because you don't have a series of grammatical equals. "a hot shower" is a noun with modifiers. "flossing and brushing your teeth" is a gerund phrase. "to get your clothes ready for the next morning" is an infinitive phrase.   One way to improve it is to make all your items gerund phrases, like the sentence below. Or you could make all your items infinitives. Try that.)

A good bedtime routine is <u>taking</u> a hot shower, <u>flossing</u> and <u>brushing</u> your teeth, and <u>getting</u> your clothes organized for the next morning.

COMMA RULE 2:   **The "buzzword" for this rule is** *TWO ADJECTIVES with "AND TEST"*: you SOMETIMES use a comma to separate two or more adjectives preceding a noun. The "and test" works like this: If it sounds very natural to put "and" between the two adjectives, you need a comma. If "and" sounds awkward at all, forget the comma.

EXAMPLE #1: That is a rough narrow dangerous road.

(...a rough and narrow road?...sounds okay - you need a comma)

(...a narrow and dangerous road?...sounds okay - you need a comma)

That is a rough, narrow, dangerous road.

EXAMPLE #2: I saw a little old man.

(...a little and old man?...sounds weird - forget it.)

(over)

COMMA RULE 3:   **The buzzword for this rule is** *COMPOUND SENTENCE:* use a comma before the conjunction when it joins independent clauses (or sentences).

EXAMPLE: Brian changed the oil on the old Chevy, and Joe checked the plugs on the Pontiac.

(There is a complete sentence on either side of the conjunction, so you need a comma.)

EXAMPLE: Brian changed the oil on the old Chevy and checked the plugs on the Ford.

(There is NOT a complete sentence on either side of the conjunction, so do not put a comma.)

EXCEPTION TO THIS RULE: IF....you are using the conjunction *and*

and

IF...either one of the sentences contains four words or less,

DO NOT USE A COMMA.

EXAMPLE: Brian changed the oil and Joe checked the plugs on the Pontiac.
                (The first independent clause contains only FOUR WORDS and the conjunction is *and*; that's why there's no comma.)

WHEN YOU'RE USING ANY OTHER CONJUNCTION BESIDES *AND*, YOU MUST USE A COMMA IF YOU HAVE A COMPOUND SENTENCE.

COMMA RULES 1, 2, & 3: EXERCISE #1

NAME:_____DATE:_____

DIRECTIONS: Insert commas where they are needed.

1.   We had lessons in swimming, canoeing, archery, and handicrafts.

2.   Mary and Frances and Ted dashed out of the car, down the beach, and into the water.

3.   Our school has organized clubs for music, art, radio, and computers.

4.   The high school orchestra includes violins, cellos, clarinets, saxophones, trumpets, and drums.

5.   I've planted seedlings, fertilized them carefully, and watered them daily.

6.   The children played happily on the swings, on the slide, and in the pool.

7.   Science and Latin and algebra are all included in next year's curriculum.

8.   Do you know how to pitch a tent, how to build a campfire, or how to cook outdoors?

9.   I enjoy swimming, boating, and surfing more than skiing, sledding, or skating.

10.   Find out who is going to the picnic, what we must take, and when we are going.

11.   This morning Tom will wash the car, Mary will pack the lunch, and then we'll go for a drive.

12.   In spite of bad predictions, the fog lifted, the sun shone, and everyone was happy.

13.   Science teaches us how to conserve our forests, how to prevent erosion of the soil, and how to control our

        water supplies.

14.   I would like to visit England, France, Spain, and Norway, the "Land of the Midnight Sun."

15.   Soccer, basketball, and football are all strenuous sports.

DIRECTIONS: The sentence below is not parallel. Rewrite it.

        The smell of cookies, going Christmas shopping, and how to keep a secret are part of what

        the holidays are all about.

(Answers will vary. Here are two possibilities.)
Smelling cookies, going Christmas shopping, and keeping secrets are part of what the
holidays are all about.
or
To smell cookies, go Christmas shopping, and keep a secret are part of what the holidays are
all about.

(over)

249

DIRECTIONS: *In each sentence below there is a COMMA SPLIT. Write the number which is under the comma split in the space at the left. Then in the space below each sentence, write what the comma is splitting.*

EXAMPLE:_____**3**_____ The happy, carefree, enthusiastic kids, enjoyed the picnic.
                                         1   2   3

splits subject and verb

- -

____**1**____ 1. The old, dog trotted slowly into the beautiful, elegant, immaculate house.
                          1   2   3

splits modifier (old) and its noun (dog)

.____**4**____ 2 The rain stopped, the sun came out, and the children continued their vigorous,
                                          1   2   3

strenuous, game.
          4

splits modifier (strenuous) and its noun (game)

____**1**____ 3. The gym teacher is carefully teaching during the course of this semester, wrestling, gymnastics,
                                                                                                         1   2   3

and tumbling.

splits verb (is teaching) and direct object (wrestling, gymnastics, and tumbling)

COMMA RULES 1, 2, & 3: EXERCISE #2

NAME:_____DATE:_____

DIRECTIONS: *Insert commas where they are needed.*

1.   John was the popular, efficient president of the senior class.

2.   The cold, dry northern air is very invigorating.

3.   We loved running barefoot over the damp, cool sand.

4.   What a stern, dignified manner that soldier has!

5.   The dark, dingy, musty attic seemed spooky.

6.   The noisy, carefree fans cheered when they saw the bright blue uniforms of the band.

7.   Have you read about the strong, courageous man who climbed the sheer, icy slopes of Mt.

        Everest?

8.   An alert, hard-working, businesslike leader is needed.

9.   A dark, squatty-looking iron stove stood in the corner of the cabin.

10.   Alfred Hitchcock fascinated us with his thrilling, blood-curdling films.

11.   It was a bright, brisk, beautiful autumn day.

12.   A little old man knocked at the door.

13.   That was a long, hard, exhausting train ride.

14.   Jupiter is a large, mysterious planet.

15.   Althea Gibson played a powerful, brilliant game.

DIRECTIONS: *The sentence below is not parallel. Rewrite it.*

        I love to eat, playing with my kitten, and a good conversation with a friend.

(Two possible correct responses are below)
I love eating, playing with my kitten, and having a good conversation...
or
I love to eat, play with my kitten, and have a good conversation...

(over)

DIRECTIONS: *In each sentence below there is a COMMA SPLIT. Write the number which is under the comma split in the space at the left. Then in the space below each sentence, write what the comma is splitting.*

____**1**____1. That, is a good, long, tough hike!
　　　　　　　1　　　2　　3

　　　　　splits subject (That) and verb (is)

____**3**____2. The young, inexperienced boys are working on a new, innovative, computer.
　　　　　　　　　1　　　　　　　　　　　　　2　　　　3

　　　　splits modifier (innovative) and its noun (computer)

____**3**____3. The dark, wet, musty tank smelled, terrible.
　　　　　　　1　　2　　　　　　　3

　　　　splits linking verb (smelled) and complement (terrible)

　　　　Photocopying this product is strictly prohibited by copyright law.

COMMA RULES 1, 2, & 3: EXERCISE #3

NAME:_____DATE:_____

DIRECTIONS: *Insert commas where they are needed.*

1.   There are many beautiful beaches along the coast, but one must get used to the cold water.

2.   Henry came over, but Tom stayed at home.

3.   I used steel traps to catch muskrats, but my friend said that was cruel.

4.   Astronomy is an old science, yet it is now one of the most exciting.

5.   Our teacher is using videos and cd-roms in our Social Studies class, and we are really

     enjoying them.

6.   She tried on eight pairs of shoes and didn't buy any of them!

7.   A robin has a nest in a tree near our porch, and we watch her feeding the baby birds.

8.   Harry lived on a farm and had to get up early in the morning to do chores.

9.   I will explain this theory once more, but you must listen.

10.   The teacher explained the project and we went to work.

11.   I'd love to go to the movies, but I have too much work to do.

12.   The movie was excellent, but I didn't enjoy waiting in line.

13.   We stopped on the side of the road and ate our lunch.

14.   On the moon the temperature rises to over 200 degrees in the daytime but drops far

     below zero at night.

15.   There was an annoying noise in the car, but we could not locate the cause.

16.   The coach drew a diagram and the players studied it.

DIRECTIONS: *The sentence below is not parallel. Rewrite it.*

A car that is poorly maintained, operating it beyond the speed limit, and to drink and drive can all be very dangerous.

(Two possible reponses are below)
To maintain a car poorly, operate it beyond the speed limit, and drive while drinking can all...
or
Maintaining a car poorly, operating it beyond the speed limit, and driving while drinking can all...

(over)

DIRECTIONS: *In each sentence below there is a COMMA SPLIT. Write the number which is under the comma split in the space at the left. Then in the space below each sentence, write what the comma is splitting.*

_____**1**_____1. The girl who was very verbal, talked too fast, but she told fascinating, interesting stories.
                                    1   2   3

splits subject (girl) and verb (talked)

_____**3**_____2. I craved a hot, delicious, cheesy pizza and drove in the pouring rain, ten miles.
                          1   2   3

splits verb (drove) and direct object (miles)

_____**1**_____3. My mother gave the girl who was just learning how to cook, the orders, but I followed them.
                                                                          1   2

splits indirect object (girl) and direct object (orders)

COMMA RULES 1, 2, & 3: TEST

NAME:_____ DATE:_____

(RAW SCORE:_____ */79* GRADE:_____)

PART I: DIRECTIONS: COMMA RULE #1: *Insert commas where they are needed.*

—3 1.   Students, teachers, parents, and visitors attended the picnic.

—3 2.   They roamed over the hills, through the fields, down to the lake, and across the bridge.

—1 3.   I bought a suit and a tie and a dress shirt yesterday.

—3 4.   George Washington Carver derived from the peanut such items as ink, coffee, beauty

creams, and pigments.

—1 5.   Do you want French or ranch or Catalina dressing on your salad?

—2 6.   Mosquitoes hummed, crickets chirped, and mockingbirds sang.

—2 7.   Robert Browning said that youth is good, that middle age is better, and that old age is best.

—3 8.   Those who had walked to the picnic, who had brought small children, who had no umbrellas,

or who had worn good clothes dashed to a nearby farmhouse.

—2 9.   The smell of peanuts, the music of a calliope, and the feel of sawdust under my feet always

remind me of the circus.

—2 10. I got <u>Gone With the Wind</u>, <u>The Grapes of Wrath</u>, and <u>The Hobbit</u> from the library.

==
22   ***PART II: COMMA RULE #2:*** *Insert commas where they are needed.*

—2 1.   My aunt is a kind, generous, warm-hearted person.

—1 2.   I need the help of three willing young men.

—1 3.   A vain, talkative disc jockey annoys me.

—1 4.   Anna fluttered her gorgeous black eyelashes.

—1 5.   We chose a beautiful mahogany end table.

(over)

255

—6.   Round, deep craters and steep, rugged mountains dot the surface of the moon.
2

—7.   We passed the warm, humid afternoon playing "Monopoly."
1

—8.   What a wide, smooth highway this is!
1

—9.   If one is not in a hurry, the quaint little streets of old Alexandria are very inviting.
1

—10.   The crowded, uncomfortable dining car was no pleasure for anyone.
==
12   **PART III: COMMA RULE #3:** *Insert commas where they are needed.*

—1.   Everyone was at the game, but Quincy arrived an hour late.
1

—2.   Either the gift was lost in the mail, or he had forgotten to thank me.
1

—3.   Into the garbage pail she flung the burned cake and immediately started work on another.
1

—4.   The critics hated the play, but it ran for six months.
1

—5.   Ethan whispered something to Philip and quickly left the stadium.
1

—6.   Jan picked the flowers and Mary arranged them.
1

—7.   Beaumont led in the first inning by two runs, but Houston was leading in the second
1

    by a score of 6-2.

—8.   Rescue workers helped farmers to clear away debris and to replant their ruined crops after the flood.
1

—9.   The *Titanic* was considered an unsinkable ship, but she sank in the North Atlantic on
1

    April 14, 1912.

—10.   At last the weather became more merciful and settled down to normal.
==
1
10   **PART IV: ALL COMMA RULES:** *Insert commas where they are needed.*

—1.   A beach party was planned for Saturday, but the weather looked bad.
1

—2.   We had invited Mary, Tom, Jane, and Jason.
3

—3.   Mom helped us with the refreshments, and Jason brought a couple of videos.
1

—4.   We ate pizza, played "Trivial Pursuit," and watched a funny old beach-blanket movie.
2

—5.   It was actually a fun, lazy, relaxing afternoon.
2

—6.   Tom said he was bored and tried to organize a game of touch football.
1

—7.   Before we could play, we had to look all over the house to find the football, locate warm
2

    clothing, and find some shoes for Mary.

—8.   After the football game Jane stretched out on the couch and took a brief, blissful snooze.
1

    Photocopying this product is strictly prohibited by copyright law.

—9. The boys waited until she was fast asleep and then painted a moustache on her upper lip.
1

—10. Jane woke up, saw the moustache and took off after Jason and Tom!
2

==
16

PART V: NON-PARALLEL SENTENCES: *Re-write the following sentences to make them parallel.*

1. To learn some new words, writing a good essay, and how to analyze our language are major parts of Mrs. Finley's curriculum.

—   *Learning some new words, writing a good essay, and analyzing our language...*
5   *or*
       To learn somenew words, write a good essay, and analyize our language...

2. My home town has all the advantages: the weather is good, friendly neighbors, with excellent schools, and fine shopping.

—   *...good weather, friendly neighbors, excellent schools, and fine shopping*
5   *or*
       ...the weather is good, the neighbors are friendly, the schools are excellent, and the shopping is fine.

==
10

PART VI: COMMA SPLITS: *In each sentence below there is a COMMA SPLIT. Write the number which is under the comma split in the space at the left. Then in the space below each sentence, write what the comma is splitting.*

—   **1**   1. The man who lives next door, wants his children to excel in school, but he fails to give them careful,
2   1   2   3

consistent help.

—
1   ***splits subject (man) and verb (wants)***

—   **1**   2. The students in this class are reading in the spring semester, a wonderful book which contains
2   1

adventure, fantasy, and romance.
        2   3

—
1   ***splits verb (are reading) and direct object (book)***

—   **3**   3. The frigid, icy air made it difficult for people to breathe, but coach kept us out to practice for our
2   1   2

upcoming, match against South High.
        3

—   ***splits modifier (upcoming) and its noun (match)***
1

==
9

Raw		Score	Grade		%
79	-	77	= A++	=	98+
76	-	75	= A+	=	95
74	-	71	= A	=	90
70	-	67	= B+	=	85
66	-	63	= B	=	80
62	-	59	= C+	=	75
58	-	55	= C	=	70
54	-	51	= D+	=	65
50	-	47	= D	=	60

COMMA RULE 4

The "buzzword" for this rule is *NONESSENTIAL MODIFIERS:* use a comma to separate nonessential adjective clauses and nonessential participial phrases from the rest of the sentence.

ADJECTIVE CLAUSES and PARTICIPIAL PHRASES are groups of words that act like adjectives. In other words, they MODIFY NOUNS AND PRONOUNS.

> EXAMPLE: My English teacher, who loves books, reads all the time.

The group of words "who loves books" is there to describe the noun "teacher." You will notice that the noun being described is almost always located in front of the phrase or clause that modifies it.

HOW TO IDENTIFY AN ADJECTIVE CLAUSE:
> An adjective clause almost always begins with a RELATIVE PRONOUN. The relative pronouns are **WHO, WHOSE, WHOM, WHICH,** and **THAT.**

HOW TO IDENTIFY A PARTICIPIAL PHRASE:
> A participial phrase begins with a PARTICIPLE. There are two kinds of participles:
> 1.)   PRESENT PARTICIPLES are verbs that end in "ing."
> 2.)   PAST PARTICIPLES are verbs that fit into the phrase "I have_____."

Once you have located the participial phrase or adjective clause, you have to decide if it's ESSENTIAL or NONES-SENTIAL. If it's nonessential, the reader doesn't need it to understand what the sentence is really saying.

> EXAMPLE: Jim Riley, who skips school repeatedly, will be expelled.

> Try taking the modifier "who skips school repeatedly" out of the sentence. What is left? "Jim Riley will be expelled." Even without the adjective clause, we still know who will be expelled. That clause is therefore NONES-SENTIAL and that's why we have commas around it.

> EXAMPLE: Students who skip school repeatedly will be expelled.

> Try taking the modifier "who skip school repeatedly" out of this sentence. What is left? "Students will be expelled." Do we know which students will be expelled without that modifier? No, we don't. It is therefore ESSENTIAL and that's why there are no commas around it.

HERE'S A TRICK: One way to tell if a clause is essential or not is to read the sentence with as much natural expression as you can (pretend you're a TV news announcer). If the modifier is nonessential, your voice will just naturally pause right where the commas go. If it is essential, there will be no tendency to pause at all.

Photocopying this product is strictly prohibited by copyright law.

COMMA RULE 4: EXERCISE #1

NAME:_____DATE:_____

DIRECTIONS: *Underline the adjective clause or participial phrase in each sentence below. After each sentence, write "AC" if it's an adjective clause and "PART" if it's a participial phrase. Then separate all the NONESSEN-TIAL modifiers from the rest of the sentence with commas.*

1.   Senator Stewart, hoping for a compromise, began an impassioned speech. *part*

2.   I bought all the books written by John Grisham at a garage sale. *part*

3.   The Foresman Building, which has become a firetrap, will be torn down. *AC*

4.   Sometimes I feel like throwing every outfit that I buy on sale into the trash! *AC*

5.   Students who watch television until late at night are not going to do their best. *AC*

6.   My grandfather Ben, sitting in his favorite chair, would always tell us stories before bedtime. *part*

7.   Give this note to the girl sitting on the sofa. *part*

8.   The senior representative from Zambia, dressed in his native costume, made a colorful sight. *part*

9.   The kids who sing in the choir enjoy performing for the other students. *AC*

10.   The candidate of my choice, kissing babies like a seasoned campaigner, was learning about politics quickly. *part*

(over)

DIRECTIONS: *In each sentence below there is a comma split. In the spaces below each sentence are the numbers of all the commas in the sentence. Find the comma split and write its number in the space at the left. Write what it is splitting beside that comma's number below the sentence. By the other numbers, write the "buzzwords" of the correct commas.*

EXAMPLE:

___*1*___   Students who skip school repeatedly, will be expelled, but our enthusiastic, dedicated
                                                              1   2   3

            students never skip.

            #1 ___*splits subject and verb*___

            #2 ___*compound sentence*___

            #3 ___*two adjectives with "and test"*___

- -

___*3*___   1.   John Wilson, elected by a large majority, began planning, a huge victory celebration.
                                        1   2   3

            #1 ___*Nonessential modifier*___

            #2 ___*Nonessential modifier*___

            #3 ___*splits verb (planning) and direct object (celebration)*___

___*1*___   2.   We have, a soft, luxurious carpet in our living room, dining room, and hall.
                              1   2   3   4

            #1 *splits verb (have) and direct object (carpet)*

            #2 *Two adjectives "and" test*

            #3 *Items in a series*

            #4 *Items in a series*

___*1*___   3.   Students, who have a lot of homework should budget their time, but often they waste
                            1   2

            their energy in useless, futile procrastination.
                                            3

            #1 ___*splits subject (students) and verb (should budget)*___

            #2 ___*Compound sentence*___

            #3 ___*Two adjectives "and" test*___

Photocopying this product is strictly prohibited by copyright law.

COMMA RULE 4: EXERCISE #2

NAME:_____DATE:_____

DIRECTIONS: *Underline the participial phrases and adjective clauses below. Identify them as you did on Exercise #1. Insert commas where they are needed.*

1.   The pitcher, thinking the runner was out, started off the field.   *part*

2.   Here is my cousin James, whom you met yesterday.   *AC*

3.   Mary, who enjoys her class in physics, will be an excellent engineer.   *AC*

4.   Louis Pasteur, striving to save a little boy from death by rabies, used a vaccine which   *part*
        finally conquered that dread disease.   *AC*

5.   The man and woman who discovered radium were Pierre and Marie Curie.   *AC*

6.   E. T. Seton, who was a famous artist-naturalist, was born in England in 1860.   *AC*

7.   *Wild Animals I Have Known,* which is one of his most popular works, was his first book.   *AC*

8.   The boy or girl who enjoys reading usually does well in school.   *AC*

9.   The boy playing left end is our best tackle.   *part*

10.   The winning runners, breathing hard and visibly tired, broke the tape at the same time.   *part*

11.   Lake Superior, covering an area of 30,000 square miles, is the largest Great Lake.   *part*

12.   The girl working next to you is my sister.   *part*

13.   The students, having gorged themselves on junk food, called the picnic a huge success.   *part*

14.   My turquoise and silver ring, which we bought in Mexico, is my favorite.   *AC*

15.   A meal cooked by my mother is always a treat.   *part*

16.   Only the students gathered in the auditorium got to hear the guest speaker.   *part*

17.   John, cramming for the history exam, wished he had kept up with his reading.   *part*

18.   My parents always loved the gifts that I made myself.   *AC*

19.   Our new school library, which has just been opened, is a great asset to our school.   *AC*

20.   The cat took a snooze in the warm sunlight streaming through the living room window.   *part*

(over)

DIRECTIONS: *In each sentence below there is a comma split. In the spaces below each sentence are the numbers of all the commas in the sentence. Find the comma split and write its number in the space at the left. Write what it is splitting beside that comma's number below the sentence. By the other numbers, write the "buzzwords" of the correct commas.*

2   1.   I have a huge, overpowering urge to tell that rude man to go jump off the incredibly tall,
                              1   2
                    Empire State Building, which is located in New York City.
                                                    3

#1 *Two adjectives "and" test*

#2 *splits modifier (tall) and its noun (Empire State Building)*

#3 *Nonessential modifier*

1   2.   I was reading, a really thrilling, mysterious book, but my mom, my dad, and my big
                                            1   2   3   4   5
                    sister told me how it came out!

#1 *splits verb (was reading) and direct object (book)*

#2 *Two adjectives "and" test*

#3 *Compound sentence*

#4 *Items in a series*

#5 *Items in a series*

1   3.   The kids in the band, decided to raise money, and their idea was to have a dance, a bake
                                                    1   2   3
                    sale, and a car wash.
                          4

#1 *splits subject (kids) and verb (decided)*

#2 *Compound sentence*

#3 *Items in a series*

#4 *Items in a series*

Photocopying this product is strictly prohibited by copyright law.

COMMA RULE 4: EXERCISE #3

NAME:_____DATE:_____

DIRECTIONS: *Insert commas where they are needed. Circle the word the phrase or clause modifies.*

1.   Ruth Snyder, who is my second cousin, will visit me next year.

2.   We take the *Shreveport Times*, which is an excellent newspaper.

3.   All highways that have eight lanes are very safe.

4.   You're a lot like my dad, who loves to tinker with old cars.

5.   I think all girls who dye their hair platinum blonde look funny.

6.   Hepzibah Humperdinck, who has a short haircut, looks funny.

7.   I attend Cranford High School, which has an enrollment of 598.

8.   All contestants answering this question correctly will win a prize.

9.   The hog-nosed snake, feared by many, is not poisonous.

10.   In *The Man of Feeling*, which is a very sentimental book, the hero who is extremely

        romantic, drops dead when his sweetheart says she loves him.

DIRECTIONS: *You are to write four sentences. In the first sentence, use the adjective clause "who passed this grammar unit" in a sentence where it is nonessential (with commas). In the second sentence use "who passed this grammar unit" as an essential adjective clause(no commas). In the third sentence the participial phrase "running in the house" must be nonessential (with commas). In the fourth sentence "running in the house" should be an essential phrase (no commas).*

> *Here are some examples:*
> *Jim Smith, who passed this grammar unit, is becoming a good writer.*
> *Students who passed this grammar unit did not have to take the remedial writing class.*
> *My younger brother, running in the house, slipped and fell.*
> *Children running in the house are often injured.*

DIRECTIONS: *Write four sentences of your own (try not to be boring...) in which you...*

1.   ...demonstrate "items in a series"

2.   ...demonstrate "two adjective with 'and test'"

3.   ...demonstrate "compound sentence"   *Answers will vary.*

4.   ...demonstrate "nonessential modifier"

(over)

DIRECTIONS: *In each sentence below there is a comma split. In the spaces below each sentence are the numbers of all the commas in the sentence. Find the comma split and write its number in the space at the left. Write what it is splitting beside that comma's number below the sentence. By the other numbers, write the "buzzwords" of the correct commas.*

2   1.   The delicious, succulent turkey that was cooked by Chef Andre, won first
                              1   2

                     prize, but Georgine's souffle won second prize.
                              3

                     #1 *Two adjectives "and" test*

                     #2 *splits subject (turkey) and verb (won)*

                     #3 *Compound sentence*

1   2.   The woman in the store looked, incredibly angry at the poor clerk, who
                                              1   2
                     was trying desperately to wrap an awkward, bulky package.
                                                                       3

                     #1 *splits linking verb (looked) and complement (angry)*

                     #2 *Nonessential modifier*

                     #3 *Two adjectives "and" test*

3   3.   Bruce Willis, Kevin Costner, and Tom Cruise, are all big stars now.
                                  1   2   3

                     #1 *Items in a series*

                     #2 *Items in a series*

                     #3 *splits subject (Bruce Willis, etc) and verb (are)*

COMMA RULE 4: TEST

NAME:_____DATE:_____

(RAW SCORE:_____ /80 GRADE:_____)

PART I: DIRECTIONS: *Underline the participial phrase or adjective clause in the sentences below. Circle the noun or pronoun each phrase or clause modifies. Insert commas where they are needed.*

EXAMPLE: My brother, who is an excellent basketball player, got a scholarship to Temple.

—1.
3   In my day a teenager liked to single out a hero who could sing or act.

—2.
4   This hero worship, which our parents said was a common affliction of teenagers, took many forms.

—3.
4   For example, when Elvis moaned and jerked his way through a song, his female audience, reacting

hysterically to his singing, screamed or fainted.

—4.
4   During his reign, which lasted longer than anyone expected, his followers imitated his hairstyle and way of

speaking and moving.

—5.
7   Then the Beatles, blasting onto the rock-and-roll scene in the early 60's, stole much of the limelight from

Elvis, who didn't have a cute English accent or a "choirboy" hairdo.

—6.
4   Within a short time Beatle posters, which were a necessity to every fan, were pushing Elvis items off

the shelves.

—7.
3   Every young man who wanted to be "cool" had a Beatle haircut.

—8.
3   In time, however, even the almighty Beatles had to make way for those who were now taking the

music-buying public by storm.

—9.
3   In my opinion, the attention that we paid to our singing idols was more beneficial than harmful.

—10.
3   A young person interested in guitars and music was probably less likely to get into serious trouble.

==
38   *(over)*

—1.   All students planning to attend the Student Council meeting are excused at 2:00.
1

—2.   Louis Pasteur ‚working in his laboratory ‚took time out to treat people for rabies.
2

—3.   The fifty-story Civic Center ‚located on the corner of Main and Daniels ‚was evacuated this afternoon due
2

   to a small fire in the lobby.

—4.   Every child enrolling in school for the first time must have a smallpox vaccination.
1

—5.   Their youngest daughter ‚loved by everyone ‚is not at all spoiled.
2

—6.   Anyone seeing a suspicious character should notify police immediately.
1

—7.   A long-distance telephone call wishing you a happy birthday is always a nice surprise.
1

—8.   My left index finger ‚badly bruised by the blow ‚began to swell.
2

—9.   Miss Danby ‚trying not to laugh ‚offered to help us with the stage makeup.
2

—10. The "House of Tiles" ‚built in Mexico City in the sixteenth century ‚is now known as Sanborn's.
2

==
16   **DIRECTIONS:** *In each sentence below there is a comma split. In the spaces below each sentence are the numbers of all the commas in the sentence. Find the comma split and write its number in the space at the left. Write what it is splitting beside that comma's number below the sentence. By the other numbers, write the "buzzwords" of the correct commas.*

— **1**   1.   The All-Breed Dog Show this weekend, will begin at 9:00 on Friday morning,
2   1   2
            10:00 on Saturday morning, and noon on Sunday.
                                    3

         — #1 *splits subject (All-Breed Dog Show) and verb (will begin)*
         1 _____

         — #2 *Items in a series*
         1 _____

         — #3 *Items in a series*
         1 _____

— **2**   2.   The beautiful, elegant, model walked gracefully across the stage, but she stopped and
2   1   2   3
            posed when she saw the camera.

         — #1 *Two adjectives "and" test*
         1 _____

         — #2 *splits modifier (elegant) and its noun (model)*
         1 _____

         — #3 *Compound sentence*
         1 _____

$\frac{3}{2}$ 3.   The winning student, who made a terrific speech, told me, a very funny story about how
                                    1   2   3
              he prepared for it.

              $\frac{}{1}$ **#1   *Nonessential modifier***

              $\frac{}{1}$ **#2   *Nonessential modifier***

              $\frac{}{1}$ **#3   *splits indirect object (me) and direct object (story)***

$\frac{1}{2}$ 4.   I am definitely, a real fan of old movies, early 50's rock-and-roll, and vintage clothes.
                                    1   2   3
              $\frac{}{1}$ **#1   *splits linking verb (am) and complement (fan)***

              $\frac{}{1}$ **#2   *Items in a series***

              $\frac{}{1}$ **#3   *Items in a series***

$\frac{3}{2}$ 5.   John, having seen "Star Trek" four times, doesn't want, to see it again, but I could see it
                                    1   2   3   4
              ten more times!

              $\frac{}{1}$ **#1   *Nonessential modifier***

              $\frac{}{1}$ **#2   *Nonessential modifier***

              $\frac{}{1}$ **#3   *splits verb (does want) and direct object (to see it again)***

==
26            $\frac{}{1}$ **#4 *Compound sentence***

Raw		Score		Grade	%
80	-	78	=	A++	=98+
77	-	76	=	A+	= 95
75	-	72	=	A	= 90
71	-	68	=	B+	= 85
67	-	64	=	B	= 80
63	-	60	=	C+	= 75
59	-	56	=	C	= 70
55	-	52	=	D+	= 65
51	-	48	=	D	= 60

COMMA RULE 5

Use a comma to set off certain INTRODUCTORY ELEMENTS (things which come at the beginning of the sentence). There are four separate "buzzwords" for this rule.

A.   **The "buzzword for this rule is *INTRODUCTORY SINGLE WORD:***

This rule applies to words which come at the beginning of the sentence and serve no function in the sentence, words such as *yes*, *well*, *no*, *why*, etc.

EXAMPLE: Why, you must be exhausted!

B.   **The "buzzword" for this rule is *INTRODUCTORY PARTICIPIAL PHRASE:***

Put a comma after an introductory participial phrase. (Remember, a participle is a verb that either ends in "ing" or fits into "I have _____.")

EXAMPLE: Pausing for a moment in the doorway, the new student smiled timidly.

C.   **The "buzzword" for this rule is *INTRODUCTORY ADVERB CLAUSE:***

Put a comma after an introductory adverb clause. (Remember the "thumb test" for finding out if a group of words is an adverb clause. Try this with the sentence below: #1: Put your left thumb over the subordinating conjunction *After.* #2: Put your right thumb over everything that follows the comma. Between your thumbnails you have "Bill hit the ball," right? That's a sentence, isn't it? That's how the "Thumb Test" works: if what's left between your thumbnails is a sentence, then that introductory group of words is an adverb clause.)

EXAMPLE: After Bill hit the ball, the crowd cheered.

D.   **The "buzzword" for this rule is *TWO OR MORE INTRODUCTORY PREPOSITIONAL PHRASES:***

Put a comma after TWO OR MORE introductory prepositional phrases.

EXAMPLE: Near the gate at the end of the corral, the horse stood quietly.

NOTE: If there is only one prepositional phrase at the beginning of the sentence, no comma is necessary **unless the sentence would be confusing without it.** Look at the sentence below and try to imagine it without the comma. Why would it be confusing if there were no comma in it?

In our state, sales tax is rather rare.

If the comma were not there, would you - at first - think that this sentence is about "state sales tax"? If the last word of the prepositional phrase looks like it might modify the next word, then you need a comma there to avoid confusion.

COMMA RULE 5: EXERCISE #1

NAME:_____DATE:_____

DIRECTIONS: *Underline and identify the introductory element in each sentence below. (sw=single word; part=participial phrase; prep=prepositional phrase(s); a.c.= adverb clause) Insert commas where they are needed.*

1.   <u>Yes,</u>Paula is my sister.
      sw

2.   <u>Climbing down a tree,</u>I ripped my pocket on a sharp twig.
      part

3.   <u>Since you collect coins,</u>you might want this one.
      a.c.

4.   <u>While we were vacationing in Montreal,</u>we met many French-speaking people.
      a.c.

5.   <u>In the morning,</u>mail is delivered to our house.
      prep

6.   <u>When we entered,</u>the room was empty.
      a.c.

7.   <u>In a corner of the garden,</u>the dog had buried all his bones.
      prep

8.   <u>While she was painting,</u>my sister accidentally broke a window.
      a.c.

9.   <u>On the morning of the third day,</u>the stranded hikers began to worry.
      prep

10.   <u>Say,</u>do you know where the key to the clock is?
      sw

DIRECTIONS: *In each sentence below there is a comma split. In the spaces below each sentence are the numbers of all the commas in the sentence. Find the comma split and write its number in the space at the left. Write what it is splitting beside that comma's number below the sentence. By the other numbers, write the "buzzwords" of the correct commas.*

___**1**___   1.   After Bill, hit the ball, the enthusiastic, exuberant crowd cheered, but the home team lost
                              1   2   3   4
                      anyway.

                      #1 *splits subject (Bill) and verb (hit)* _____

                      #2 *Intro adverb clause* _____

                      #3 *Two adjectives "and" test* _____

                      #4 *Compound sentence* _____

(over)

269

__3__   2.   John, who scored the top grade on the math final, has been given, the opportunity to
                                   1   2   3
                         attend a special math camp this summer.

                         #1   *Nonessential modifier*

                         #2   *Nonessential modifier*

                         #3   *splits verb (has been given) and direct object (opportunity)*

__1__   3.   Henry told Jill, a silly, ridiculous joke that really wasn't funny, but she laughed anyway.
                                           1   2   3
                         #1 *splits indirect object (Jill) and direct object (joke)*

                         #2 *Two adjectives "and" test*

                         #3 *Compound sentence*

COMMA RULE 5: EXERCISE #2

NAME: _____DATE:_____

DIRECTIONS: *Underline and identify the introductory elements in the sentences below, using the abbreviations you were given in Exercise #1. Insert commas where they are needed.*

1.   Known in China thousands of years ago, falconry is an ancient sport.
        part

2.   Like the hawk a falcon has a crooked beak.
        prep

3.   Although falconry is an ancient art, many people still enjoy it today.
        a.c.

4.   Having sharp claws and hooked beaks, falcons are naturally good hunters.
        part

5.   In the place of guns, some sportsmen use falcons for hunting.
        prep

6.   After she has learned to fly, a female falcon is taken from the nest and tamed.
        a.c.

7.   Until the falcon becomes accustomed to living around men, she wears a hood.
        a.c.

8.   Covering the eyes and head, this leather hood helps the hunter control the bird.
        part

9.   When the falcon has the hood on, the hunter carries the bird into the field.
        a.c.

10.   In the field the desired game is located.
        prep

11.   When the hunter sees his prey and takes the hood off, the falcon instinctively attacks.
        a.c.

12.   In addition to a hood, other implements are used in falconry.
        prep

13.   During a hunt a falconer usually wears a heavy leather gauntlet or glove.
        prep

14.   When he is training a young falcon to hunt, he also uses lures.
        a.c.

15.   Used properly, lures teach falcons to attack certain birds.
        part

16.   Containing pieces of meat and feathers, the lure quickly attracts the falcon.
        part

17.   Within seconds a hungry falcon usually pounces upon the lure.
        prep

18.   Yes, falcons become trained hunters in a short time.
        sw

19.   Since the falcon's speed and accuracy are extremely effective, guns are unnecessary.
        a.c.

20.   In a field with a falcon, hunters often use a dog to retrieve the game.
        prep

(over)

DIRECTIONS: *In each sentence below there is a comma split. In the spaces below each sentence are the numbers of all the commas in the sentence. Find the comma split and write its number in the space at the left. Write what it is splitting beside that comma's number below the sentence. By the other numbers, write the "buzzwords" of the correct commas.*

__1__   1.   Three students in Mrs. Finley's 3rd hour class have received this month, awards for
                                                                                          1
                attendance, courtesy, and academic excellence.
                                  2   3

                #1   *splits verb (have received) and direct object (awards)*

                #2   *Items in a series*

                #3   *Items in a series*

__2__   2.   The happy, excited, fans ran out onto the football field, and they carried the triumphant
                               1   2   3
                coach around the track.

                #1   *Two adjectives "and" test*

                #2   *splits modifier (excited) and its noun (fans)*

                #3   *Compound sentence*

__4__   3.   In a drawer in my dresser, I keep my diary, which contains my innermost thoughts, but
                                            1   2   3
                no one but me, is allowed to see it.
                             4

                #1   *Intro prep*

                #2   *Nonessential modifier*

                #3   *Compound sentence & Nonessential modifier*

                #4   *splits subject (no one) and verb (is allowed)*

Photocopying this product is strictly prohibited by copyright law.

COMMA RULE 5: EXERCISE #3

NAME:_____DATE:_____

DIRECTIONS: *Underline and identify the introductory elements in the sentences below, using the abbreviations you were given for Exercise #1. Insert commas where they are necessary.*

1.   <u>Why,</u>the entire story is false!
        sw

2.   <u>Washing and polishing the car for hours,</u>the boys found that they were tired.
                part

3.   <u>While Mario put the costume on,</u> the accompanist played "Rhapsody in Blue."
                a.c.

4.   <u>At the edge of the deep woods near Lakeville in Cumberland County,</u>they built a small cabin.
                prep

5.   <u>Among the weak and cowardly,</u> competition is usually unpopular.
                prep

6.   <u>Oh,</u>I wouldn't be too sure of that!
        sw

7.   <u>Behaving like a spoiled child,</u>he sulked and pouted for hours.
                part

8.   <u>When we had finished playing,</u>the piano was rolled offstage to make room for the next act.
                a.c.

9.   <u>On the afternoon of the first day of school,</u>the halls are filled with confused 7th graders.
                prep

10.   <u>Driven beyond her patience,</u>the teacher slammed her book upon the desk.
                part

11.   <u>In a minute</u> I will leave for home.
                prep

12.   <u>In the dark,</u>shadows can appear to be monsters.
                prep

PART II: DIRECTIONS: *Write sentences according to the following instructions.*

1.   A sentence with a single-word introductory element.

2.   A sentence with an introductory participial phrase.

3.   A sentence with two or more introductory prepositional phrases.

4.   A sentence with an introductory adverb clause.   *Answers will vary*

5.   A sentence demonstrating "items in a series."

6.   A sentence demonstrating "two adjectives with 'and test.'"

7.   A sentence demonstrating "compound sentence."

8.   A sentence demonstrating "nonessential modifier."

(over)

DIRECTIONS: *In each sentence below there is a comma split. In the spaces below each sentence are the numbers of all the commas in the sentence. Find the comma split and write its number in the space at the left. Write what it is splitting beside that comma's number below the sentence. By the other numbers, write the "buzzwords" of the correct commas.*

__4__   1.   Speaking on the intercom, Mr. Campbell, who is our principal, read us in his clear
                 1   2   3

voice, the morning announcements.
   4

#1   *Intro part*

#2   *Nonessential modifier*

#3   *Nonessential modifier*

#4   *splits indirect object (us) and its direct object (announcements)*

__5__   2.   Well, I have a particular reason, which I certainly don't have to explain, for not doing my
               1   2   3

boring, stupid, homework!
   4   5

#1   *Intro s. w.*

#2   *Nonessential modifier*

#3   *Nonessential modifier*

#4   *Two adjectives "and" test*

#5   *splits modifier (stupid) and its noun (homework)*

__2__   3.   The short, dumpy woman in the line at the bakery sounded completely, idiotic when she
                1   2

asked for some bread, which was the only product they sold in the store.
                              3

#1   *Two adjectives "and" test*

#2   *splits linking verb (sounded) and complement (idiotic)*

#3   *Nonessential modifier*

    Photocopying this product is strictly prohibited by copyright law.

COMMA RULE #5: TEST

NAME:_____DATE:_____

(RAW SCORE:_____*/104*__GRADE:_____)

PART I: *ITEMS IN A SERIES: Insert commas where they are needed.*

___3___ 1.   She was formerly on the staff of the embassies in Moscow, Berlin, Vienna, and Madrid.

___2___ 2.   There were toys for the children, books for Mom and Dad, and a stereo for me!

___2___ 3.   During the summer, workers installed a new gym floor, an improved heating system,

and green chalkboards in the high school.

___1___ 4.   The weather forecaster predicted rain or sleet or snow for tomorrow.

== ___3___ 5.   We walked, we played, we ate, and we had a great time.
11

PART II: *TWO ADJECTIVES WITH "AND TEST": Insert commas where they are needed.*

___1___ 1.   She is an alert, lively girl.

___2___ 2.   We patiently sat through a long, dull, amateurish performance.

___2___ 3.   It was a raw, cold, dark November day.

___1___ 4.   She is a bright, talented young woman.

== ___1___ 5.   He wore a new blue blazer to the concert.
7

PART III: *COMPOUND SENTENCE: Insert commas where they are needed.*

___1___ 1.   I grabbed the wet dog, and Susie slammed the door before he could get away.

___1___ 2.   I gave some good advice to Jim and got some from him in return.

___1___ 3.   The first two acts were slow-moving, but the third act is full of action.

___1___ 4.   You go ahead and I'll follow you.

== ___1___ 5.   The train pulled out of the station and left me stranded there with no luggage.
5

PART IV: *NONESSENTIAL MODIFIERS: Insert commas where they are needed.*

___2___ 1.   John Thomas, who was offered scholarships to two colleges, will go to Yale in September.

___1___ 2.   John Thomas is the only senior who was offered two scholarships.

___2___ 3.   My youngest brother, who was playing in the street, was almost struck by a car.

___1___ 4.   Animals frightened by thunder often try to hide.

== ___1___ 5.   Friends who do favors for you may expect you to do favors for them.
7

(over)

PART V: *INTRODUCTORY ELEMENTS: Underline and identify the introductory element in each sentence below, using the following abbreviations:(sw=single word; part=participial phrase; prep=prepositional phrase; ac=adverb clause.) Insert commas where they are necessary.*

__1.　　Well, be sure to ask if you need help. _____*sw*_____
3

__2.　　In the second half of the first period, Johnson slam-dunked the ball to put our team in the lead.
3

　　　　_____*prep*_____

__3.　　Speaking in the assembly, Katy Stover urged students to continue to keep the school clean.
3

　　　　_____*part*_____

__4.　　In the newspaper, writers seldom make grammatical errors. _____*prep*_____
3

__5.　　When Bill was driving, our truck lurched alarmingly. _____*a.c.*_____
3

__6.　　Having studied the commas rules in detail, Jean aced the test. _____*part*_____
3

__7.　　Why, anyone can see the child is ill! _____*sw*_____
3

__8.　　Since we were leaving in the morning, we went to bed early. _____*a.c.*_____
3

__9.　　By the end of the class, the students were extremely restless. _____*prep*_____
3

__10.　　Finished at the last minute, the assignment was poorly done. _____*part*_____
3

==
30

PART VI: ALL COMMA RULES COMBINED: *Insert commas where they are needed.*

__1.　　Looking for the lost car keys, we searched under the car, in the house, on the porch, and
4

　　　　among the weeds.

__2.　　Well, I guess that about does it!
1

__3.　　Among the synonyms are "humor", "wit", "sarcasm", and "irony."
3

__4.　　After we had placed an ad in the paper, we found the owner of the puppy.
1

__5.　　I sold three tickets, Jason sold four, Jill sold ten, and Myra sold twelve.
3

__6.　　Wanting to gain attention, the child talked loudly and interrupted our conversation.
1

__7.　　In the second section on page 23, notice the list of helping verbs.
1

__8.　　Students going on the field trip must be at the bus at 9:00 sharp.
1

__9.　　In the wild, animals must kill for food.
1

__10.　　The teacher read us an excerpt from the speech, yet we were not able to recognize it later.
1

==
17

　　　　Photocopying this product is strictly prohibited by copyright law.

PART VII: DIRECTIONS: *In each sentence below there is a comma split. In the spaces below each sentence are the numbers of all the commas in the sentence. Find the comma split and write its number in the space at the left. Write what it is splitting beside that comma's number below the sentence. By the other numbers, write the "buzzwords" of the correct commas.*

<u>2</u>⁵ 1. The exhausted, exasperated, teacher walked quickly to the faculty lounge, which was the only
              ¹   ²   ³
          place where she could get away from kids for a while.

          <u>#1</u>₁ *Two adjectives "and" test* _____

          <u>#2</u>₁ *splits modifier (exasperated) and its noun (teacher)* _____

          <u>#3</u>₁ *Nonessential modifier* _____

<u>2</u>⁵ 2. In a kingdom by the sea, the boy in the poem, loved the main character, who was called
                               ¹   ²   ³
          Annabel Lee.

          <u>#1</u>₁ *Intro prep phrases* _____

          <u>#2</u>₁ *splits subject (boy) and verb (loved)* _____

          <u>#3</u>₁ *Nonessential modifier* _____

<u>2</u>⁶ 3. Determined to catch students running in the halls, Mr. Calderera suspended, John Griffith, Jason
                                                        ¹   ²   ³
          McGrath, and Tina Matthews.
                   ⁴
          <u>#1</u>₁ *Intro part phrase* _____

          <u>#2</u>₁ *splits verb (suspended) and direct object (John Griffith, etc)* ___

          <u>#3</u>₁ *Items in a series* _____

          <u>#4</u>₁ *Items in a series* _____

<u>3</u>⁵ 4. The Great Bandini, who is undoubtedly the greatest magician on earth, showed his enraptured
                            ¹   ²
          audience, the most amazing trick of all time.
                   ³
          <u>#1</u>₁ *Nonessential modifier* _____

          <u>#2</u>₁ *Nonessential modifier* _____

          <u>#3</u>₁ *splits indirect object (audience) and direct object (trick)* _____

$\frac{1}{6}$ 5.   The student who wrote the best essay was, the winner of the Literary Award, and he received a
                                                            1   2

scholarship, a cash prize, and a certificate.
                    3   4

$\frac{}{1}$ #1   *splits linking verb (was) and complement (winner)*

$\frac{}{1}$ #2   *Cmpound sentence*

$\frac{}{1}$ #3   *Items in a series*

$\frac{}{1}$ #4   *Items in a series*

==
27

Raw		Score		Grade	%
104	-	101	=	A++	=98+
100	-	98	=	A+	= 95
97	-	93	=	A	= 90
92	-	88	=	B+	= 85
87	-	83	=	B	= 80
82	-	78	=	C+	= 75
77	-	72	=	C	= 70
71	-	67	=	D+	= 65
66	-	62	=	D	= 60

COMMA RULES 6, 7, & 8

These comma rules have to do with things that INTERRUPT the sentence. There are three things that, because they "interrupt" the structure of the sentence, are set off by commas.

RULE #6: **The "buzzword" for this rule is either *APPOSITIVES* or *APPOSITIVE PHRASES*.** These are usually set off by commas.

An APPOSITIVE is a noun or pronoun. An APPOSITIVE PHRASE is a noun or pronoun plus anything that modifies it. It is located (usually) after another noun or pronoun and helps to describe it by giving further information about it.

EXAMPLE: I often play tennis, a lively game. (The appositive phrase "a lively game" is another way of saying "tennis" and further describes it.)

NOTE: Sometimes an appositive is so closely related to the noun it restates that it should not be set off by commas. You can usually tell when this is the case by reading the sentence "a la network newscaster." If there is no <u>need</u> to pause, there should not be commas to set it off.

EXAMPLES: My sister Elizabeth is left-handed. (appositive=Elizabeth)
We girls are going shopping. (appositive=girls)
The writer Mark Twain is dead. (appositive=Mark Twain)

NOTE: If the appositive phrase is a title which is already "set off" by either italics or quotation marks, then the commas around that title should be eliminated.

EXAMPLE: My favorite book <u>Gone With the Wind</u> was a national sensation.

Since the title of the book is underlined (or in italics), it is already "set off" from the rest of the sentence, so no commas are necessary.

RULE #7: **The "buzzword" for this rule is *DIRECT ADDRESS*.** Words used in **direct address** are set off by commas.

DIRECT ADDRESS means any name you call someone when you are DIRECTLY ADDRESSING them.

EXAMPLES: The program, Jean, has been changed.(direct address = Jean)
Miss Bates, may I leave early? (direct address=Miss Bates)
Please answer the doorbell, Honey. (direct address=Honey)

RULE #8: **The "buzzword" for this rule is *EXPRESSIONS*.** Expressions are set off by commas.

This rule applies to EXPRESSIONS that are inserted into sentences - not really necessary information - but the kind of information you might put in parentheses. These are often commonly used expressions like "after all," or "on the other hand," or "I think."

EXAMPLES: He didn't, however, keep his promise.(expression=however)
After all, you won the contest! (expression = after all)
Men, in general, like dark suits. (expression = in general)

COMMA RULES 6, 7, & 8: EXERCISE #1

NAME:_____DATE:_____

DIRECTIONS: *Underline the appositive or appositive phrase, draw an arrow to the noun or pronoun it restates, and insert commas where they are necessary.*

1.   Jack, my little cousin, still prefers nursery rhymes.

2.   My friend Mary Jo will visit us soon.

3.   Carolyn Keene, author of the Nancy Drew stories, is a popular writer.

4.   Have you met Gail Phillips, my best friend?

5.   Science, my favorite subject, gets more fun each year.

6.   The Smith twins, members of the rugby team, have to report for practice soon.

7.   Archimedes, the Greek physicist, made a great discovery by placing a gold crown in a tub of water.

8.   The boys had fun working on the car, a dilapidated old wreck.

9.   Only two of the animals, a horse and a cow, were saved from the fire.

10.   A black funnel-shaped cloud, sign of a tornado, sent everyone running for shelter.

DIRECTIONS: *Rewrite each pair of sentences into a single sentence containing an appositive or appositive phrase.*

EXAMPLE: Jill Douglas is mayor of our town. She will speak next.

             Jill Douglas, mayor of our town, will speak next.

1.   The fastest runner is Penny Tate. She is on the track team.
          The fastest runner, Penny Tate, is on the track team.
2.   We have a favorite horse. Her name is Daisy and she won the race.
          Our favorite horse, Daisy, won the race.
3.   The author is Mark Twain. He knew a lot about people.
          The author Mark Twain knew a lot about people.
4.   The girl in the third row is Paula. She likes to hike.
          Paula, the girl in the third row, likes to hike.
5.   There was only one hit against Wills. It was a single.
          There was only one hit against Wills, a single.

Answers may vary, but be sure each sentence contains an appositive phrase and doesn't change the meaning of the original two sentences.

DIRECTIONS: *Insert commas where they are needed.*

1.   Mother, have you met Mrs. Gillespie?

2.   On the other hand, I'd rather have the day off.

3.   Dinner, Madame, is served.

(over)

DIRECTIONS: *In each sentence below there is a comma split. In the spaces below each sentence are the numbers of all the commas in the sentence. Find the comma split and write its number in the space at the left. Write what it is splitting beside that comma's number below the sentence. By the other numbers, write the "buzzwords" of the correct commas.*

_1_   1.   Since the boy who was the winner of the skating competition, had only been training for a short
                                                                    1

while, some of the other competitors were jealous, or at least they resented his apparently
        2   3

effortless, natural style.
            4

#1   *splits subject (boy) and verb (had been training)*

#2   *Intro a. c.*

#3   *Compound sentence*

#4   *Two adjectives "and" test*

_5_   2.   In a short, clear memo to his workers, Mr. Baldwin described all the things he thought were
                    1   2

wrong with the company, how they had gotten that way, and exactly what, could be done
                            3   4   5

about them.

#1   *Two adjectives "and" test*

#2   *Intro prep*

#3   *Items in a series*

#4   *Items in a series*

#5   *splits subject (what) and verb (could be done)*

_4_   3.   Jackie, my little cousin, still enjoys nursery rhymes, yet he is growing every day, more and
                1   2   3   4

more mature.

#1   *Appositive*

#2   *Appositive*

#3   *Compound sentence*

#4   *splits linking verb (is growing) and complement (mature)*

281

COMMA RULES 6, 7, & 8: EXERCISE #2

NAME:_____DATE:_____

DIRECTIONS: *Underline the appositives and appositive phrases below. Insert commas where they are needed.*

Yesterday at dawn my family was startled out of bed by a loud screech of tires, my uncle Jasper's car pulling into our driveway. Soon we heard voices in the hallway, our relatives all talking at once. Sadie, my aunt, asked, "Oh, is this pretty house where your brother Bob lives? Won't they be surprised to see us, their favorite relatives?"

Sparky, our little cocker spaniel, expressed our surprise by barking noisily at the intruders, our uninvited and unexpected relatives. Then Bonecrusher, their Saint Bernard, lumbered forward and tried to make breakfast out of Sparky! Dad untangled the snarling animals and tied both of them, Sparky and Bonecrusher, in the backyard. Mortal enemies on sight, the dogs spent the rest of the day growling and yapping at each other.

A minor incident, that fight was only the beginning of the turmoil in our house. Wilbur, Uncle Jasper's youngest boy, took an immediate liking to a handpainted vase, a treasured heirloom, and dashed it to smithereens. While Aunt Sadie was apologizing for Wilbur, Uncle Jasper was chasing Sylvester, his oldest boy. Sylvester, meanwhile, was chasing my sister Beth so he could cut her hair with the kitchen scissors!

Just before leaving the house, a place I used to call "Home Sweet Home", Uncle Jasper said, "We're going to spend our vacation, two whole weeks, with you!" To be polite, we have to stay home and play nifty games, particularly Monopoly and Chinese checkers. Even our family's bedtime, formerly 10:00, has changed to midnight. And, since Aunt Sadie has insomnia, a condition which prevents her from sleeping past 5:00 a.m., everybody gets up for an early breakfast. My stomach turns when I think about their visit, a full two weeks.

But yesterday Mother, a wonderfully wise person, smiled at my complaints. "Take heart, Daniel my son," she said. "Remember that we will have our revenge! Our day will come at about 2:00 p.m. on a Thursday in November, Thanksgiving, when - totally unannounced - we'll just drop in on THEM!!!"

DIRECTIONS: *Use each of the following items as an APPOSITIVE or APPOSITIVE PHRASE in a sentence of your own. Write 10 separate sentences, one for each item below.*

1.   Linda   4.   a good teacher   7.   a girl sitting near me
2.   a nuisance   5.   Austin and Victor   8.   the candidate to select
3.   my neighbor   6.   the life of the party   9.   a book for children
                                                            10.   the man you should meet

EXAMPLE: Mrs. Finley, a good teacher, is also a wonderful person.(...your sentences don't have to be true...)

(over)

Photocopying this product is strictly prohibited by copyright law.

DIRECTIONS: *In each sentence below there is a comma split. In the spaces below each sentence are the numbers of all the commas in the sentence. Find the comma split and write its number in the space at the left. Write what it is splitting beside that comma's number below the sentence. By the other numbers, write the "buzzwords" of the correct commas.*

3   1.   My neighbor's relatives, an interesting group, visit them each summer with an
                                           1   2
           assortment of equally peculiar, friends.
                                                       3

   #1   *Appositive*

   #2   *Appositive*

   #3   *splits modifier (peculiar) and its noun (friends)*

3   2.   During the early part of last June, they were looking forward to a few weeks of complete, total
                                                 1   2
           relaxation when they answered, an unwelcome knock at the door.
                                                     3

   #1   *Intro prep*

   #2   *Two adjectives "and" test*

   #3   *splits verb (answered) and direct object (knock)*

4   3.   Standing there in all their splendor of baggy Bermuda shorts, knobby knees, and friendly grins
                                                                            1   2
           were his uncle Herbert and his large, obnoxious, family.
                                                       3   4

   #1   *Items in a series*

   #2   *Items in a series*

   #3   *Two adjectives "and" test*

   #4   *splits modifier (obnoxious) and its noun (family)*

283

COMMA RULES 6, 7, & 8: EXERCISE #3

NAME:_____DATE:_____

DIRECTIONS: *Underline the interrupters in the sentences below. Identify them in the space below as follows:* *appos = appositive or appositive phrase, da = direct address, expr = expression. Insert commas where they are needed.*

1.   The story, in my opinion, is much too long and complicated. **_Expression_**

2.   You scoundrel, what do you mean by trying to cheat your friends? **_Direct address_**

3.   When Mr. Kean, my geography teacher, visited Indiana, he toured the campus of Purdue.

        Appositive

4.   Richie, leave the room and shut the door. **_Direct address_**

5.   Mathematics, I'm afraid, is my hardest subject. **_Expression_**

6.   *Little Women*, a classic book for young people, was part of my growing up. **_Appositive_**

7.   You will stay, I hope, as long as you possibly can. **_Expression_**

8.   Do you remember, Patty, what Romeo's last name was? **_Direct address_**

9.   Modern highways, for example, are marvelous feats of engineering. **_Expression_**

10.   May I go to the movies, Dad? **_Direct address_**

DIRECTIONS: *This is an activity you and your teacher will do tomorrow. You don't have to do anything for homework.*

1.	as I was saying	4.	for instance	7.	on the other hand
2.	on the contrary	5.	if you ask me	8.	however
3.	of course	6.	to tell the truth	9.	for example
				10.	in fact

(over)

Photocopying this product is strictly prohibited by copyright law.

DIRECTIONS: *In each sentence below there is a comma split. In the spaces below each sentence are the numbers of all the commas in the sentence. Find the comma split and write its number in the space at the left. Write what it is splitting beside that comma's number below the sentence. By the other numbers, write the "buzzwords" of the correct commas.*

4   1.   What, in your opinion, was the cause of the economic crash of 1929, and why didn't the people in
                   1   2   3
           charge of the Stock Market, do anything about it?
                                      4

   #1   *Expression*

   #2   *Expression*

   #3   *Compound sentence*

   #4   *splits subject (people) and verb (do)*

6   2.   My hair dryer, which I bought three years ago, has put out more hot air than all Presidential
                          1   2
           candidates put together, but this morning, if you can believe it, it decided, to poop out on me!
                                   3   4   5   6

   #1   *Nonessential modifier*

   #2   *Nonessential modifier*

   #3   *Compound sentence*

   #4   *Expression*

   #5   *Expression*

   #6   *splits verb (decided) and direct object (to poop out...)*

1   3.   Anybody who has ever tried to eat spaghetti at a fancy restaurant, knows that, no matter what,
                                                                               1   2   3
           you'll end up with spots of sauce all over your chin, down your shirt, and on the tablecloth.
                                                              4   5

   #1   *splits subject (anybody) and verb (knows)*

   #2   *Expression*

   #3   *Expression*

   #4   *Items in a series*

   #5   *Items in a series*

285

PLAYING WITH TRANSITIONAL DEVICES

What you see below is a conversation about Mrs. Dragonbottom, the evil grammar teacher. Do you find it difficult to follow? Doesn't it appear to be saying one thing and then saying just the opposite? Now, using the transitional devices at the bottom of Exercise #3, put the first expression in front of the first sentence below; put the second expression in front of the second sentence, and so on. Is it hard to follow now? That's how valuable these transitional devices are; you should make an effort to use them in your writing until they become second nature.

SAMPLE CONVERSATION

Mrs. Dragonbottom is the meanest teacher in this whole school!

She's an absolute sweetiepie!

She can be rather vindictive when she is crossed.

She gave me a detention just for setting fire to Martha Sue's pigtails!

She's a mean old witch!

I don't think I've ever known anybody as mean as Mrs. Dragonbottom.

She rescued that poor little lost puppy last week.

That doesn't excuse all the other stuff she does.

When Billy knocked over the outhouse, she called his mom!

Billy was grounded until his 21st birthday!

NOW - TRY IT WITH THE EXPRESSIONS!

we always have a lot of fun with this exercise, but its primary purpose is for students to see how important it is to insert "transitional devices" into their writing to enhance clarity. After we've gone through the above conversation, I usually start one with something like "If you ask me, _____over there is a real pain in the neck!" Immediately the conversation starts rolling, with people either agreeing with me or defending the person, depending on the transitional device that's next. Try it!

COMMA RULES 6, 7, & 8: TEST

NAME:_____ DATE:_____

(RAW SCORE:_____ */82* GRADE:_____)

PART I: DIRECTIONS: *Insert commas where they are needed.*

$\frac{2}{}$ 1.   Shana Alexander, one-time editor of <u>McCall's</u>, was the main speaker.

$\frac{1}{}$ 2.   We have a figurine made of clay from Kilimanjaro, Africa's highest mountain.

$\frac{1}{}$ 3.   The whole class listened to my best friend Jane give her speech.

$\frac{2}{}$ 4.   Saint Augustine, the oldest city in the United States, has many very narrow streets.

$\frac{2}{}$ 5.   Sugar cane, an important Florida crop, may be shipped refined or raw.

$\frac{1}{}$ 6.   Do you own a thesaurus, a dictionary of synonyms and antonyms?

$\frac{2}{}$ 7.   At North Cape, the northernmost point of Europe, the sun does not set from the middle

of May until the end of July.

$\frac{2}{}$ 8.   The American mastodon, an extinct, elephantlike animal, was hunted by primitive man.

$\frac{1}{}$ 9.   John F. Kennedy's brother Robert was assassinated during a Presidential campaign.

$\frac{2}{}$ 10.   At Thermopylae, a narrow pass in Eastern Greece, a band of three hundred Spartans faced

==
16   an army of thousands from Persia.

PART II: DIRECTIONS: *Insert commas where they are needed.*

$\frac{1}{}$ 1.   Sandra, why do you call your cat Cleopatra?

$\frac{1}{}$ 2.   Stop this incessant chatter, class.

$\frac{2}{}$ 3.   We, my fellow graduates of the class of 2000, will be the leaders of the 21st century.

$\frac{1}{}$ 4.   Professor Adams, when was the Battle of Marathon?

$\frac{1}{}$ 5.   What is your opinion of the candidates, Laura?

$\frac{1}{}$ 6.   Dad, may I borrow the car?

$\frac{2}{}$ 7.   Where, my dear Mr. Ditherington, do you think you are going?

$\frac{1}{}$ 8.   Senator Smith, I have a proposal for improving our state.

$\frac{1}{}$ 9.   Lisa, you really must apologize.

$\frac{1}{}$ 10.   You know that dogs aren't allowed on the couch, Snoopy!

==
12

(over)

PART III: DIRECTIONS: *Insert commas where they are needed.*

$\frac{}{1}$ 1.   Yes, there are many constellations visible in the summer.

$\frac{}{1}$ 2.   For instance, on a summer night you can see the Scorpion and the Serpent.

$\frac{}{1}$ 3.   To be sure, we should not fail to mention the Milky Way.

$\frac{}{2}$ 4.   The Milky Way, in fact, is more impressive in the summer than at any other time.

$\frac{}{1}$ 5.   Of course, Hercules is an interesting constellation.

$\frac{}{2}$ 6.   Studying the constellations is, in my opinion, a most interesting pastime.

$\frac{}{2}$ 7.   It does take some imagination, however, to pick out some of them.

$\frac{}{2}$ 8.   The Archer, for example, is hard to perceive.

$\frac{}{2}$ 9.   The Scorpion, on the other hand, is quite clearly outlined.

$\frac{}{2}$ 10.   Astronomy, I think, is a fascinating science.

$==$
16

PART IV: DIRECTIONS: *Insert commas where they are needed.*

$\frac{}{2}$ 1.   The whole family, several friends, and some relatives from out-of-state came for dinner

on Sunday.

$\frac{}{1}$ 2.   Mom made a delicious gourmet meal, and we sat down to a table loaded with food.

$\frac{}{1}$ 3.   Yes, we all ate way too much!

$\frac{}{2}$ 4.   I especially loved the golden-brown, piping-hot, home-baked rolls.

$\frac{}{2}$ 5.   My dad, who is trying to lose a few pounds, started off with a generous serving of salad.

$\frac{}{1}$ 6.   Since he'd eaten only salad, he decided to have a "tiny taste" of everything else.

$\frac{}{2}$ 7.   The "tiny taste", a generous serving of everything edible on the table, filled his plate!

$\frac{}{2}$ 8.   His diet, needless to say, was blown sky-high for the day.

$\frac{}{1}$ 9.   Cutting himself a large piece of lemon-meringue pie, Dad declared that his diet would

start first thing the next morning.

$\frac{}{1}$ 10.   Dinners eaten on festive occasions in our house are always fatal to Dad's diet!

$==$
15

****

DIAGRAM FOR 5 POINTS EXTRA CREDIT:

Any student of this course in grammar should know the structure of the sentence and the function of every word

in it.

DIRECTIONS: *In each sentence below there is a comma split. In the spaces below each sentence are the numbers of all the commas in the sentence. Find the comma split and write its number in the space at the left. Write what it is splitting beside that comma's number below the sentence. By the other numbers, write the "buzzwords" of the correct commas.*

$\frac{4}{2}$ 1. Yes, we all sat around looking at old yearbooks, laughing at the funny hair styles we wore, and
            1   2   3
    secretly wishing with all our hearts, that we could go back to those good old days for a while.
                                          4

$\frac{}{1}$ #1 ***Intro s. w.***

$\frac{}{1}$ #2 ***Items in a series***

$\frac{}{1}$ #3 ***Items in a series***

$\frac{}{1}$ #4 ***splits verb (wishing) and direct object (that we could go...)***

$\frac{1}{2}$ 2. The character in the play who had all the money and fame, was the one whom we most suspected,
                                                      1   2
    but the real murderer was a quiet, mousy person that no on even noticed!.
                          3

$\frac{}{1}$ #1 ***splits subject (character) and verb (was)***

$\frac{}{1}$ #2 ***Compound sentence***

$\frac{}{1}$ #3 ***Two adjectives "and" test***

$\frac{4}{2}$ 3. John, the most able debater on the team, appeared to be stumped for an answer until one of the
          1   2
    youngest, least-experienced, members of the team saved the day.
            3   4

$\frac{}{1}$ #1 ***Appositive***

$\frac{}{1}$ #2 ***Appositive***

$\frac{}{1}$ #3 ***Two adjectives "and" test***

$\frac{}{1}$ #4 ***splits modifier (least-experienced) and its noun (members)***

$\frac{4}{2}$ 4. Before Albert was old enough to get a license, he had already picked out his car, a used Chevrolet
                                          1   2
    with 40,000 miles on it, and started with his own money, a savings account for the down payment.
                          3   4

$\frac{}{1}$ #1 ***Intro a. c.***

$\frac{}{1}$ #2 ***Appositive***

$\frac{}{1}$ #3 ***Appositive***

$\frac{}{1}$ #4 ***splits verb (started) and direct object (account)***

$\frac{==}{23}$

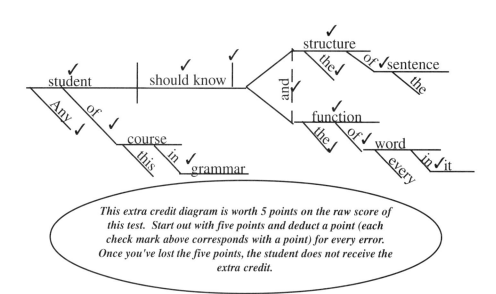

This extra credit diagram is worth 5 points on the raw score of this test. Start out with five points and deduct a point (each check mark above corresponds with a point) for every error. Once you've lost the five points, the student does not receive the extra credit.

Raw		Score		Grade	%
82	-	80	=	A++	= 98+
79	-	77	=	A+	= 95
76	-	73	=	A	= 90
72	-	69	=	B+	= 85
68	-	65	=	B	= 80
64	-	61	=	C+	= 75
60	-	57	=	C	= 70
56	-	53	=	D+	= 65
52	-	49	=	D	= 60

COMMA RULES 9, 10, & 11

COMMA RULE #9:   **The "buzzword" for this rule is** *DATES & ADDRESSES:* use commas to separate items in dates and addresses.

          EXAMPLE: My family moved to Knoxville, Tennessee, on Monday, May 4, 1964.

                                  On May 4, 1964, I bought a car at Cisco Cadillac, 645 Commerce Street, Knoxville, Tennessee 20200.

If the items in your address or date are separated by prepositions, they should not also be separated by commas.

          EXAMPLE: I moved to 330 Elm Street in Waynesville, Illinois. (no comma after Elm Street)

                                 (NOTE: There is no comma between the state and zip code.)
(ALSO NOTE: When a date or an address is part of a sentence, you must put a comma AFTER the last item in the date or address, if the sentence continues on. Look at the comma after "Tennessee" and the one after "1964" in the sentences above.)

COMMA RULE #10:   *The "buzzword" for this rule is SALUTATIONS & CLOSINGS:* use a comma after the salutation of a friendly letter (use a colon after the salutation of a business letter) and after the closing of any letter.

          EXAMPLE: Dear Jim, (friendly letter)
Dear Mr. Jones: (business letter)
Truly yours,
Loves and kisses,

COMMA RULE #11:   *The "buzzword" for this rule is NAMES & ABBREVIATIONS:* use a comma between a name and Jr., Sr., M.D., etc.

          EXAMPLE: Allen Davies, Jr.
Stanley Browne, M. D.

                                 (NOTE: Do not use a comma between a name and a Roman numeral - Jonathan Sanders III; Henry VIII; Elizabeth I)

COMMA RULES 9, 10, & 11: EXERCISE #1

NAME:_____DATE:_____

DIRECTIONS: *Insert commas where they are needed.*

1.   443 North University Avenue, Lansing, Michigan 48103

2.   1900 Logan Road, Linden, New Jersey 07036

3.   Monday, August 5, 1991

4.   after January 1, 1984

5.   379 Scott Avenue, Salt Lake City, Utah 85115

6.   Michigan Avenue at Twelfth Street, Chicago, Illinois

7.   Thanksgiving Day, 1978

8.   from June 23, 1989, to January 2, 1990

9.   either Tuesday, September 3, or Saturday, September 7

10.   Box 147, Rapid City, South Dakota

11.   The building on the corner of Market Street and Highland Avenue in Akron, Ohio, is where my

      grandfather was born.

12.   Sincerely yours,

13.   Dear Jean, (in a letter thanking her for a baby shower gift.)   *

14.   Dear George: (in a letter asking your tax man for information on the stock market)   *

15.   The Founding Fathers of our nation signed the Declaration of Independence in Philadelphia,

      Pennsylvania, on July 4, 1776.

16.   The party will be on Friday, July 9, in Wheeling, West Virginia, at 7:00 in the evening.

---

* *What determines whether or not a letter is a business letter or a friendly letter is not how well you know the person to whom you are writing; it is determined by the intent of the letter. If the letter's content is social, it is a friendly letter (even if you're writing to someone you've never met). If the content is business, it's a business letter (even if you're writing to your old college roommate who does your taxes!)*

(over)

DIRECTIONS: *In each sentence below there is a comma split. In the spaces below each sentence are the numbers of all the commas in the sentence. Find the comma split and write its number in the space at the left. Write what it is splitting beside that comma's number below the sentence. By the other numbers, write the "buzzwords" of the correct commas.*

___3___ 1.   In July, 1776, Thomas Jefferson and the other Founding Fathers, gave us the Declaration of
                   1   2   3
              Independence.

              #1 - dates & addresses

              #2 - dates & addresses

              #3 - splits subject (T.J. and the F.F.) & verb (gave)

___1___ 2.   The men at the Continental Congress in Philadelphia, voted on a document which remains to this
                                                                   1
              day one of the most famous, revered writings of all time, but they probably didn't realize that at
                                          2   3
              the time.

              #1 - splits subject (men) & verb (voted)

              #2 - 2 adjectives with "and test"

              #3 - compound sentence

___3___ 3.   When the Declaration was finally signed on July 4, 1776, they surely thought, that the world
                                                              1   2   3
              would soon forget what they had done on that hot, humid day.
                                                              4

              #1 - dates & addresses

              #2 - dates & addresses and/or introductory adverb clause

              #3 - splits verb (thought) & direct object (that the ...)

              #4 - 2 adjectives with "and test"

COMMA RULES 9, 10, & 11: EXERCISE #2

NAME:_____DATE:_____

DIRECTIONS: *Insert commas where they are needed.*

1.   The first Boston Marathon was held on April 19, 1897.

2.   Are you talking about Kansas City, Kansas, or Kansas City, Missouri?

3.   Sherlock Holmes supposedly lived at 221B Baker Street, London, England.

4.   Send your reply to Campbell and Jones, Inc., 135 South LaSalle Street, Chicago, Illinois

        60603.

5.   He was born on April 3, 1963, which makes him an Aries.

6.   Ed's address is 4652 Orchard Street, Oakland, California.

7.   We're going to the museum on Thursday, May 5.

8.   Does this address say Gary, Indiana, or Cary, Illinois?

9.   My older brother hasn't had many birthdays because he was born on February 29, 1960.

10.   Someday my address will be 1600 Pennsylvania Avenue, Washington, D. C.

DIRECTIONS: *Insert commas where they are needed and be prepared to tell why you used each comma.*

                intro. adverb clause
1.   Since Susan's visit was to be a short one, we wanted to do something special each day.

2.   A luncheon was held in her honor, and all of her high school buddies were there.   *compound sentence*

         intro. participial phrase
3.   Claiming to be totally surprised, Susan had a terrific time.

              items in a series
4.   At her table were Marie, Stacey, Beth, and Renee.

        intro. adverb clause
5.   Since no one had plans for the evening, we talked until it was quite late.

6.   The waiter cleared our table, but we sat over our coffee and talked for hours.   *compound sentence*

7.   Susan, who was a very appreciative guest, said she had never had so much fun.   *nonessential modifier*

8.   On Saturday, June 10, we got together with some of our old neighbors.   *dates & addresses*

9.   Yes, even old Mrs. Bates was there!   *intro. single word*

          items in a series
10.   After many hours of gossip, memories, and laughter, we took Susan to the airport.
        intro prep. phrase

(over)

DIRECTIONS: *In each sentence below there is a comma split. In the spaces below each sentence are the numbers of all the commas in the sentence. Find the comma split and write its number in the space at the left. Write what it is splitting beside that comma's number below the sentence. By the other numbers, write the "buzzwords" of the correct commas.*

__4__   1.   John, my next-door neighbor, is giving a party this weekend, but he is extremely, nervous about
                  1   2   3   4
            the arrangements.

            ___#1 - appositive phrase_____

            ___#2- appositive phrase_____

            ___#3 - compound sentence_____

            ___#4 - splits linking verb (is) & complement (nervous)___

__1__   2   He has invited, all his closest, most intimate friends to a gathering on Friday, February 6th.
                          1   2   3
            ___#1 - splits verb (invited) & direct object (friends)___

            ___#2 - 2 adjectives with "and test"_____

            ___#3 - dates & addresses_____

__3__   3.   The refreshments, the music, and all the games, have been gathered together, and we all expect
                              1   2   3   4
            to have a wild, crazy time.
                          5

            ___#1 - items in a series_____

            ___#2 - items in a series_____

            ___#3 - splits subject (games) & verb (have ...)_____

            ___#4 - compound sentence_____

            ___#5 - 2 adjectives with "and test"_____

295

COMMA RULES 9, 10, & 11: EXERCISE #3

NAME:_____DATE:_____

DIRECTIONS: *Insert commas where they are needed.*

1. My cousins were both born on September 6, 1962.

2. Why is 10 Downing Street, London, famous?

3. Eleanor Roosevelt was born on October 11, 1884, and died on November 7, 1962.

4. Where were you on Friday, June 23, 2000?

5. Reno, Nevada, is farther west than Los Angeles, California.

6. Saturday, July 26, is Kathryn's birthday party.

7. The best hot dogs on earth are at Petey's, 110 Washington Street, Elm Forest, Illinois.

8. Address your letter to the *Chicago Sun-Times*, 401 North Wabash Avenue, Chicago, Illinois 60611.

9. We lived at 130 Rand Road, Austin, Texas, from May 1, 1993, to April 30, 1997.

10. The only historical date I can remember is July 4, 1776.

DIRECTIONS: *Insert commas where they are needed and be prepared to tell which rule is used.*

intro. participial phrase
1. Completely exhausted by our day outdoors, we were happy to tumble into bed early.

compound sentence
2. Susan lived on a farm, and she invited us to visit her on another weekend.

intro. adverb clause
3. Although we had seen many farms, visiting one was a new experience.

expressions   *items in a series*
4. It was great fun, in my opinion, to see all the cows, horses, pigs, and chickens.

intro.adverb clause
5. When the roosters began to crow at dawn, the farm seemed to come to life.

items in a series
6. Breakfast was very early so that we could get to the barn to see the milking machine, feed the pigs,

     and scatter feed for the chickens.

items in a series
7. Dinner was at noon and we had never had such heaping platters of mashed potatoes, fried chicken, fresh

     peas, and homemade blueberry muffins.

intro.adverb clause   *2 adjectives with"and test"*
8. After we had eaten our dessert, we stretched out under a big, leafy tree and went to sleep.

2 adjectives with"and test"   *intro. adverb clause*   *2 adjectives with"and test"*
9. Since it was a warm, humid afternoon, we were glad to go for a cool, refreshing swim.

intro. participial phrase
10. Getting ready for bed that night, we decided that the farm was the perfect vacation spot.

(over)

     Photocopying this product is strictly prohibited by copyright law.

DIRECTIONS: *In each sentence below there is a comma split. In the spaces below each sentence are the numbers of all the commas in the sentence. Find the comma split and write its number in the space at the left. Write what it is splitting beside that comma's number below the sentence. By the other numbers, write the "buzzwords" of the correct commas.*

___*3*___ 1. Sherlock Holmes, who is one of my favorite fictional characters, solved with the help of
                                    1   2
                Dr. Watson, hundreds of difficult mysteries.
                          3

    #1 - nonessential modifier

    #2 - nonessential modifier

    #3 - splits verb (solved) & direct object (hundreds)

___*1*___ 2. Holmes and Watson were, extremely clever when it came to dealing with dangerous, vicious
                                          1   2
                criminals, and they put their share of them behind bars.
                          3

    #1 - splits linking verb (were) & complement (clever)

    #2 - 2 adjectives with "and test"

    #3 - compound sentence

___*3*___ 3. Since the middle of the 19th century, readers have thrilled to the workings of Holmes' precise,
                                                1   2
                computer-like, mind as he solved crime after crime.
                            3

    #1 - introductory prepositional phrases

    #2 - 2 adjectives with "and test"

    #3 - splits modifier and its noun

ALL COMMA RULES TEST

NAME:_____DATE:_____

(RAW SCORE:_____ */138* GRADE:_____)

PART I: Items in a Series: *Insert commas where they are needed.*

___ 1.   Jim and Ted and Bill are my best friends among all my classmates.
1

___ 2.   Today's symbols of success in the home include personal computers, VCR's, and electronic games.
2

___ 3.   A considerate person listens when others are speaking, thinks carefully before saying
2
            anything, and tries not to hurt anyone's feelings.

___ 4.   We noticed unsightly beer cans, candy wrappers, and refuse paper all along the road.
2

___ 5.   I want a stereo or a mountain bike or cross-country skis for my birthday.
1

===
8

PART II: Two Adjectives with "AndTest": *Insert commas where they are needed.*

___ 1.   Everyone stared at the king's priceless crown.
1

___ 2.   The wagon train approached wild, lonely, mountainous country.
2

___ 3.   Port Townsend is a friendly, unsophisticated little town.
1

___ 4.   The beautiful blond lady had a short, peculiar-looking older brother.
1

___ 5.   The old grandfather clock struck midnight.
1

===
6

PART III: Compound Sentence: *Insert commas where they are needed.*

___ 1.   The long drought that had worried the farmers finally ended, and day after day the rain came
1
            down in sheets.

___ 2.   The beds of streams that had been dry came to life, and the caked soil became green again.
1

___ 3.   Small streams became raging rivers and greedily engulfed the countryside.
1

___ 4.   The levees broke and towns were flooded.
1

___ 5.   We thought the drought would never end, but it finally did.
1

===
5

(over)

PART IV: Nonessential Modifiers: *Insert commas where they are needed*

___ 1.   Students who cut school should be expelled.
1

___ 2.   Senator Stevens **,** hoping for passage of his bill **,** talked to several legislators.
2

___ 3.   All buildings which had been declared unsafe were torn down.
1

___ 4.   I wish the boy that I met at Sandy's party would call me.
1

___ 5.   The young salesman **,** trying desperately to make a sale **,** talked for five minutes.
2

== **PART V: Introductory Element:** *Insert commas where they are needed.*
7

___ 1.   Why **,** everyone knows what happened in 1776!
1

___ 2.   When we were watching television last night **,** I felt an earthquake.
1

___ 3.   In a dark corner of the deserted building **,** a kitten was crying pathetically.
1

___ 4.   Walking slowly through the museum **,** the man searched for a particular painting.
1

=== ___ 5.   For walking **,** shoes should be comfortable and sturdy.
5 **1**

PART VI: Appositives, Direct Address, Expressions: *Underline the interrupter in each sentence below. Insert commas where they are needed. Identify the interrupter in the space provided. (appos = appositive; da = direct address; expr = expression)*

___ 1.   Today's movies **,** <u>if you want my opinion</u> **,** contain too much violence. ____*expr*____
4

___ 2.   John Glenn **,** <u>America's first astronaut to orbit the earth</u> **,** became a United States Senator.
4
         _____*appos*_____

___ 3.   <u>Class</u> **,** today we'll be studying the use of the semicolon. _____*da.*_____
3

___ 4.   Your room **,** <u>sir</u> **,** is ready for you. _____*da*_____
4

___ 5.   The Waldorf **,** <u>one of New York's oldest hotels</u> **,** has all the charm of yesteryear. ____*appos*____
4

___ 6.   <u>By the way</u> **,** have you met my aunt?____*expr*____
3

___ 7.   It is **,** <u>after all</u> **,** your turn to wash the dishes. ____*expr*____
4

___ 8.   Last fall I read *Tom Sawyer* by Mark Twain **,** <u>America's foremost 19th century humorist.</u>
3
         _____*appos*_____

___ 9.   Have you seen the car keys **,** <u>Mom</u>? _____*da*_____
3

___ 10.   The final game **,** <u>however</u> **,** was called because of rain. ____*expr*____
4

===
36

299

PART VII: Dates & Addresses, Salutations & Closings, Names & Abbreviations: *Insert commas where they are needed.*

___
2   1.   Our idea was to hold a reunion on June 22, 2001, at the old high school.

___
3   2.   Write to me at 222 Oak Road, Akron, Ohio 81007, after the first of March.

___
4   3.   Their baby was born on Monday, May 1, 1959, in Baltimore, Maryland.

___
1   4.   It was on May 10th in 1948 that they began work on the project.

___
1   5.   She lived at 330 Main Street in Westfield, New Jersey.

___
1   6.   Henry III was a monarch about whom Shakespeare wrote plays.

___
5   7.   Maria had moved to Tampa, Florida, on November 19, 1995, and in 1996 she moved again to

Columbus, Ohio.

___
2   8.   Present at the reception for Senator and Mrs. Stevens were Mr. and Mrs. Henry Worth, Jr. and

Martin Feldstein, M. D.

___
3   9.   The Constitution of the United States was signed on September 17, 1787, in Philadelphia, Pennsylvania.

___
2   10.   Dear John,

===
24   Last night I heard what I thought was a cat in severe pain outside my window. Imagine my surprise when
            my mother told me it was you serenading me! If you promise never to sing to me again for as long as we
            live, I accept your proposal of marriage!

                                                                      Love and kisses,

                                                                      Marcia

PART VIII: All Comma Rules: *Insert commas where they are needed.*

___
3   1.   We left Moravia, which is a resort town in New York, and drove to Owasco Lake, which is near Syracuse.

___
3   2.   Michael, you know I hate tea parties, receptions, and formal dinners!

___
5   3.   This letter is addressed to Mr. Nick Walters, P. O. Box 429, Culver City, California 90014, and is dated

July 14, 1991.

___
1   4.   When people say I resemble my mother, I always feel flattered.

___
1   5.   A simple, clear writing style is always appropriate.

___
1   6.   The class studied all the comma rules in detail, and the teacher gave them a big test.

___
1   7.   A boy riding a red bicycle was seen leaving the scene of the accident.

=
___
2   8.   That dress, my dear Miss Ames, looks like a dream on you!

___
2   9.   Paul Bunyan, the legendary giant of the Northwest, had a blue ox for a pet.

___
1   10.   Mrs. Hood said she wasn't mad about the window and invited us in for cookies.

                                                                                          (over)

PART IX:
DIRECTIONS: *In each sentence below there is a comma split. In the spaces below each sentence are the numbers of all the commas in the sentence. Find the comma split and write its number in the space at the left. Write what it is splitting beside that comma's number below the sentence. By the other numbers, write the "buzzwords" of the correct commas.*

___2___   1.   On our trip around the country, we were really and truly, disgusted to see the litter that
                               1   **2**

       thoughtless, selfish people had dropped along the wayside.
            3

         #1 - introductory prepositional phrases

___5___   *#2 - splits linking verb (were) & complement (disgusted)*

         #3 - 2 adjectives with "and test"

___4___   2.   We saw beer cans, candy wrappers, and all sorts of filthy, unsightly, garbage.
                         1   **2**   **3**   **4**

         #1 - items in a series

         #2 - items in a series

___6___   *#3 - 2 adjectives with "and test"*

         #4 - splits modifier and its noun

___2___   3.   Because of public awareness of this problem, people all over the country, are getting fed up with
                                       1   **2**

       litterers, who should know better.
            3

         #1 - introductory prepositional phrases

___5___   *#2 - splits subject (people) & verb (are getting)*

         #3 - nonessential modifier

___3___   4.   Signs, commercials, and articles have increased in recent years, our determination to do
          1   **2**   **3**

       something about this problem.

         #1 - items in a series

___5___   *#2 - items in a series*

         #3 - splits verb (increased) & direct object (determindation)

___2___   5.   Hoping the message will get out, the media is trying to convince "litterbugs" to leave us, a
                                1   **2**

       cleaner, more beautiful country, but we all have to help.
            3   **4**

         #1 - introductory participial phrase

         #2 - splits indirect object (us) & direct object (country)

___6___   *#3 - 2 adjectives with "and test"*

         #4 - compound sentence

===
27

RAW			
SCORE		GRADE	%
138 - 135	=	A++	= 98+
134 - 131	=	A+	= 95
130 - 124	=	A	= 90
123 - 117	=	B+	= 85
116 - 110	=	B	= 80
109 - 103	=	C+	= 75
102 - 96	=	C	= 70
95 - 89	=	D+	= 65
88 - 82	=	D	= 60

PUNCTUATING QUOTATIONS

First of all, there are four terms we will be using in this unit which you must understand: they are DIRECT QUOTE , INDIRECT QUOTE, DIALOGUE, and NARRATIVE. The following four lines should make these terms clear to you.

DIRECT QUOTE: Jackie said, "I am going to Palmer on Saturday."
        (DIALOGUE is what we call the words that Jackie is saying = *I am going to Palmer on Saturday*)
        (NARRATIVE is what we call what the narrator is saying = *Jackie said*)

INDIRECT QUOTE: Jackie said that she is going to Palmer on Saturday.

I. You use quotation marks ("-open quotes," - close quotes) to enclose a person's exact words.

    EXAMPLE: "We're learning about punctuation," said Joe.

II. A direct quote begins with a capital letter <u>if the quote is a sentence</u>.

    EXAMPLE: Maria said, "<u>T</u>he frame is not strong enough."

III. THE BROKEN QUOTE: When a quoted <u>sentence</u> of dialogue is divided into two parts by narrative, the second part of the dialogue begins with a lower case letter.

    EXAMPLE: "The time has come," said Joe, "to finish my term paper." (note the lower case *t* in *to*)

IV. When you go from dialogue to narrative or from narrative to dialogue - unless other punctuation is present - you need a comma to "change gears" from one to the other.

    EXAMPLE: "Science is more interesting than history," said Bernie.
          (note the location of the comma after "history")

          I asked, "Who is your science teacher?"
          (note the location of the comma after "asked")

          "Does she let you do experiments?" asked Debbie.
          (note that no comma is necessary after "experiments" because there is other punctuation there.)

V. A period or comma following a quotation is ALWAYS placed INSIDE the close quotes.

    EXAMPLE: "It's time to go," said the guide.

          The man replied, "I'm ready."

See how the period and the comma are inside the close quote?

       Photocopying this product is strictly prohibited by copyright law.

VI.   Question marks and exclamation marks should be placed <u>inside</u> the close quotes IF THE DIALOGUE IS A QUESTION OR EXCLAMATION. Question marks and exclamation marks should be place <u>outside</u> the close quotes IF THE NARRATIVE IS A QUESTION OR EXCLAMATION. Study the following quotations very carefully.

        EXAMPLE: "How far have we come?" asked the man. (dialogue is a question)

                        Who said, "Go west, young man"? (narrative is a question)

                        "Jump!" screamed the woman. (dialogue is an exclamation)

                        I nearly died when he said, "Time's up"! (narrative is an exclamation.)

VII.   When your dialogue consists of several sentences, open quotes at the beginning and don't close them until the end of the dialogue.

        EXAMPLE: "I'll wait for you at the Mall. Get there as soon as you can. Try not to be late," he said and rushed off down the hill.

VIII.   A QUOTE WITHIN A QUOTE: Use single quotes (' - open quote,'- close quote) to enclose dialogue inside other dialogue.

        EXAMPLE: "Let's all yell, 'You won!' when Jack comes in," said Dad.

                        "Did I really hear Mrs. Neuman say, ' You may use books on the test'?" asked Sally.

A good way to handle quotations is to think of them as sentences inside other sentences. In the sentence -

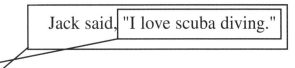

Jack said, "I love scuba diving."

The "inside" sentence is "I love scuba diving."   Any punctuation for the inside sentence goes <u>inside the quotes.</u>

    I is the subject, *love* is the verb, and *scuba diving* is the direct object.

The "outside" sentence is "Jack said, 'I love scuba diving.'" Any punctuation for this sentence goes <u>outside the double quotes</u>, unless it is a period or a comma which go inside the close quote no matter what.

    Jack is the subject, *said* is the verb and the quoted sentence is the direct object.

Be sure, when you're dealing with quotations, that you punctuate each sentence - both the inside one and the outside one - correctly.

A couple of handy items: You never have two "end marks" of punctuation together, unless one of them is a question mark and one of them is an exclamation mark. Example: *"Did Jane scream, 'Help!'?" asked Mr. Bates.* Notice that Mr. Bates is asking a question, so his sentence needs a question mark. Jane is screaming, so her sentence needs an exclamation mark.

In any other situation, a question or exclamation mark would "cancel out" a period or comma. Example: *"Did Jane say, 'I'm going out'?" asked Mr. Bates.* Notice that Jane's sentence loses its punctuation to the question mark.

PUNCTUATING QUOTATIONS: EXERCISE #1

NAME:_____DATE:_____

DIRECTIONS: *Copy the following sentences in the space provided below each sentence, inserting commas, quotation marks, and capitals where they are needed. Do not recopy the ones that are correct as they are.*

1.   The librarian told me to be quiet.

2.   At the same time Mike whispered hush up!

       At the same time Mike whispered, "Hush up!"
3.   He asked can't you see that people are trying to study?

       He asked, "Can't you see that people are trying to study?"
4.   I replied in a whisper I'm sorry that I disturbed you.

       I replied in a whisper, "I'm sorry that I disturbed you."
5.   I should have known better, I said to myself, than to raise my voice.
     *

       "I should have known better," I said to myself, "than to raise my voice."
6.   Next I quietly asked the girl across from me for her science book.

7.   She whispered I'll give it to you in a minute.

       She whispered, "I'll give it to you in a minute."
8.   But I need it now I explained.

       "But I need it now," I explained.
9.   She muttered something about people who can't remember to bring their stuff.

10.   About that time the bell rang and the librarian called out it's time to go, kids.

       About that time the bell rang, and the librarian called out, "It's time to go, kids!"

  * *Sometimes authors use italics for thoughts, especially when it's important to differentiate between what is* <u>*spoken*</u> *and what is* <u>*thought.*</u>

     I should have known better, **I said to myself,** *than to raise my voice.*

  In the ordinary course of events, however, you treat a thought as an ordinary quotation.

PUNCTUATING QUOTATIONS: EXERCISE #2

NAME:_____DATE:_____

DIRECTIONS: *Rewrite the following sentences in the space provided, inserting proper punctuation and capitalization.*

1. What do you know about the life of Mark Twain our teacher asked Lydia.
    "What do you know about the life of Mark Twain?" our teacher asked Lydia.

2. Did you mean it when you said I'll help you with that assignment
    Did you mean it when you said, "I'll help you with that assignment"?

3. Look out screamed the man on the dock.
    "Look out!" screamed the man on the dock.

4. What a relief it was to hear the timekeeper say put down your pencils now (Sentences worded in this manner [What a day it was!] should be treated as exclamations.
    What a relief it was to hear the timekeeper say, "Put down your pencils now"!

5. Do you remember asked Mrs. Bates the story of the tortoise and the hare
    "Do you remember," asked Mrs. Bates, "the story of the tortoise and the hare?"

6. I leaned over and whispered are you going to be busy this afternoon
    I leaned over and whispered, "Are you going to be busy this afternoon?"

7. Did anybody notice that sign that said last chance for gas for 100 miles
    Did anybody notice that sign that said, "Last chance for gas for 100 miles"?

8. If you think shouted Bill I'm going to help you now, you're crazy
    "If you think," shouted Bill, "I'm going to help you now, you're crazy!"

9. When was the last time you heard a teacher say no homework tonight, class
    When was the last time you heard a teacher say, "No homework tonight, class"?

10. The next person who says loan me a pen is going to regret it
    The next person who says, "Loan me a pen," is going to regret it!

> *It's useful to point out that, unless the speaker is directly identified in the sentence, you are to assume that it's a narrator talking, so there would be no need to enclose the entire sentence in punctuation marks.*

PUNCTUATING QUOTATIONS: EXERCISE #3

NAME:_____DATE:_____

DIRECTIONS: *Rewrite the following sentences, punctuating them correctly. Be careful, they're sneaky!*

1.   Noel, have you seen my catcher's mitt asked Jim it's been missing since Monday. I need it for practice today.

      "Noel, have you seen my catcher's mitt?" asked Jim. " It's been missing since Monday. I need it for practice today."

2.   In what poem did Longfellow write the thoughts of youth are long, long thoughts asked Bill

      "In what poem did Longfellow write, 'The thoughts of youth are long, long thoughts'?" asked Bill.

3.   Is his motto still stay in the game and pitch I asked Bob

      "Is his motto still, 'Stay in the game and pitch'?" I asked Bob.

4.   How I laughed when my science teacher referred to Bob as the young Einstein in my class exclaimed Tip

      "How I laughed when my science teacher referred to Bob as 'the young Einstein in my class'!" exclaimed Tip.

5.   Did Jack shout bring my book or did he yell ring my cook asked the Duke
      "Did Jack shout, 'Bring my book!' or did he yell, 'Ring my cook!'?" asked the Duke.

DIRECTIONS: If a sentence below is an INDIRECT QUOTE, rewrite it to be a DIRECT QUOTE. If it's a DIRECT QUOTE, rewrite it to be an INDIRECT QUOTE.

1.   My brother said he would miss the rehearsal.
            "I'll miss the rehearsal," said my brother.
2.   "What is your excuse?" asked the principal.
            The principal asked him what his excuse was.
3.   "Sam," asked Mia, "why aren't you playing soccer this year?"
            Mia asked Sam why he wasn't playing soccer this year.
4.   The thicf finally admitted that he stole the furs.
            "I stole the furs!" admitted the thief.
5.   I told Dad I needed fifteen dollars.
            "Dad, I need fifteen dollars," I said.
6.   "How did you manage to get that answer?" asked the teacher.
            The teacher asked him how he managed to get that answer.
7.   Bill yelled that the score was tied again.
            "The score's tied again!" yelled Bill.
8.   Grandpa said he could feel snow in the air.
            "I can feel snow in the air," said Grandpa.
9.   Jim said he thought he could win.

            "I think I can win," said Jim.
10.   "That," said Mr. Turner with a grin, "is the first mistake I've made in ten years!"
      Grinning, Mr. Turner said that it was the first mistake he'd made in ten years.

These

answers

will

vary

Photocopying this product is strictly prohibited by copyright law.

PUNCTUATING QUOTATIONS: TEST

NAME:_____DATE:_____

(RAW SCORE:_____/185 GRADE:_____)

PART I: DIRECTIONS: *Rewrite the following sentences NEATLY on a separate sheet of paper. Put in the necessary capitalization and punctuation. Keep in mind, as you do this, that this is a story which BEGINS WITH NARRATIVE and contains a conversation between TWO PEOPLE.*

6 —— 1.   Do you often hear your fellow students whining, " My teachers give too much homework" ?

7 —— 2.   Have you ever heard students shout , " Down with homework ! " ?

4 —— 3.   " I'm drowning in homework ! " I hear students cry .

4 —— 4.   How pathetic it is to hear a student say , " I can't do any more " !

6 —— 5.   The first thing you usually hear a student say is , " What's the homework tonight ? "

4 —— 6.   " I think I have homework tonight , " said Jean .

4 —— 7.   " Bob, do we have any homework tonight in Mr. Gaal's class ? " she asked .

9 —— 8.   " Sure , " Bob replied . " He told us to read Chapter Twelve and answer the questions . "

8 —— 9.   " Chapter Twelve ! " shrieked Jean . " Doesn't that man think we have personal lives ? "

8 —— 10. " That man , " replied Bob , " is a sadist . " **

8 —— 11. " I know that , Bob , " groaned Jean . " I wish there was a way to get him locked up . "

6 —— 12. " I know what we could do ! We could drive him right over the edge ! " shouted Bob .

8 —— 13. " How ? " asked Jean, looking hopefully at Bob . " Tell us how ! "

8 —— 14. " If we all did our homework every single night , " said Bob, rubbing his hands gleefully

together , " he'd probably have a nervous breakdown trying to keep up with the grading ! "

5 —— 15. Jean stared at Bob with disgust. " Is THAT your great idea ? " she asked .

9 —— 16. " When you said , ' Is THAT your great idea ? ' it means you're not thrilled with it, right ? " said Bob .

8 —— 17. " Bob , " said Jean , " go soak your head. Your idea stinks ! "

112

* *Could end in an exclamation point or a period (which becomes a comma) - give credit either way.*

** *It's important to stress that there are only two people involved in this conversation; otherwise, this sentence comes out like this: That man replied, "Bob is a sadist." (I only give 3 points if it's like that.) We always have a good giggle about this perfect stranger who walks in, declares Bob a sadist, and is never heard from again!!*

(over)

PART II: DIRECTIONS: *Recopy the following sentences on a separate sheet of paper, punctuating and capitalizing them properly. If the sentence is correct as it is, write the letter C next to that number on your paper.*

$\frac{}{8}$ 1.   " Did you notice , " Inspector Brewer asked , " anything peculiar about the suspect ? "
          =   = =   = = =   = =

$\frac{}{4}$ 2.   " Just that he wore a raincoat and a hat that hid his face , " I replied .
          =   = =   =

$\frac{}{4}$ 3.   " Right ! " said the Inspector .
          =   = =   =

$\frac{}{4}$ 4.   " I also believe he limped on his left foot , " I said .
          =   = =   =

$\frac{}{8}$ 5.   " Did you say he was tall , " Brewer asked , " and are you certain about the limp? "
          =   = =   = = =   = =

$\frac{}{1}$ 6.   I reminded the Inspector that I had only caught a glimpse of the man.(CORRECT)

optional

$\frac{}{8}$ 7.   " Oh, by the way , " I added , " he was carrying a small suitcase too . "
          =   = =   = = =   = =

$\frac{}{4}$ 8.   " Would you mind coming down to the station to make a statement ? " Brewer asked .
          =   = =   =

$\frac{}{1}$ 9.   I told him I didn't mind, but that I preferred to keep my name out of the papers. (CORRECT)

$\frac{}{4}$ 10.   " No need to worry , " he remarked as he opened the squadcar door for me .
          =   = =   =

$\frac{}{1}$ 11.   I thanked him for his courtesy and got in. (CORRECT)

====
47

PART III: DIRECTIONS: *Rewrite the following sentences on a separate sheet of paper. Be careful; they're sneaky!*

$\frac{9}{}$ 1.   Jack asked , " Are you sure Mr. Phillips said , ' Hand in your term papers tomorrow, class ' ? "
             = = =   = = =   = = =

$\frac{}{8}$ 2.   " Who said , ' I wear the chain I forged in life , ' in Dickens' famous story ? " asked Mrs. Bailey .
         =   = =   = =   = =   =

$\frac{}{9}$ 3.   " I always crack up when James asks , ' What page are we on ? ' ! " exclaimed Sue .
         =   = = =   = = = =   =

====
26

RAW SCORE		GRADE		%
185	- 181 =	A++	=	98+
180	- 175 =	A+	=	95
174	- 166 =	A	=	90
165	- 157 =	B+	=	85
156	- 148 =	B	=	80
147	- 138 =	C+	=	75
137	- 129 =	C	=	70
128	- 120 =	D+	=	65
119	- 111 =	D	=	60

PUNCTUATING DIALOGUE

I.   When you write dialogue (two or more persons having a conversation), begin a new paragraph each time the speaker changes. Remember, the narrator is a speaker too. Pay special attention to which narrative goes in a paragraph by itself and which narrative goes in the same paragraph with the dialogue.

"Hi," said Sean to the boy trying to open the locker next to him. "Need some help?"

The boy looked up. "Yeah," he said, "I'm new here and - I know this sounds dumb - but I've never had a locker before! I don't really understand how to open this thing!"

Sean stared at the new boy. He LOOKED normal. American accent, American clothes. How could he have gotten through junior high without having a locker? "I don't get it," said Sean. "Did you go to school on Mars?"

"You're not too far off!" laughed the boy. "My folks are with the Peace Corps in West Africa. I've never gone to school before. My mom and dad taught me at home.   I feel like I am from Mars!" He blushed and glanced at Sean uneasily. He hoped this boy, the first person who'd spoken to him in the new school, wouldn't think he was weird. He really wanted to have some friends in this new place.

"Gosh!" said Sean. "People are really going to make a big deal out of you! Wait'll our Social Studies teacher hears about this!"

The two boys walked off together down the hall, Sean asking questions as fast as he could get them out of his mouth. The new boy, Eric, was answering them the best he could - a huge grin on his face. It was going to be all right!

NOTE: If you look at the above passage, you will notice that sometimes the narrative is in the same paragraph as a speech, and sometimes it's in a separate paragraph. Imagine that you are a television director and that each paragraph is a camera angle. In the first paragraph above, you would have one camera shot of Sean by himself. In the next sentence, which is narrative, you would change your camera angle (or paragraph) because it's about Eric and what he's doing and saying. The last paragraph would require a new "camera angle" because it's about what both boys are doing. So if you just visualize when a new camera angle would be needed, that's where you need a new paragraph!

II.   When a quoted passage consists of more than one paragraph, put quotation marks at the BEGINNING OF EACH PARAGRAGH and at the END OF THE ENTIRE PASSAGE. Do NOT put quotation marks at the end of any paragraph but the last.

EXAMPLE:

"After dinner this evening," said Jack, leaning back contentedly in his easy chair, "Denise and I decided to make a list of all the jobs that need doing around here.

"We first inspected the house. The major jobs were the following: mending the hole in the sofa cushion, washing Grandma's crystal, sorting out the sheets and towels, dusting Mom's china collection, and re-potting the African violets. Of course, I insisted on helping. After all, I live here too!

"Well, I broke a crystal wine glass and a china teacup and dumped our favorite African violet out on the living room carpet. What can I say? I guess I'm just too clumsy to do delicate work like this! I tell ya," Jack said with a wink, as he watched Denise scurrying madly around the house, "a homeowner's work is NEVER done!"

Notice that there are "open quotes" at the beginning of each of Jack's three paragraphs, but the close quotes don't appear until the very end of his entire speech.

PUNCTUATING DIALOGUE: EXERCISE #1

I usually "eyeball" the homework assignment to see if it is generally correct (ie: I can see that the student has put the separate speakers in separate paragraphs, etc.) If, in my judgment, the homework doesn't look like the students have generally gotten the point, I have been known to tell them to take out a piece of paper and I DICTATE the exercise, complete with paragraphing and punctuation. They really HATE having to write something twice, but I've noticed that the 2nd exercise is done correctly!

Christmastime had finally arrived and Jim and Susan asked their parents if they could take their Christmas money out of savings to go shopping.

"We'll have to make a list first," said Jim.

"Do you think we'll have enough to buy something for everybody?" asked Susan.

"I'm not sure, Susie, but if we don't, maybe we could go in together on some of the presents."

"That's a great idea, Jim!" said Susan.

Their parents gave them permission to get their money out of savings and drove them to the mall the next Saturday morning.

"Okay," said Jim. "Now that we have our money, where do you want to go first?"

"Well, why don't we try the toy store to take care of the kids on our list. We HAVE to buy for the kids."

"That's true," said Jim. "We'll REALLY be in trouble if we forget any of them!"

The two kids shopped all day. When their parents picked them up at four o'clock, two very tired youngsters climbed wearily into the car.

"Well," said Susan, "we did it. We got something for everyone on our list."

"That's fantastic!" said Mom. "You must be pretty good money managers to make your money go that far! The whole family is going to be so pleased that you remembered them."

Susan thought for a moment. "That's true," she said, "which probably means that they'll get us something really nice in return."

"Well, you don't sound very happy about that," observed Dad.

"But, Dad!" cried Jim. "Don't you understand? That just means that we'll have to be sure and get them something really nice in return NEXT year!!"

PUNCTUATING DIALOGUE: EXERCISE #2

"Good morning, class," said Mrs. Finley.

"Good morning, Mrs. Finley!" sang the class in chorus.

"Today we are going to study the correct punctuation of dialogue."

"Yeccchhh!" said Sean.

"We always study the same old junk," said Stacy.

"You NEVER show us any movies," said Becky.

"Yeah," said Jason, "Mr. Johnson's class ALWAYS has movies. How come we never see any movies in here?"

"But, dear students!" cried Mrs. Finley. "I thought you LOVED my class. You know how much I care. You know I just want you to be happy and have fun all the time. Don't you enjoy learning all this valuable educational material?"

"Not really," said Becky.

"We want to play games and read plays and see movies!" shouted Chris.

"Yeah, who wants to be educated anyway?" said Tanya.

"We'd much rather be ignorant and have fun!" yelled Bryce.

"Oh, I see," said Mrs. Finley. "Ignorance is bliss, is that it?"

"You got it, Mrs. Finley!"

"Well, it grieves me deeply to see you so unhappy," said Mrs. Finley, " but I'd really hate to see you MISERABLE in a few short years when you hit the REAL WORLD and can't handle it!! So let's get started."

There is no test for this unit. They will be tested on this in the next unit.

PUNCTUATING TITLES

I.   Use quotation marks to enclose the titles of articles, short stories, essays, poems, songs, chapters, and television and radio programs.

EXAMPLES:

articles:	"The Truth About OPEC"
short stories:	"The Monkey's Paw"
essays:	"A Modest Proposal"
poems:	"The Cremation of Sam McGee"
songs:	"Hello Dolly"
chapters:	Chapter 10, "The Industrial Revolution"
TV or radio shows:	"The Howdy Doody Show"

II.   Use underlining (when you are handwriting or typing) or *italics* (when you're using either print or computer) for the titles of books, plays, movies, periodicals, works of art, long musical compositions, ships, aircraft, and spacecraft.

EXAMPLES:

books:	Tom Sawyer	*Tom Sawyer*
plays:	Romeo and Juliet	*Romeo and Juliet*
movies:	The Blob Eats Cleveland	*The Blob Eats Cleveland*
periodicals:	the Anchorage Times	the *Anchorage Times*
works of art:	the Mona Lisa	the *Mona Lisa*
symphonies, etc.:	Beethoven's Erioca	Beethoven's *Erioca*
ships:	the Titanic	the *Titanic*
aircraft:	the Spirit of St. Louis	the *Spirit of St. Louis*
spacecraft:	Columbia	*Columbia*

REMEMBER: If the title is also an appositive phrase, "set it off" with either italics or quotation marks, but DO NOT put commas around it.

EXAMPLE: My favorite book *Anne of Green Gables* is set on Prince Edward Island.
(*Anne of Green Gables* is an appositive, but the italics set it off; you don't need commas)

III.   Use underlining or italics for words, letters, and figures referred to AS SUCH and for foreign words and expressions. When words, letters, and figures are referred to "as such," it means that the word, etc. is being discussed in the sentence as a word and not as its meaning.

EXAMPLES:

Does the word judgement have one or two e's?

I never could write a 5 very nicely.

In chewing gum at the interview, I was guilty of a horrible faux pas.

REMEMBER: UNDERLINING IS TO HANDWRITING AND TYPING AS ITALICS IS TO PRINT OR COM-
PUTER. If you have access to italics, you should use them. If you don't, then underline instead. NEVER do both.

PUNCTUATING TITLES:EXERCISE #1

NAME:_____DATE:_____

DIRECTIONS: *Punctuate the following sentences correctly.*

1.   Is it true your ancestors came over on the <u>Mayflower</u>?

2.   The foreign phrase <u>de riguer</u> refers to something which is fashionable and proper.

3.   Mother was completely engrossed in an article entitled "The New Wonder Diet" in this month's issue of

        <u>Woman's Day.</u>

4.   Many jokes have been made about Rodin's magnificent sculpture <u>The Thinker.</u>

5.   The quartet sang "Sweet Adeline" at the close of the program.

6.   The Latin terms <u>cum laude</u>, <u>magna cum laude</u>, and <u>summa cum laude</u> usually appear on the diplomas of

        the best students.

7.   The soprano sang the aria "One Fine Day" from the opera <u>Madame Butterfly</u>.

8.   After seeing Shakespeare's <u>Julius Caesar</u>, I wrote an essay entitled "The Bard of Avon," but I was

        embarrassed to see that I had omitted the first <u>e</u> in his name.

9.   The teacher read "The Adventure of the Speckled Band" from her anthology <u>The Complete Sherlock Holmes</u>

10.   I spent my afternoon at the library reading one-hundred-year-old copies of the <u>New York Times</u>.

PUNCTUATING TITLES: EXERCISE #2

NAME:_____DATE:_____

DIRECTIONS: *Punctuate the following sentences correctly.*

1.   The senior class play this year is <u>Arsenic and Old Lace</u>.

2.   "Class, open your books to the chapter entitled 'A House Divided' in your history books," said Mrs. Mendez, holding up a copy of <u>The American Story.</u>

3.   The sinking of the <u>Andrea Doria</u> in the mid-fifties was a terrible tragedy.

4.   Billy walked slowly up to the chalkboard and wrote <u>kat</u>, <u>peepul</u>, and <u>teechur</u> in a childish scrawl.

5.   Did you see the final episode of "The Winds of War" on television last night?

6.   I think my favorite piece of music is the <u>Pastoral</u> symphony by Ludwig Von Beethoven.

7.   Mom, do you pronounce the <u>e</u> in <u>calliope</u>?

8.   My subscription to <u>Newsweek</u> magazine runs out next month.

9.   "I'll never forget seeing Julie Andrews in <u>My Fair Lady</u>," said Janet. "My mother took me to see several Broadway plays that year, but it was my favorite."

10.   Edgar Allen Poe is probably best remembered for his poem "The Raven."

PUNCTUATING TITLES: EXERCISE #3

NAME:_____DATE:_____

DIRECTIONS: *Punctuate the following sentences correctly.*

1.   "Nina, did you see 'Designing Women' this week?" asked Janie. "It's my favorite show."

2.   "The Long Search" was the most exciting chapter in the story about the lion cubs.

    (Question)
3.   "In what poem did Longfellow write, 'The thoughts of youth are long, long thoughts'?" asked Jane.

    (Answer)
4.   "I think it was in 'My Lost Youth,'" replied Mother.

5.   "Have you read 'Congress's License to Lie' in the latest <u>Reader's Digest</u>?" asked Lee.

6.   "What did Romeo mean when he said, 'It is the east and Juliet is the sun,' in the second act of <u>Romeo and Juliet</u>?" asked Bill.

7.   The tour group stood silently gazing at the magnificence of Michelangelo's <u>David.</u>

8.   "Sometimes when I watch 'Saturday Night Live,' I laugh until I cry," said Grace.

9.   Pulling on the oars, the boys took the <u>Ginger Lee</u> out to the middle of the lake.

10.   "Why doesn't anybody pronounce the <u>r</u> in <u>February</u> so a person can remember to spell it correctly?" wailed Sherry.

PUNCTUATING TITLES: TEST

NAME:_____ DATE:_____

(RAW SCORE: _____/141 GRADE: _____)

PART I: DIRECTIONS: *Punctuate the following sentences correctly. Don't change punctuation which is already there.*

(— 1 pt. —)

___1. 1. Diana Ross made the song "Stop in the Name of Love" popular.

___4 2. "The Catbird Seat" is a funny short story by James Thurber," said Tim in his oral report.

___1 3. Did you see Jean's picture in today's Times?

___1 4. Eric had to read the novel My Darling, My Hamburger for a book report.

___4 5. "The drama department is presenting The Miracle Worker for their spring play," announced Mr. Conklin.

(— 1 pt. —)

___1 6. Mr. Gates assigned the fifth chapter "Lee and His Generals" in our history textbook.

___2 7. Norman Lear changed television history with the series "All in the Family." *close quotes must be to right of period.*

___2 8. Esther used an article called "The Persian Gulf: What Next?" from Newsweek as the basis for her history

report.

(— 1 pt. —)

___9 9. "Hey, Patty," asked Jean, "you didn't happen to read the article 'Are You a Good Friend?' in this month's

Young Miss, did you?"

___9 10. "If you're looking for a shocking ending," said my English teacher, "you should read Shirley Jackson's

famous short story 'The Lottery.'" *close quotes must be to right of period.*

close quotes must be to right of comma

___5 11. "I'll never forget when my teacher read us 'An Occurrence at Owl Creek Bridge,' a famous short story,"

said Kelly.

___2 12. Vincent Van Gogh's famous Sunflowers was the first painting which sold for over a million dollars.

___2 13. The plane which dropped the atomic bomb on Hiroshima was called the Enola Gay.

___1 14. The Latin term non sequitur refers to a statement which is not logical.

___5 15. "Mozart's comic opera The Magic Flute has always been a favorite of mine," said Sean.

___3 16. "I'll never forget how embarrassed I was when I learned I had been mispronouncing epitome. It was a big

word I used all the time to try and impress people!" laughed Jill.

(over)

 4 17. Dr. Gates announced," Since you obviously have studied Shakespeare's <u>Othello</u> so thoroughly,

I will assign no further reading for the weekend."

 1 18. Lance proudly displayed his diploma on which were the Latin words <u>summa cum laude</u>,

meaning "with highest honors."

 4 19. Henry Higgins worked day and night to teach Eliza Doolittle to pronounce <u>rain</u>, <u>Spain</u>,

and <u>plain</u> so that the long <u>a</u> was pronounced correctly.

 7 20. "Oh look!" exclaimed Charles as we leafed through the stack of old magazines. "This 1963

issue of <u>Life </u>magazine has an article in it entitled' Loch Ness Secret Solved.'" *or* (!")

68

PART II: *On a separate sheet of paper, copy the following dialogue, punctuating and paragraphing it correctly. Assume that the punctuation you see written here is correct. (For Key, see next page.)*

It was a typical Saturday night at the dorm. All the guys who had dates had already gone out, but

a few remained in the lounge Hey said Jim does anybody want to go see a movie tonight Tom, who

was dozing in a huge easy chair, opened one eye. I'll go he said I'm just sitting around

staring at the walls anyway great said Jim do you want to drive or shall I heaving himself out

of the chair, Tom said no I'll drive Why asked Jim. Because I don't want to be seen in that heap

of yours I have an image to protect Jim picked up a cushion and heaved it at Tom trust me, pal

he laughed just be seen with me and your image is set for life oh yeah? Yeah! okay said (Who is speaking here?

Jim or Tom?) you drive

RAW SCORE			GRADE		%
141	-	138	= A++	=	98+
137	-	133	= A+	=	95
132	-	126	= A	=	90
125	-	119	= B+	=	85
118	-	112	= B	=	80
111	-	105	= C+	=	75
104	-	98	= C	=	70
97	-	91	= D+	=	65
90	-	84	= D	=	60

DIALOGUE KEY: Sometimes we have to discuss whether or not a sentence should end with a period or an exclamation mark. As long as the rest of the punctuation and capitalization is consistent with whichever they've chosen, I give credit.

2 — ¶ It was a typical Saturday night at the dorm. All the guys who had dates had already gone

out, but a few remained in the lounge .

9 — ¶ " Hey , " said Jim . "Does anybody want to go see a movie tonight ? "

8 — ¶ Tom, who was dozing in a huge easy chair, opened one eye. " I'll go , " he said . " I'm just

sitting around staring at the walls anyway . "

9 — ¶ " Great ! " said Jim . " D o you want to drive or shall I ? "

7 — ¶ H eaving himself out of the chair, Tom said , " No, I'll drive . "

4 — ¶ " Why ? " asked Jim.

5 — ¶ " Because I don't want to be seen in that heap of yours . I have an image to protect ! "

11 — ¶ Jim picked up a cushion and heaved it at Tom . " Trust me, pal ! " he laughed . " Just be

seen with me and your image is set for life ! "

4 — ¶ " Oh yeah? "

3 — ¶ " Yeah! "

11 — ¶ " Okay , " said **Tom** , " you drive ! "

73

1. Could be either (. "D) or (, "d)

2. Could be "Okay! or Okay," said Tom. " You drive!"

TEACHER NOTE: It's a bit challenging to have kids grade these papers, but I think it's worth it. I know some teachers worry about students' accuracy, but I think the positive effect of seeing one's successes and failure immediately is a sufficient trade-off. If student "short changes" himself, he'll usually let you know, and you can fix it then.

I just tell them what each paragraph is worth. Then I read through the paragraph, mentioning all the paragraphing, punctuation, and capitalization. I tell the student to draw a circle around whatever is wrong. When I get to the end of that paragraph, I just tell him to deduct all the mistakes from whatever the paragraph is worth. That way, if the student has put in some extra punctuation that doesn't belong, he loses points. Tell your student, "Bad punctuation cancels out good punctuation."

SEMICOLONS & COLONS

I.   SEMICOLONS (;)

    A.   Use a semicolon between independent clauses (sentences) if they are NOT joined by a conjunction.

        EXAMPLE: Mary enjoys romantic novels; her brother likes fantasy.

    B.   Use a semicolon between independent clauses joined by such words as *for example, for instance, therefore, that is, besides, accordingly, moreover, nevertheless, furthermore, otherwise, however, consequently, instead, hence.*

        The italicized words above are very useful when a writer is trying to show the relationship between one idea and another. They are often called TRANSITIONAL DEVICES because they help the reader make the transition from one thought to another.

        EXAMPLE: Jane showed me in many ways that she was still my friend. She saved me a seat on the bus. (It's a bit difficult to perceive the relationship between these two ideas.)

                      Jane showed me in many ways that she was still my friend; for example, she saved me a seat on the bus. (Now the relationship between the two ideas is very clear)

    C.   A semicolon (call this a "SUPERCOMMA") may be used to separate the independent clauses of a compound sentence <u>if there are commas within the clauses</u> and there might be some confusion about where the first sentence ends and the second sentence begins.

        EXAMPLE:
        (confusing)   She will invite Elaine, Kim, and Stacey, and Val will ask Molly.

        (clear)   She will invite Elaine, Kim, and Stacey; and Val will ask Molly.

    D.   A semicolon (call this a "SUPERCOMMA") may be used to separate items in a series <u>if there are commas within the items.</u>

        EXAMPLE:
        (confusing)   The dates of the Iowa testing will be Monday, April 4, Tuesday, April 5, and Wednesday, April 6.

        (clear)   The dates of the Iowa testing will be Monday, April 4; Tuesday, April 5; and Wednesday, April 6.

II.   COLONS (:)

    A.   Use a colon to mean "note what follows." A colon should be used before a list of items, especially after expression like *as follows* and *the following*.

          EXAMPLES: You will need to take the following things: a heavy jacket, boots, a sleeping bag, a hunting knife, and a backpack.

                            I have three extracurricular activities: reading, skiing, and playing computer games.

          NOTE: If you look carefully at the sentences above, you will notice that THE WORDS IN FRONT OF THE COLON MAKE UP A COMPLETE SENTENCE. A colon should never SPLIT a sentence.

          EXAMPLES: My extracurricular activities are: reading, skiing, and playing computer games.
(Note that the colon splits the linking verb and complement. The colon should be LEFT OUT of this sentence.)

                            Mix the sifted flour with: cinnamon, nutmeg, ginger, and sugar.
(Note that the colon splits the preposition and its object. The colon should be LEFT OUT of this sentence.)

    B.   Use a colon before a quotation when the narrative which introduces the quotation makes up a complete sentence. This is especially true of a long quotation.

          EXAMPLE: Horace Mann had this to say about dealing with those who disagree with you: "Do not think of knocking out another person's brains because he differs in opinion from you. It would be as rational to knock yourself on the head because you differ from yourself ten years ago."

    C.   Use a colon in the following situations:

          1.   Between the hour and the minute when you write the time. (7:30 etc.)

          2.   Between the chapter and verse when referring to passages from the Bible, the Koran, or other books organized in this manner. (Genesis 2:2)

          3.   Use a colon after the salutation of a business letter. (Dear Sir:)

SEMICOLONS & COLONS: EXERCISE #1

NAME:_____DATE:_____

DIRECTIONS: *Some of the sentences below require semicolons, some have semicolons that should not be there, some have semicolons that should be commas, and some of the sentences are correct. Put in the missing semicolons, cross out or change the incorrect ones, and leave the sentences which are correct as they are.*

1.   Many people feel insecure about punctuation; they never know whether they're right or wrong!

2.   In ancient times writers didn't use punctuation; therefore ,their writings are difficult to read.

3.   As a matter of fact, writers during the days of ancient Greece and Rome didn't even put a space between each word!

4.   Life moved at a much slower pace than it does today ;hence, it wasn't that important to be able to read something quickly.

5.   The ability to read and write was a rare one; consequently , few people depended on the written word as we do today.

6.   Most people lived their entire lives without ever sending or receiving a letter; they didn't need to know how to read and write.

7.   Although people honored and respected those who could read⤫ they didn't see the need for it in their own lives.

8.   Toward the latter part of the Middle Ages, nations began to trade widely with each other; literacy became a necessity for success in business.

9.   A merchant could expect to receive several written messages in a day ; it became important to be able to read something quickly.

10. Earlier in ancient times, some genius figured out that, if he left a space between words, his writing could be read more quickly ;we're all very grateful to this obscure writer!

11. There has to be something to tell us when a sentence ends ;otherwise, we might think that the end of one sentence is the beginning of another.

12. Somewhere along the line a writer decided to put a dot at the end of each sentence ;this made his writing much clearer.

13. In time other "end marks" of punctuation appeared; one of these is the question mark.
.

14. When these writers used certain marks they found it easier to convey their true meaning; other people saw the value of it and simply copied what the other guy did!

15. Eventually writers began to use many punctuation marks ;therefore, it became necessary to agree upon some rules.

16. In the early days punctuation was pretty "free-wheeling"; Shakespeare used it pretty much as he pleased!

(over)

17. Commas began to be used in a more orderly way ; for example , commas were used to separate items used in a series.

18. Other situations where a comma became necessary were appositives , which are groups of words that restate other nouns ; nonessential modifiers , which are word groups used to modify other nouns ; and direct address , which is a word or words used to refer to the person to whom one is speaking.

19. Everybody needs to know how to punctuate correctly ; otherwise , other people will have a hard time understanding their writing.

20. So next time you get tired of doing these punctuation worksheets, remember what punctuation is really for ; it helps us all communicate more quickly and clearly!

SEMICOLONS & COLONS: EXERCISE #2

NAME:_____DATE:_____

*DIRECTIONS: **Decide where colons should appear in the following sentences and write them in.***

1.   Reading Proverbs 3:13, the minister supported his main point with the following quotation :"Happy is the
      man that findeth wisdom and the man who getteth understanding."

2.   In science class we have to learn the meaning of the following words :*amphibian, chromosome, neutron,*
      oxidation, and *vertebrae.*

3.   Miss Thomson invited Alden, Richard, and Sammy.

4.   The farmer explained the uses of the various parts of the plow :landslide, clevis, jointer, and beam.

5.   Experts can identify a fingerprint by observing the nature of the following: arches, whorls, loops, and
      composites.

6.   At 10:45 the teacher closed the lesson by reading Exodus 20:12:"Honor thy father and thy mother, that thy
      days may be long upon the land which the Lord thy God giveth thee."

7.   At 8:20 the agent told us that the 6:10 train would not arrive before 9:15.

8.   Along the midway were several kinds of rides :a roller coaster, a ship, two merry-go-rounds, and a
      Ferris wheel.

9.   There were sandwiches, cold drinks, and candy on our trays.

10.   At an airport I like to listen to the many noises: motors roaring before take-off, loudspeakers announcing
      departures and arrivals, and telephones ringing at every counter.

323

SEMICOLONS & COLONS: EXERCISE #3

NAME:_____DATE:_____

DIRECTIONS: *Using semicolons and colons, correctly punctuate the following sentences. You may have to change punctuation that is already there into something else.*

1. A scrawny, friendly stray dog wandered onto the field ; the umpire stopped the game.

2. Because they do not conduct electricity, the following materials can be used as insulators : rubber , glass , cloth , and plastics.

3. There are only three primary colors in painting : red, blue, and yellow.

4. Other colors are mixtures of primary colors ; for instance , purple is a mixture of red and blue.

5. The ten-gallon hat of the cowboy was used as a protection from the sun, a dipper for water, and a pan for washing his hands ; and leather chaps protected him from thorny bushes.

6. The minister began her sermon by quoting these two verses from the Bible : Matthew 23 : 39 and John 16 : 27.

7. In his speech to the Thespian Society, Mr. Stevenson quoted from several Shakespearean plays : *Romeo and Juliet, The Tempest, Macbeth,* and *Julius Caesar.*

8. Captain James Cook explored much of the Pacific Ocean ; he found the Hawaiian Islands in 1778.

9. From 1851 to 1864, the United States had four Presidents : Millard Fillmore, a Whig from New York ; Franklin Pierce, a Democrat from New Hampshire ; James Buchanan, a Democrat from Pennsylvania ; and Abraham Lincoln, a Republican from Illinois.

10. From 1 : 15 to 1 : 50 p.m., I was so sleepy that my mind wandered ; I rested my head on my right palm and let my eyelids sag to half-mast.

SEMICOLONS & COLONS: TEST

NAME:_____DATE:_____

(RAW SCORE:_____ *$/120$* GRADE:_____)

PART I: *Insert semicolons where they are needed. You may need to change some commas to semicolons.*

___1. Take Mom's suitcase upstairs **;** you can leave Dad's in the car for now.
1

___2. I wrote to Anne, Beth, and Meghan **;** and Jean notified Ted and Sue.
1

___3. The Stone of Scone was used in ancient Scottish coronations **;** for years it lay beneath the coronation chair
1   in Westminster Abbey.

___4. Alaska is huge and wild **;** it is also modern and sophisticated.
1

___5. Mother threw the coat away **;** it was worn out.
1

___6. Janet did as she was told **;** however, she grumbled ungraciously.
1

___7. From 1968 to 1988 the Presidents were Richard Nixon, a Republican from California **;** Gerald Ford, a
3   Republican from Michigan **;** Jimmy Carter, a Democrat from Georgia **;** and Ronald Reagan, a Republican
        from California.

___8. Mr. Baxter, who never raised his voice in the classroom, began to shout **;** obviously he had been
1   pushed beyond his limit.

___9. After the fire, the family stood in the smoke-blackened dining room **;** and the house, now a smoking shell,
1   no longer looked like their own.

___10. Never be afraid to admit that you don't know something **;** always be ashamed to admit that you don't care.
1

====
12

PART II: *Some of the sentences below need colons; if so, insert them. Some of them have colons which should not be there; if so, cross them out. Some of them are correct; if so, write C in the space provided.*

___ _____ 1. A search showed that Jack's pocket contained the following **:** a knife, half an apple, a piece of
1   gum, a dime, and a nickel.

___ _____ 2. These cookies are made o̶f̶ flour, brown sugar, butter, eggs, and nuts.
1

___ *C* 3. At the drug store I bought a comb, a lipstick, and a box of tissues.
1

___ *C* 4. The following students will report to the main office: Anne Brown, Pete Kendall, Mary Jo Derum,
1   and Lane Williams.
1

(over)

___-_____ 5. The minister opened the service with a reading from John 10 **:** 16.
1

___-_____ 6. I have always wanted to do three things **:** climb a mountain, ride a race horse, and take a hot-air
1
balloon ride.

___ **C** 7. We have studied the following kinds of punctuation marks: commas, quotation marks, colons,
1
and semicolons.

___ **C** 8. To succeed in sports, one should be disciplined, well-coordinated, and motivated.
1

___-_____ 9. You need these supplies for this class **:** white lined notebook paper, a blue or black pen, and a
1
pencil.

___-_____ 10. At exactly 3 **:** 15 we will begin our meeting.
1

══
10

PART III: *Punctuate the following sentences correctly, using all the punctuation marks we have studied.*

___ 1. One of my favorite cowboy movies is called The 3**:** 10 to Yuma **;** it's about a law officer who must get his
3
prisoner on the train that leaves for Yuma at ten minutes after three.

___ 2. **"** Lightning has always awed people **,"** explained Mrs. Belmont **,"** and many of us are still frightened by it **."**
7

___ 3. **"** Have you read Poe's short story **'** The Pit and the Pendulum **'** ? **"** asked Jenna.
4

___ 4. **"** You'll need the following materials for the art course **:** a brush **,** an easel **,** and some watercolors **,"**
6
announced Mr. Greene.

___ 5. **"** Have you seen this month's issue of Seventeen **?"** asked Gloria.
4

___ 6. At 8 **:** 15 on March 1 **,** 1980 **,** we ate the last of our provisions.
3

___ 7. We thought we were taking a short cruise **;** however **,** it turned out to be quite a long trip.
2

___ 8. Robert Burns **,** a Scottish poet **,** wrote the poem **"** Flow Gently, Sweet Afton. **"**
4

___ 9. In the novel Little Women there are four sisters **:** Meg **,** Jo **,** Beth **,** and Amy.
5

___ 10. **"** Sally **,** who is my older sister **,** is coming home from college tonight **,"** announced Janet.
5

___ 11. Lenore was a poised **,** self-confident young woman **;** her ambition was to get involved in local politics.
2

___ 12. The finalists in the Miss Stuffed Artichoke contest were Pearl Button , a stunning blonde from West
8

Mudsling , Wisconsin ; Ima Sweathog , a dainty brunette from Gnawbone , Indiana ; and Reina Ponderoof ,

a pert redhead from Lower Intestine , Nevada.

___ 13. My brothers and sisters have these characteristics in common : kindness , unselfishness , and loyalty.
3

___ 14. " This morning's sermon ," said Reverend Jenkins , our new minister ," will be based on Luke 4 : 18. "
8

___ 15. Opening his copy of the <u>Wall Street Journal</u> , Dad settled back in his chair and announced , " I do not wish to
6

be disturbed ; I have had a difficult day. "

___ 16. " Open your books , but don't start yet ," said Miss Ames , my math teacher.
5

___ 17. The members of the senior class , who had been working very hard , had a great time at the Prom ; and the
5

Winter Ball , which was put on by the juniors , was also a big success.

___ 18. Professor Hensley , hurrying down the corridor with his nose buried in Steinbeck's great novel <u>The Grapes</u>
5

<u>of Wrath</u> , bumped right into Miss Peabody , the tall , muscular physical education teacher.

___ 19. " Since I had planned to stay home and watch ' Saturday Night Live ,' I decided to make some popcorn ; that
7

was my first mistake ," explained Gail.

___ 20. " The next morning one of the crew shouted , ' Land ho ! '" said Jim.
6

===
98

RAW SCORE			GRADE		%
120	-	117	= A++	=	98+
116	-	114	= A+	=	95
113	-	108	= A	=	90
107	-	102	= B+	=	85
101	-	96	= B	=	80
95	-	90	= C+	=	75
89	-	84	= C	=	70
83	-	78	= D+	=	65
77	-	72	= D	=	60

327

FORMING THE POSSESSIVE

When we want to indicate that something belongs to or is owned by somebody or something, we use the POSSESSIVE. We form the possessive by adding either ' or 's to a noun.

I.   POSSESSIVE PRONOUNS

These pronouns are already possessive in form. We do not need to add apostrophes to them to make them possessive.

mine	ours	yours	theirs	your
his	hers	its	whose	yours

II.   POSSESSIVE NOUNS: To form the possessive you...

A.   ...take the SINGULAR NOUN and add 's.

EXAMPLES: lady's dress
              baby's toys
              Marcia's book

B.   ...take the PLURAL NOUN ENDING IN S and add '.

EXAMPLES: ladies' room
              four days' delay
              girls' soccer team

C.   ...take the PLURAL NOUN NOT ENDING IN S and add 's.

EXAMPLES: children's choir
              men's room
              people's choice

D.   ...take the NAME ENDING IN S OF MORE THAN ONE SYLLABLE and add '.

EXAMPLES: Mr. Ellis' house
              Hercules' journey

When a one-syllable name ends in S, you add 's. (Example: Chris's house)

HERE'S A TRICK: Rather than trying to remember all those rules, learn to "flip the possessive phrase around." For example, suppose you were dealing with

THE GIRLS BASKETBALL TEAM WON THEIR GAME.

Just "flip the phrase around" like this: "The girls basketball team is the basketball team of the girls." Now "freeze frame" the "word-in-the-box" in your "mind's eye." You have to add to that word to make it possessive, and there are only two possibilities: s or '. Which one "looks right"? Right! It must be GIRLS' because GIRLS'S "looks wrong." Now go back and put the apostrophe where it belongs in the sentence above.

POSSESSIVES: EXERCISE #1

NAME:_____DATE:_____

PART I: *Find and underline the possessive phrase in each sentence below. Then in the space provided, "flip" the phrase and write the "word-in-the-box" in the box provided.*

EXAMPLE: The boys basketball team won.	**the basketball team of the**	**boys**
1. Toms team won the game.	*the team of*	*Tom*
2. The boys soccer tryouts will be next week.	*soccer for*	*boys*
3. I sell mens clothing in my store.	*clothing for*	*men*
4. The store next door sells ladies clothing.	*clothing for*	*ladies*
5. Mr. Gates is in the teachers lounge.	*lounge for*	*teachers*
6. The girls locker room is locked.	*locker room for*	*girls*
7. Jesus disciples traveled with Him.	*disciples of*	*Jesus*

PART II: *Using the technique of "flipping the possessive phrase," correctly punctuate the following sentences. Remember to "freeze frame" the word-in-the-box", then add either ' or 's.*

1.   Bonnie's team won the spelling match.

2.   Tammy's little sister got lost in the store.

3.   My two brothers' clothes were all over the floor.

4.   That girl's book fell out of the car.

5.   The doctor gently felt the dog's paw.

6.   I left my sweater at the dentist's office.

7.   Richard's hobby is collecting ballplayers' autographs.

PART III: *Rewrite the sentences below. These sentences are already "flipped," so you need to put them back the way they were before they were flipped. Your rewritten sentence must say the same thing as the original sentence, but it must contain a possessive.*

1.   The hat of that fat man blew down the street.
         That fat man's hat blew down the street.
2.   There are the coats of two girls in the closet.
              two girls' coats
3.   We found the bike which belongs to Ramon in the basement.
              Ramon's bike
4.   It was "The Day for Ladies" at Yankee Stadium.
              Ladies' Day

329

POSSESSIVES: EXERCISE #2

NAME:_____DATE:_____

PART I: *Correctly form the possessives in the sentences below:*

1.   The children's presents are in the hall closet.

2.   Ann's store sells maps and travel books.

3.   Ross's golf bag is in my father's car.

4.   That architect's designs have won many awards.

5.   Many campers' tents were destroyed by the forest fire.

6.   We used Trish's scarf as a bandage.

7.   Louis' phone number has been changed.

8.   The boys' basketball team was undefeated.

9.   Tess's butterfly collection has two dozen specimens.

10.   The sailors' raincoats protected them from the spray.

PART II: *Rewrite the following sentences so that they say the same thing but contain possessives.*

1.   The library for children closes at five o'clock.   ***children's library***

2.   We found the mittens of George.   ***George's mittens***

3.   Which department sells cribs for babies?   ***babies' cribs***

4.   Where are the tickets of the women?   ***women's tickets***

5.   The house of George Jones is on this street.   ***George Jones's house***

6.   The house of the Joneses is on this street.   ***the Joneses' house***

7.   I will be with you again in the time of two days.   ***in two days' time***

8.   I can only take a vacation of one week this year.   ***one week's vacation***

9.   Please give me the worth of two dollars in quarters.   ***two dollars' worth***

10.   The teachings of Socrates are still studied today.   ***Socrates' teachings***

(over)

PART III: Write words according to the following directions:

WORD	POSSESSIVE	PLURAL	PLURAL POSSESSIVE
LADY	lady's	ladies	ladies'
CHILD	child's	children	children's
MAN	man's	men	men's
GIRL	girl's	girls	girls'
WOMAN	woman's	women	women's

POSSESSIVES: EXERCISE #3

NAME:_____DATE:_____

PART I: *Write words according to the following directions:*

WORD	POSSESSIVE	PLURAL	PLURAL POSSESSIVE
BABY	*baby's*	*babies*	*babies'*
SHEEP	*sheep's*	*sheep*	*sheep's*
TOM SMITH	*Smith's*	THE SMITHS	*Smiths'*
MOUSE	*mouse's*	*mice*	*mice's*
BOY	*boy's*	*boys*	*boys'*

PART II: *Place apostrophes in the proper places in the sentences below:*

1. The governor's mansion was lit by floodlights.

2. Three policemen's uniforms were in the back of the car.

3. My aunt's favorite color is magenta; what's yours?

4. We need a stretcher to carry the team's mascot into the locker room.

5. John took three weeks' vacation to Tahiti this year.

6. Please give me two dollars' worth of change.

7. Let's go to the old swimming hole just for old times' sake.

8. Julie's skirt was shorter than hers.

9. In college we studied Aristophanes' speeches.

10. Coach Gillis' daughter is coming to the game this week.

PART III: *Rewrite the following sentences using the possessive.*

1. Tonight we are having dinner at the house of the Finleys.   *the Finleys' house*

2. Janie suddenly found herself in the locker room for the boys.   *boys' locker room*

3. I asked for the worth of a dollar in change.   *a dollar's worth*

4. I said I would see him in the time of two months.   *in two months' time*

5. After the study of four years, I considered myself an expert in economics.   *four years' study*

PART IV: *On the back compose your own possessive sentences using the following nouns:*   *(Answers will vary)*

1. Sally   2. Socrates   3. any singular noun   4. Ross   5. any plural noun not ending in S.

Photocopying this product is strictly prohibited by copyright law.

POSSESSIVES: TEST

NAME:_____ DATE:_____

(RAW SCORE:_____*/70* GRADE:_____)

PART I: *Write words according to the following directions:*

		WORD	**POSSESSIVE**	**PLURAL**	**PLURAL POSSESSIVE**
(3	1.	TOOTH	*tooth's*	*teeth*	*teeth's*
	2.	BOX	*box's*	*boxes*	*boxes'*
points	3.	NURSE	*nurse's*	*nurses*	*nurses'*
	4.	JONES	*Jones's*	*Joneses*	*Joneses'*
each)	5.	KISS	*kiss's*	*kisses*	*kisses'*
	6.	WITCH	*witch's*	*witches*	*witches'*
	7.	COUNTRY	*country's*	*countries*	*countries'*
	8.	PUPPY	*puppy's*	*puppies*	*puppies'*
	9.	MAN	*man's*	*men*	*men's*
	10.	WOMAN	*woman's*	*women*	*women's*

===

30

PART II: *Place apostrophes where they are needed in the sentences below:*

1. Dierdre couldn't wait to see her parents' reaction.

2. Our school band 's original song was quite good.

(1

3. All the horses' stalls need to be cleaned out.

4. Are all pigs' tails curly?

point

5. My mom's new job begins today.

6. Are you going over to Bob White's house?

each)

7. The three new students' work was best.

8. The two guests' gifts were funny.

9. We have to make fifteen other dancers' costumes.

10. My dog's left paw is injured.

RAW SCORE		GRADE		%
70 - 68	=	A++	=	98+
67 - 66	=	A+	=	95
65 - 63	=	A	=	90
62 - 59	=	B+	=	85
58 - 56	=	B	=	80
55 - 52	=	C+	=	75
51 - 49	=	C	=	70
48 - 45	=	D+	=	65
44 - 42	=	D	=	60

(over)

11.   Give me four dollars' worth of quarters please.

12.   Those countries' main exports are oil and coal.

13.   Tony's speech was the best in the class.

14.   The ladies' room is locked.

===
15

15.   The women's room is locked.

PART III: *Rewrite the following sentences so that they say the same thing but have possessives.*

1.   Hank did the laundry of the whole family last week.   ***the whole family's laundry***

2.   The hands of the pianist were long and slender.   ***the pianist's hands***

3.   Glenn likes the symphonies of Beethoven.   ***Beethoven's symphonies***

4.   You should change the water of the goldfish.   ***the goldfish's water***

5.   Bob isn't getting his usual vacation of three weeks this year.   ***three weeks' vacation***

6.   The dishes of the cats are empty.   ***the cats' dishes***

7.   Tonight we're going to a party at the house of the Joneses.   ***the Joneses' house***

8.   The house of Ross is on the next street.   ***Ross's house***

9.   Someone has borrowed the skates of Lee.   ***Lee's skates***

10.   The lounge of the teachers is located near the office.   ***the teachers' lounge***

11.   The sails of all three boats need fixing.   ***all three boats' sails***

12.   Where is the room of the men?   ***the men's room***

13.   The mother of Curtis is late.   ***Curtis' mother***

14.   We say this prayer in the name of Jesus.   ***Jesus' name***

===
15

15.   There are two kids in the office of the nurse right now.   ***the nurse's office***

334   *Photocopying this product is strictly prohibited by copyright law.*

PART IV: *Write original sentence using the words below as possessives. Be sure you are using the word as a possessives, not a plural.*

(Worth

one

point

each.)

1.   Hercules

     Hercules'

2.   boy (singular)

     boy's

3.   boys (plural)

     boys'

4.   lady (singular)

     lady's

5.   lady (plural)

     ladies'

6.   Mr. Ellis

     Mr. Ellis'

7.   Chris

     Chris's

8.   week (singular)

     week's

9.   week (plural)

     weeks'

10. Sheila

     Sheila's

Answers will vary,

but possessives must

look like this.

===
10

CAPITALIZATION

I. *Capitalize the names of persons.*

EXAMPLES: Sandra Wilson   MacDonald (the M and the D are capitalized)

Mr. Charles F. Skinner   O'Brien   John McCaffrey, Jr.

Initials & abbreviations
after names are capitalized

II. *Capitalize geographical names*

EXAMPLES: (towns, cities)   Anchorage, Kansas City

(counties)   Harrison County

(states)   Alaska, New Hampshire

(sections)   the East, the Midwest, the South

NOTE: the words <u>north</u>, <u>west</u>, <u>southeast</u>, etc. are not capitalized when they indicate
direction, such as"the south of town" or "traveling northwest."

(countries)   the United States of America, Brazil

(continents)   Asia, Antarctica

(islands)   Prince Edward Island, the Hawaiian Islands

(mountains)   Mount McKinley, Mount Ararat, the Alps

(bodies of water)   the Indian Ocean, Lake Hood, Columbia River

(roads, highways)   Route 10, New Seward Highway, Elm Street

Twenty-first Street

**Note that "first" is
not capitalized.**

(parks)   Yellowstone National Park

NOTE: words like <u>city</u>, <u>park</u>, <u>street</u>, etc. are capitalized if they are part of a name. If
they are not part of a name, they are just ordinary common nouns.

III. *Capitalize proper adjectives* **(when you make an adjective out of a proper noun)**

EXAMPLE: Greek theatre, English literature, Indian maiden, Italian shoes

IV. *Capitalize names of organizations, business firms, institutions, and governmental bodies.*

EXAMPLES: (organizations)   American Red Cross, Boy Scouts of America

(business firms)   Nordstrom, J.C. Penney, Western Airlines

(institutions)   Columbia University, Service High School,
Providence Hospital

NOTE: Do NOT capitalize words like <u>hotel, theater, high school</u> unless they are part of
a name.

EXAMPLES: West High School   high school teacher

Sheraton Hotel   a hotel in town

Fourth Avenue Theatre   a movie theater

(government bodies)   Congress, Federal Bureau of Investigation

V. *Capitalize the names of historical events and periods, special events, and calendar items.*

EXAMPLES: (historical events)   Boston Tea Party, the Middle Ages, World War I

(special events)   Fur Rendezvous, Homecoming, Super Bowl

(calendar items)   Sunday, May, Halloween, Fourth of July

NOTE: Do not capitalize the names of seasons (summer, spring, etc.) unless they are
part of the names of an event. (Winter Carnival)

VI.   *Capitalize the names of nationalities, races, and religions.*
EXAMPLES: (nationalities)   Canadians, an American, a European
            (races)   Indian, African-American, Asian
            (religions)   Moslem, Presbyterian, a Christian Scientist

VII. *Capitalize the brand names of business products.*
EXAMPLES: Fritos, Cocoa Puffs, Toyota

NOTE: Do not capitalize the noun that often follows a brand name (Chevy truck, Guess jeans)

VIII. *Capitalize the names of ships, planets, monuments, awards, and any other particular place, thing, or event.*
EXAMPLES: (ships, trains)   the *Mayflower*, the *Silver Streak*
            (aircraft, missiles)   the *Enola Gay*, the *Titan*
            (planets, stars)   the North Star, Jupiter, the Milky Way

NOTE: *Sun* and *moon* are only capitalized when they are listed with the other bodies in our solar system. Earth is capitalized when it is a name (I will return to Earth.) but not when it's preceded by an article (I will return to the earth.).

            (monuments, etc.)   Washington Monument, Viet Nam Memorial
            (buildings)   the Eiffel Tower, Taj Mahal, World Trade Center
            (awards)   the Oscar, Congressional Medal of Honor

IX.   *Do not capitalize the names of school subjects except languages and the names of particular courses.*
EXAMPLES: Presently I am taking English, science, Geography I, Spanish, and economics.

NOTE: Do not capitalize the members of a class (freshman, sophomore, junior, senior) unless it is part of a proper noun (Junior Prom, Senior Picnic)

X.   *Capitalize titles*
   A.   *Capitalize the title of a person when it comes before a name:*
        EXAMPLES: President Bush
                    Mrs. Morrison
                    Dr. Jenkins
                    Professor Wright

   B.   *Capitalize a title used alone or following a person's name only if it refers to a high official or to someone to whom you wish to show special respect:*
        EXAMPLES: Can you name our thirtieth President? (a high official)
                    The General regrets he will be unable to attend.(special respect)
                    The president of our club read the minutes.(not a high official)

   NOTE: When a title is used alone in direct address, it is usually capitalized.
          EXAMPLES: I'm pleased to see you, Doctor.
                      Tell me, Coach, what are our chances?

   C.   *Capitalize words showing family relationship used with or as a person's name but NOT when preceded by an adjective.*
        EXAMPLES: Aunt Mabel, Cousin Enid, Mom
                    my mother, your father, Frank's sister

XI.   *Capitalize the first word and all words in titles of books, periodicals, etc. EXCEPT ARTICLES, PREPOSITIONS, AND CONJUNCTIONS.*

        EXAMPLES: *Gone with the Wind*
                             "The Adventure of the Speckled Band"
                             "Just Tell Me That You Love Me"
                             Pride and Prejudice

The Bible and the books of the Bible are always capitalized.

XII.   *Capitalize words referring to the Diety; do not capitalize the word "god" when referring to a polytheistic pantheon of gods.*

        EXAMPLES: God and His universe.
                             The people came to Jesus and they worshipped Him.
                             The God of Islam is Allah.
                             The Aztec god in the form of a feathered serpent was Quetzalcoatl.

CAPITALIZATION: EXERCISE #1

NAME:_____DATE:_____

DIRECTIONS: *In each of the following items, you are to choose the correct one of the two forms. Circle the letter of the correct item and be prepared to tell me why the other one is wrong.*

1. ✔a. His store is on Front Street in Burlington.
   b. His store is on front street in Burlington.

2. a. We crossed the Snake river.
   ✔b. We crossed the Snake River.

3. a. He now lives in california.
   ✔b. He now lives in California.

4. ✔a. Did you fly over South America?
   b. Did you fly over south America?

5. ✔a. He took a picture of Pike's Peak.
   b. He took a picture of Pike's peak.

6. ✔a. City streets in the West are often wide.
   b. City streets in the west are often wide.

7. ✔a. Yellowstone National Park has many geysers.
   b. Yellowstone national park has many geysers.

8. ✔a. The city of Columbus is the capital of Ohio.
   b. The City of Columbus is the capital of Ohio.

9. a. The hurricane swept over the gulf of Mexico.
   ✔b. The hurricane swept over the Gulf of Mexico.

10. ✔a. Drive east on U.S. Highway 35.
    b. Drive East on U.S.Highway 35.

11. a. We are proud of our State parks.
    ✔b. We are proud of our state parks.

12. a. I live on Forty-Fifth Street.
    ✔b. I live on Forty-fifth Street.

13. ✔a. The headquarters is in Travis County.
    b. The headquarters is in Travis county.

14. a. The Vikings called the atlantic ocean the sea of darkness.
    ✔b. The Vikings called the Atlantic Ocean the Sea of Darkness.

15. ✔a. The states of the Midwest are referred to as the nation's breadbasket.
    b. The states of the midwest are referred to as the nation's breadbasket.

16. a. A three-lane Highway is dangerous.
    ✔b. A three-lane highway is dangerous.

17. ✔a. I have a map of the Virgin Islands.
    b. I have a map of the Virgin islands.

18. a. New York city is the largest city in the east.
    ✔b. New York City is the largest city in the East.

19. ✔a. The Great Salt Lake is near the Nevada border.
    b. The Great Salt lake is near the Nevada Border.

20. ✔a. His address is 2009 Bell Avenue.
    b. His address is 2009 Bell avenue.

Photocopying this product is strictly prohibited by copyright law.   **339**

CAPITALIZATION: EXERCISE #2

NAME:_____DATE:_____

DIRECTIONS: *Circle the letters which should be capitalized in the sentences below.*

1.   mr. ronson mentioned the fact that mercury and venus are closer to earth than jupiter.

2.   every freshman at jefferson high school knows he will take at least three years of english and two years of

    mathematics.

3.   while in the city of washington, we saw the ford theater where lincoln was shot.

4.   a methodist, a moslem, and a roman catholic conducted an interesting panel discussion.

5.   since I plan to study medicine at northwestern university, I'm taking latin and biology I.

6.   after I had gone to the grocery store at the corner of thirty-first street and stonewall avenue, I stopped at the

    twin oaks lumber company, which is two blocks south of cooper avenue.

7.   vacationing in the west, we saw electric peak, which is on the northern boundary of yellowstone national

    park; we also saw the devil's tower, which is in northeastern wyoming.

8.   later we drove along riverside drive and saw the lincoln memorial, which is the site of dr. martin luther

    king, jr.'s famous "I have a dream" speech.

9.   in the spring, usually the first saturday after easter, the women's missionary society, a baptist organization,

    gives a picnic for our class.

10.   leaving ecuador in south america on a banana boat named *bonanza*, they went through the panama canal

    and sailed through the caribbean sea to nassau in the bahamas.

CAPITALIZATION: EXERCISE #3

NAME:_____DATE:_____

DIRECTIONS: *Circle the letters which should be capitalized in the sentences below.*

1   speaking to the seniors of westfield high school, mr. carter praised *the tragedy of american compassion*, a

      book by marvin olasky.

2.   on the sunday before labor day, we drove as far as the murphy motel, a mile west of salem, virginia; the

      manager, mr. kelly, proudly announced that he was a member of the virginia tourist court association.

3.   waiting for a city bus at the corner of twenty-first street and hampton drive, we admired the anne klein

      clothes in dillard's window display.

4.   father and his brother, my uncle julian, told me about rockefeller center and about the shops on fifth avenue

      in new york city.

5.   professor massey studied at the library of congress and the folger shakespeare library during july and

      august.

                                                     ✲

6.   althea gibson's autobiography *I always wanted to be somebody* was published by harper & row.

7.   I especially like the photograph - made by alaska airlines - of mt. mckinley in alaska.

8.   in his junior year at sheridan high school, uncle rufus studied latin, french, english, geometry, and art.

9.   the reverend walker said that the gods of the ancient greeks did not offer the promise of immortality that

      our god does.

10.   after the texans so bravely fought against the forces of general santa anna in 1836, the alamo became

      famous as a memorial to texas liberty, a symbol of american freedom like the statue of liberty.

✲   *Your students will probably want to leave the word to in lower case. Tell them it*
      should be capitalized and ask them why. See if anybody can tell you that it's not a
      short preposition here but part of the infinitive to be. So, since it's a verbal, both "to"
      and "be" should be capitalized.

CAPITALIZATION: TEST

NAME:_____DATE:_____

(RAW SCORE:_____ /89 GRADE:_____)

PART I: DIRECTIONS: *Some of the following sentences are correct and some need capitalization.*
If the sentence is correct, write a C in the space provided; if it is not correct, circle the letters to be capitalized.

1/1. In the fall everyone looks forward to the football season. _C_

2/2. Football fans can see their favorite high school or college team play on saturday and their favorite

professional teams on sunday. _____

3/3. Last weekend I saw ohio state play michigan. _____

2/4. Kay's aunt introduced her to the captain of one of the world's largest passenger ships, the *queen*

elizabeth II. _____

4/5. The greeks believed that their various dieties met on mount olympus to listen to zeus, the king of the

gods. _____

2/6. Ann likes geography and history, but she does the best in english and french. _____

4/7. The chief justice explained the ruling of the supreme court. _____

1/8. On July 4 the Bayshore Mall puts on a spectacular fireworks display. _C_

2/9. The *titanic* sank after hitting an iceberg off the coast of newfoundland. _____

5/10. My aunt went to amsterdam to see rembrandt's *the night watch.* _____

====
26

PART II: DIRECTIONS: *Circle any letter that should be capitalized in the sentences below.*

5/1. Mail the letter to the union of south africa and the package to genoa, italy.

4/2. This year palm sunday is the last sunday in march.

3/3. Among the early settlers were roman catholics and congregationalists.

5/4. like other north american indians, the ancient iriquois believed in many gods.

2/5. The department of agriculture publishes many pamphlets that are useful to the home gardener.

3/6. Did aunt josie send you that mexican straw hat?

2/7. The *windy jane* is a small white sailboat.

Just as in punctuation tests, in this test BAD capitalization cancels out GOOD capitalization. I never give
a sentence lower than a zero; in other words, there are no "minus balances" on test sentences.

(over)

$\overline{2}$ 8. Last winter Carrie had an iceboat on greenwood lake.

$\overline{3}$ 9. In history and in spanish, we are studying the same european renaissance.

$\overline{2}$ 10. One woman is an armenian; the other is a greek.

====

31 **PART III: DIRECTIONS:** *If a sentence is correct, write C in the space. If it needs capitalization, circle the letter that should be capitalized.*

$\overline{5}$ 1. nan and I are spending the summer at camp medomak in washington, maine. _____

$\overline{1}$ 2. Tommy has a new English bicycle, a gift from his aunt. __*C*__

$\overline{1}$ 3. Suddenly I saw the boeing 747 darting across the sky. _____

$\overline{1}$ 4. Here is a new series of Norwegian airmail stamps. __*C*__

$\overline{1}$ 5. The waters of the Mediterranean are very blue. __*C*__

$\overline{1}$ 6. The table is made of asian teakwood. _____

$\overline{1}$ 7. The Acme Tractor Company is looking for a qualified computer analyst. __*C*__

$\overline{1}$ 8. Have you ever seen a Mexican jumping bean? __*C*__

$\overline{1}$ 9. We heard the performance of Verdi's *aida*. _____

$\overline{3}$ 10. My sister is taking english, math II, social studies, biology, and french. _____

$\overline{1}$ 11. Just then I noticed her new persian rug. _____

$\overline{3}$ 12. Is the goldstar bus company still on strike? _____

$\overline{1}$ 13. Silk is an important Japanese export. __*C*__

$\overline{2}$ 14. Jerry lives on the west side of oak street. _____

$\overline{1}$ 15. Sometimes the boys go fishing on Lake Oswego. __*C*__

$\overline{1}$ 16. At Aspen, Colorado, I learned to ride a horse. __*C*__

$\overline{2}$ 17. She is traveling by northwest airlines. _____

$\overline{2}$ 18. My favorite program is sponsored by cocoa crispies cereal. _____

$\overline{1}$ 19. Colgate has introduced a new kind of toothpaste. __*C*__

$\overline{2}$ 20. Octopuses lurk in the mediterranean sea. _____

====

32

RAW SCORE		GRADE		%
89	- 87	=	A++	=	98+
86	- 84	=	A+	=	95
83	- 80	=	A	=	90
79	- 75	=	B+	=	85
74	- 71	=	B	=	80
70	- 66	=	C+	=	75
65	- 62	=	C	=	70
61	- 57	=	D+	=	65
56	- 53	=	D	=	60

PUNCTUATION REVIEW: EXERCISE #1

NAME:_____DATE:_____

DIRECTIONS: *Punctuate the following sentences correctly, using everything you have been taught about punctuation and capitalization.*

1.   Our national heroes , people like abraham lincoln , martin luther king , jr. , and cesar chavez , fought for these rights : life , liberty , and equality.

2.   Rod evans , sailing over the last hurdle , won the race easily ; roger evans , his brother , came in a slow second.

3.   " I knew you'd make it , rod ! shouted winston . when are you headed for the olympics ? your father said last night , my son rod is going to be all-american this year ! ' " *

4.   Rosemary is knitting her first sweater , a soft , cuddly wool one with no sleeves. She is making it according to directions in the may issue of <u>seventeen</u> magazine.

5.   John does , I believe , still live at 268 fairway lane , fairbanks , alaska.

6.   Father's day comes on the third sunday in june ; mother's day comes on the second sunday in may.

7.   Jim dreams of doing research at the rockefeller national laboratory in albany , new york.

8.   I've carefully studied chapter 23 , " punctuating quotations , " in our textbook <u>adventures in punctuation</u> ; therefore , I feel prepared for the test tomorrow.

9.   Wisteria , a lovely purple flower , was named after caspar wistar , an 18th century anatomist , and jimson weed was named after jamestown , virginia .

10.   A computer can be used for making lists of things to do , keeping track of household accounts , and doing your homework ; and term papers done on a computer always look nicer.

*In this you have an exclamation inside another exclamation. It's also possible to have a question inside of another question. When this occurs, you only want one exclamation or question mark.

Whether you put it inside the quotes or outside is a judgement call on the part of the writer.

PUNCTUATION REVIEW: EXERCISE #2

NAME:_____DATE:_____

DIRECTIONS: *Add all the necessary punctuation and capitalization you have been taught to the sentences below.*

1.   The race was over; the jockey leaped from her horse and smilingly accepted the glittering, shimmering gold cup.

2.   Mr. Cameron, our shop teacher, announced, "Bring the following supplies: wood, nails, and glue."

3.   "The girls' mittens are missing," said Mother. "They said they left them in the pockets of their gap jackets."

4.   "Have you seen Kevin Costner's movie <u>Dances With Wolves</u>?" Cara asked.

5.   Casey's story "The Night They Burned the Outhouse" will appear in this month's issue of <u>Sanitation Gazette</u>.

6.   "I think I should point out," said Mr. Henries, the store manager, "that Michael's dog isn't welcome here."

7.   "Watch out for shaving cream!" yelled Mike. "It's Halloween, you know!"

8.   "Did Mrs. Finley say, 'In my opinion, Tom Selleck is a dweeb,' asked John, "or am I hearing things?"

9.   "First I read the sports section of today's <u>Washington Post</u>," said Jim, "and then I did the crossword puzzle."

10.   The judge, staring with a ferocious scowl at the skinny, terrified prisoner, asked, "do you plead guilty or not guilty?"

"The Night They Burned the Outhouse" is an appositive, which would ordinarily be "set off" by commas; however, because this title is already "set off" by quotation marks, the commas should be eliminated.

PUNCTUATION REVIEW: EXERCISE #3

NAME:_____DATE:_____

DIRECTIONS: *Add all the necessary punctuation and capitalization you have been taught to the sentences below.*

1. "can you lend me five dollars for a week or so, old buddy?" asked mr. gardner, father's best friend.

2. "Jim, the cleaning woman is here, but she says she doesn't do windows!" yelled mom.

3. His program, which we watch regularly, is on sunday afternoons.

4. "People who live in glass houses shouldn't throw stones," said miss phillips.

5. "why, even you can work this gadget, mary!" cried elaine.

6. "it was jean, as a matter of fact, who memorized the poem 'stopping by woods on a snowy evening' from our poetry anthology america's major poets," said robert.

7. The test was long and difficult; however, everyone finished.

8. His grades are as follows: english, his favorite class, an A; history, a really tough class, a B; science, his least favorite, a C; and math, a B.

9. The sermon opened with a reading of deuteronomy 3:24 from the king james version of the holy bible.

10. "how," richard asked, mopping his brow listlessly, "do you people stand this climate?"

* "Stopping by Woods on a Snowy Evening" is an appositive, which would ordinarily be "set off" by commas; however, because this title is already "set off" by quotation marks, the commas should be eliminated. The case is the same for the title America's Major Poets.

Photocopying this product is strictly prohibited by copyright law.

PUNCTUATION/CAPITALIZATION REVIEW:TEST

NAME:_____DATE:_____

(RAW SCORE:_____ /342 GRADE:_____)

PART I: *Add the necessary punctuation and capitalization to the sentences below.*

7 1. "the teacher said , I will assign no homework tonight !" she yelled jubilantly.

12 2. "over the drinking fountain at school," said bob, "there is a sign that says 'old faceful.'"

10 3. as the president of the united states entered , the band played "hail to the chief."

10 4. john adams and thomas jefferson, old rivals, died on the same day , the fourth of july.

4 5. most of the engineers were pleased with the new design, but helen had doubts about it.

4 6. to eat, the little old man from china used chopsticks.

5 7. mrs. curtis' shoes hurt her feet, but she wore them anyway.

8 8. "the parents are invited to the teachers' meeting," said mrs. haynes.

4 9. the new high school has many excellent features ; however, it needs more equipment in the gymnasium.

21 10. this traffic control system will be introduced in the following cities : buffalo, new york; st. louis, missouri; dallas, texas; and los angeles, california.

8 11. "we'll soon catch this culprit ; he has left several fingerprints on this glass," said detective grogan.

11 12. the following were thomas' ambitions : to go to harvard , to graduate summa cum laude, and to get a job in a prestigious new york law firm.

16 13. "I did not read this week's newsweek," said frank, "but I heard there was an article called 'life on other planets.'"

10 14. "the waitresses' names appear on their checks," said the manager. "please let us know if there is any problem."

2 15. we were so thirsty after our run that milk or water or even ink would have tasted good.

4 16. the happy, tired, victorious crew staggered over the rocks and fell on the sand.

9 17. roy shouted in anger, "you heard my dad say, 'I won't allow you boys to go out tonight'!"

* *Students may prefer to make two separate sentences here.*

(over)

18. "we can now hope," said dr. peters, chief of surgery at harbor general hospital," for a complete recovery."

19. the call of the wild, jack london's great novel, is a popular favorite with alaskans.

20. "the man or woman who enjoys reading is never lonely," said my english teacher.

PART II: *Punctuate the following **possessive** situations correctly.*

1. The three contestants' entries were all good.

2. The judges' work could be observed by visiting their courtrooms.

3. One judge's choice was different from the rest.

4. That is one of this year's best new television series.

5. The story's ending leaves many readers puzzled.

6. The four ships' cargoes are on the pier.

7. The drill team girls' jackets are at the cleaners.

8. Three women's cars were left in the parking lot.

9. That customer's complaints did not impress the manager.

10. Have you read the exciting tales of Ulysses' adventures?

PART III: *Put **colons** where they are needed in the sentences below.*

1. The book has photographs of some of the most beautiful mountain ranges in the world: the Himalayas, the Andes, the Alps, and the Rockies.

2. Here is a list of the possible times for our meeting: 12:30, 2:00, or 5:30.

3. I arrived at the station at 3:30 in the morning.

4. You will need to find the following: a fishing rod, some night crawlers, a few hooks, and a bag to take home any fish we catch.

5. If I wake up after 7:30, I can't get to school before 9:00.

6. Whenever I see a poster of Italy, I think of all the wonderful food I ate there: delicious cream sauces, ripe black olives, succulent meats, and golden cheeses.

7. The train will depart from Anchorage at 7:15 and arrive in Fairbanks at 4:30.

8. Please give this message to all the following people: Sandy Pressman, Judy Pruitt, Mike Scott, and Alex Wolfson.

__2__ 9.   If you want to be in Fresno before 4:00, you should leave here by 10:30.

__1__ 10.   Tell me which of these presents you would prefer: a bicycle, a canoe, a radio, or a dog.

===

16   *PART IV: Insert semicolons where they are needed in the sentences below.*

__1__ 1.   The team members are on the field; they are ready to play.

__3__ 2.   Mr. Short ordered several new model kits: Skyblaster, a delta-winged aircraft,; Killer Diller, a new chopper

            bike,; Conquerer, an interplanetary cruiser,; and Conestoga, a replica of a covered wagon.

__1__ 3.   Traveling was Mary's hobby; she planned a trip to Paris last year.

__1__ 4.   The test, a review of all the rules of punctuation and capitalization, was a tough one; I think I did well on it.

__1__ 5.   The math problem was solved by Tom, Andrea, and James,; and Brandon did it in two minutes.

__1__ 6.   Sylvia is still looking for the solution; she has tried almost everything.

__3__ 7.   My favorite books as a child were *Anne of Green Gables*, the story of a red-haired orphan,; *Daddy-Long-*

            Legs, the story of an orphan who was sent to college,; and *Elsie Dinsmore*, the story of a rich little orphan

            whose relatives are trying to get her money; I guess I was fascinated by orphans!

__1__ 8.   A storm is coming; black clouds are forming.

__1__ 9.   Frank picked beans, cauliflower, and broccoli,; and Mary hoed the other end of the garden.

__1__ 10.   Something is wrong with my computer; it keeps making mistakes!

===

14   *PART V: Insert commas where they are needed.*

__2__ 1.   We first heard this story in Sydney, Australia, during our vacation.

__3__ 2.   On December 31, 1977, a stranger arrived in Nestor, North Dakota.

__4__ 3.   Between January 31, 1978, and February 23, 1978, he worked in the garage of his house.

__3__ 4.   On November 22, 1978, the stranger went to Grand Rapids, Michigan.

__2__ 5.   He returned on December 1, 1978, with a large box.

__2__ 6.   On December 10, 1978, young Tim Hartley peeked into the garage.

__2__ 7.   From that day until the Hartleys moved to Kingsport, Tennessee, Tim told wild tales of what he had seen in

            that garage.

__4__ 8.   Between February 24, 1979, and March 15, 1979, neighbors heard strange noises coming from the garage.

__2__ 9.   The neighbors met on March 16, 1979, and decided to complain to the police.

(over)

    349

____4 10. The police visited the house on March 16,1979, and on March 17,1979,but no one

seemed to be at home.

____1 11. The police obtained a search warrant on March 18,1979.

____2 12. Half the people of Nestor,North Dakota,were watching as the police entered the garage.

____1 13. All they found was an empty box and a newspaper dated February 28,2089.

====

32   PART VI: DIRECTIONS: In each sentence below there is a comma split. In the spaces below each sentence
are the numbers of all the commas in the sentence. Find the comma split and write its number in the space at
the left. Write what it is splitting beside that comma's number below the sentence. By the other numbers,
write the "buzzwords" of the correct commas.

____2____ 1. In the business world of the future, machines designed for specific functions, will do a lot of the
                                                    1   2
work which we now do ourselves, but I don't believe the human mind can ever be completely
                                  3
replaced.

____5____   #1 - introductory modifier (2 prep. phrases)

               #2 - splits subject (machines) & verb (will do)

               #3 - compound sentence

____5____ 2. Yes, we have machines which can do math functions, keep track of data, and check our spelling,
              1   2   3   4
but only a human being can perform, certain types of work.
                                      5

               #1- introductory single word

____7____   **#2 - items in a series**

               #3-- items in a series

               #4 - compound sentence

               #5 - splits verb (perform) & direct object (types)

____5____ 3. If we wish to communicate ideas to other people, we often use jokes, examples, and analogies as
                                                            1   2   3
a means of explaining complex, detailed, concepts.
                      4   5

               #1 - introductory modifier (adverb clause)

____7____   **#2 - items in a series**

               #3- items in a series

               #4 - 2 adjectives with "and test"

               #5 - splits modifier and its noun.

___1___ 4. Even a machine which has been programmed to write, could not come up with jokes or plays on
                                                                                          1
              words, those little extras that even an average, well educated person would use.
                 2   3

___   #1 - splits subject (machine) & verb (could come)
 5
              #2 - appositive phrase

              #3 - 2 adjectives with "and test"

___1___ 5. Whenever our future employment is looking more and more, doubtful because machines are
                                                                              1
              taking over, remember that an educated human being, using all his or her creative talents to the
                 2   3
              utmost, can never be completely replaced by a machine.
                 4

___   #1 - splits linking verb (looking) & complement (doubtful)
 6
              #2 - introductory adverb clause

              #3 - nonessential modifier

====
 30   #4 - nonessential modifier

PART VII: *On a piece of lined notebook paper, write the following dialogue, using correct paragraphing, capitalization, and punctuation.*

Sean and Jason walked slowly into Mrs. Finley's classroom Sean sat down, put his books under his desk, and leaned over to Jason hey he said are you as worried about this test as I am are you kidding said Jason I worked until midnight you mean you studied asked Sean, beginning to chew his fingernails I kind of thought I'd try to fake it are you out of your mind Jason hissed I studied for two hours I looked over all my notes and went over the review worksheets Sean smiled weakly at Jason wow he said looking over your notes and going over the review sheets what a great idea wish I'd thought of it Jason stared at Sean in disgust it's a little late now, pal

See Key

¶ Sean and Jason walked slowly into Mrs. Finley's classroom.   Sean sat down, put his books under his

_12_   desk, and leaned over to Jason.   "Hey," he said, "are you as worried about this test as I am?"

*

— could also be !

_9_   ¶ "Are you kidding?" said Jason.   "I worked until midnight."

_9_   ¶ "You mean you studied?" asked Sean, beginning to chew his fingernails.   "I kind of thought I'd try to

fake it."

_10_   ¶ "Are you out of your mind?" Jason hissed.   "I studied for two hours.   I looked over all my notes and

went over the review worksheets."

_14_   ¶ Sean smiled weakly at Jason.   "Wow!" he said.   "Looking over your notes and going over the review

**

**

sheets!   What a great idea!   Wish I'd thought of it."

_6_   ¶ Jason stared at Sean in disgust.   "It's a little late now, pal."

====

60

* could also be: said. "Are

** these could be punctuated with periods (commas) or
exclamation marks.

RAW SCORE		GRADE		%
342 -	335 =	A++	=	98+
334 -	324 =	A+	=	95
323 -	307 =	A	=	90
306 -	290 =	B+	=	85
289 -	273 =	B	=	80
272 -	256 =	C+	=	75
255 -	239 =	C	=	70
238 -	222 =	D+	=	65
221 -	205 =	D	=	60

NOTES FOR TEACHERS

By now you have no doubt worked out a method for delivery of this curriculum that works for you and your student, so I really have no brilliant suggestions for these units. Just so you don't have to "reinvent the wheel," however, I have a tentative schedule for these units on the next page.

I have devised some ways of reinforcement that I like, however, For example, I give extra credit if the student can find usage errors in the newspaper or in magazines (and there are plenty of 'em!). The student must cut the error out and glue it to a piece of paper. He must highlight the error and then, at the bottom of the paper, he must rewrite the offending sentence with the usage error corrected.

Since few things are so delightful as correcting one's elders, this usually appeals strongly to students! And it does make them aware of the way they speak which, in the words of Professor 'Enry 'Iggins, "absolutely classifies them"!

This is a topic which is rarely mentioned in schools today because we have become so hesitant to risk offending anyone. But not to mention how important it is to speak clear, standard English is to do your student a tremendous disservice. He wants to get ahead and be successful, and it's our job to give him the tools to do that. If we give him the impression that he will not be judged by the way he speaks, we really are lying to him!

Sometime I tell my students to be on the listen because I will be committing some "usage sin" today - and if they can spot it and correct it (in writing, as above), they get extra credit.

SUGGESTED WORK SCHEDULE
FOR ANALYTICAL GRAMMAR: UNITS 29 - 34

(** means it's a homework assigbnment)

There are six units on usage. There are two cumulative exams, after Units #31 and #34.

DAY	ASSIGNMENT	POINTS
1	Go over Notes carefully until concept is understood (Unit #29)	These points are optional
2	Review and Correct Ex. 1 ** Ex. 2	5 points for completed assgmnt
3	Review and Correct Ex. 2 Introduce new concept (Unit #30) ** Ex. 1	5 points
4	Review and Correct Ex. 1 ** Ex. 2	5 points
5	Review and Correct Ex. 2 Introduce new concept (Unit #31) ** Ex. 1	5 points
6	Review and Correct Ex. 1 ** Ex. 2	5 points
7	Review and Correct Ex. 2 Review for Test (Units #29, 30, & 31)	5 points
8	Test: Units #29, 30, & 31	
9	Correct Test Introduce new concept (Unit #32) ** Ex. 1	20 points

REPEAT THE ABOVE PROCESS FOR UNITS #32, 33, & 34.

You will find that these units are not very time-consuming, if they are taught after the student has the grammatical background to grasp them.   Congratulations! You have completed Analytical Grammar! Check our website, www.analyticalgrammar.com, for reinforcement activities to keep your student's grammar and usage skills sharp.

PRONOUN-ANTECEDENT AGREEMENT

I.   When we learned about pronouns, we learned that an antecedent is the noun that the pronoun stands for. A pronoun must agree with its antecedent in NUMBER, GENDER, and PERSON.

A.   NUMBER refers to whether a pronoun is singular or plural.

      1.   The following pronouns are SINGULAR:

each	one	everybody	someone
either	anybody	everyone	nobody
neither	anyone	somebody	no one

      EXAMPLES: EACH of the men had HIS rifle ready for inspection.
                         EVERYONE has a right to HIS own opinion.
                         SOMEONE had left HIS OR HER books under a tree.

      2.   The following pronouns are either singular or plural depending on the antecedent.

all	any	some	none

      EXAMPLES: SOME of the STUDENTS looked tired when THEY were finished.
                         SOME of the SYRUP looks funny when IT is poured.

      3.   Two or more singular antecedents joined by <u>or</u> or <u>nor</u> are treated as singular.

      EXAMPLES: Either Jack OR Hal will bring HIS tape recorder.
                         Neither the teacher NOR his aide would repeat what HE had said.

B.   GENDER refers to whether the pronoun is MASCULINE, FEMININE, or NEUTER.

      EXAMPLES: The whale was fighting for ITS life. (neuter gender)
                         The postman said HE was tired. (masculine gender)
                         The waitress took HER time. (feminine gender)

When an antecedent is meant to indicate both masculine and feminine, it is correct to use masculine pronouns. However, to be "politically correct," it is often advisable to use the phrase "his or her."

    355

C.   PERSON refers to the following:

        I, me are in the FIRST PERSON

        you, your, yours are in the SECOND PERSON

        he, she, him, her, his, hers are in the THIRD PERSON

EXAMPLES: (WRONG) ONE should never let YOUR disappointment show.

        This sentence starts off in 3rd person and switches to 2nd!

    (RIGHT) ONE should never let HIS (OR ONE'S) disappointment show.

    (WRONG) I find that night driving is hard on YOUR eyes.

        This sentence starts off in 1st person and ends up in 2nd!

    (RIGHT) I find that night driving is hard on MY eyes.

PRONOUN-ANTECEDENT AGREEMENT: EX. #1

NAME:_____DATE:_____

DIRECTIONS: *Change whatever you have to change in the sentences below to correct any errors in agreement.*

1.   Neither the buyer nor the seller had made up ~~their~~ *his* mind.

2.   Everyone has a right to ~~their~~ *his* own opinion.

3.   Each of the winning essays had ~~their~~ *its* good points.

4.   Will each student please turn in ~~their~~ *his* schedule tomorrow?

5.   One should always write ahead for ~~their~~ *one's or his* hotel reservations.

6.   Each of us needs to start thinking about ~~their~~ *his* career now.

7.   If one tries hard enough, ~~you can~~ *one or he* can usually finish the reports in an hour.

8.   Everyone applying for the scholarship must bring ~~their~~ *his* birth certificate.

9.   Neither Lynn nor Sue has written ~~their~~ *her* thank-you notes.

10.   Everybody in the office has made ~~their~~ *his* vacation plans.

DIRECTIONS: *In each blank write a pronoun that will agree with its antecedent.*

1.   A person should not expect too much from ___*his*___ friends.

2.   The postman brought Jack and Ray the books that ___*they*___ had ordered.

3.   Either Norma or Jill will stay after school so that ___*she*___ can help decorate.

4.   Several of the convicts refused to eat ___*their*___ food.

5.   Each of the seals caught the fish that were thrown to ___*it*___.

PRONOUN-ANTECEDENT AGREEMENT: EX. #2

NAME:_____DATE:_____

DIRECTIONS: *Some of the sentences below contain errors in agreement. If so, cross out the incorrect pronoun and write in the correct form.*

1.   One of my aunts takes a great deal of pride in her furniture.

2.   Knowing this, nobody in our family puts ~~their~~ *his* feet on chairs or sits on beds at her house.

3.   One of her brothers used to think ~~they~~ *he* could be an exception to the rule.

4.   Uncle Charlie would come home late at night, undress in the dark, and dive into his bed, nearly knocking

        every slat out of ~~their~~ *its* place.

5.   Each of these plunges left ~~their~~ *its* mark on the rickety bed.

6.   At first, both Aunt Mary and my mother offered their advice and asked him to be careful.

7.   Anybody else would have mended ~~their~~ *his* ways, but not Charlie; he needed discipline!

8.   Late one night there was a loud crash, and everyone ran out of ~~their~~ *his or her** room to investigate.

9.   No one could believe ~~their~~ *his* eyes! Lying on the floor was Charlie, groaning loudly.

10.   If anybody asks you why Charlie suddenly reformed, tell ~~them~~ *him* that one day Aunt Mary

        merely decided to rearrange her furniture.

DIRECTIONS: *In each blank write a pronoun that will agree with its antecedent.*

1.   Both of the boys forgot ____*their*____ promises.

2.   Everyone needs ___*his*___ own pen.

3.   Neither apologized for _____*his*_____ blunder.

4.   Each of the players felt that ___*he*___ had failed the coach.

5.   When Susan sees one of her girlfriends, she always stops and talks to ___*her*___.

* When you're telling a story, and it's obvious that your "cast of characters" includes both males and females, then you really have no choice but to use "his or her."

SUBJECT-VERB AGREEMENT

Verbs have number too. In other words, a singular subject (boy) takes a singular verb (runs). BOY RUNS.
A plural subject (boys) takes a plural verb (run). BOYS RUN. This is usually not a problem except in
these cases:

I.   When there are modifiers between the subject and verb.

        EXAMPLE: A **GROUP** of demonstrators **WAS** starting a sit-in.

II.   When the subject is an indefinite pronoun. In the last unit you learned which of these pronouns is
        singular and which is plural. Refer to that list again.

        EXAMPLE: **EACH** of the girls **IS** an excellent student.

                        BOTH of the girls **ARE** excellent students.

III.   When singular subjects are joined by OR or NOR - they need a singular verb.

        EXAMPLE: **NEITHER** the customer **NOR** the clerk **IS** always right.

                        BOTH the customer **AND** the clerk **ARE** right.

IV.   When the sentence begins with HERE, THERE, WHERE, WHEN, WHY, or HOW, be sure that
        the verb agrees with the subject. In these sentences the subject is usually located after or to the
        right of the verb.

        EXAMPLE: There **ARE** two **ATHLETES** in this race.

                        When **IS** the **CURTAIN GOING** up?

V.   When a sentence has a compound subject joined by "or" or "nor" - and one subject is singular and
        the other one is plural - then the verb agrees with the subject closest to it.

        EXAMPLE: Either my uncle or my **COUSINS ARE** coming for a visit.

                        Neither the drill team girls nor the marching **BAND IS** participating in the
                        parade.

    359

SUBJECT-VERB AGREEMENT: EX. #1

NAME:_____DATE:_____

DIRECTIONS: *Underline the correct verb in the sentences below.*

1.   Cells in your brain (needs, need) oxygen.

2.   Our boys, in position at the line of scrimmage, (was, were) awaiting the snap.

3.   Broadway, with its flashing lights and bright colors, (impress, impresses) a visitor.

4.   A change in the rules often (confuse, confuses) the spectators.

5.   The silence inside the Carlsbad Caverns (is, are) awe-inspiring.

6.   There (is, are) many vacation destinations to choose from.

7.   Where (was, were) your ancestors from?

8.   The flowers in the garden at the back of my house (is, are) excellent for cutting.

9.   The crowd at the Homecoming Game (was, were) in excellent spirits.

10.   These exercises on the proper way to speak English (is, are) not what I call great fun!

DIRECTIONS: *Rewrite the following sentences, changing the conjunction from AND to OR or vice versa. Change the verb to agree with the new situation.*

1.   Ned and Larry have gone to the science fair.

        EXAMPLE: EITHER Ned OR Larry HAS gone to the science fair.

2.   Either rain or snow has been predicted for tomorrow.
        Rain and snow have been predicted for tomorrow.

3.   Either Jane or Mary has prepared the lunch.
        Jane and Mary have prepared the lunch.

4.   The car in front of us and the car on the other side of the street are to blame.
        Either the car in front of us or the car on the other side of the street is to blame.

5.   The house on the hill and the cottage in the valley are for sale.
        Either the house on the hill or the cottage in the valley is for sale.

SUBJECT-VERB AGREEMENT: EX. #2

NAME:_____DATE:_____

DIRECTIONS: *Underline the correct verb in the sentences below.*

1.   Many of us (like, likes) long books.

2.   There (is, are) many reasons why I can't go.

3.   Somebody among the spectators (was, were) snoring.

4.   (Has, Have) all of the senators returned?

5.   Nobody in my family (is, are) able to remember phone numbers.

6.   (Have, Has) either of you been to Mexico before?

7.   Where (is, are) the ingredients for this recipe?

8.   Each of the girls (was, were) eligible for the award.

9.   People in the position in which you find yourself often (try, tries) to find new jobs.

10.   The author who had written all those books (don't, doesn't) like to sign autographs.

DIRECTIONS: *Rewrite the following sentences, changing the conjunction from AND to OR or vice versa. Change the verb to agree with the new situation.*

1.   Venus and Mars do not seem far away when you consider the vast distances of outer space.
        Venus or Mars does not seem far away...

2.   Each week a poem and an essay appear in the school newspaper.
        Each week either a poem or an essay appears ...

3.   Both the boy in the third row and the girl at the door have been called to the office.
        Either the boy in the third row or the girl at the door has been called ...

4.   Either my uncle or my father-in-law was present when Kennedy was shot.
        My uncle and my father-in-law were ...

5.   Both my brother and my sister have graduated *magna cum laude*.
        Either my brother or my sister has graduated ...

WHICH PRONOUN?

I. When using the personal pronouns I or ME along with another noun, always **PUT THE OTHER GUY FIRST.**

> EXAMPLE: (wrong) He told <u>me and Jim</u> to return after lunch.
>   (right)   He told <u>Jim and me</u> to return after lunch.

II. When listing multiple subjects, place them in the appropriate "social" order. In other words, **LADIES BEFORE GENTLEMEN AND OLDER FOLKS BEFORE YOUNGER.**

> EXAMPLE: (wrong) My dad, my mom, my grandma, and I went out for brunch on Sunday.
>   (right) My grandma, my mom, my dad, and I went out for brunch on Sunday.

III. Does one say, "Give this book to either Bob or I," or "Give this book to either Bob or me"? Does one say, "We girls had a great time," or "Us girls had a great time"?

TAKE THE OTHER GUY OUT: In most instances, there is a simple, easy-to-use trick which is helpful in solving this problem. The trick is called "**TAKE THE OTHER GUY OUT.**" In the first example above, take "either Bob or" out. Would you ever say, "Give this book to I"? Of course not. So, you wouldn't say, "Give this book to either Bob or I" either. You would say,"Give this book to either Bob or me."

In the second example above, just take the "girls" out and you immediately know which pronoun to use.

In some cases, however, the above "TAKE THE OTHER GUY OUT" trick won't work. In these cases, you have to know your grammar to solve the problem. You already know enough about the structure of the sentence. The only other thing you need to know is that pronouns come in two CASES: the NOMINATIVE (sometimes called the SUBJECTIVE) case and the OBJECTIVE case.

The nominative case is used for the job of SUBJECT or PREDICATE NOMINATIVE.

The objective case is used for the job of DIRECT OBJECT, INDIRECT OBJECT, or OBJECT OF THE PREPOSITION.

NOMINATIVE PRONOUNS: I, we, you, he, she, it, they, who, whoever

OBJECTIVE PRONOUNS: me, us, you, him, her, it, them, whom, whomever

Notice how this works: look at the sentence, "Give this book to either Bob or *me*." What job is *me* doing? Correct; it's being the **object** of the preposition. That's why you need the **object**ive pronoun *me*.

IN ANY CASE, IT'S A TOTAL "COP-OUT" TO USE THE WORD "MYSELF" INSTEAD OF "I" AND "ME"!!

In the sentence, "We girls had a great time," *we* is the subject of the sentence (*girls* is an appositive); therefore, you need the nominative pronoun *we*.

IV. PRONOUN AS PREDICATE NOMINATIVE: Is it correct to say, "It was me whom they wanted," or "It was I whom they wanted"?

In informal speech, we would usually say, "It was me," and - even though technically this is incorrect - it is now acceptable. However, in formal written work (and in grammar tests), we need to know that, since *I* is the predicate nominative in the above sentence, the nominative form is correct.

EXAMPLE: The documents proved that it was he who committed the crime.

WHICH PRONOUN: EXERCISE #1

NAME:_____DATE:_____

DIRECTIONS: *Circle the right pronoun in parentheses. If the pronouns are in the wrong ORDER, rewrite the sentence.*

1.   *Tom and I*
           Next Saturday (I, me) and Tom will make all the arrangements.

2.   *her and me*
           Ted invited (I, me) and (she, her) to the party.

3.   *Harry and I*
           The guests of honor were (I, me) and Harry.   *(I is predicate nominative)*

4.   *he*
           How many goals did (he, him) and Chuck make?

5.   *her*
           Tell Betty and (she, her) the whole story.

6.   *She and I*
           (I, me) and (she, her) volunteered to help in the Red Cross blood drive.

7.   *They*
           (They, Them) and the Clark boys were to blame.

8.   *me*
           Dad gave Chuck and (I, me) a ride to town.

9.   *he*
           Was it (he, him) who called the fire department?

10.   *She*   *he*
           (She, her) and (he, him) were on the bus.

DIRECTIONS: *Rewrite the sentences below to make them correct.*

1.   Me and Janie went to the Mall yesterday.
           Janie and I went to the Mall yesterday.

2.   Either Jason, Wendy, or myself will be there to be sure the doors are open.
           Either Wendy, Jason, or I will be there ...

3.   Please give your tickets to either Julie, Crystal, or I.
           Please give your tickets to either Julie, Crystal, or me.

4.   Me, my mom, my dad, and my grandma went to Gallo's for dinner.
           My grandma, my mom, my dad, and I went to Gallo's ...

5.   Mrs. Phillips gave Bob and I a makeup test.
           Mrs. Phillips gave Bob and me a makeup test.

363

WHICH PRONOUN: EXERCISE #2

NAME:_____DATE:_____

DIRECTIONS: *Circle the correct pronoun in parentheses. Rewrite the sentence if the people are in the wrong order.*

         John and I
1.   (Me, I) and John are going to the mall this afternoon.

                  my brother and me.
2.   My grandpa loves to read stories to (I, me) and my brother.

         she and I
3.   Mom said (I, me) and (she, her) were not going to need more money.

                      me
4.   We distributed the money amongst Sally, Diane, and (I, me).

   We
5.   (We, Us) Alaskans are an independent bunch!

           him   *her*
6.   Dad packed a lunch for (he, him) and (she, her).

        Bev and me
7.   Will you help (I, me) and Bev clean the recreation room?

          us
8.   Jerome wrote a poem to (we, us) girls in the senior class.

  She   *I*
9.   (She, Her) and (I, me) will join you later for lunch.

       him   *me*
10.   Mr. Wilson gave (he, him) and (I, me) a few pointers about football.

DIRECTIONS: *Rewrite the sentences below to make them correct.*

1.   Mr. Bates gave a copy of the Winners' List to Mrs. Sampson and myself.
      Mr. Bates gave a copy of the Winners' List to Mrs. Sampson and me.

2.   Either Erin or myself will see you later.
      Either Erin or I will see you later.

3.   Me, my uncle, and my aunt went to Disney World last summer.
      My aunt, my uncle, and I went to Disney World ...

4.   Him and John were the ones who had their notes typed.
      He and John were the ones who had their notes typed.

5.   John, my grandpa, me, and my dad all went to the baseball game last night.
      My grandpa, my dad, John, and I all went ...

        Photocopying this product is strictly prohibited by copyright law.

USAGE FINAL #1

NAME:_____DATE:_____

(RAW SCORE:_____ */67* GRADE:_____)

PART I: PRONOUN-ANTECEDENT AGREEMENT: *Circle the correct pronoun.*

1.   Neither Bill nor Mark had told me what (he, they) wanted.

2.   I had to read each of the essays carefully before I could grade (it, them).

3.   Jim and Mike will lend us (his, their) history notes.

4.   If one makes the effort, (he, they, you) can usually accomplish a goal.

5.   I feel that cleaning (my, your, one's) room is my least favorite chore.

===
5

PART II: *Write the correct pronoun in the blank space.*

1.   Angelo and Mario will attend with _____*their*_____parents.

2.   Either Tim or Tyler will sponsor _____*his*_____ own team this year.

3.   Neither Ray nor Brad will do _____*his*_____ homework alone.

4.   Is either Beth or Betsy going to read _____*her*_____ essay aloud?

5.   Neither this dish nor that plate is in _____*its*_____ regular place on the shelf.

6.   Either Mr. Marley or Mr. Engels parked _____*his*_____ car in the driveway.

7.   Did either Earl or Dave turn in _____*his*_____ book report early?

8.   Both Wes and Paul came to run _____*their*_____ laps on the track.

9.   Should either Al or Jane call _____*his or her*_____ parents before we begin?

10.   Neither Sarah nor Marian wants _____*her*_____ name called.

===
10

PART III: SUBJECT-VERB AGREEMENT: *Circle the correct verb in parentheses.*

1.   John, as well as some of the other club members, (plans, plan) to ask questions.

2.   As each one of you students (know, knows), your reports will be due on Friday.

3.   There (is, are) some leftover sandwiches in the refrigerator.

4.   Nobody in my family (is, are) any good at video games.

===
5   5.   (Has, Have) all of the team members suited up?

(over)

365

PART IV: Read the sentences below carefully. If the verb agrees with its subject, write Y in the space; if it does not agree, write N in the space.

__*Y*__ 1.   One of the cabinets contains the club's banner and membership rolls.

__*N*__ 2.   Each of the hostesses are standing in the doorway.

__*N*__ 3.   The numbers on the license plate was covered with mud.

__*N*__ 4.   Every one of the clerks have to punch the time clock.

__*Y*__ 5.   The bridges on Highway 34 are extremely narrow.

__*N*__ 6.   One of the assistants answer the telephone.

__*N*__ 7.   Our assignment for the next two days cover events during the French Revolution.

__*N*__ 8.   A bag of golf clubs, as well as two tennis rackets, stand in the corner of the closet.

__*Y*__ 9.   Each of the farmers uses modern machines.

__*Y*__ 10.   Does either of the girls play the piano?

===
10

PART V: *Rewrite these sentences, following the directions in parentheses. You will have to change the verb accordingly.*

EXAMPLE:The boys have finished delivering the papers.(Change BOYS to EACH OF THE BOYS)
Each of the boys has finished delivering the papers.

1.   My sister is planning to attend summer school.(Change SISTER to SISTERS)
My sisters are planning to attend summer school.

2.   Nobody in our town intends to participate in the ceremony.(Change NOBODY to MANY)
Many in our town intend to participate in ...

3.   Most of the money was contributed by children.(Change MONEY to QUARTERS)
Most of the quarters were contributed by children.

4.   Neither the students nor the teacher has found the missing book. (Remove NEITHER and change NOR to AND)
The students and the teacher have found the missing book.

5.   Some of the workers spend too much time in the snack bar. (Change SOME to ONE)
One of the workers spends too much time in the snack bar.

===
5

PART VI: *The sentences below contain unnecessary changes in VERB TENSE. Change either verb so that it matches the other in tense.*

EXAMPLE: Patty spoke so quickly that no one understands her.

Patty speaks so quickly that no one understands her. or
Patty spoke so quickly that no one understood her.

1.   Paul walks into the room and we all looked up.
      Paul walks and we look - or - Paul walked and we looked

2.   There was a great movie on TV, but Leah has to work.
      There is a movie, but Leah has - or - There was a movie, but Leah had to work.

3.   Time is running out and we were still three points behind.
      Time was running and we were - or - Time is running and we are ...

4.   Rick played Romeo and Keith plays Tybalt.
      Rick plays and Keith plays - or Rick played and Keith played ...

5.   Toni didn't understand the question, so she raises her hand.
      Toni doesn't ... so she raises - or - Toni didn't ... so she raised ...

===
5

PART VII: *Circle the correct pronoun in parentheses. If the pronoun is in the wrong place, rewrite the sentence and put the words in the correct order.*

him and me
___ 3   1.   The accident taught (I, me) and (he, him) a lesson.

her and me
___ 3   2.   The waiter asked (I, me) and (she, her) what we wanted.

Jack and me?
___ 2   3.   Have you been avoiding (I, me) and Jack?

___ 1   4.   Have you and (her, she) had an argument?

___ 1   5.   It was (he, him) who notified the police.

___ 1   6.   Is it (she, her) whom you are marrying?

Ben and me
___ 2   7.   Sam helped (I, me) and Ben paint the garage.

___ 1   8.   I haven't heard a word from either Judy or (her, she).

___ 1   9.   The letters are for you, Paula, and (I, me).

Frank and me
___ 2   10.   Please give (I, me) and Frank another chance.

Clara and me.
___ 2   11.   He rode his bike between (I, me) and Clara.

Jerry and me.
___ 2   12.   The job of buying refreshments was assigned to (I, me) and Jerry.

her and me.
___ 3   13.   You have to choose between (I, me) and (she, her).

___ 1   14.   (We, Us) three have to sing the solo parts.

Grandma, Mom, and I
==== 2   15   (Me, I), Mom, and Grandma all went on the ferris wheel.

27

Raw		Score	Grade		%
67	to	65	=	A++ =	98+
64	to	63	=	A+ =	95
62	to	60	=	A =	90
59	to	56	=	B+ =	85
55	to	53	=	B =	80
52	to	50	=	C+ =	75
49	to	46	=	C =	70
45	to	43	=	D+ =	65
42	to	40	=	D =	60

WHO AND WHOM

In the previous unit, you were taught a trick to help you decide which pronoun to use called TAKE THE OTHER GUY OUT. When deciding when to use WHO and when to use WHOM, however, there is no nifty little trick. People who know when to use WHO and when to use WHOM show that they are well educated because they understand the structure of the sentences they are using. To solve this problem, you must analyze the sentence grammatically and figure out what job that pronoun is doing In time, the correct pronoun choice will "sound right" to you.

WHO is used when the pronoun is being a subject or a predicate nominative. That's why it's called the SUBJECTIVE or NOMINATIVE CASE.

WHOM is used when the pronoun is being an object (direct object, indirect object, or object of the preposition). That's why it's called the OBJECTIVE case.

Look at these example sentences. In each one the word *WHO* or *WHOM* is doing a specific job. If that job is subject or predicate nominative, *WHO* is used. If it's some kind of object, *WHOM* is used.

EXAMPLES: To WHOM are you speaking? (*WHOM* is the object of the preposition *to*)

WHO are those men? (*WHO* is the subject of *are*)

WHOM was the speaker attacking? (*WHOM* is the direct object of *attacking*)

We did not know WHOM the man wanted. (*WHOM* is the direct object of *wanted*)

John is the boy WHO needs your help. (*WHO* is the subject of *needs*)

Do not be mislead by interrupting expressions such as "do you think," "shall I say," or do you suppose."

EXAMPLES: WHO do you suppose will be elected? (*WHO* is the subject of *will be elected*)

WHOM do you think he meant? (*WHOM* is the direct object of *meant*)

WHO shall I say is calling? (*WHO* is the subject of *is calling*)

NIFTY TRICK DEPARTMENT: One quick way to find out what job the pronoun is doing is to **"match up" all the subjects and verbs** in the sentence. Find all the verbs and look for their subjects. If you find a verb without a subject, your pronoun *WHO* is probably it. Also, watch out for those linking verbs - because *WHO* could be a predicate nominative. If it's not a subject, it's probably an object - so it should be *WHOM*.

Sometimes it helps if you think of *WHO* as *HE* and *WHOM* as *HIM*

WHO AND WHOM: EXERCISE #1

NAME:_____DATE:_____

DIRECTIONS: *Circle the correct pronoun in parentheses. In the space provided below each sentence, write what job it's doing. If it's a subject, write the word that it's the subject of, etc.*

1.   (Who, Whom) did you see at the station?

_____***Whom is the direct object of "did see"***_____

2.   He is the one (who, whom) we least suspected.

_____***Whom is the direct object of "suspected."***_____

3.   To (who, whom) did you apply for a job?

_____***Whom is the object of the preposition "to"***_____

4.   Please support (whoever, whomever) is elected.

_____***Whoever is the subject of "is elected."***_____

5.   I shall support (whoever, whomever) the class chooses.

_____***Whomever is the direct object of "chooses."***_____

6.   (Whom, Who) do you think will win the election?

_____***Who is the subject of "will win."***_____

7.   We nominated candidates (who, whom) we thought would win.

_____***Who is the subject of "would win."***_____

8.   From (who, whom) did you get that information?

_____***Whom is the object of the preposition "from."***_____

9.   Sam says "hello" to (whoever, whomever) he sees.

_____***Whomever is the direct object of "sees."***_____

10.   The door is open to (whoever, whomever) wants to come.

_____***Whoever is the subject of "wants."***_____

369

WHO AND WHOM: EXERCISE #2

NAME:_____DATE:_____

DIRECTIONS: *Circle the correct pronoun in parentheses. In the space provided below each sentence, write what job it's doing. If it's a subject, write the word that it's the subject of, etc.*

1.   Most of the people (who, whom) are hired are under thirty.

   Who is the subject of "are hired."

2.   Most of the people (who, whom) they hire are under thirty.

   Whom is the direct object of "hire."

3.   Give this report to (whoever, whomever) is in the office.

   Whoever is the subject of "is."

4.   (Who, Whom) do you need to see, Mr. Jones?

   Whom is the direct object of "to see."

5.   (Who, Whom) do you suppose is the winner of the contest?

   Who is the subject of "is."

6.   I don't remember (who, whom) you want to invite.

   Whom is the direct object of "to invite."

7.   (Who, Whom) do you think called the police?

   Who is the subject of "called."

8.   Do you know (who, whom) the police suspect?

   Whom is the direct object of "suspect."

9.   (Who, Whom) do you want to speak to?

   Whom is the object of the preposition "to."

10.   She is the one (who, whom) we must stop.

   Whom is the direct object of "must stop."

ADJECTIVE OR ADVERB?

I.   Another common usage problem is when people use an <u>adjective</u> when they should use an <u>adverb</u>.

      EXAMPLE: (substandard)   That dress fits perfect.
                        (standard)   That dress fits perfectly.

The word *perfect* is an adjective and modifies a noun, as in "a perfect fit." *Perfectly*, however, is an adverb. In the sentence above, the adverb *perfectly* is there to describe HOW the dress "fits."

NOTE: Remember that when your sentence (or clause) contains a linking verb, the complement may be a predicate adjective. In this case you don't want an adverb.

      EXAMPLE: (wrong)   That dress looks well on her.
                        (right)   That dress looks good on her.

II.   People seem to have the most trouble choosing between the adjectives *GOOD* and *BAD* and the adverbs *WELL* and *BADLY*.

      A.   *GOOD* and *BAD* are adjectives that either modify nouns or complete linking verbs.

            EXAMPLE: It was a GOOD (or BAD) day for a picnic.

      B.   *WELL* and *BADLY* are adverbs that modify verbs or other modifiers.

            EXAMPLE: He did WELL (or BADLY) on the test.

      C.   *WELL* is used as an adjective only when it means "in good health."

            EXAMPLE: Mrs. Thatcher does not look well today.

                            I haven't felt well for several days.

III.   When using comparatives and superlatives, be sure you are using the correct form for either an adjective or an adverb. Look at the following examples:

ADJECTIVE	COMPARATIVE	SUPERLATIVE	ADVERB	COMPARATIVE	SUPERLATIVE
quiet	quieter	quietest	**quietly**	more quietly	most quietly

(wrong) This engine will run quieter than that one.

(right) This engine will run more quietly than that one.

ADJECTIVE OR ADVERB: EXERCISE #1

NAME:_____DATE:_____

DIRECTIONS: *Underline the correct word in parentheses. In the space provided below each sentence, write either ADJECTIVE or ADVERB and what it modifies. If it's a predicate adjective following a linking verb, write PREDICATE ADJECTIVE and the verb it completes.*

1.   You can finish the job (easy, <u>easily</u>) in an hour.

   ___*Adverb modifying "can finish"*_____

2.   The sky remained (<u>clear</u>, clearly) all day long.

   ___*predicate adjective of "remained."*_____

3.   The mechanic stayed (steady, <u>stead</u>ily) on the job until it was finished.

   ___*adverb modifying "stayed."*_____

4.   The rancher acted (<u>uneasy</u>, uneasily) about the weather bureau's storm warning.

   ___*predicate adjective of "acted."*_____

5.   Mary felt (<u>unhappy</u>, unhappily) about her report card.

   ___*predicate adjective of "felt."*_____

DIRECTIONS: If the capitalized word is incorrect in the sentence below, substitute the correct form.

   angry
1.   Harry sounded A̶N̶G̶R̶I̶L̶Y̶ over the phone.

   carefully
2.   The repair job was done C̶A̶R̶E̶F̶U̶L̶.

   perfectly
3.   The left shoe now seemed to fit P̶E̶R̶F̶E̶C̶T̶.

4.   Football is played DIFFERENTLY in Canada.

   unhappily
5.   Jane gazed U̶N̶H̶A̶P̶P̶Y̶ at her ruined dress.

ADJECTIVE OR ADVERB: EXERCISE #2

NAME: _____ DATE: _____

DIRECTIONS: *Underline the correct word in parentheses. In the space provided below each sentence, write either ADJECTIVE or ADVERB and what it modifies. If it's a predicate adjective following a linking verb, write PREDICATE ADJECTIVE and the verb it completes.*

1.   Doris picked up her purse (quick, <u>quickly</u>), threw on a coat, and ran out the door.

    adverb modifying "picked."

2.   You can run a small car more (economical, <u>economically</u>) than a large one.

    adverb modifying "can run."

3.   The poem sounds (<u>different</u>, differently) in French.

    predicate adjective of "sounds."

4.   Mark's knee was hurt (bad, <u>badly</u>) during the first game.

    adverb modifying "was hurt."

5.   Students should talk (quieter, <u>more quietly</u>) in the halls during classes.

    adverb modifying "should talk."

DIRECTIONS: *If the capitalized word is incorrect in the sentence below, substitute the correct form.*

1.   Stir the mixture ~~GOOD~~ *well* before adding the milk.

2.   Caroline did ~~BAD~~ *badly* on the exam.

3.   Be sure and mix the sand and cement ~~GOOD~~ *well*.

4.   You can see just as WELL from the balcony.

5.   Harriet feels ~~BADLY~~ *bad* about losing your earring.
       ↑
    linking verb

373

TRANSITIVE/INTRANSITIVE VERBS & ASSORTED ERRORS

I.   Transitive verbs are verbs which can take a direct object; in other words, they "transport" the action of the subject to the direct object.

Try using the verb *have* in a sentence that doesn't have a direct object. Can't be done, can it? That's because you must **have** something; you can't just **have.**

II.   Intrasitive verbs are verbs which do not take a direct object.

Try using the verb *arrive* in a sentence which has a direct object. Can't do it, can you? That's because you don't ever **arrive** anything; you just **arrive**.

III. Many verbs can be transitive in some sentences and intransitive in others.

In the sentence, "He eats lunch with me," the verb is transitive because it takes the direct object *lunch.* In the sentence, "He eats with me," the verb is intransitive because it has no direct object.

IV: There is a relatively small group of verbs with which people have difficulty. Three of the most common will be discussed in this unit. They are *lie/lay, sit/set*, and *rise/raise*.

PRESENT	PAST	PAST PARTICIPLE
lay	laid	laid
lie	lay	lain

To lay is a transitive verb which can take a direct object; *to lie* is intransitive and cannot take a direct object.

I <u>am laying</u> the cup on the table	I <u>laid</u> the book down.	The hen <u>has laid</u> an egg.
She <u>lies</u> on the sofa.	We <u>lay</u> in the sun.	He <u>has lain</u> in bed for a month.

raise	raised	raised
rise	rose	risen

To raise is a transitive verb which can take a direct object; *to rise* is intransitive and cannot take a direct object.

Vern <u>is raising</u> alfalfa this year.	He <u>raised</u> his eyebrows.	We <u>have raised</u> greyhounds for years.
The sun <u>rises</u> in the east.	Al <u>rose</u> to make a speech.	The temperature <u>has risen</u> since noon.

sit	sat	sat
set	set	set

To sit is an intransitive verb which cannot take a direct object; *to set* is transitive and must take a direct object.

We always <u>sit</u> on the porch.	Joe <u>sat</u> in the third row.	You <u>have sat</u> in front of that TV all day.
Renee <u>set</u> a record today.	I <u>set</u> the cup on the table.	<u>Have</u> you two <u>set</u> a date yet?

V.   THIS, THAT, THESE, and THOSE:

THIS and *THAT* are singular modifiers; *THESE* and *THOSE* are plural modifiers.

EXAMPLES: (wrong) These kind are my favorites.
                (right) This kind is my favorite. (Notice that everything agrees:modifier,subject, verb)

                (wrong) These sort of shoes hurt my feet.
                (right)   This sort of shoe hurts my feet. (Notice, everything agrees)

VI.   FEWER and LESS

FEWER is a plural modifier; *LESS* is a singular modifier. (*FEWER* modifies things that <u>can be counted</u>;
        LESS modifies things which <u>cannot be counted</u>.)

EXAMPLES: Jack had FEWER colds this year. (Can you count "colds"?)
                There is LESS snow this year than last. (Can you count "snow"?)
                This product contains LESS fat. (Can you count "fat"?)
                This cheese has FEWER calories. (Can you count "calories"?)

VII.   The following is a list of serious usage errors to avoid:

AIN'T   Once acceptable, but no longer so. Now replaced by *AM NOT, IS NOT,* or
                        ARE NOT.

IT, HE, SHE DON'T   Misused for "it, he, or she <u>doesn't"</u>

SEEN for SAW   I seen that movie" is incorrect. *SEEN* can only be used with *HAVE*:
                        "I have seen that movie." In this context, the correct usage is "I saw
                        that movie."

DOUBLE SUBJECT   Tracy she got an A on the test. (Just take out the *SHE*)

THEM   Misused for *THOSE*, as in "Give me them gloves," instead of "Give me
                        those gloves." *THEM* is a pronoun in the objective case, never a modifier.

GOT   Misused for *HAVE*. "Do you got your homework?" is incorrect. "Do you have
                        your homework?" is correct. *GOT* means RECEIVED, as in "I got an A on the
                        test."

SHOULD OF   There is no such construction. It sounds like *SHOULD OF* when you say
                        SHOULD'VE, but what you are really saying is *SHOULD HAVE.*

DOUBLE NEGATIVE   As in "I didn't do nothing." Should be "I did nothing," or "I didn't do
                        anything."

                        HARDLY, BARELY, or *SCARCELY* are negative words that should not be
                        used with another negative. "There wasn't hardly anyone on the tennis court,"
                        is incorrect. It should be "There was hardly anyone on the tennis court."

TRANSITIVE/INTRANSITIVE VERBS & ASSORTED ERRORS: EXERCISE #1

NAME:_____DATE:_____

DIRECTIONS: *Correct the following sentences by rewriting them in the space provided below each sentence.*

1.   That there is my new jacket.
      That is my new jacket.

2.   It really don't matter if you come or not.
      It really doesn't matter if you come or not.

3.   We don't want no trouble here.
      We don't want any trouble here. - or we want no trouble.

4.   You should of seen that movie!
      You should have seen that movie.

5.   We don't got no assignment in math tonight.
      We don't have any assignment in math tonight.

DIRECTIONS: *Circle the correct form of the verb in the sentences below.*

1.   The mother goose (lay, laid) her eggs in the tall grass.

2.   The moon (raises, rises) in the night sky like a white balloon.

3.   We (sat, set) in the rocking chairs on the front porch last evening.

4.   Sally had (laid, lain) down to take a nap.

5.   Winston always (raises, rises) to the occasion.

DIRECTIONS: *Circle the correct word in parentheses.*

1.   The advertisers say there are (fewer, less) types of tar in these cigarettes.

2.   He certainly ate enough of (that, those) (kind, kinds) of cookies.

3.   Ted had (fewer, less) first-place votes than George.

4.   You will have (fewer, less) interruptions in the library.

5.   I have never seen (these, this) (types, type) of notebook before.

6.   We have never eaten (these, this) kind before.

7.   We have had (fewer, less) tourism in Alaska this year.

TRANSITIVE/INTRANSITIVE VERBS & ASSORTED ERRORS: EXERCISE #2

NAME:_____DATE:_____

DIRECTIONS: *Circle the correct word in parentheses.*

1.   The store does not sell (this, these) (type, types) of stoves any more.

2.   Next time you bake a cake, use (fewer, less) eggs.

3.   Next time you bake a cake, use (fewer, less) vanilla.

4.   This beverage is less filling because it has (fewer, less) calories.

5.   (That, Those) (sort, sorts) of candies upset my stomach.

DIRECTIONS: *Correct the following sentences by rewriting them in the space provided below each sentence.*

1.   Do you got any homework in math tonight?
      Do you have any homework in math tonight?

2.   We didn't have barely any candy left after the kids finished
      We had barely any candy left after ...

3.   There wasn't hardly no people left on the beach.
      There were hardly any people left on the beach.

4.   You should of gone to the party.
      You should have gone to the party. (or should've)

5.   It's really important to speak and write English good, ain't it?
      It's really important to speak and write English well, isn't it?

DIRECTIONS: *Circle the correct form of the verb in the sentences below.*

1.   The little girl (lay, laid) her toy gently on the shelf.

2.   Sarah has (lain, laid) out in the sun too long without sunscreen!

3.   The temperature has (raised, risen) by at least twenty degrees.

4..   We (set, sat) the statue carefully on its platform.

5.   Josephine (rose, raised) teacup poodles.

A transitive verb   ***takes a direct object***   .

An intransitive verb ***does not take a direct object***   .

377

USAGE FINAL #2

NAME:_____ DATE:_____

(RAW SCORE:_____ */71* GRADE:_____)

PART I: *If necessary, correct the double negative in the sentence below.*

1.   We couldn't hardly hear the speaker.

2.   The car didn't stop for ~~no~~ stoplights.

3.   Connie hadn't never flown in an airplane.   ***(or hadn't ever)***

4.   The injured horse couldn't barely walk.

5.   Seniors don't have ~~nothing~~ **anything** to complain about.   ***(or "Seniors have nothing ...")***

___
5

PART II: *If necessary, correct the usage errors in the sentence below.*

1.   We could ~~of~~ **have** gone to see the Beach Boys, but we couldn't get tickets.

2.   Do you ~~got~~ **have** your homework for math class today?

3.   Jack ~~he~~ said he ~~seen~~ **saw** the car speeding southbound on Main Street.

4.   Has anybody seen my math book?

5.   When we got to the house, there wasn't nobody there. ***(or "wasn't anybody")***

___
5

PART III: *If necessary, correct the following sentences in any way that's needed.*

1.   With algebra you can solve this problem ~~easy~~ **easily**.

2.   Football is played differently in Canada.

3.   The driver turned ~~quick~~ **quickly** at the corner and sped away.

4.   Run ~~quick~~ **quickly** and see if the mail is here.

5.   Lynn's feelings were hurt ~~bad~~ **badly** when Sherry laughed at her.

6.   I think she did very ~~bad~~ **badly** last night.

7.   Does she always sing so ~~good~~ **well**?

8.   Mrs. Hoffman argued her point well.

9.   Mike plays basketball almost as ~~good~~ **well** as his brother.

___ 10.   I slept so well last night!

10

(over)

PART IV: *Rewrite the sentences in the space provided. If it is correct, leave it alone.*

1.   Me and him went to the mall.
      He and I went to the mall.

2.   Her and her best friend are having a fight.
      She and her best friend are having a fight.

3.   The test was retaken by John, Brandon, and me.

4.   Give that book to me and him.
      Give that book to him and me.

===
5

5.   Them and us have to leave early.
      They and we have to leave early.

PART V: *In the space provided, write what job the capitalized pronoun is doing. (SUBJECT, PREDICATE NOMINATIVE, DIRECT OBJECT, INDIRECT OBJECT, OBJECT OF THE PREPOSITION)*

1.   Mr. Doyle is a man WHO likes young people. _____*subject*_____

2.   Mr. Doyle is a man WHOM young people like. _____*direct object*_____

3.   The girl WHO spoke to me has just won a prize. _____*subject*_____

4.   The girl WHOM I spoke to has just won a prize. _____*object of the preposition*_____

5.   Can you tell me WHO that player is? _____*predicate nominative*_____

===
5

PART VI: *Circle the correct words in parentheses.*

2 1.   Our gym class does (that, <u>those</u>) (kind, <u>kinds</u>) of exercises.

3 2.   (<u>This</u>, These) (<u>brand</u>, brands) of tape (have, <u>has</u>) inferior sound quality.

2 3.   Nurses wear (<u>this</u>, these) type of (<u>shoe</u>, shoes.)

2 4.   Campers use (this, <u>these</u>) (sort, <u>sorts</u>) of tents.

2 5.   Lola can perform (<u>that</u>, those) (<u>sort</u>, sorts) of back dive.

===
11

PART VII: *Circle the correct modifier in parentheses.*

1.   We have (less, <u>fewer</u>) school holidays this year.

2.   Unfortunately, there seems to be (<u>less</u>, fewer) volunteerism on my committee.

3.   The commercials say there are (less, <u>fewer</u>) problems with this model.

4.   This frozen dinner has (less, <u>fewer</u>) calories than the other.

5.   We have had (less, <u>fewer</u>) inches of snow this year.

===
5

379

PART VIII: *Choose which pronoun is correct. Then in the space provided, write what job that pronoun is doing.*

1. Ladies (who, whom) lived during the fifteenth century painted their teeth instead of their nails.

    _____ *subject* _____

2. Her older sister, to (who, whom) she sent the article, has moved to Santa Fe.

    _____ *object of the preposition* _____

3. It was Napoleon (who, whom) invaded Spain in 1808. ____ *subject* _____

4. Maureen finally guessed (who, whom) it was. _____ *predicate nominative* _____

5. I visited with Mr. Winslow, (who, whom) was mowing his lawn. _____ *subject* _____

6. Mr. Ross, (who, whom) I work for, owns two wheat farms. ___ *object of the preposition* ____

7. Is there anyone (who, whom) plans to leave early? _____ *subject* _____

8. He is a teacher (who, whom) I respect. _____ *direct object* _____

9. There is the man (who, whom) you were asking about. _____ *object of the preposition* ____

10. Francis Drake, (who, whom) Queen Elizabeth I knighted, defeated the Spanish Armada.

    _____ *direct object* _____

===
20

PART IX: *Circle the correct word in parentheses.*

1. Each of the boys finished (his, their) hotdogs.

2. Both of my uncles went to (his, their) college reunion.

3. Either Janie or Tracy got an A on (her, their) exam.

4. Several of the players renegotiated (his, their) contracts.

===
5. A person should know what (he wants, they want) in life.

5 **PART X** *Circle the correct word in parentheses.*

Raw		Score		Grade		%
76	to	74	=	A++	=	98+
73	to	72	=	A+	=	95
71	to	68	=	A	=	90
67	to	65	=	B+	=	85
64	to	61	=	B	=	80
60	to	57	=	C+	=	75
56	to	53	=	C	=	70
52	to	49	=	D+	=	65
48	to	45	=	D	=	60
44	and lower	=	F			

1. George has (risen, raised) the flag every morning for ten years.

2.. My grandparents love to (set, sit) on their front porch in the cool of the evening.

3. Try not to kill the goose that (lies, lays) the golden egg!

4. Has Penelope (raised, risen) from her "bed of pain" yet?

5. He (lay, laid) a bet on Knuckleduster to win the third race.

===
5

380

ACTIVE & PASSIVE VOICE

Active and passive voice are terms you will hear a LOT when you write. It's important to know what active and passive voice is, when each is appropriate, and how to fix a passive sentence (because in writing the active voice is usually preferred).

I. ACTIVE VOICE: In general you'll hear that **active voice is better than passive**. What does it mean when a sentence is in **active voice**?

A sentence in active voice means that the **subject is performing the action of the verb**. Here arc some examples:

The boy threw the ball.
My mother sings beautifully.
Watch your step. (This subject is the understood "you" but still performs the action.)

Use of the active voice generally makes your writing more vivid and clear.

II. PASSIVE VOICE: A sentence in passive voice has the **object of an action acting as the subject.** Many times this results in the subject not being in the sentence at all. Here are passive versions of the above sentences:

The ball <u>was thrown</u> by the boy. OR *The ball was thrown.*
A song <u>was beautifully sung</u> by my mother.
Steps <u>should be taken</u> carefully.

III. SPOTTING THE PASSIVE VOICE: Passive voice can be spotted (WAIT! That's passive! Let's try again …)

You can spot passive voice by looking for this verb construction:

form of "to be" + past participle

("To be" forms can include *are, am, is, was, were, has been, had been, will be, will have been, being*, etc.)

Also, does the sentence end with a preposition phrase using the preposition *by*? Many passive voice sentences put the do-er of the action at the end of the sentence as the object of the prepositional phrase. Here's an example:

The exercise was written by the teacher. or *The test was taken by the student.*

IV. IS PASSIVE VOICE ALWAYS INCORRECT? Not always. It should be avoided in general, but there are times when it is necessary or appropriate. There are times when you need to put the emphasis on the object rather than the subject. Let's say you were writing a murder mystery, the

381

murder having taken place in a hotel room. The forensics teams is there, looking for clues. The following sentence -

> *The room had been cleaned an hour prior to the murder.*

is preferable to

> *The maid had cleaned the room an hour prior to the murder.*

because you don't want to bring attention to the maid in as a character in your story.

Or let's say you're writing an obituary. You might use the sentence -

> *The body was interred at Forest Lawn Cemetery.*

rather than -

> *The gravediggers interred the body at Forest Lawn Cemetery.*

I expect the reasons for the choice of the passive voice would be obvious in this case!

V. WHY DO PEOPLE USE THE PASSIVE VOICE? You need to become aware of how people use language to shape the way the sentence is perceived. Because it's easy to leave the do-er of the action out of a passive sentence, some people use the passive voice to avoid mentioning who is responsible for certain actions. Here are some examples:

> *Mistakes were made.*
> *Tthe Acme Oil Company stipulates that a few gallons of crude might have been spilled.*

ACTIVE & PASSIVE VOICE: EX. #1

NAME:_____DATE:_____

DIRECTIONS: *Identify whether each sentence is active or passive by wring A (active) or P (passive" in the space provided next to each sentence.*

   A 1.   The man painted the room and bright shade of blue.

   P 2.   The book was put on the shelf.

   P 3.   Cars were made on the factory line by the workmen.

   A 4.   I bought a brand new car this weekend.

   A 5.   We've all made mistakes.

   P 6.   Errors were made along the way.

   P 7.   The results are being tabulated as we speak.

   A 8.   I'm writing a new book about my trials and tribulations in college.

   P 9.   The refrigerator was plugged into the wrong socket.

   A 10.   I am going to write my paper after lunch.

DIRECTIONS: *In the space provided, re-write the above sentences. If they're passive, re-write them in the active voice; if the active, re-write them in the passive voice. Try to include all the elements in the original sentence, although when you re-write into passive voice, the subject frequently disappears. Because passive voice sentences are often unclear, a subject has to be inserted.*

1.   ***The room was painted a bright shade of blue. (answers may vary somewhat)***

_____

2.   ***I put the book on the shelf. (answers may vary somewhat)***

_____

3.   ***The workmen made the cars on the factory line. (answers may vary somewhat)***

_____

4. _A new car was purchased this weekend. (answers may vary somewhat)_

5. _Mistakes were made by all of us. (answers may vary somewhat)_

6. _We made errors along the way. (answers may vary somewhat)_

7. _Precinct workers are tabulating the results as we speak. (answers may vary_

somewhat)

8. _A new book was written about my trials and tribulations in college. (answers_

may vary somewhat)

9. _I plugged the regrigerator into the wrong socket. (answers may vary somewhat)_

10. _My paper will be written after lunch. (answers may vary somewhat)_

ACTIVE & PASSIVE VOICE: EX. #2

NAME:_____DATE:_____

DIRECTIONS: Identify whether each sentence is active or passive by wring A (active) or P (passive" in the space provided next to each sentence. Then re-write the sentence in the opposite voice on the lines provided.

_P_ 1. At this evening's concert selected famous arias will be sung by our star soprano.

At this evening's concert our star soprano will sing selected famous arias. (answers may vary somewhat)

_A_ 2. Beginning tomorrow morning, workmen will begin the removal of the windows.

Beginning tomorrow morning the windows will be removed by the workmen. (answers may vary somewhat)

_P_ 3. Although Melissa took great care in washing the dishes, a treasured wine glass was broken.

Although she took great care in washing the dishes, Melissa broke a treasured wineglass.. (answers may vary somewhat)

_P_ 4 Using Brad's telephone touchpad, all his spring semester classes were chosen in one hour.

Using his telephone touchpad, Brad chose all his spring semester classes in one hour. (answers may vary somewhat)

_P_ 5. The packages were wrapped and taken to the post office by our shipping clerk yesterday.

Our shipping clerk wrapped and took all the packages to the post office yesterday. (answers may vary somewhat)

_A_ 6. Using their state-of-the-art 3D glasses, the audience saw the new action thriller.

Using state-of-the-art 3D glasses, the new action thriller was seen by the audience. (answers may vary somewhat)

_**A**_ 7. The CEO and the Vice-President of Operations planned all the next year's conventions.

All next year's conventions were planned by the CEO and the Vice-Presdient of Operations.

(answers may vary somewhat)

_**P**_ 8. The crumpled party dressed was washed,and ironed by the maid before the next evening.

Tthe maid had washed and ironed the crumpled party dress before the next evening.

(answers may vary somewhat)

_**P**_ 9. While the fascinated science class watched, the secret ingredient was stirred into the mixture.

While the fascinated science class watched, the teacher stirred the secret ingredient into the

mixture. (answers may vary somewhat)

_**P**_ 10. By ten a.m. of the third day of their camping trip, the tents had been packed neatly away.

By ten a.m. of the third day of their trip, the campers had packed their tents neatly away.

(answers may vary somewhat)

ACTIVE & PASSIVE VOICE: EXERCISE #3

NAME:_____DATE:_____

DIRECTIONS: *In the space provided, re-write the sentences below. If they're passive, re-write them in the active voice; if the active, re-write them in the passive voice. Try to include all the elements in the original sentence, although when you re-write into passive voice, the subject frequently disappears. Because passive voice sentences are often unclear, a subject has to be inserted.*

___*P*___ 1. Despite the massive public protests, the bill was passed by the Senate and the House.

__*Despite the massive public protests, the Senate and House passed the bill. (answers may vary*__

__*somewhat)*__

___*P*___ 2. Even though the pitcher was trying to pitch a fair game, the batter was hit by a fast ball.

__*Even though the pitcher was trying to pitch a fair game, he hit the batter with a fastball.*__

__*(answers may vary somewhat)*__

___*A*___ 3. Why did the chicken cross the road?

__*Why was the road crossed by the chicken? (answers may vary somewhat)*__

___*A*___ 4. Even though Meg, Jo, Beth, and Amy didn't let on, they surprised Marmee with gifts.

__*Even though Meg, Jo, Beth, and Amy didn't let on, Marmee was surprised with gifts.*__

__*(answers may vary somewhat)*__

___*P*___ 5. At the expense of the federal taxpayers, a fence has been built across our southern border.

__*At the expense of the taxpayers, the federal government has built a fence across our southern*__

__*border. (answers may vary somewhat)*__

_**A**__6 The outside "prejudice reduction"consultant damaged many relationships in our office .

Many relationships in our office were damaged by the outside "prejudice reduction" consultant.

(answers may vary somewhat)

_**P**__7. A huge new marketing plan has been put into place in our company.

The marketing department in our company has put a huge new marketing plan in place.

(answers may vary somewhat)

_**A**__8. Some of today's champions on Civil Rights voted against the Civil Rights Act of 1964.

The Civil Rights Act of 1964 was voted against by some of today's champions on Civil Rights.

(answers may vary somewhat)

_**P**__9. Prior to 1920 women in the United States were denied the right to vote.

Prior to 1920 the law in the United States denied women the right to vote.

(answers may vary somewhat)

_**A**__10. While they were on the raft, Tom and Huck shielded each other from the evils of civilization.

While they were on the raft, Tom and Huck were shielded from the evils of civilization.

(answers may vary somewhat)

ACTIVE & PASSIVE VOICE: TEST

NAME:_____DATE:_____

RAW SCORE: _____/120 = GRADE:_____PERCENTAGE: _____

DIRECTIONS: *In the space provided, re-write the sentences below. If they're passive, re-write them in the active voice; if the active, re-write them in the passive voice. Try to include all the elements in the original sentence, although when you re-write into passive voice, the subject frequently disappears. Because passive voice sentences are often unclear, a subject has to be inserted.*

P 1. Two key findings are indicated by the results of this test.

The results of this test indicate two key findings. (answers may vary somewhat)

_____

== 6

— 1
— 3
— 2

2. Researchers have found that heart disease is the leading cause of death in the USA.

Heart disease has been found to be the leading cause of death in the USA.

(answers may vary somewhat)

== 6

— 1
— 3
— 2

A 3. Why did you pack my stuff and leave it on the front lawn?

Why was my stuff packed and left on the front lawn? (answers may vary somewhat)

_____

== 6

— 1
— 3
— 2

A 4. Dr. Huang delivered the twins at 5:30 a.m. on May 5, 2010.

The twins were delivered by Dr. Huang at 5:30 a.m. on May 5, 2010. (answers may vary

somewhat)

== 6

— 1
— 3
— 2

P 5. Before he left the theater the rock star was beseiged by screaming fans.

Before he left the theater, screaming fans beseiged the rock star. (answers may vary somewhat)

_____

== 6

— 1
— 3
— 2

P 6. A souvenir of her trip to give to her nephew was purchased by Nikki

Nikki purchased a souvenir of her trip to give to her nephew. (answers may vary somewhat)

_____

== 6

— 1
— 3
— 2

Photocopying this product is strictly prohibited by copyright law.   **389**

__−__ __A__ 7. Before the test began, the students read the directions very carefully.
1

== __−__   ***Before the test began, the directions were read very carefully by the students. (answers may***
6 **3**   ***vary***

__−__   ***somewhat)***
2

__−__ __P__ 8. The U.S. Constitution was signed on September 17, 1787.
1

== __−__   ***Tthe Founders signed the U.S. Constitution on September 17, 1787. (answers may vary***
6 **3**

__−__   ***somewhat)***
2

__−__ __A__ 9. Witnesses saw a man wearing a hooded sweatshirt and jeans leaving the scene of the crime.
1

== __−__   ***A man wearing a hooded sweatshirt and jeans was seen leaving the scene of the crime.***
6 **3**

__−__   ***(answers may vary somewhat)***
2

__−__ __P__ 10. As a result of our baseball game, Mrs. Hawkins' window was broken.
1

== __−__   ***As a result of our baseball game, we broke Mrs. Hawkins' window. (answers may vary somewhat)***
6 **3**

__−__
2

__−__ __P__ 11. The girl sitting next to me was asked to share her notes from the prior lecture.
1

== __−__   ***I asked the girl sitting next to me to share her notes from the prior lecture.***
6

__−__   ***(answers may vary somewhat)***
3

__−__
2

__−__ __A__ 12. When the bell rang, the teacher told the class that they could leave.
1

== __−__   ***When the bell rang, the class was told by the teacher that they could leave.***
6

__−__   ***(answers may vary somewhat)***
3

__−__
2

__−__ __A__ 13. When were you planning to tell me about the broken vase?
1

== __−__   ***When was I going to be told about the broken vase? (answers may vary somewhat)***
6

__−__
3

__−__
2

__−__ __A__ 14. The man carrying the marked $100 bills finally admitted that he had stolen them.
1

== __−__   ***The man carrying the marked $100 bills finally admitted that they were stolen. (***
6

__−__   ***answers may vary somewhat)***
3

__−__
2

___*A*___ 15. The college athletic department has awarded James a full-ride scholarship for soccer.

James was awarded a full-ride soccer scholarship by the college athletic department.

(answers may vary somewhat)

== 6   1̄ 3̄ 2̄

___*P*___ 16. The Christmas money had been saved by the children all year long.

The children had been saving the Christmas money all year long. (answers may vary somewhat)

== 6   1̄ 3̄ 2̄

___*P*___ 17. Mrs. Dragonbottom's sarcasm had been patiently endured by the students for a month.

For a month the students had patiently endured Mrs. Dragonbottom's sarcasm.

(answers may vary somewhat)

== 6   1̄ 3̄ 2̄

___*A*___ 18. The drama class presented their spring play *The Crucible* for the student body.

The drama class's spring play **The Crucible** *was presented for the student body.*

(answers may vary somewhat)

== 6   1̄ 3̄ 2̄

___*P*___ 19. My senior class trip began with a tour of D.C. which was taken by everybody in the group.

My senior class trip began with a tour of D.C. which everybody in the group took.

(answers may vary somewhat)

== 6   1̄ 3̄ 2̄

___*P*___ 20. In ancient times punctuation wasn't used, which makes their writing hard for us to read.

In ancient times writers didn't use punctuation, which makes their writing hard for us to read.

(answers may vary somewhat)

== 6   1̄ 3̄ 2̄

(Correctly identifying the "voice" of the sentence = 1 point.
Re-writing the sentence into the oppositie "voice" = 3 points.
Including all the elememts of the original sentence = 2 points.)

Raw		Score		Grade		%
120	-	118	=	A++	=	98+
117	-	114	=	A+	=	95
113	-	108	=	A	=	90
107	-	102	=	B+	=	85
101	-	96	=	B	=	80
95	-	90	=	C+	=	75
89	-	84	=	C	=	70
83	-	78	=	D+	=	65
77	-	72	=	D	=	60
71 and below			=	F		